משנה

ArtScroll Mishnah Series®
A rabbinic commentary to the Six Orders of the Mishnah

Rabbis Nosson Scherman / Meir Zlotowitz

General Editors

the mishnah

ARTSCROLL MISHNAH SERIES / A NEW TRANSLATION WITH A COMMENTARY **YAD AVRAHAM** ANTHOLOGIZED FROM TALMUDIC SOURCES AND CLASSIC COMMENTATORS.

Published by

Mesorah Publications, ltd

ששה סדרי **משנה**

THE COMMENTARY HAS BEEN NAMED **YAD AVRAHAM**
AS AN EVERLASTING MEMORIAL AND SOURCE OF MERIT
FOR THE *NESHAMAH* OF
אברהם יוסף ע״ה בן הר״ר אליעזר הכהן גליק נ״י
AVRAHAM YOSEF GLICK ע״ה
WHOSE LIFE WAS CUT SHORT ON 3 TEVES, 5735

FIRST EDITION
First Impression ... March, 1986

Published and Distributed by
MESORAH PUBLICATIONS, Ltd.
1969 Coney Island Avenue
Brooklyn, New York 11223

Distributed in Israel by
MESORAH MAFITZIM / J. GROSSMAN
Rechov Harav Uziel 117
Jerusalem, Israel

Distributed in Europe by
J. LEHMANN HEBREW BOOKSELLERS
20 Cambridge Terrace
Gateshead
TYNE AND WEAR
England NE8 1RP

THE ARTSCROLL MISHNAH SERIES®
SEDER NEZIKIN Vol. I(a): *BAVA KAMMA*
© Copyright 1986
by MESORAH PUBLICATIONS, Ltd.
1969 Coney Island Avenue / Brooklyn, N.Y. 11223 / (718) 339-1700

All rights reserved. This text, the new translation, commentary, and prefatory comments
— including the typographic layout, illustrations, charts, appendices, and cover design —
have been edited and revised as to content, form and style
and are fully protected against copyright infringement.

No part of this book may be reproduced **in any form**
— **including photocopying and retrieval systems** —
without **written** permission from the copyright holder,
except by a reviewer who wishes to quote brief passages in connection with a review
written for inclusion in magazines or newspapers.

THE RIGHTS OF THE COPYRIGHT HOLDER WILL BE STRICTLY ENFORCED.

ISBN
0-89906-289-X (hard cover)
0-89906-290-3 (paperback)

Typography by CompuScribe at ArtScroll Studios, Ltd.
1969 Coney Island Avenue / Brooklyn, N.Y. 11223 / (718) 339-1700

Printed in the United States of America by Moriah Offset
Bound at Sefercraft, Brooklyn, NY

✥ Seder Nezikin Vol. I(a):
מסכת בבא קמא
Tractate Bava Kamma

Translation and anthologized commentary by
Rabbi Avrohom Yoseif Rosenberg

Edited by:
Rabbi Tzvi Zev Arem

The Publishers are grateful to
TORAH UMESORAH
and
YAD AVRAHAM INSTITUTE
for their efforts in the publication of the
ARTSCROLL MISHNAH SERIES

ספר זה הוקדש לעילוי נשמת
משרת נאמן לקונו ועמו
הרב שמעון ב״ר נחמיה הלוי ע״ה
שנחטף בדמי ימיו כ״א כסלו תשמ״ו

This volume is dedicated to the memory of
Rabbi Shimon Zweig ע״ה

*All his life, R' Shimon was appointed and elected
to positions of leadership, but always he remained
a servant of those who needed him.*

*No goal was too lofty and no task too menial for him.
If it was good for his people and beneficial to others,
he would plan it, fight for it, work for it, do it.*

*Whether a gavel or a broom, he would wield it
with the same zeal and pride —
because he saw everything as a tool for the
glory of Hashem and the welfare of His people.*

*As a husband, father, son, friend, colleague, or official,
when he was needed he was there.
Of that, there was never a doubt.*

*He is gone too soon.
His memory and example endure.
And always will.*

תנצב״ה

הסכמה

הנה ידידי הרב הגאון ר' אברהם יוסף ראזענבערג שליט״א אשר היה מתלמידי החשובים ביותר וגם הרביץ תורה בכמה ישיבות ואצלינו בישיבתנו בסטעטן איילאנד, ובזמן האחרון הוא מתעסק בתרגום ספרי קודש ללשון אנגלית המדוברת ומובנת לבני מדינה זו, וכבר איתמחי גברא בענין תרגום לאנגלית וכעת תרגם משניות לשפת אנגלית וגם לקוטים מדברי רבותינו מפרשי משניות על כל משנה ומשנה בערך, והוא לתועלת גדול להרבה אנשי ממדינה זו שלא התרגלו מילדותם ללמוד המשנה וגם יש הרבה שבעזר השי״ת התקרבו לתורה ויראת שמים כשכבר נתגדלו ורוצים ללמוד שיוכלו ללמוד משניות בנקל בשפה המורגלת להם, שהוא ממזכי הרבים בלמוד משניות וזכותו גדול. ואני מברכו שיצליחהו השי״ת בחבורו זה. וגם אני מברך את חברת ארטסקרול אשר תחת הנהלת הרב הנכבד ידידי מוהר״ר מאיר יעקב בן ידידי הגאון ר' אהרן שליט״א זלאטאוויץ אשר הוציאו כבר הרבה חבורים חשובים לזכות הרבים וכעת הם מוציאים לאור את המשניות הנ״ל.

ועל זה באתי על החתום בז' אדר תשל״ט בנוא יארק.

נאום משה פיינשטיין

מכתב ברכה

יעקב קמנצקי

RABBI J. KAMENECKI
38 SADDLE RIVER ROAD
MONSEY, NEW YORK 10952

בע"ה

יום ה' ערב חג השבועות תשל"ס, פה מאנסי.

כבוד הרבני איש החסד שוע ונדיב מוקיר רבנן מר אלעזר נ"י גליק
שלו' וברכת כל טוב.

מה מאד שמחתי בהודעי כי כבודו רכש לעצמו הזכות שייקרא ע"ש
בנו המנוח הפירוש מבואר על כל ששת סדרי משנה ע"י "ארטסקראל"
והנה חברה זו יצאה לה מוניטין בפירושה על תנ"ך, והנה נקוה שכשם
שהצליחה בתורה שבכתב כן תצליח בתורה שבע"פ. ובהיות שאותיות
"משנה" הן כאותיות "נשמה" לפיכך טוב עשה בכוונתו לעשות זאת לעילוי
נשמת בנו המנוח אברהם יוסף ע"ה, ומאד מתאים השם "יד אברהם" לזה
הפירוש, כדמצינו במקרא (ש"ב י"ח) כי אמר אין לי בן בעבור הזכיר
שמי וגו'. ואין לך דבר גדול מזה להפיץ ידיעת תורה שבע"פ בקרב
אחינו שאינם רגילים בלשון הקדש. וד' הטוב יהי' בעזרו ויוכל לברך
על המוגמר. ויראה רוב נחת מכל אשר אתו כנפש מברכו.

יעקב קמנצקי

Approbation/מכתב ברכה

מכתב ברכה

בע"ה — ד' בהעלותך — לבני א"י, תשל"ט — פה קרית טלז, באה"ק

מע"כ ידידי האהובים הרב ר' מאיר והרב ר' נתן, נר"ו, שלום וברכה נצח!

אחדשה"ט באהבה ויקר,

לשמחה רבה היא לי להודע שהרחבתם גדול עבודתכם בקודש לתורה שבע"פ, בהוצאת המשנה בתרגום וביאור באנגלית, וראשית עבודתכם במס' מגילה.

אני תקוה שתשימו לב שיצאו הדברים מתוקנים מנקודת ההלכה, וחזקה עליכם שתוציאו דבר נאה ומתוקן.

בפנותכם לתורה שבע"פ יפתח אופק חדש בתורת ה' לאלה שקשה עליהם ללמוד הדברים במקורם, ואלה שכבר נתעשרו מעבודתכם במגילת אסתר יכנסו עתה לטרקלין חדש וישמשו להם הדברים דחף ללימוד המשנה, וגדול יהי' שכרכם.

יהא ה' בעזרכם בהוספת טבעת חדשה באותה שלשלת זהב של הפצת תורת ה' להמוני עם לקרב לב ישראל לאבינו שבשמים בתורה ואמונה טהורה.

אוהבכם מלו"ח,
מרדכי

[x]   מכתב ברכה/Approbation

מכתב ברכה

בשורת התרחבות עבודתם הגדולה של סגל חבורת ,,ארטסקרול'', המעתיקים ומפרשים, לתחומי התורה שבע"פ, לשים אלה המשפטים לפני הציבור כשלחן ערוך ומוכן לאכול לפני האדם [ע' רש"י], ולשימה בפיהם — לפתיחת אוצרות בשנות בצורת ולהשמיעים בכל לשון שהם שומעים — מבשרת צבא רב לתורה ולימודה [ע' תהלים ס"ח י"ב בתרגום יונתן], והיא מאותות ההתעוררות ללימוד התורה, וזאת התעודה על התנוצצות קיום ההבטחה ,,כי לא תשכח מפי זרעו''. אשרי הזוכים להיות בין שלוחי ההשגחה לקיומה וביצועה.

יה"ר כי תצליח מלאכת שמים בידם, ויזכו ללמוד וללמד ולשמור מסורת הקבלה כי בהרקת המים החיים מכלי אל כלי תשתמר חיותם, יעמוד טעמם בם וריחם לא נמר. וע' משאחז"ל בכ"מ ושמרתה זו משנה — וע' חי' מרן רי"ז הלוי עה"ת בפ' ואתחנן] ותהי' משנתם שלמה וברורה, ישמחו בעבודתם חברים ותלמידים, ,,ישוטטו רבים ותרבה הדעת'', עד יקויים ,,אז אהפוך אל העמים שפה ברורה וגו' '' [צפני' ג' ט', עי' פי' אבן עזרא ומצודת דוד שם].

ונזכה כולנו לראות בהתכנסות הגליות בזכות המשניות כל' חז"ל עפ"י הכתוב ,,גם כי יתנו בגויים עתה אקבצם'', בגאולה השלמה בב"א.

הכו"ח לכבוד התורה, יום ו' עש"ק לס' ,,ויצא פרח ויצץ ציץ ויגמל שקדים'', ד' תמוז התשל"ט

יוסף חיים שניאור קוטלר
בלאאמו"ר הגר"א זצוק"ל

מכתב ברכה

ב"ה
לכבוד ידידי וידיד ישיבתנו, מהראשונים לכל דבר שבקדושה
הרבני הנדיב המפורסם ר' אליעזר הכהן גליק נ"י
אחדשה"ט באהבה,

בשורה טובה שמעתי שכב' מצא את המקום המתאים לעשות יד ושם להנציח זכרו של בנו **אברהם יוסף** ע"ה שנקטף בנעוריו. "נתתי להם בביתי ובחומתי יד ושם". אין לו להקב"ה אלא ד' אמות של הלכה בלבד. א"כ זהו בית ד' לימוד תורה שבע"פ וזהו המקום לעשות יד ושם לנשמת בנו ע"ה.

נר ד' נשמת אדם אמר הקב"ה נרי בידך ונרך בידי. נר מצוה ותורה אור, תורה זוהי הנר של הקב"ה וכשמשומרים נר של הקב"ה שעל ידי הפירוש "**יד אברהם**" בשפה הלעוזית יתרבה לימוד ושקיעת התורה בבתי ישראל. ד' ישמור נשמת אדם.

בנו אברהם יוסף ע"ה נתברך בהמדה שבו נכללות כל המדות, לב טוב והיה אהוב לחבריו. בלמדו בישיבתנו היה לו הרצון לעלות במעלות התורה וכשעלה לארצנו הקדושה היתה מבוקשו להמשיך בלמודיו. ביקוש זה ימצא מלואו על ידי הרבים המבקשים דרך ד', שהפירוש "**יד אברהם**" יהא מפתח להם לים התלמוד.

התורה נקראת "אש דתי", ונשמלה לאש יש לה הכח להפעפע בכל לפעיל פעולה גדול לפצוע בכחות האדם, הניצוץ שהאיר בך רבנו הרב שרגא פייוועל מנדלוביץ זצ"ל שמרת עליו, ועשה חיל. עכשיו אתה מסייע להאיר נצוצות בנשמות בני ישראל שיעשה חיל ויהא לאור גדול.

תקותי עזה של כל התלמידי חכמים שנדבה רוחם להוציא לפועל מלאכה ענקית זו לפרש המשניות כולה, יצא עבודתם ברוח פאר והדר ויכוונו לאמיתה של תורה ויתקדש שם שמים על ידי מלאכה זו.

יתברך כב' וב"ב לראות ולרוות נחת רוח מצאצאיו.
הכו"ח לכבוד התורה ותומכיה עש"ק במדבר תשל"ט

אלי' שוויי

Approbation/מכתב ברכה

מכתב ברכה

דוד קאהן   ביהמ"ד גבול יעבץ
                         ברוקלין, נוא יארק

בס"ד כ"ה למטמונים תשל"ט

כבוד רחימא דנפשאי, עושה ומעשה
ר' אלעזר הכהן גליק נטריה רחמנא ופרקיה

שמוע שמעתי שכבר תקעת תקיעת כפיך לתמוך במפעל האדיר של חברת ארטסקרול — הידוע בכל קצווי תבל ע"י עבודתה הכבירה בהפצת תורה — לתרגם ולבאר ששה סדרי משנה באנגלית. כוונתך להנציח זכר בנך הנחמד אברהם יוסף ז"ל שנקטף באבו בזמן שעלה לארץ הקודש בתקופת התרוממות הנפש ושאיפה לקדושה, ולמטרה זו יכונה הפירוש בשם "יד אברהם"; גם האיר ה' רוחך לגרום עילוי לנשמתו הטהורה שעי"ז יתרבה לימוד התורה שניתנה בשבעים לשון, על ידי כלי מפואר זה.

מכיוון שהנני מכיר היטיב שני הצדדים, אוכל לומר לדבק טוב, והנני תקוה שיצליח המפעל הלזה לתת יד ושם וזכות לנשמת אברהם יוסף ז"ל. חזקה על חברת ארטסקרול שתוציא דבר נאה מתוקן ומתקבל מתחת ידה להגדיל תורה ולהאדירה.

והנני מברך אותך שתמצא נוחם לנפשך, שהאבא זוכה לברא, ותשבע נחת — אתה עם רעיתך תחיה — מכל צאצאיכם היקרים אכי"ר

ידידך עז
דוד קאהן

Approbation/מכתב ברכה

Preface

אָמַר ר׳ יוֹחָנָן: לֹא כָרַת הקב״ה בְּרִית עִם יִשְׂרָאֵל אֶלָּא עַל־תּוֹרָה שֶׁבְּעַל פֶּה שֶׁנֶּאֱמַר: ״כִּי עַל־פִּי הַדְּבָרִים הָאֵלֶּה כָּרַתִּי אִתְּךָ בְּרִית ...״

R' Yochanan said: The Holy One, Blessed is He, sealed a covenant with Israel only because of the Oral Torah, as it is said [Exodus 34:27]: For according to these words have I sealed a covenant with you ... (Gittin 60b).

With gratitude to Hashem Yisborach we present the Jewish public with Bava Kamma, the first volume of Seder Nezikin. This begins the third seder to be published in the ArtScroll Mishnah Series, and it follows the successful completion of Moed and Nashim. In addition to Nezikin, work is proceeding on the three other sedarim. All of this is thanks to the vision and commitment of MR. AND MRS. LOUIS GLICK. In their quiet, self-effacing way, they have been a major force for the propagation of Torah knowledge and the enhancement of Jewish life for a generation. The commentary to the mishnayos bears the name YAD AVRAHAM, in memory of their son AVRAHAM YOSEF GLICK ע״ה. An appreciation of the niftar will appear in Tractate Berachos. May this dissemination of the Mishnah in his memory be a source of merit for his soul. תנצב״ה.

By dedicating the ArtScroll Mishnah Series, the Glicks have added a new dimension to their tradition of service. The many study groups in synagogues, schools and offices throughout the English-speaking world are the most eloquent testimony to the fact that thousands of people thirst for Torah learning presented in a challenging, comprehensive, and comprehensible manner.

We are proud and grateful that such venerable luminaries as MARAN HAGAON HARAV YAAKOV KAMINETZKI זצ״ל and להבל״ח MARAN HAGAON HARAV MORDECHAI GIFTER שליט״א have declared that this series should be translated into Hebrew. Boruch Hashem, it has stimulated readers to echo the words of King David: גַּל־עֵינַי וְאַבִּיטָה נִפְלָאוֹת מִתּוֹרָתֶךָ, *Uncover my eyes that I may see wonders of Your Torah* (Psalms 119:18).

May we inject two words of caution:

First, although the Mishnah, by definition, is a compendium of laws, the final halachah does not necessarily follow the Mishnah. The development of halachah proceeds through the Gemara, commentators, codifiers, responsa, and the acknowledged poskim. Even when our commentary cites the Shulchan Aruch, *the intention is to sharpen the reader's understanding of the Mishnah, but not to be a basis for actual practice. In short, this work is meant as a first step in the study of our recorded Oral Law — no more.*

Second, as we have stressed in our other books, the ArtScroll commentary is not meant as a substitute for the study of the sources. While this commentary, like others in the various series, will be immensely useful even to accomplished scholars and will often bring to light ideas and sources they may have overlooked, we strongly urge those who can, to study the classic seforim in the original. It has been said that every droplet of ink coming from Rashi's pen is worthy of seven days' contemplation. Despite the exceptional caliber of our authors, none of us pretends to replace the study of the greatest minds in Jewish history.

The author of this volume, RABBI AVROHOM YOSEIF ROSENBERG, *is familiar to ArtScroll Mishnah readers; in fact, he wrote three earlier volumes including the very first in the Series. His manuscript was edited by* RABBI TZVI ZEV AREM, *whose work is well known from earlier volumes of the Mishnah Series.*

We are also grateful to the staff of Mesorah Publications: RABBI HERSH GOLDWURM, *whose encyclopedic knowledge is always available;* REB ELI KROEN *whose very fine graphics production of this volume, carries on the tradition of* REB SHEAH BRANDER *who remains a leader in bringing beauty of presentation to Torah literature;* RABBI AVIE GOLD, STEPHEN BLITZ, SHIMON GOLDING, YOSAIF TIMINSKY, MICHAEL ZIVITZ, LEA FREIER, MRS. ESTHER FEIERSTEIN, MRS. MALKA HELFGOTT, SIMIE GLUCK, MRS. FAIGIE WEINBAUM, MRS. JUDI DICK, *and* ESTIE ZLOTOWITZ.

Finally, our gratitude goes to RABBI DAVID FEINSTEIN שליט״א *and* RABBI DAVID COHEN שליט״א, *whose concern, interest, and guidance throughout the history of the ArtScroll Series have been essential to its success.*

Rabbi Nosson Scherman / Rabbi Meir Zlotowitz

ט׳ אדר ב׳ תשמ״ו / March 20, 1986
Brooklyn, New York

As this volume goes to press, the Torah world
is thrust into mourning
at the passing of the גדולי ומאורי האומה
מרן הגאון רשכבה״ג ר׳ משה בן הרב דוד זצוק״ל
מרן הגאון מו״ר ר׳ יעקב בן הרב בנימין זצוק״ל

ימלא ה׳ חסרוננו
תנצב״ה

מסכת בבא קמא

Tractate Bava Kamma

[Note: The following verses are those which are most often cited in the Mishnah and the commentary in this tractate.]

שמות כא:כח-לז; כב:ג-ה

כא [כח] וְכִי־יִגַּח שׁוֹר אֶת־אִישׁ אוֹ אֶת־אִשָּׁה וָמֵת סָקוֹל יִסָּקֵל הַשּׁוֹר וְלֹא יֵאָכֵל אֶת־בְּשָׂרוֹ וּבַעַל הַשּׁוֹר נָקִי. [כט] וְאִם שׁוֹר נַגָּח הוּא מִתְּמֹל שִׁלְשֹׁם וְהוּעַד בִּבְעָלָיו וְלֹא יִשְׁמְרֶנּוּ וְהֵמִית אִישׁ אוֹ אִשָּׁה הַשּׁוֹר יִסָּקֵל וְגַם־בְּעָלָיו יוּמָת. [ל] אִם כֹּפֶר יוּשַׁת עָלָיו וְנָתַן פִּדְיֹן נַפְשׁוֹ כְּכֹל אֲשֶׁר־יוּשַׁת עָלָיו. [לא] אוֹ־בֵן יִגָּח אוֹ־בַת יִגָּח כַּמִּשְׁפָּט הַזֶּה יֵעָשֶׂה לּוֹ. [לב] אִם־עֶבֶד יִגַּח הַשּׁוֹר אוֹ אָמָה כֶּסֶף שְׁלֹשִׁים שְׁקָלִים יִתֵּן לַאדֹנָיו וְהַשּׁוֹר יִסָּקֵל.

[לג] וְכִי־יִפְתַּח אִישׁ בּוֹר אוֹ כִּי־יִכְרֶה אִישׁ בֹּר וְלֹא יְכַסֶּנּוּ וְנָפַל־שָׁמָּה שּׁוֹר אוֹ חֲמוֹר. [לד] בַּעַל הַבּוֹר יְשַׁלֵּם כֶּסֶף יָשִׁיב לִבְעָלָיו וְהַמֵּת יִהְיֶה־לּוֹ.

[לה] וְכִי־יִגֹּף שׁוֹר־אִישׁ אֶת־שׁוֹר רֵעֵהוּ וָמֵת וּמָכְרוּ אֶת־הַשּׁוֹר הַחַי וְחָצוּ אֶת־כַּסְפּוֹ וְגַם אֶת־הַמֵּת יֶחֱצוּן. [לו] אוֹ נוֹדַע כִּי שׁוֹר נַגָּח הוּא מִתְּמוֹל שִׁלְשֹׁם וְלֹא יִשְׁמְרֶנּוּ בְּעָלָיו שַׁלֵּם יְשַׁלֵּם שׁוֹר תַּחַת הַשּׁוֹר וְהַמֵּת יִהְיֶה־לּוֹ.

[לז] כִּי יִגְנֹב־אִישׁ שׁוֹר אוֹ־שֶׂה וּטְבָחוֹ אוֹ מְכָרוֹ חֲמִשָּׁה בָקָר יְשַׁלֵּם תַּחַת הַשּׁוֹר וְאַרְבַּע־צֹאן תַּחַת הַשֶּׂה. **כב** ... [ג] אִם־הִמָּצֵא תִמָּצֵא בְיָדוֹ הַגְּנֵבָה מִשּׁוֹר עַד־חֲמוֹר עַד־שֶׂה חַיִּים שְׁנַיִם יְשַׁלֵּם.

[ד] כִּי יַבְעֶר־אִישׁ שָׂדֶה אוֹ־כֶרֶם וְשִׁלַּח אֶת־בְּעִירֹה וּבִעֵר בִּשְׂדֵה אַחֵר מֵיטַב שָׂדֵהוּ וּמֵיטַב כַּרְמוֹ יְשַׁלֵּם.

[ה] כִּי־תֵצֵא אֵשׁ וּמָצְאָה קֹצִים וְנֶאֱכַל גָּדִישׁ אוֹ הַקָּמָה אוֹ הַשָּׂדֶה שַׁלֵּם יְשַׁלֵּם הַמַּבְעִר אֶת־הַבְּעֵרָה.

[Note: The following verses are those which are most often cited in the Mishnah and the commentary in this tractate.]

Exodus 21:28-37; 22:3-5

21 [28] *If a bull gores a man or a woman, and he dies, the bull shall surely be stoned, and its flesh shall not be eaten, and the owner of the bull is quit. [29] But if the bull was a habitual gorer from yesterday and the day before, and its owner was warned, but he did not watch it, and it kills a man or a woman, the bull shall be stoned, and also its owner shall be put to death. [30] A ransom shall be imposed upon him; he shall give the redemption of his soul according to whatever be imposed upon him. [31] Whether it gores a male child or it gores a female child, according to this judgment shall be done to it. [32] If the bull gores a male slave or a female slave, he shall give his master thirty silver shekels, and the bull shall be stoned.*

[33] *If a man opens a pit or if a man digs a pit, and he does not cover it, and a bull or a donkey falls therein, [34] the owner of the pit shall pay; he shall give money to its owner, and the dead one shall be his.*

[35] *If a man's bull gores another's bull, and it dies, they shall sell the live bull and divide the money of it and also divide the dead one. [36] But if it was known that the bull was a habitual gorer from yesterday and the day before, and its owner does not watch it, he shall surely pay a bull for the bull, and the dead one shall be his.*

[37] *If a man steals an ox or a lamb and slaughters it or sells it, he shall pay five cattle instead of the ox and four sheep instead of the lamb.* **22** ... [3] *If the stolen article is found in his hand alive, whether a bull, a donkey or a lamb, he shall pay twofold.*

[4] *If a man causes a field or vineyard to be grazed, and shall let his animal loose, and it grazes in another's field, the best of his field or the best of his vineyard he shall pay.*

[5] *If a fire goes forth and comes across thorns, and a stack of grain, or standing grain, or a field is consumed, the one who ignited the fire shall surely pay.*

General Introduction to Bava Kamma

৺ঌ The Tractate

The first tractate of *Seder Nezikin* is the tractate *Nezikin*, which is divided into three parts: *Bava Kamma* [the first gate], *Bava Metzia* [the middle gate], and *Bava Basra* [the last gate]. It is a common practice among authors to divide their work into sections called 'gates' [e.g., *Shaarei Teshuvah, Chovos Halevavos*]. The term 'gate' is certainly a most appropriate description of the Mishnah in general because it is a gateway to the understanding of laws of the Torah *(Tos. Yom Tov*, Introduction to *Seder Nezikin)*.

In counting the number of tractates comprising the Mishnah, some count these parts as three tractates; others, as one. *Ri Migash* and *Ritva* consider the entire *Seder Nezikin* as one long tractate (see first *Tosafos* to *Bava Basra; Yad Malachi*, p. 80).

Bava Kamma deals mainly with liabilities and payments of damages, devoting also three chapters to laws of theft and robbery.

৺ঌ Liability for Damages

The Torah holds a person liable for damages inflicted by himself, as well as by his chattels.

Just as one is prohibited to steal or rob the property of others, so is he prohibited to damage their property. If he does so, whether he derives benefit from it or not, whether it was done intentionally or unintentionally, he must pay for the damage *(Tur Choshen Mishpat* 378). Just as one is prohibited to do damage to another, and if he does so, he is liable to pay, so must he guard his property lest it damage — whether they be living creatures, such as cattle, beasts, and fowl,[1] or objects such as pits in the ground, fires that he starts, and the like. If any of these damages another's property, its owner is liable to pay.

One is not liable, however, for damages done by his gentile slave, because if he were, we fear that in the event he would provoke the slave, the latter would deliberately go and cause damage to others in order to make his master liable (ibid. 389 from *Yadayim* 4:7, *Gemara* 4a). One is not responsible for damages caused by his עֶבֶד עִבְרִי, *Jewish bondman*, because the latter is not truly his property (see ArtScroll *Kiddushin*, footnote to p. 9).

---

1. Although Scripture *(Exodus* 21:28ff., 35f.) deals only with damages done by one's bull, the laws apply equally to any living creature, as stated in mishnah (5:7). The Torah specifies the bull only because that was the animal usually involved in such a case *(Tur* ad loc.).

משניות / בבא קמא [4]

❧ Avos and Tolados

The various types of damagers mentioned explicitly in the Torah are known as אָבוֹת, *avos* (lit., *fathers*) — that is, primary damagers. Each *av* has תּוֹלָדוֹת, *tolados* (lit., *descendants*) — that is, secondary types of damagers that possess the same basic characteristics as that *av*.

The *avos* are:

1) אָדָם הַמַּזִּיק, *a man who damages:* This includes damages done to other people, to livestock, or to inanimate objects. (See commentary to 1:1, s.v. *The Dispute between Rav and Shmuel,* for the Biblical sources from which this is derived.) From the *Gemara* it is not clear what the *tolados* of this *av* are (see ibid.).

2) קֶרֶן, *keren* (horn): This is described in *Exodus* (loc. cit.), and includes injuries inflicted by an animal goring either a man or another animal. The first three times the animal gores, it is considered a תָּם, *tam* (lit., *innocent, tame*), and, as a fine to its owner *(Gem.* 15b), the damagee in each case is awarded half the damages. As will be explained in the preface to 4:1, according to some *Tannaim,* this means that the damagee becomes a partner in the animal that gored for that amount; according to others, he merely has a lien on it for that amount. After the animal gores three times — its owner having been warned to watch it after each time — the animal becomes a מוּעָד, *muad* (lit., *forewarned*), and if it does damage subsequently, its owner must pay the full damages from the best of his property (see commentary to end of 1:1).

The *tolados* of *keren* include: an animal pushing with its body, biting, lying down, and kicking. All these resemble goring in that they are unusual and are done with intent to damage.

3) שֵׁן, *shen* (tooth): This is based on *Exodus* 22:4, and refers to an animal that eats produce in a field belonging to someone other than its owner. The *tolados* of *shen* are other types of damage which the animal does in order to derive pleasure, such as rubbing against a wall, thereby knocking it down, or against produce, thereby soiling it *(Rav* 1:1).

4) רֶגֶל, *regel* (foot): Derived from the same verse as *shen,* this category is comprised of damages committed by the animal with its foot while walking. Its *tolados* include other damages done by the animal as it walks (see commentary ibid., s.v. הַשּׁוֹר).

5) אֵשׁ, *eish* (fire): That is, if someone ignites a fire — even in his own property — and it spreads to his neighbor's area and does damage. This is discussed in *Exodus* 22:5. Its *tolados* are any items that are carried by a normal wind, such as a stone, knife, or bundle, placed on a roof, which causes damage while flying *(Rav* 1:1).

6) בּוֹר, *bor* (pit): This refers to the cases, mentioned in *Exodus* 21:22f., in which one digs or uncovers a pit in public property. If the pit is ten handbreadths deep, and a person falls into it and is injured, or an animal falls into it and is injured or dies, the one who dug or uncovered the pit is

liable. By Scriptural decree, however, he is not liable if a person is killed by falling into his pit (see commentary to 1:1, s.v. *Bor*). If the pit is less than ten handbreadths deep, he is liable only if the person or animal is injured, but does not die; should death occur, he is exempt (see commentary to 5:5). The *tolados* are any obstacles lying on the ground upon which people or animals can stumble and injure themselves *(Rav loc. cit.)*.

Although the first mishnah lists only four *avos*, the other two are — according to one opinion — omitted, or — according to another — included among the others (see commentary to 1:1, s.v. *The Dispute between Rav and Shmuel*).

◆§ הַמּוֹצִיא מֵחֲבֵרוֹ ... / The Burden of Proof ...

A basic principle in Jewish law regarding monetary litigations is הַמּוֹצִיא מֵחֲבֵרוֹ עָלָיו הָרְאָיָה, *The burden of proof lies on the one who seeks to exact something from the other* (3:11). That is, if one of a person is in possession of something, and another claims that it is his, the latter must bring witnesses or other substantial evidence in order to prove his claim.

One opinion in the *Gemara* (46b) derives this from the verse (*Exodus* 24:14): מִי־בַעַל דְּבָרִים יִגַּשׁ אֲלֵיהֶם, *Whoever has matters shall approach them*, which is interpreted as meaning that whoever claims that something in someone else's possession is his *(Rashi ad loc.)* must bring proof that it is so to the judges (cf. *Sifrei* to *Deuteronomy* 1:16).

Another view in the *Gemara* is that this principle is logical, and needs no Scriptural support.

◆§ Summaries of Chapters

One is liable only for certain types of damagers that damage certain types of property in certain places. Chapter 1 discusses these and also enumerates when one is liable for half the damages, and when for the full damages.

Chapter 2 elaborates on topics mentioned in the final mishnah of the first chapter: when the various *avos* are considered to be in the *muad* category, the controversy whether or not the damages done by a *tam* in the property of the damagee incur liability for the full damages, and the laws concerning a man who damages.

Chapter 3 deals with obstacles placed in a public place; damages caused by the collision of two persons; those originating in one domain and causing damage in another; those caused by animals or men to one another; instances in which one is liable for his own deeds, but not for those of his animal, and vice versa; and cases of doubtful liability.

Chapter 4 deals with the case of a *tam* that gored many times and yet remained in the status of a *tam*; an animal that is considered a *muad* for some cases, but not for others; those animals which do not incur liability for their owners, either because of their own status or that of their owners; the payment of ransom when an animal kills a man; when the ownership of a condemned bull terminates; when a שׁוֹמֵר, *guardian*, takes the place of the owner with regard to liability for damages; and what degree of watching is required to exempt the owner from payment of damages.

Chapter 5 completes the laws of the animal that damages, and also deals with those of the pit in all its details.

Chapter 6 discusses the measures one must take to prevent his animal from causing damages in the categories of *shen* and *regel*; how the payments for these damages are computed; when an animal's owner is liable for what it eats in his own domain; and details of the liability for a fire.

Chapter 7 deals with the laws of theft, primarily with כֶּפֶל [*kefel*], the *twofold payment*, and אַרְבָּעָה וַחֲמִשָּׁה, *the fourfold and fivefold payments*. The last mishnah also lists types of animals that may not be raised in certain places.

Chapter 8 is entirely devoted to the subject of wounds inflicted by one man on another.

Chapter 9 deals with the laws of robbery, mainly with cases in which the robber made changes on the stolen article. In certain such cases, the robber may keep the article and compensate the owner with a monetary payment instead.

Chapter 10 discusses other laws of robbery.

❈ ❈ ❈

Notes Regarding the Commentary

As in the previous volumes of the Mishnah Series, every entry in the commentary has been carefully documented. Where the author has inserted a comment of his own, it is surrounded by brackets.

Untranslated Hebrew terms found in the Commentary are defined in the glossary at the end of the tractate.

בבא קמא א/א

[א] אַרְבָּעָה אֲבוֹת נְזִיקִים: הַשּׁוֹר, וְהַבּוֹר, וְהַמַּבְעֶה, וְהַהֶבְעֵר. לֹא הֲרֵי הַשּׁוֹר כַּהֲרֵי הַמַּבְעֶה, וְלֹא הֲרֵי הַמַּבְעֶה כַּהֲרֵי

יד אברהם

Chapter 1

1.

אַרְבָּעָה אֲבוֹת נְזִיקִים — *The four primary damagers are:*

There are four types of damagers mentioned explicitly in the Torah. These are designated as אֲבוֹת, *avos* — (primary damagers; lit., *fathers*) because there are תּוֹלָדוֹת, *toldados* (secondary types of damagers; lit., *descendants*) — possessing the same characteristics as these *avos* (*Rav*; *Rashi*).

The translation follows *Rosh*, who renders נְזִיקִים as *damagers*.[1]

Meiri observes that — like the word נְזִיקִים — נְזִיקִין, too, is commonly translated as *damages*.

The mishnah now lists the four primary damagers.

הַשּׁוֹר — *the bull*,[2]

[Actually, the same laws apply to all animals and birds. The mishnah specifies the example of a bull only because that was the usual case (see *Rambam*, *Hilchos Nizkei Mamon*; *Tur* *Choshen Mishpat* 389; mishnah 5:7).]

This category comprises the damages perpetrated by an animal with its foot while walking, such as breaking utensils by stepping on them. These laws are based on *Exodus* 22:4, וְשִׁלַּח אֶת בְּעִירֹה [*If a man*] ... *shall let his animal loose*, which is interpreted as a reference to damages done with the foot. Since this type of damage, which is referred to throughout the tractate as רֶגֶל, *regel* (foot), is characterized by unintentional damage caused by the animal while walking, the *toldados* of *regel* include other damages committed by the animal as it walks, such as those done with the body, the hair [utensils become entangled in its hair and it drags them and breaks them], the burden on its back, or the bell on its neck (*Rav* from *Gemara* 3a-b). [As discussed below, there is an opinion in the *Gemara* which interprets the mishnah differently.]

Since *regel* occurs frequently, all the aforementioned damages, which are also

---

1. The word נְזִיקִים is grammatically constructed in the pattern of נְזִירִים, *those who separate themselves* (e.g., Nazirites), and חֲסִידִים, *those who perform* חֶסֶד, *kindness*. Here, too, נְזִיקִים denotes those who perform נֶזֶק, *damage*. Rather than choose the usual term, מַזִּיקִים, the Tanna — a Jerusalemite — chose the form to which he was accustomed (*Rosh*, quoted by *Shitah Mekubetzes*). In fact, the first three mishnayos were composed by this *Tanna* from Jerusalem (*Maharatz Chayos* to 6b).

Another theory is that, strictly speaking, the word מַזִּיקִים bears the connotation of *willful damagers*, a description that applies only to the קֶרֶן, *horn*, and אָדָם, a *man* who intentionally damages [see below], but not to the other *avos* (*Meiri*).

2. [We have generally translated שׁוֹר as *bull*, rather than *ox*, because the latter is defined as either an adult castrated male of the genus *Bos*, or as any member of the bovine family. It appears more likely that שׁוֹר, which — as described in Scripture and the Mishnah — seems to be one that is wont to gore and commit other such damages, is the *bull*, the uncastrated male of a bovine animal. To be sure, there are some exceptions; see, for example, 5:6.]

משניות / בבא קמא — פרק א: ארבעה אבות [8]

1. The four primary damagers are: the bull, the pit, the *maveh*, and the fire. The bull is not like the *maveh*, nor is the *maveh* like the bull. These two,

YAD AVRAHAM

common and are done with the foot, are regarded as *tolados* of *regel*.

Although the term *regel* would appear to us to be more explicit than the term שׁוֹר, *shor* [bull] to denote this category of damages the *Tanna* chose to use the latter word in the mishnah, because we might erroneously interpret *regel* as *kicking*, which — since it is done with the intention of damaging — is, in fact, a *toladah* of קֶרֶן, *horn*, as explained in mishnah 4 *(Tiferes Yisrael).*

וְהַבּוֹר, — *the pit,*

If one digs or uncovers a pit ten handbreadths deep in public property, and an animal falls into it and dies, he is liable. If the pit is less than ten handbreadths deep, he is liable only if the animal is injured; should it die, however, he is exempt from payment. [See commentary to 5:5, s.v. הָיוּ.] These laws are derived from *Exodus* 21:33f., וְכִי־יִפְתַּח אִישׁ בּוֹר ..., *If a man opens a pit* ....

This category of damagers is characterized as having been prone to cause damage from the moment they were made or placed, without any motion on their part or the assistance of any other force. Its *tolados* are: phlegm, mucus, or any obstacle — such as a stone, a knife, or a bundle — lying on the ground, upon which a person or an animal can stumble and be injured *(Rav, Tif. Yis., Gem.* 3b, *Rashi* ad loc.).

וְהַמַּבְעֶה, — *the maveh,*

This refers to the tooth of an animal that eats the produce in a field belonging to someone other than its owner. The laws of this category are derived from another phrase in *Exodus* 22:4: וּבִעֵר בִּשְׂדֵה אַחֵר, *and it grazes in another's field.* The *Tanna* calls this category *maveh*, from the root בעה, meaning *to uncover,* as in the phrase *(Ovadiah* v. 6) נִבְעוּ מַצְפֻּנָיו, *his hidden places uncovered.* In the mishnah, *maveh* refers to the tooth, which is sometimes covered by the mouth, and sometimes uncovered *(Rav from Gem.* ibid., *Rashi* ad loc.).

He did not explicitly call it שֵׁן, *shen* (tooth), lest we think that this category also includes damages done with the teeth, but not for the animal's enjoyment [e.g., biting, and chewing inedible items, such as clothing and utensils *(Tif. Yis.)*]. By stating *maveh* we understand that the reference is to eating, when the tooth is sometimes uncovered and sometimes covered *(Tosefos Yom Tov* from *Nimmukei Yosef).*

Others explain that the animal's tooth is described as *maveh* because the latter term means *searching;* i.e., it seeks food to eat[1] *(Rambam Commentary.).*

The tooth is characterized as deriving benefit from the damage it causes, since the animal derives benefit from eating the produce. Its *tolados*, therefore, are other types of damage which the animal does in order to derive pleasure, such as rubbing against a wall, thereby knocking it down, or against produce, thereby soiling it *(Rav from Gem.* 3a; see *Tosefos R' Akiva).*

---

1. [Although *Rambam* etymologizes the word as being related to *searching* and *seeking*, we have found no evidence that he had reason to dispense with the *Gemara's* relating it to *uncovering.* To be sure, the two terms are consanguineous; an animal, for example, in its *search* for food will constantly be *uncovering* things. Interestingly, *Rashi* to the quoted verse in *Ovadiah* cites both translations of נבעו — *uncovered* and *sought.* Indeed, *Tiferes Yisrael* to our mishnah seems to attempt a reconciliation of *Rambam's* interpretation with that of *Nimmukei Yosef.*]

יד אברהם

◆§ The Dispute between Rav and Shmuel

Up to this point, we have explained the mishnah according to Shmuel's interpretation in the *Gemara* (3b). According to Rav,[1] however, *maveh* refers to אָדָם, *adam* (man); i.e., damages perpetrated by man upon other people, animals, or inanimate objects. The laws of the latter two categories are based on *Leviticus* 24:21: וּמַכֵּה בְהֵמָה יְשַׁלְּמֶנָּה, *If one strikes a beast, he shall pay for it*. The laws of the first category are derived from *Exodus* 21:24: עַיִן תַּחַת עַיִן, *Eye for eye*, which means that if one blinds the eye of another, he must pay him for the value of an eye. The appellation *maveh* is derived from the root בעה, used in Scripture to mean *to pray*. Since man is the only species that prays, the *Tanna* uses that term to refer to him.[2]

He does not use the common word, אָדָם, *man*, since that term could also include gentile slaves, leading us to believe that one is responsible for the damages perpetrated by his gentile slaves [and, in fact, he is not (*Gem.* 4a from *Yadayim* 4:7, see General Introduction, s.v. *Liability for Damages*)]. He therefore chose the term מַבְעֶה which is used in *Isaiah* 21:12 and refers strictly to Jews (*Nimmukei Yosef*).

From the *Gemara*, it is not clear what the *tolados* of *adam* are. *Pnei Yehoshua* suggests that any damage inflicted by man's power — not directly by his body — is a *toladah* of *adam*. The example given in the *Gemara* (3b) is that of someone spitting on silks or into beverages, and spoiling them. Since his body does not come in contact with the damaged article, this is not a damage in the primary category, but rather a *toladah*.

According to Rav, *shor* includes three *avos*: *keren* [horn], *shen*, and *regel*. According to Shmuel, who interprets *maveh* as tooth, and *shor* as *regel*, man is not included in the mishnah, since the *Tanna* here deals only with damages inflicted by one's possessions, not those caused by the person himself. Similarly, *keren* is not mentioned here, since the *Tanna* lists only such damagers that are deemed to be *muad* (forewarned) from the beginning, whereas a bull is generally considered tame with regard to goring and its owner is therefore liable only for half the damage it causes by goring, until the fourth time that it damages in this manner (*Gem.* 3b).

וְהַהֶבְעֵר. — *and the fire.*

That is, if someone ignited a fire in his own property, and it spread to his neighbor's area and inflicted damage. This is based on *Exodus* 22:5, כִּי־תֵצֵא אֵשׁ ... שַׁלֵּם יְשַׁלֵּם הַמַּבְעִר אֶת־הַבְּעֵרָה, *If a fire goes forth and comes across thorns, and a stack of grain, or standing grain, or a field is consumed, the one who ignited the fire shall surely pay* (Rav; Rashi).

Tos. Yom Tov explains that the *Tanna* chose the word הַבְעֵר instead of the familiar term אֵשׁ, *eish*, to refer to fire, because the latter might be misconstrued to mean that the mishnah is discussing only a case in which the fire was started on the property of the damagee. The truth is, however, that the Torah requires restitution even if he lights the fire in his own property, and it spreads to that of his neighbor, as is deduced from the aforementioned verse. The *Tanna*, therefore, chooses the word הַבְעֵר, alluding to *Exodus* 35:3: לֹא תְבַעֲרוּ אֵשׁ בְּכֹל מֹשְׁבֹתֵיכֶם, *You shall not kindle fire in all your dwellings* — which, of course, refers primarily to one igniting a fire in his own property — in order to make this implication.

Later commentators challenge *Tos. Yom Tov's* interpretation, because if the intent of the *Tanna's* choice of words were merely to include a fire that spreads from one field to another, as described in *Exodus* 22:5 — he

---

1. [To avoid confusion between Rav, the Talmudic sage, and *Rav*, the commentator to the Mishnah: the latter name is *italicized*; the former is in regular type.]

2. For a philosophic discussion of this thought, see Overview to ArtScroll *Siddur*.

משניות / בבא קמא — פרק א: ארבעה אבות [10]

could just as well have used the more familiar term אש, which is in that verse.

Tiferes Yisrael suggests that the *Tanna's* use of the word אש would intimate that the initiator of the fire would be liable only if a flame connected to his fire caused damage. Should a glowing coal detach itself from his fire, however, we would think that he is not responsible for it, since that is not called *fire*. The *Tanna* therefore chose the term הִבְעִר, *igniting*, to point out that one is responsible for an ignited coal as well as for fire [see *Lechem Shamayim*].

Since fire inflicts damage through being carried by the wind, any damage caused in this manner is a *toladah* of this category. Included are a stone, a knife, or a bundle, placed on the roof, which is blown off by a normal wind and inflicts damage while flying (*Rav* from *Gem.* 3b).

[At this point, the *Tanna* explains the necessity for the Torah to state each of the various *avos*, and why it would not have been possible to derive one from another.]

לֹא הֲרֵי הַשּׁוֹר כַּהֲרֵי הַמַּבְעֶה, — *The bull is not like the maveh,*

The *Tanna* questions the necessity for the Torah to state *maveh*, since the liability of *maveh* could be derived from that of *shor*. To this, he replies that the aspects of *shor* are not like the aspects of *maveh*; therefore, the latter could not be derived from the former (*Rav* from *Gem.* 5a).

The intention is that *maveh* is more lenient than *shor*. Consequently, were the Torah to state only *shor*, *maveh* could not be derived therefrom, because we would say that one is liable only for *shor*, which is more stringent, but not for *maveh*. Therefore, the Torah states *maveh*, to teach us that one is liable for it, too. According to the view of Shmuel mentioned above, *shor* means *regel* [foot], and *maveh* refers to *shen* [tooth]. Accordingly, we explain the mishnah as follows: Should the Torah state only *regel*, we would say that one is liable for it, because it occurs frequently, but not for *shen*, which is not that common. Therefore, it was necessary for the Torah to state that *shen* is also liable (*Rav* from *Gem.* 4a).

Tiferes Yisrael expatiates upon the *Gemara's* explanation: If the Torah would mention only *regel*, we would believe that this type of damage — since it is common and always prone to occur when the animal is walking — should incur liability, because the animal's owner should have watched it carefully. As for *shen*, however, although a hungry animal is apt to help itself to fruits belonging to a stranger, one that is not particularly hungry will not do so, and might not require such careful watching.

[*Rav's* interpretation of the mishnah will be explained below.]

וְלֹא הֲרֵי הַמַּבְעֶה כַּהֲרֵי הַשּׁוֹר. — *nor is the maveh like the bull.*

It was necessary for the Torah to mention *shor*; it could not have been derived from *maveh*, because it is more lenient than *maveh* in one respect. Therefore, had the Torah stated only *maveh*, we might think that only it is subject to liability because it has this stringency, but not *shor* which does not.

According to Shmuel, who interprets *shor* as *regel* [foot], and *maveh* as *shen* [tooth], the mishnah is explained as follows: *Shen* is not as lenient as *regel*, since the animal derives benefit from its *shen* damages, but not from those of *regel*. [That is, when an animal is hungry, it has a strong desire to eat, and requires strict watching against partaking of crops belonging to a stranger; that does not apply to *regel* however, (*Tif. Yis.*).] Therefore, we could not deduce *regel* from *shen* (*Rav* from *Gem.* 3a).

According to Rav, who interprets *shor* as referring to all the *avos* related to the bull — viz., *keren* [horn], *shen*, and *regel* — and *maveh* as referring to man, the mishnah is explained as follows:

Were the Torah to state only that one is liable for *shor*, we could not derive the

בבא קמא א/א

הַשּׁוֹר. וְלֹא זֶה וָזֶה, שֶׁיֵּשׁ בָּהֶן רוּחַ חַיִּים, כַּהֲרֵי הָאֵשׁ, שֶׁאֵין בּוֹ רוּחַ חַיִּים; וְלֹא זֶה וָזֶה, שֶׁדַּרְכָּן לֵילֵךְ וּלְהַזִּיק, כַּהֲרֵי הַבּוֹר, שֶׁאֵין דַּרְכּוֹ לֵילֵךְ

יד אברהם

liability of man from it, since the former category contains the stringency that if an animal kills a person, its owner must pay כֹּפֶר, *kofer* [ransom from the death penalty at the hands of Heaven (*Ex.* 21:30)]. Therefore, we would believe that one is liable for the damages inflicted by his animal, but not for the damages he himself inflicts.

On the other hand, were the Torah to state only that man is liable for the damages he himself inflicts, we would not know that he is also liable for the damages inflicted by his animal. We would think that liability for damages applies only to man — who is liable to pay for the five categories enumerated in 8:1 — but not to *shor*, whose owner is not liable to pay for the five categories. Therefore, the Torah must state both *shor* and *maveh* (*Gem.* 4a).

The *Tanna* merely tells us that *shor* and *maveh* are unlike, but does not specify in what ways, because it is easy to find a stringency in one type of damager that another one does not have, and he relies on the reader to do so. In the latter part of the mishnah, on the other hand, where we are dealing with the rarer instance of a stringent quality that two or three *avos* have over one *av*, it was necessary for the *Tanna* to elaborate (*Tos. Yom Tov* quoting *Tos.*).

In explaining the necessity for the Torah to enumerate each of the four *avos*, the *Tanna* did not follow the order he had used to list them, and state: *The bull is not like the pit.* This is because he would not be able to continue with his next statement — *Neither are these two, which are living things* — since the pit is not a living thing.

Alternatively, the mishnah deviates from the order to stress that the Torah had to specify even the bull and *maveh*, both of which are living things, and one could not be derived from the other (*Tos. Yom Tov* from Rashi).

וְלֹא זֶה וָזֶה, — *These two* [lit., *this and this*],

Namely, *shor* and *maveh* — i.e., *regel* and *shen*, according to Shmuel; the bull and the man, according to Rav (*Rav* from *Gem.* 4a).

שֶׁיֵּשׁ בָּהֶן רוּחַ חַיִּים, — *which are living things* [lit., *which have in them the spirit of life*],

They, therefore, have their own will, and may want to damage out of anger, hunger, or the like; hence, they must be watched carefully (*Tif. Yis.*).

כַּהֲרֵי הָאֵשׁ, שֶׁאֵין בּוֹ רוּחַ חַיִּים; — *are not like the fire, which is not a living thing;*

Therefore, were the Torah to state only *shor* and *maveh*, we would not know that a person is liable for the damages of a fire which he starts since the latter is not a living thing (*Rav*); i.e., it has no desire of its own to damage (*Tif. Yis.*).

Surprisingly, the *Tanna* does not continue with the reverse statement: *Nor is the fire like these ...*, which would mean that we cannot derive *shor* and *maveh* from *eish*. *Tosafos* (2a, s.v. ולא) explain that fire has no stringent aspects that are not found in *shor* and *maveh*. Although fire is unique in that it has another force combined with it — namely, the wind, which spreads it — that is not regarded as a stringency. On the contrary, the fact that this other force does not emanate from the fire itself is a leniency. [The Torah, however, holds the one who lit the fire liable as though it would spread by its own power.] Accordingly, we would, indeed, be able to derive *shor* and *maveh* from *eish*. In fact, the *Gemara* (5b) concludes that all the *avos* could have actually been derived from a combination of *bor* (pit) and any one of the others. They were written only because each one differs from the others in a particular law.

1
1
which are living things, are not like the fire, which is not a living thing; nor are these, whose manner is to go forth and damage, like the pit, whose manner is not to go forth and damage. The common feature in

YAD AVRAHAM

Nimmukei Yosef, however, maintains that the *Tanna* merely did not bother to continue with the reverse statement. *Tos. Yom Tov* notes that *Nimmukei Yosef,* unlike *Tosafos* apparently deems the fact that fire is joined by another force to be a stringency.

Tiferes Yisrael explains that, since the wind may blow at anytime, the fire must be watched more closely than *shen* and *regel,* since the animal does not commit these damages unless they are possessed with the desire to eat or to walk, respectively.

וְלֹא זֶה וָזֶה, — *nor are these,*
That is, these three [*shor, maveh,* and *eish*] (*Rashi*).

Despite the fact that this group includes both living and inanimate things, they have one common feature (*Tif. Yis.*):

שֶׁדַּרְכָּן לֵילֵךְ וּלְהַזִּיק, — *whose manner is to go forth and damage,*
Therefore, one must watch them carefully (*ibid.*).

כַּהֲרֵי הַבּוֹר, שֶׁאֵין דַּרְכּוֹ לֵילֵךְ וּלְהַזִּיק. — *like the pit, whose manner is not to go forth and damage.*

Therefore, had the Torah not written that one is liable for damages caused by a pit which he had dug or opened, we would not be able to derive it from the other three *avos.* It was therefore necessary to specify all four *avos* in the Torah (*Rav*).

Had Scripture discussed only *bor* [pit], we would not be able to derive the other three *avos* therefrom, since a pit is unique in that, from its very inception, it is prone to cause damage (*Tos. Yom Tov* from *Tos.* 2a).

As mentioned above, the *Gemara* concludes that, although none of the *avos* can be derived from each other, and neither can all be derived from *bor* or from *eish,* had the Torah specified only *bor* and any one of the other *avos,* the remaining two could have been derived from them (see *Rashi* 5b). Nonetheless, the Torah discusses all of them, because each one has a unique feature not found in the others:

◆§ **Shen** and **Regel:** One is not liable for these damages if they are perpetrated on public property.

◆§ **Bor:** A person is not liable if he opens a pit and a man falls into it and is killed, or if utensils fall into it and are broken. We derive this from *Exodus* 21:33, וְנָפַל־שָׁמָּה שׁוֹר אוֹ חֲמוֹר, *and a bull or a donkey fall therein.* The Rabbis expound that the specification of *a bull* is meant to exclude man — i.e., if a man falls into the pit, and is killed, the one who opened the pit is not required to pay ransom or any other payment to the victim's heirs. The term *a donkey* excludes utensils — i.e., if any inanimate object falls into the pit and is broken, torn, or destroyed in any way, the one who opened the pit is exempt.

◆§ **Eish:** One who starts a fire is exempt from paying for the damages it causes if hidden things are burnt — e.g., garments that are hidden in a stack of grain. This is based on the phrase (*ibid.* 22:5): אוֹ הַקָּמָה, *or standing grain,* which teaches us that one is responsible only if the fire damages exposed objects like grain standing in the field, and not objects that are hidden (*Rav* from *Gem.* 5b, *Rashi ad loc.*).

◆§ **Keren:** The first three times an animal inflicts damage by goring, its owner is liable to pay half the damages; if it gores again subsequently, he must pay the full damages.

[13] THE MISHNAH/BAVA KAMMA – Chapter One: *Arbaah Avos*

בָּבָא קַמָּא א/א

וּלְהַזִּיק. הַצַּד הַשָּׁוֶה שֶׁבָּהֶן שֶׁדַּרְכָּן לְהַזִּיק וּשְׁמִירָתָן עָלֶיךָ, וּכְשֶׁהִזִּיק, חָב הַמַּזִּיק לְשַׁלֵּם תַּשְׁלוּמֵי נֶזֶק בְּמֵיטַב הָאָרֶץ.

יד אברהם

Man: If one wounds another, he is liable to pay the five types of indemnity delineated in 8:1.

Although it was necessary in any case for the Torah to specify all the *avos* because of their various halachos, the *Tanna* nevertheless took the pains of demonstrating why the *avos* could not be derived from one another as one more reason that the Torah mentions all the *avos* in the spirit of יַגְדִּיל תּוֹרָה וְיַאְדִּיר, *that the Torah be made great and glorious* [Isaiah 42:21] (*Tos. Yom Tov* from *Tos.* 5b).

הַצַּד הַשָּׁוֶה שֶׁבָּהֶן — *The common feature in them*

[That is, the feature in which all four *avos* are alike.]

שֶׁדַּרְכָּן לְהַזִּיק, וּשְׁמִירָתָן עָלֶיךָ, — *is that their manner is to damage, and you are responsible to watch them,*

[*You* refers to the owner or initiator of the animals or things that cause the damage.]

The mishnah states this to teach us that there are other things besides these *avos* that fit this description, and that, like the *avos*, if they cause damage, the owner or initiator is liable to make restitution for it (*Rav* from *Gem.* 6a).

The *Gemara* explains the mishnah's point to be that one is liable for any type of damage, although it does not resemble any of the four mentioned in the mishnah, as long as it can be derived from a common feature in two, three, or even all four of them (*Tos. Yom Tov* from *Nimmukei Yosef*).

[The צַד הַשָּׁוֶה, common-feature interpretation, is one of the methods of exegetically interpreting Scripture (see *Gateway to the Talmud,* p. 137).].

An example of this is the case of a stone, knife, or bundle left on the roof, which is blown off by a normal wind, and someone comes along and stumbles on it. This would not be considered a *toladah* of the pit, since, unlike the latter, another force — the wind — is necessary to join with it in order to inflict damage. It is also not a *toladah* of *eish*, since — unlike fire — it does not inflict damage while moving, but only after it has stopped moving. From a combination of *bor* and *eish*, however, whose common feature is *that their manner is to damage, and you are responsible to watch them,* we derive liability in this case.

The mishnah states, *and you are responsible to watch them,* to indicate that one is not liable for damages inflicted by animals or things unless he is responsible to watch them for one of the following reasons: (1) he owns it (e.g., his animals); (2) he accepts responsibility to watch another's possession so that it should not cause any damage; (3) he performs an act which makes him liable for damages [such as digging a pit or igniting a fire].

Should he be guilty of negligence in his watching, he is obliged to make restitution for the damage. If he entrusts the damager to a responsible person, asking him to watch it, the latter assumes the responsibility, and the owner is exempt. The owner is also exempt if he watches the damager properly, as is required in that particular case, and it nevertheless inflicts damage (*Tos. Yom Tov* from *Nimmukei Yosef*).

וּכְשֶׁהִזִּיק, — *and when it damages,*

[That is, when one of these *avos* damages.]

משניות / בבא קמא — פרק א: ארבעה אבות [14]

1 1

them is that their manner is to damage, and you are responsible to watch them, and when it damages, the damager is obligated to pay for the damage with the best of the land.

YAD AVRAHAM

חָב הַמַזִיק — *the damager is obligated*
[I.e., the owner or initiator of the thing that inflicts the damage is obligated.[1]]

לְשַׁלֵּם תַּשְׁלוּמֵי נֵזֶק — *to pay for* [lit., *to pay the payments of*] *the damage*
The *Gemara* (10b) interprets the expression תַּשְׁלוּמֵי, *restitution*, as one denoting *completion*, rather than payment. This means, for example, that in a case in which one's thing caused the death of another person's animal, the carcass is given to its owner, and the damager is required to pay the difference between its value and the value of the animal prior to its death. The same is true of any instance in which the damaged item still has some value; it is returned to its owner, and the damager is responsible to compensate him only for the difference between its current value and that which it was worth originally.

Since the damaged item is given to its original owner, if it depreciates between the time of the damage and the time the case is brought to court, he suffers the loss. The damager need only pay the difference between the item's value prior to the damage and its value after the damage, regardless of its present worth (*Tos. Yom Tov* from *Nimmukei Yosef*).

בְּמֵיטַב הָאָרֶץ. — *with the best of the land.*
This is based on the verse (*Ex.* 22:4) מֵיטַב שָׂדֵהוּ וּמֵיטַב כַּרְמוֹ יְשַׁלֵּם, *the best of his field or the best of his vineyard he shall pay.* The intention is that [if the damager wishes to pay with real property, as explained below] he must pay from the best of his fields or vineyards (*Rav*). *His field* means the one belonging to the damager (*Tos. Yom Tov* from *Gem.* 6b). Although this verse deals specifically with *shen* and *regel*, the *Gemara* (5a) applies it to all types of damages.

This ruling is applicable only if the damager chooses to pay with real estate. Should he wish to pay with movables, however, he is free to pay with items of any quality. This is based on the maxim that all chattels are considered to be of the best quality, for if they cannot be sold in one place, they can be sold elsewhere. He may even pay with bran, the cheapest part of the wheat. Only if the damager chooses to pay with real estate, which obviously cannot be taken to another place and sold there, must he pay with the best quality, so that it can be easily sold (*Rav* from *Gem.* 7b).

Some authorities rule that if the damager owns both chattels and real estate, the damagee may demand that he pay with the former (*Tif. Yis.* from *Choshen Mishpat* 419:1).

This ruling applies only to damages. In the case of loans, however, if the debtor has money, he must pay the debt with it; otherwise, he must pay with movables of whatever quality he wishes. If he pays with real estate, he may give the creditor properties of at least medium quality. In the case of paying a hired worker, on the other hand, he must do so with money. If he has none, he must sell his property in order to pay the worker with money (*Rav*; *Tos.* 9a).

---

1. Although the usual term for *obligated* is חַיָב, this *Tanna* uses the Jerusalemitic form חָב (*Tos. Yom Tov* from *Gem.* 6b; see *Maharatz Chayos* to 6b.).

[15] THE MISHNAH/BAVA KAMMA — Chapter One: *Arbaah Avos*

בבא קמא א/ב

[ב] כֹּל שֶׁחַבְתִּי בִּשְׁמִירָתוֹ הִכְשַׁרְתִּי אֶת־נִזְקוֹ. הִכְשַׁרְתִּי בְּמִקְצָת נִזְקוֹ, חַבְתִּי בְתַשְׁלוּמִין כְּהֶכְשֵׁר כָּל־נִזְקוֹ. נְכָסִים שֶׁאֵין בָּהֶן מְעִילָה, נְכָסִים שֶׁל בְּנֵי בְרִית,

יד אברהם

2.

After delineating the various primary types of damagers in the first mishnah, the *Tanna* proceeds to expound the general requisites for liability applying to these damagers: namely, when a person is accountable for damages caused by his possessions, for damaging what types of property, and on whose premises must the damages be committed.

כֹּל שֶׁחַבְתִּי בִּשְׁמִירָתוֹ — *Anything that I am obligated to watch*

That is, if something that I am responsible to watch so that it not inflict any damages did, in fact, cause damage (*Tif. Yis.*).

הִכְשַׁרְתִּי אֶת־נִזְקוֹ — *I have perpetrated its damage.*

If I did not watch it adequately, and it inflicted damage, it is as if I perpetrated the damage, and I am liable to pay for it. The *Gemara* gives an example of one who entrusted his bull to a deaf-mute, a mentally deranged person, or a minor, and then the animal did some damage. The owner is liable, since he is obliged to watch it, and giving it over to such individuals is not considered proper watching (*Rav* from *Gem.* 9b).

Rashi quotes his teacher, who renders: *It is incumbent upon me to make reparations for its damage.* In other words, since I was responsible to watch it and I neglected to do so, I must compensate for the damage.

הִכְשַׁרְתִּי בְּמִקְצָת נִזְקוֹ — [*If*] *I partially perpetrated its damage* [lit., *I perpetrated part of its damage*],

Although I did not completely perpetrate the damage (*Rav*).

חַבְתִּי בְתַשְׁלוּמִין כְּהֶכְשֵׁר כָּל־נִזְקוֹ — *I am obligated to pay as though I had completely perpetrated its damage* [lit., *had perpetrated its entire damage*].

That is, if I am even partially responsible for the damage, I am obliged to pay for the entire damage as though I were completely responsible. For example, if one digs a pit in public property nine handbreadths deep — a depth capable of causing injury — and someone else digs one more handbreadth, bringing its total to ten handbreadths — a depth capable of killing — and an animal falls into it and is killed, all *Tannaim* agree that the one who completed the pit is fully responsible, since a pit of nine handbreadths, as a rule, cannot kill an animal (*Rav* from *Gem.* 10a).

Should the animal be injured and not die, however, Rabbi holds that they are both responsible, while the Sages rule that even in this case, the second one is completely responsible (*Gem.* ibid.).

The latter view is based on the phrase (*Ex.* 21:33) כִּי־יִכְרֶה אִישׁ בֹּר, *If a man digs a pit*, implying that only one of those who digs a pit is responsible for it, and no more. The end of the next verse, וְהַמֵּת יִהְיֶה־לּוֹ, *and the dead one shall be his*, is exegetically interpreted to mean that the person responsible for the pit is the one who created a pit capable of killing (*Tos.* from *Gem.* 51a).

This ruling is rationalized by *Maggid Mishneh* (*Hil. Nizkei Mamon* 12:12), who explains that since the pit was initially of such depth that it could only injure, and the second person was the one who had

2. Anything that I am obligated to watch I have perpetrated its damage. [If] I partially perpetrated its damage, I am obligated to pay as though I had completely perpetrated its damage.

[The law of damages applies to] property that is not [subject to] *me'ilah*, property of Jews, property

YAD AVRAHAM

converted it into a pit that could cause death, he is completely responsible for any damages (*Tos. Yom Tov*, as explained by *Shoshannim LeDavid*).

נְכָסִים שֶׁאֵין בָּהֶן מְעִילָה, — [*The law of damages applies to*] *property that is not* [*subject to*] *me'ilah*,

One is responsible for damaging property only if the law of מְעִילָה, *me'ilah* — the prohibition to steal or derive benefit from consecrated objects (*Lev.* 5:15) — does not apply to it. If one transgresses the law of *me'ilah*, he must pay not only for the value of the object, but he is obliged to pay an additional one-fifth of that amount as well, and bring an אָשָׁם, *guilt-offering*. The mishnah teaches us that if a person or something belonging to him damages consecrated property, he is exempt from paying for it.

The Torah [*Ex.* 21:35] states this ruling regarding the law of *keren* [horn]: וְכִי־יִגֹּף שׁוֹר־אִישׁ אֶת־שׁוֹר רֵעֵהוּ, *If a man's bull gores another's bull*, which is interpreted to mean that the owner of the bull is liable only if it injures a bull belonging to another person. If, however, it injures a consecrated bull, he is not liable. Although this ruling is stated regarding *keren*, it applies equally to all damagers (*Rav* from *Gem.* 6b, *Rashi* ad loc.; cf. *Ravad*, cited by *Meiri* ibid.).

Rav follows *Rava's* explanation (cited in the *Gemara* 13a) of the mishnah — that one is exempt from recompensing for the damage of any consecrated object, even those that are not subject to *me'ilah*, such as קָדָשִׁים קַלִּים, *kodoshim kallim* (offerings of lesser sanctity). The expression in the mishnah, *property that is not* [*subject to*] *me'ilah*, refers only to private property, to which *me'ilah* is not applicable.

Tos. Yom Tov, however, quotes R' Yochanan's view (*Gem. loc. cit.*) that one is exempt for damaging only those offerings which are subject to *me'ilah*. Should he or one of his things damage *kodoshim kallim*, however, since there is no *me'ilah* involved, he is indeed liable for the damages. This is in accordance with the opinion of R' Yose the Galilean, who considers *kodoshim kallim* to be private property. It appears that *Rambam* concurs with this view in *Hilchos Nizkei Mamon* 8:1, according to *Lechem Mishneh* and *Beur HaGra*.

In his *Commentary*, however, *Rambam* appears to explain the mishnah as discussing the animal that *inflicts* the damage. He states that there are five conditions requisite for the damager to be liable for the damage perpetrated by his belongings; should one of these conditions be lacking, he is exempt. The first is that they not be consecrated, for if the animal were consecrated — e.g., as a חַטָּאת, *sin-offering*, or an אָשָׁם, *guilt-offering* — and it caused damage, he is not liable. This is what the *Tanna* means by *property that is not* [*subject to*] *me'ilah*.

נְכָסִים שֶׁל בְּנֵי בְרִית, — *property of Jews* [lit., *children of the covenant*],

This comes to exclude the case of property of a Jew that damaged property of a gentile. Since the gentile is not included in the covenant between God and the Jewish people, the *Tanna* exempts the damager from liability (*Rav, Gem.* 13b).

[17] THE MISHNAH/BAVA KAMMA – Chapter One: *Arbaah Avos*

בבא קמא א/ג

נְכָסִים הַמְיֻחָדִים, וּבְכָל־מָקוֹם חוּץ מֵרְשׁוּת הַמְיֻחֶדֶת לַמַּזִּיק וּרְשׁוּת הַנִּזָּק וְהַמַּזִּיק. וּכְשֶׁהִזִּיק, חָב הַמַּזִּיק לְשַׁלֵּם תַּשְׁלוּמֵי נֶזֶק בְּמֵיטַב הָאָרֶץ.

[ג] שׁוּם כֶּסֶף, וְשָׁוֶה כֶסֶף, בִּפְנֵי בֵית־דִּין, וְעַל־

יד אברהם

[This is explained at length in the commentary to 4:3.]

נְכָסִים הַמְיֻחָדִים — *property that is owned*.

One is liable for damaging property only if it has an owner; should he damage ownerless property, however, he is exempt (*Rav; Rashi*).

Tos. Yom Tov strongly challenges this interpretation. Although this is indeed the apparent meaning of the mishnah, the *Gemara* (13b) refutes it, since it is obvious that the damager is exempt, there being no one to institute an action against him.

Instead, the *Gemara* explains the mishnah to mean that, for example, an ownerless bull gores a bull which has an owner. Immediately after the goring, a stranger takes possession of the bull that gored, thus preventing the owner of the gored bull from taking it and thereby receiving restitution for the damage. The *Tanna* teaches us that since the damaging bull had no owner, it cannot be taken as restitution if someone else already acquired it. Alternatively, if the owner of a bull that gored relinquished his ownership of the bull or consecrated it after the goring, but prior to the final verdict of the court, he is not responsible, since the damager must have an owner at the time the verdict is delivered. [See *Lechem Shamayim.*]

The *Gemara* (13b) also offers an alternative interpretation of the mishnah: Liability is applicable only if it is known who the owner of the goring bull is. Should two bulls pursue a third one and gore it, and each of the owners claims that the other's bull inflicted the damage, they are both exempt. [This is discussed at length in the commentary to 3:11.]

וּבְכָל־מָקוֹם — *and anywhere*.

That is, wherever one's possessions inflict damage to another's property, he is liable (*Rav; Rashi*).

חוּץ מֵרְשׁוּת הַמְיֻחֶדֶת לַמַּזִּיק — *except [on] the premises owned by the damager*.

If, for example, a person's bull enters someone else's property, and a bull belonging to the owner of that property gores it, the property owner is exempt from payment, since he can claim, 'What was your bull doing in my property?' (*Rav, Rashi* from *Gem.* 13b).

This ruling applies only if one's possessions cause the damage. Should the owner of the premises himself intentionally injure another person who entered without permission, however, he is liable, for the injured person can claim, 'You have only the right to evict me; you have no right to injure me' (*Rav* from *Gem.* 48a).

The same applies if a person injures another's animal, which enters his premises without permission. The owner of the animal can claim, 'You have only the right to evict my animal from your property; you have no right to injure it' (*Tos. Yom Tov* from *Rambam Commentary* and *Hil. Nizkei Mamon* 7:7, *Tur Choshen Mishpat* 378, *Nimmukei Yosef*).

וּרְשׁוּת הַנִּזָּק וְהַמַּזִּיק — *and the premises of the damagee and the damager*.

If a yard was owned jointly by two partners, and an animal owned by one of them damaged the property of the other in that yard, if it damaged through *shen* and *regel* — i.e., if the animal ate

משניות / בבא קמא — פרק א: ארבעה אבות [18]

that is owned, and anywhere except [on] the premises owned by the damager and the premises of the damagee and the damager. When he damages, the damager is obligated to pay for the damage with the best of the land.

3. The evaluation is in money, and [the payment is made with] money's worth, in the presence of

YAD AVRAHAM

fruit belonging to the other partner, or trampled it — its owner is exempt. This ruling applies only if the yard was designated for animals as well as produce. However, should the yard be designated for produce, but not for animals, and one partner's animal ate or trampled the other's produce, he is liable. On the other hand, if one partner's animal caused damages in the category of *keren* (horn), he is liable in all cases (*Rav* from *Gem.* 13b).

These rulings are based on the verse (*Ex.* 22:4): וּבִעֵר בִּשְׂדֵה אַחֵר, *and it grazes in another's field,* from which the Sages deduce that if a yard is designated for fruit only and not for animals, since animals are not supposed to be there, it is considered *another's field,* even in regard to the animal of one of the yard's partners, and he is liable if it causes damage. Should the yard be designated for animals as well, since they are permitted to enter the yard, it is not regarded as *another's field,* but as his own field, and he is exempt from paying for damages committed by his animals (*Tos. Yom Tov* from *Rashi* to *Gem.* ad loc.).

If the yard is designated for the animals of both partners (e.g., Reuven and Shimon), but for the fruit of only one of them (Reuven), and Shimon's animal enters the yard and destroys Reuven's fruit with *shen* or *regel* — according to *Rif* and *Rambam* (loc. cit. 1:9), since only Reuven has the right to bring in fruit, it is regarded as *another's field,* and Shimon is liable. According to *Rabbeinu Tam,* however, since Shimon has a right to bring his animal into the yard, it is not regarded as *another's field,* and he is exempt (*Tos. R' Akiva*).

וּכְשֶׁהִזִּיק, חָב הַמַּזִּיק לְשַׁלֵּם תַּשְׁלוּמֵי נֶזֶק בְּמֵיטַב הָאָרֶץ. — *When he damages, the damager is obligated to pay for the damage with the best of the land.*

Although this was already stated in the previous mishnah, it is repeated here to include *keren* (horn), not mentioned in the above mishnah, which — according to Shmuel — deals only with damagers that are considered *muad* (forewarned) from the beginning, and excludes *keren,* since an animal is considered a *tam* with regard to goring until it gores three times (*Tos. Yom Tov* from *Gem.* 4a, 13b). The mishnah teaches us that even the damages of *keren* must be paid from the best of the land (*Tif. Yis.*).

3.

The following mishnah proceeds to discuss the rules concerning the types of damages, how the amount of the damage is determined, and what type of witnesses are accepted to offer testimony in such cases.

שׁוּם כֶּסֶף, — *The evaluation is in money,*

The evaluation of damages is made in amounts of money; i.e., the court evaluates how much the damage amounts to, and the damager pays that amount. For example, if Reuven's cow entered Shimon's premises and trampled his garment — thereby tearing it —

א/ג   פִּי עֵדִים בְּנֵי חֹרִין בְּנֵי בְרִית. וְהַנָּשִׁים בִּכְלַל הַנֶּזֶק.
יד אברהם

and on a later occasion, Reuven's cow tripped on that very garment in public property — which is considered like a pit in public property (see below) — and broke its leg, we do not say that, since each one injured the other, let one damage cancel out the other. Rather, we evaluate both damages, and the one who damaged more must pay the difference (*Rav* and *Rashi* to *Gem.* 14b).

Tos. Yom Tov explains that any item lying in a place where it is liable to cause injury is similar to a pit, and is deemed its *toladah*.

Although the two injuries appear to be equal, we do not say that one cancels out the other; rather, we submit the case to the court for exact evaluation, and in the event that the damages are not equal, the perpetrator of the greater damage pays the difference. If, indeed, the damages are equal, both are exempt (*Tos. Yom Tov* from *Nimmukei Yosef*).

וְשָׁוֶה כֶסֶף, — and [the payment is made with] *money's worth*,

[In the following case, restitution for the damages need not be paid in money:] If Reuven damages Shimon, and dies before the case is settled, Shimon has a lien only on the real property of Reuven's estate, not the movables. The *Tanna* expresses this with the phrase שָׁוֶה כֶסֶף, *money's worth*, to denote that there is a lien only on real property, which is *worth* money. Chattels, however — because of their liquidity — are considered like money itself (*Rav* from *Gem.* 14b).

This follows the rule that movables belonging to orphans are not pledged to creditors (*Tif. Yis.*).

Rav (*Kesubos* 9:3) states that the prevailing practice in all Jewish courts is that movables of orphans are indeed pledged to creditors. *Rambam* (*Hil. Nizkei Mamon* 8:12) adds that this practice applies to all debts, including damages, a view shared by *Rif* and *Rosh* (loc. cit.). *Rosh* goes so far as to assert that — since all business is nowadays transacted with chattels, rather than with real estate — they, too, are pledged to creditors according to Talmudic law. There are, however, other interpretations of that ruling. See *Rosh, Kesubos* 6:5.

Rabbeinu Ephraim [quoted by *Tur Choshen Mishpat* 419], however, rules that the practice of mortgaging the chattels of orphans was innovated only for repaying loans, in order to maintain their availability. [Knowing that they could collect their loans even from movables of their debtor's heirs, if necessary, people would more readily agree to lend money.] Regarding damages, however, since their occurrence is relatively uncommon, this practice was not implemented (*Tos. Yom Tov*).

Since, unlike in *Kesubos* [9:3], *Rav* is silent about the current practice regarding a lien on the chattels of a damager's estate, we have no way of knowing his view on this issue (*Tos. Yom Tov*).[1]

בִּפְנֵי בֵית־דִּין, — *in the presence of a court*,

The evaluation and the payment shall be made only in the presence of a court of מֻמְחִין, *mumchin* [authorized judges], not before one of הֶדְיוֹטוֹת, *laymen* (*Rav* from *Gem.* 14b).

[*Mumchin* are those judges authorized by their predecessors, who were, in turn, authorized by their predecessors, in one continuous line, stemming from Moses, who authorized Joshua. This authorization is traditionally known as סְמִיכָה, *semichah*. Those judges who are the recipients of

---

1. [The mere fact that *Rav* is silent here on this topic is not conclusive proof that he holds damages to be different from debts, since *Rambam*, too, in his *Commentary* here does not mention this issue, although he concurs with *Rav's* view in his *Commentary* to *Kesubos* 9:2; yet, in *Hilchos Nizkei Mamon* 8:12, he states that this practice applies to all cases, including damages. Obviously, he had intended that the readers of his *Commentary* should apply his comment in *Kesubos* 9:2 to here as well.]

1 3
a court, and by the testimony of witnessess [who are] freemen [and] Jews. Women are governed by the [law

YAD AVRAHAM

semichah are empowered to judge cases of fines, such as בְּפֶל, *the twofold payment*, and אַרְבָּעָה וַחֲמִשָּׁה, *the fourfold and fivefold payments*, which the Torah imposes on a thief in certain cases (see preface to 7:1).

Hedyotos are those who have not received this traditional authorization. Although they may be accomplished scholars, they are not allowed to judge such cases.]

Notwithstanding that our mishnah does not treat cases of fines — since, according to Shmuel, *shor* refers to *regel* and *maveh* to *shen*, both of which are examples of מָמוֹן, *restitution* — it nevertheless intimates that there are other cases that require *mumchin* (Tos. 14b).

Although *keren* is alluded to at the end of the preceding mishnah (see commentary there, s.v. וּכְשֶׁהִזִּיק), and the half-damage payment for *keren* is regarded as a fine, the mishnah here refers to the full-damage payment of the *muad*, who has already gored three times. This is evident from the *Tanna's* concluding statement that the payment must be made with the best of the land, which applies only to a *muad*, and not to a *tam*, as outlined at the end of this chapter (Tos. Yom Tov).

וְעַל־פִּי עֵדִים — *and by the testimony of witnesses*

As discussed in 7:4 and in *Kesubos* 3:9, if a person admits that he is guilty of a crime punishable by a fine before witnesses attest to that fact, he is exempt from paying the fine. According to some opinions, once he admits, he is permanently exempt, even if witnesses come thereafter (Gem. 14b).

בְּנֵי חֹרִין — *[who are] freemen*

This excludes gentile slaves belonging to Jews; although they must be circumcised and observe all the commandments required of Jewish women, they are disqualified from testifying (Gem. 15a, 88a).

בְּנֵי בְרִית. — *[and] Jews.*

This statement disqualifies gentiles from testifying. Were the *Tanna* to tell us that a slave is disqualified, we would think that this is only because he has no legal pedigree, but gentiles, who have a legal pedigree, are qualified. Should the *Tanna* tell us that gentiles are disqualified from testimony, we would think that this is because they are not bound by the *mitzvos*, whereas a gentile slave — who is obligated to perform those commandments required of a woman — is qualified for testimony. Consequently, the *Tanna* must tell us that both gentiles and gentile slaves are disqualified (Gem. 15a).

Although these two groups are unfit for all types of testimony, the *Tanna* found it necessary to inform us that they are disqualified to testify in cases of damage. *Rambam (Commentary and Hil. Nizkei Mamon* 8:13) writes: You should not think that — since the only ones found in the horse stables, the cattle stalls, and the sheep pens are slaves, shepherds and the like — if they testified that this is the animal that damaged, we should believe them; or if children or women testified that this person injured that one, or if they testified concerning other damages — do not think that we should rely on them. Such is not the case; we never impose an obligation of money by the testimony of witnesses, unless they are witnesses who are qualifed to testify in other cases, and they testify in court, and the court obligates the damager to pay.

Tur [*Choshen Mishpat* 408] states that even in the case of an animal belonging to a gentile that gores an animal belonging to a Jew we must require qualified witnesses, not slaves or gentiles (Tos. Yom Tov).

Although gentiles accept gentile witnesses — when they come to our courts, we must judge them according to our laws (Tos. R' Akiva from *Yam Shel Shlomo*).

וְהַנָּשִׁים בִּכְלַל הַנֶּזֶק. — *Women are*

[21] THE MISHNAH/BAVA KAMMA – Chapter One: *Arbaah Avos*

בבא קמא א/ד

וְהַנִּזָּק וְהַמַּזִּיק בְּתַשְׁלוּמִין.

[ד] **חֲמִשָּׁה** תַּמִּין וַחֲמִשָּׁה מוּעָדִין: הַבְּהֵמָה אֵינָהּ מוּעֶדֶת — לֹא לִגַּח, וְלֹא לִגּוֹף, וְלֹא לִשּׁוֹךְ, וְלֹא לִרְבּוֹץ, וְלֹא לִבְעוֹט. הַשֵּׁן

יד אברהם

governed by the [law of] damages.

Whether she damages others or others damage her, the laws applying to men and to women are uniform (Rav).

וְהַנִּזָּק וְהַמַּזִּיק בְּתַשְׁלוּמִין. — *The damagee and the damager are included in the payment.*

Sometimes the one who is the victim of the damage must, in a sense, pay for part of it, just as the one who inflicts it. For example, if Reuven's bull killed Shimon's bull, and the carcass deteriorated before the case was brought to court, Shimon must suffer the depreciation. The result is that Reuven does not make the complete half-damage payment to which the Torah entitled Shimon if Reuven's bull is a *tam*, or the entire full-damage payment if his bull was a *muad*. Since, in this case, the damagee sustains an additional loss, we may say that he is paying for the damage along with the damager (*Rav* from *Gem.* 15a).

Although this law was already alluded to in the preceding mishnah, it is repeated here to teach us that it applies both in the case of *tam* and in the case of *muad*. Should the *Tanna* tell us this ruling regarding *tam*, we would be likely to believe that — only in this case — in which the animal's owner had not been warned after each of three gorings, does the damager not suffer the loss of the depreciation of the carcass, but that in the case of a *muad*, he does suffer that loss.

On the other hand, were the *Tanna* to state this ruling only as regards *muad* we might think that it applies only in that case, reasoning that since the owner of the injured animal receives complete compensation, he must, at least, suffer the loss of depreciation. In the case of *tam*, however, since he is compensated only for half the damages, he need not suffer the loss of depreciation.

To avoid these misconceptions, both cases must be stated in the mishnah (*Tos. Yom Tov* from *Gem.* 15a).

4.

⊰§ **תָּם/Tam and מוּעָד/Muad**

The following mishnah deals with the subject of the תָּם, *tam* [the tame damager; pl. *tamin*], and the מוּעָד, *muad* [the damager whose owner is forewarned; pl. *muadin*]. *Tam* is the term used to describe something that damages in a way it is not accustomed to, but happened to do so in this case. *Muad* notes something that constantly or usually damages in a particular way (*Rambam Commentary*).

The only case of *tam* mentioned in the Torah is that of *keren*, damage caused by a bull's horn. This includes all its *tolados* (secondary types of damages). Should an animal gore three times, and its owner was warned each time, it is deemed a *muad*.

In the words of the Torah (*Ex.* 21:35f.): *If a man's bull gores another's bull, and it dies, they shall sell the live bull and divide the money of it, and also divide the dead one. But if it was known that the bull was a habitual gorer from yesterday and the day before, and its owner does not watch it, he shall surely pay a bull for the bull, and the dead one shall be his.*

This is interpreted by the *Gemara* (23b) to mean that the first three times an animal gores or damages in any unusual way with intention to damage, the damagee

משניות / בבא קמא — פרק א: ארבעה אבות [22]

1 4 of] damages. The damagee and the damager are included in the payment.

4. [T]here are] five that are *tamin* and five that are *muadin:* An animal is not *muad* — neither to gore, nor to push, nor to bite, nor to lie down, nor to

YAD AVRAHAM

is awarded half the damages by becoming a partner in the animal for that amount. Should the entire body of the damaging animal not equal half the damages, the damagee has no recourse to obtain the difference. Once the animal gores three times, and the owner has been warned each time to watch it, the animal is regarded as a *muad*, and the fourth time it gores, the owner must pay the complete damages from the best of his property.

Other types of damagers, such as *shen, regel, eish, bor,* and man, are regarded as *muadin* from the outset, since they are accustomed to damage in this manner from their inception.

חֲמִשָּׁה תַמִּין — [There are] five that are tamin

There are five ways in which an animal is generally not accustomed to cause damage. If it does so, however, its owner is liable to pay for half the damages, (Rav).

וַחֲמִשָּׁה מוּעָדִין: — and five that are muadin:

There are five cases in which the damager is accustomed to damage in a certain manner, and must therefore pay the complete damages (Rav).

[The mishnah now proceeds to list the five acts, regarding which an animal is generally considered a *tam.*]

הַבְּהֵמָה אֵינָהּ מוּעֶדֶת — An animal is not muad —

[It is generally not considered forewarned in the following respects. However, if it already commited the act three times, and its owner had been warned each time, it is considered forewarned.]

The *Tanna* chooses the expression *is not muad* rather than *is tam* to contrast the following acts — which are all *tolados* of *keren* — with *shen* and *regel,* concerning which the mishnah states below: *Shen is muad to eat what is fit for it; regel is muad to break as it walks.*

These two are considered *muad* from the outset, unlike *keren* and its *tolados,* which are not. Had he stated, *An animal is tam as regards goring* ..., we would be led to believe that it always remained a *tam* in these respects and never pays for the complete damage in such cases (*Tif. Yis.*).

לֹא לִגַּח, — neither to gore,

With its horns (*Rav; Rashi; Rambam*).

וְלֹא לִגוּף, — nor to push,

With its body (*Rashi*). Rav describes it as *pushing with the entire body.* Rambam (*Commentary*) states that the term נְגִיפָה applies to pushing by any limb of the animal's body.

וְלֹא לִשּׁוֹךְ, — nor to bite,

Although biting is done with the teeth, it is not a *toladah* of *shen,* since the intention here is to the type of biting from which the animal derives no benefit, unlike *shen* — that refers to eating — from which the animal benefits (*Tos. Yom Tov* from *Gem.* 2b). [Rather, it is a *toladah* of *keren* as will be explained below.]

וְלֹא לִרְבּוֹץ, — nor to lie down,

The owner of an animal is not considered forewarned that it will lie down on large vessels and break them.

[23] THE MISHNAH/BAVA KAMMA – Chapter One: *Arbaah Avos*

בבא קמא א/ד

מוּעֶדֶת לֶאֱכוֹל אֶת הָרָאוּי לָהּ; הָרֶגֶל מוּעֶדֶת לְשַׁבֵּר בְּדֶרֶךְ הִלּוּכָהּ; וְשׁוֹר הַמּוּעָד; וְשׁוֹר הַמַּזִּיק בִּרְשׁוּת הַנִּזָּק; וְהָאָדָם. הַזְּאֵב, וְהָאֲרִי, וְהַדֹּב, וְהַנָּמֵר, וְהַבַּרְדְּלָס, וְהַנָּחָשׁ — הֲרֵי אֵלּוּ מוּעָדִין. רַבִּי אֱלִיעֶזֶר אוֹמֵר: בִּזְמַן

יד אברהם

He is, however, regarded as forewarned that it will lie down on small vessels. Therefore, if it indeed does so, he is liable to pay for the complete damage (Rambam, Hil. Nizkei Mamon 1:5). Rosh (1:21) and, apparently, Rif, however, make no such distinction.

Although the animal lies down by bending its legs, lying down is not a *toladah* of *regel* since it is not as usual a damage as *regel*, which refers to walking. The same is true of kicking (*Tos. Yom Tov* from *Gem.* 2b). [Instead, they are both *tolados* of *keren*, as will be explained below.]

ולא לבעוט. — *nor to kick*.

[See comment of *Tos. Yom Tov* cited in the above paragraph.]

Because the five acts listed thus far are done by the animal with intention to damage, they are *tolados* of *keren*, with the exception of goring, which is the *av* itself. These are the *five that are tamin*, and therefore, if an animal causes damage in one of these ways, its owner is liable for only half the damages (*Rav; Rashi*).

[The mishnah now proceeds to list the *five that are muadin*.]

הַשֵּׁן מוּעֶדֶת לֶאֱכוֹל אֶת הָרָאוּי לָהּ; — *Shen is muad to eat what is fit for it;*

[That is, the owner of an animal is considered to have been forewarned to prevent his animal from damaging another's property through eating what is fit for it, such as fruits and vegetables (2:2). Consequently, he is liable for the full amount of the damages.] This is true even the first time the animal causes such a damage, and even if the owner had not been warned to prevent him from doing this. [Since it is customary for the animal to damage things in this manner, the owner should have known to watch it properly.] The same applies to *regel* mentioned below (*Gem.* 16a).

[According to *Rav*, this is the first of the *five that are muadin*. Others, however, interpret the mishnah differently, as discussed below.]

הָרֶגֶל מוּעֶדֶת לְשַׁבֵּר בְּדֶרֶךְ הִלּוּכָהּ; — *regel is muad to break as it walks;*

[That is, the owner of an animal is deemed forewarned to prevent it from breaking pottery or the like unintentionally while it walks. According to *Rav*, this is the second of the *five that are muadin*. See comment of the *Gemara* (16b) cited above.]

וְשׁוֹר הַמּוּעָד; — *the muad bull;*

I.e., if a bull [or any other animal] caused damage through any of the five acts mentioned above — namely: goring, pushing, biting, lying down, or kicking — three times, and its owner had been warned after each time, he is liable to pay for the complete damages caused by such an act from then on. Although these types of damages are counted as five units in the mishnah's enumeration of those *that are tam*, they are reckoned as only one item [the third] in the list of those *that are muadin* (*Rav.*)

Since, in these cases, the owner of the animal becomes forewarned through one process — the testimony of witnesses that the animal caused damage — they are counted as one item in this list (*Rashi*).

וְשׁוֹר הַמַּזִּיק בִּרְשׁוּת הַנִּזָּק; — *the bull that damages [while] on the premises of the*

משניות / בבא קמא — פרק א: ארבעה אבות [24]

1 4 kick. *Shen* is *muad* to eat what is fit for it; *regel* is *muad* to break as it walks; the *muad* bull; the bull that damages [while] on the premises of the damagee; and man.

The wolf, the lion, the bear, the leopard, the *bardelas*, and the snake are *muadin*. R' Eliezer says:

YAD AVRAHAM

damagee;

Although one's animal never gored before, and is generally deemed tame in this respect, if it enters another person's premises and gores the latter's animal, the owner of the goring animal is adjudged as if he were forewarned, and must pay for the complete damage. This follows the view of R' Tarfon (2:5). The halachah, however, is in accordance with the opinion of the Sages (ibid.), who rule that only the visual half-damage payment is due *(Rav).*

[According to *Rav*, this is the fourth of the *five that are muadin.*]

Rav's statement that this is in accordance with R' Tarfon applies only to this segment of the mishnah. The beginning of the mishnah, however, which states, *An animal is not muad — neither to gore, nor to push ...,* deals with damages committed on the premises of the damagee. This is evident from the following segment, *Shen is muad to eat what is fit for it; regel is muad to break as it walks,* which applies only in the premises of the damagee, since there is no liability for such damages anywhere else. It follows that the beginning of the mishnah is telling us that the owner of an animal which damages while on the premises of the damagee is not considered forewarned and, hence, pays only for half the damage. Obviously, this follows the view of the Sages (quoted above), who disagree with R' Tarfon *(Tos. Yom Tov* following Shmuel in *Gem.* 15b).

וְהָאָדָם. — *and man.*

Man, too, is considered forewarned from the outset, and is always obliged to pay the full damages *(Rav).*

Thus we have *five that are muadin.* The *Tanna* does not count *the pit* and *the fire,* since he deals only with living creatures *(Rashi). Tosafos* (4a) conclude that, the reason he did not include them was that, since they are inanimate objects, there is obviously no difference between the first time they damage and the fourth time *(Tos. Yom Tov).*

Tiferes Yisrael suggests that the category of *man* includes *the pit* and *the fire,* since a man digs the pit and ignites the fire.

As mentioned above, *Rav* explains the mishnah according to Shmuel, attributing the first part to the Sages and the second part to R' Tarfon. There is another interpretation of the mishnah offered by Ravina in the *Gemara* (16a). He explains that the text of the mishnah is deficient, and should read as follows: *There are five that are tamin, and if they damage three times, the five of them become muadin. Shen and the regel, however, are muadin from the outset. This is the muad bull* (i.e., the forewarned bull discussed here is the one referred to by the Torah [*Ex.* 21:29]). *Regarding the bull that damages in the premises of the damagee — that is a controversy between R' Tarfon and the Sages.*

Rav prefers Shmuel's interpretation to Ravina's, since it does not require adding words to the mishnah *(Tos. Yom Tov).* Rambam *(Commentary)* and *Rif* however, adopt Ravina's interpretation.

הַזְּאֵב, וְהָאֲרִי, וְהַדֹּב, וְהַנָּמֵר, וְהַבַּרְדְּלָס, וְהַנָּחָשׁ הֲרֵי אֵלּוּ מוּעָדִין. — *The wolf, the lion, the bear, the leopard, the bardelas, and the snake are muadin.*

The owners of these are regarded as

[25] THE MISHNAH/BAVA KAMMA – Chapter One: *Arbaah Avos*

בבא קמא א/ד

שֶׁהֵן בְּנֵי תַרְבּוּת, אֵינָן מוּעָדִין; וְהַנָּחָשׁ מוּעָד לְעוֹלָם.
מַה־בֵּין תָּם לְמוּעָד? אֶלָּא שֶׁהַתָּם מְשַׁלֵּם חֲצִי נֶזֶק מִגּוּפוֹ, וְהַמּוּעָד מְשַׁלֵּם נֶזֶק שָׁלֵם מִן־הָעֲלִיָּה.

יד אברהם

forewarned from the outset. The *Tanna* did not reckon these together with the *five that are muadin*, which would have resulted in a total of eleven items in that category, since these animals are usually not found in civilization (*Rav, Rambam Commentary*). It is therefore seldom that they have owners to be held accountable for their damages (*Tif. Yis.*).

The text of the mishnah is deficient, and should read: *And there are others that are muadin similar to these: the wolf ...* (*Tos. Yom Tov* from *Gem.*).

The owner of any of these creatures is considered forewarned, regardless of how it inflicts damage, even by biting or some other unusual manner. In all these cases he must make restitution for the full damage (*Rashi*). This view coincides with that of *Rambam* (*Hil. Nizkei Mamon* 1:6).

These beasts are adjudged like a bull that has gored three times, for whose damages its owner must pay completely, even if they are committed in public property (*Maggid Mishneh; Lechem Mishneh*).

Tosafos (16a), however, rule that the owners are regarded as forewarned only if the animals damage in their customary manner — for example, a wolf tears his prey or a lion devours it alive or tears it to store for the future. These damages fall under the category of *shen*, and the owner is therefore liable only if they take place on the premises of the damagee. Even if a snake damages through biting — from which it does not derive any benefit — its owner is nevertheless not liable if it occurs in public property. Since that is its habit, it is deemed *regel*, which is exempt from liability anywhere but in the premises of the damagee.

On the other hand, should the lion tear its prey or the wolf devour it alive — which they are not accustomed to do — these acts are considered *keren*, and the owner is liable for only half the damages.

Our translation of נָמֵר as *leopard*, unlike that of *Tiferes Yisrael* — who renders it as *tiger* — follows *Rashi* to *Jeremiah* 13:23. *Radak* in *Sefer Hashorashim* identifies it as a spotted beast. Moreover, the Aramaic נְמוּר is the equivalent of the Hebrew נָקֹד, *spotted* (*Targum Onkelos* to *Gen.* 30:32).

Concerning *bardelas*, however, there is much controversy and conjecture. *Rashi* (*Sanhedrin* 15b) and *Be'er Hagolah* (*Choshen Mishpat* 389:80) identify it as a skunk. *Tosafos* (loc. cit.) take exception to *Rashi's* definition, since *bardelas* is listed among animals that are much fiercer than the skunk, and which customarily kill people. Rather, they conjecture that it is a species of the snake. *Aruch* renders it as *a leopardess*, which is even more ferocious than its male counterpart. Other commentators identify it as the cheetah, and some, as the hyena (*Kaffich*). See *Aruch Hashalem*.

רַבִּי אֱלִיעֶזֶר אוֹמֵר: בִּזְמַן שֶׁהֵן בְּנֵי תַרְבּוּת, — *R' Eliezer says: When they are domesticated*,

[If people raised them, and trained them not to inflict damage.]

אֵינָן מוּעָדִין; — *they are not muadin;*

That is, their owners are not considered forewarned unless the animals demonstrate that they are habitual damagers.

1 4 When they are domesticated, they are not *muadin*; but the snake is always *muad*.

What is [the difference] between a *tam* and a *muad*? Only that the [owner of the] *tam* pays half the damages from its body, and the [owner of the] *muad* pays the full damages from the best of the property.

YAD AVRAHAM

The halachah does not follow R' Eliezer's view; rather even if these animals are domesticated, their owners are considered forewarned *(Rav; Rambam).*

וְהַנָּחָשׁ מוּעָד לְעוֹלָם. — *but the snake is always muad.*
Although it is domesticated *(Tif. Yis.).* This is the conclusion of R' Eliezer's statement *(Beis David).*

מַה־בֵּין תָּם לְמוּעָד? — *What is [the difference] between a tam and a muad?*
[What are the differences between the liability of the owner of a *tam* and that of an owner who is considered forewarned to guard his animal?]

אֶלָּא שֶׁהַתָּם מְשַׁלֵּם חֲצִי נֶזֶק מִגּוּפוֹ, — *Only that the [owner of the] tam pays half the damages from its body,*
[That is, the damagee is recompensed by becoming a partner in the animal that did the damage for half the amount of the loss he incurred (see preface).]
Since his compensation is limited to a partnership in the animal that caused the damage, should the latter be lost or die, the damagee receives no restitution for the loss he suffered *(Tif. Yis.).*
[Additionally, even if half of the amount of the damages exceeds the value of the damaging animal, the owner's liability is not increased (see 3:11 and commentary there).]

וְהַמּוּעָד מְשַׁלֵּם נֶזֶק שָׁלֵם מִן־הָעֲלִיָּה. — *and the [owner of the] muad pays the full damages from the best of the property.*
Even if the animal that caused the damage is worth less than the amount of the damage, the owner must nonetheless pay the complete amount. This is derived from the verse regarding the *muad* (Exodus 21:36), *He shall surely pay a bull for the bull,* and it does not say that he should pay 'from the body of the bull' *(Rav).*
Therefore, even if the damaging bull dies, the owner must pay for the damages, unlike the case of the *tam* above *(Tif. Yis.).*

Chapter 2

1.

The following chapter elaborates on the *five that are muadin* — which are enumerated in the preceding mishnah.

Although that mishnah states *shen* before *regel,* this mishnah commences with the latter, since, following the pattern of the very first mishnah of the tractate, according to Shmuel (see commentary ibid., s.v. The Dispute between Rav and Shmuel), that is the meaning of *the bull* mentioned first there. Even according to Rav (ibid.), *regel* is included under that category. *Shen,* however, according to Shmuel, is referred to as *maveh* (Meiri; cf. Tos., quoted by Tos. Yom Tov).

[27]   THE MISHNAH/BAVA KAMMA – Chapter One: *Arbaah Avos*

בבא קמא ב/א

[א] **כֵּיצַד** הָרֶגֶל מוּעֶדֶת? לְשַׁבֵּר בְּדֶרֶךְ הִלּוּכָהּ. הַבְּהֵמָה מוּעֶדֶת לְהַלֵּךְ כְּדַרְכָּהּ וּלְשַׁבֵּר. הָיְתָה מְבַעֶטֶת, אוֹ שֶׁהָיוּ צְרוֹרוֹת מְנַתְּזִין מִתַּחַת רַגְלֶיהָ, וְשָׁבְרָה אֶת־הַכֵּלִים, מְשַׁלֵּם חֲצִי נֶזֶק. דָּרְסָה עַל־הַכְּלִי וּשְׁבָרַתּוּ, וְנָפַל עַל־כְּלִי וּשְׁבָרוֹ,

יד אברהם

כֵּיצַד הָרֶגֶל מוּעֶדֶת? — *In what way is regel [considered] muad?*

That is, for what damages in the category of *regel* is the owner of an animal considered forewarned so that he must pay for the full damage? (Tif. Yis.).

לְשַׁבֵּר בְּדֶרֶךְ הִלּוּכָהּ — *To break as it walks.*

If an animal breaks vessels or utensils while it is walking, its owner is considered forewarned regarding those damages (Rav; Rashi). Although this statement does not add anything to the preceding mishnah, it is stated here as an introduction to the following statement, which deals with the *tolados* of *regel* (Tos. Yom Tov from Nimmukei Yosef).

Tosafos explain this as part of the mishnah's question: *In what way is regel [considered] muad to break as it walks?*

הַבְּהֵמָה מוּעֶדֶת לְהַלֵּךְ כְּדַרְכָּהּ וּלְשַׁבֵּר — *The animal is muad to walk in its usual manner and break.*

Whereas the beginning of the mishnah deals with the *av* — the primary case of *regel*, in which the animal breaks something by treading upon it — this sentence deals with the *tolados* of *regel*; namely, damages done by the animal with its body, its hair [i.e., utensils became entangled in its hair, and it dragged and broke them], or the pack it was carrying, as it walked along (*Rav* from *Gem.* 17b).

According to Tosafos' interpretation, cited above, this is the *Tanna's* reply to the question: *In what way is regel [considered] muad to break as it walks?*

To this he answers that the *tolados* [enumerated above] are classified as *regel*, and the owner of the animal is considered forewarned in all those cases.

הָיְתָה מְבַעֶטֶת — *[If] it was kicking,*

And thereby damaged something (Meiri). This is an unusual occurrence, and therefore, a *toladah* of *keren*, which includes all unusual damages. Consequently, the owner pays only half the damages (Rav; Rashi; see preface to 1:4).

Although this is not one of the *tolados* of *regel* which is the subject of this mishnah, the *Tanna* mentions it nevertheless, since — like the following case — its liability is limited to half the damages (Tos. Yom Tov from Tos.).

Since this is a *toladah* of *keren*, the owner is liable even if the animal damages while on public property (Meiri).

אוֹ שֶׁהָיוּ צְרוֹרוֹת מְנַתְּזִין מִתַּחַת רַגְלֶיהָ — *or [if] pebbles were flying from under its feet,*

[This includes pebbles, splinters, or anything else that flew because of the animal's power.]

וְשָׁבְרָה אֶת־הַכֵּלִים — *and it broke vessels,*

[The pebbles or other items flew and broke vessels (see *Shinuyei Nuschaos*).]

מְשַׁלֵּם — *he pays*

[The owner of the animal pays.]

חֲצִי נֶזֶק — *half the damages.*

Although the animal broke the vessels in a usual manner, its owner pays only half the damages, for it is a הֲלָכָה לְמֹשֶׁה מִסִּינַי, *a tradition received orally by Moses at Sinai,* that if the animal damages by its power — without

משניות / בבא קמא — פרק ב: **כיצד הרגל** [28]

1. In what way is *regel* [considered] *muad*? To break as it walks. The animal is *muad* to walk in its usual manner and break.

[If] it was kicking, or [if] pebbles were flying from under its feet, and it broke vessels, he pays half the damages. [If] it stepped on a vessel and broke it, and it fell on a vessel and broke it, for the first one he

YAD AVRAHAM

its body coming in contact with the damaged object — the owner of the animal is liable for only half the damages. Since it is a *toladah* of *regel*, he is liable only if the animal commits this act in the premises of the damagee; should it occur in a public domain, he is exempt *(Rav; Rashi)*.

However, if an animal steps on pebbles in public property, causing them to fly into private property and inflict damage, its owner is liable *(Tif. Yis.* from *Gem.* 19a; *Rambam, Hil. Nizkei Mamon* 2:4).

Also, since it is a *toladah* of *regel*, the owner of the animal must pay from the best of his property, even if his animal is not worth the amount of half the damages *(Tos. Yom Tov* from *Gem.* 3b).

If the animal kicks the pebbles and thereby breaks a vessel, this is a *toladah* of *keren*, and the owner of the animal is liable even if the incident took place in a public domain. The *Gemara* (19a) discusses whether the fact that the animal caused the pebbles to fly by kicking, which is unusual, reduces the half-damage payment in this case to a quarter-damage payment, or whether there is never a payment of less than half the damages. *Rambam (Hil. Nizkei Mamon* 2:5f.) explains that the question is whether damaging with pebbles is always a *toladah* of *regel* — regardless of how it is done — and the payment for it is therefore not reduced by the fact that the kicking is unusual,

or whether it is a *toladah* of *keren* if done in an unusual manner, and the liability for it is therefore limited to only one-fourth of the damages. The *Gemara* leaves this question unresolved.

Rambam's view is that in a monetary dispute involving a halachah which is undecided by the *Gemara*, the plaintiff cannot exact any payment from the defendant. But if the former seizes that amount of money from the latter, we cannot take it away from him. Accordingly, he rules that if an animal damages by kicking pebbles in public property, its owner is exempt; but if the damagee seizes a quarter of the damages, we may not take it away from him. Should the animal damage in such a manner on the premises of the damagee, its owner is liable for one-fourth of the damages. If the damagee seizes money for half the damages, we may not take it away from him

דְּרָסָה עַל-הַכְּלִי וּשְׁבָרַתּוּ, — [*If*] *it stepped on a vessel and broke it*,

[An animal, as it was walking in the premises of the owner of a vessel, stepped on the vessel and broke it.]

וְנָפַל עַל-כְּלִי וּשְׁבָרוֹ, — *and it fell on a vessel and broke it*,

I.e., the broken vessel fell on another vessel and broke it *(Rashi to Rif;*[1] see *Dikdukei Soferim).*

The first vessel was broken by the body of the animal; the second one, by its power *(Rav; Rashi).*

---

1. [The commentary to *Rif* ascribed to *Rashi* was not written by him; its author is unknown. He adopted *Rashi's* comments to the *Gemara* to serve as an aid in the study of *Rif*. In some instances, it differs from *Rashi* to the *Gemara*. Perhaps the author had a different version.]

בבא קמא ב/ב

עַל־הָרִאשׁוֹן מְשַׁלֵּם נֶזֶק שָׁלֵם, וְעַל־הָאַחֲרוֹן מְשַׁלֵּם חֲצִי נֶזֶק. הַתַּרְנְגוֹלִים מוּעָדִין לְהַלֵּךְ כְּדַרְכָּן וּלְשַׁבֵּר. הָיָה דְלִיל קָשׁוּר בְּרַגְלָיו, אוֹ שֶׁהָיָה מְהַדֵּס, וּמְשַׁבֵּר אֶת־הַכֵּלִים, מְשַׁלֵּם חֲצִי נֶזֶק.

[ב] **כֵּיצַד** הַשֵּׁן מוּעֶדֶת? לֶאֱכוֹל אֶת־הָרָאוּי לָהּ.

יד אברהם

עַל־הָרִאשׁוֹן מְשַׁלֵּם נֶזֶק שָׁלֵם — **for the first one he pays the full damages,**

[The owner of the animal must pay for the full amount of the first vessel.] Since it broke by the animal's walking in its usual manner, the damagee is classified as *regel* (*Tif. Yis.*), and the owner is liable for the full damage (*Rav; Rashi*).

Even if the vessel rolled over and then broke, it is considered that the animal broke it with its body, and the owner is liable for the full damage (*Tos. R' Akiva from Gem.* 17b).

וְעַל־הָאַחֲרוֹן מְשַׁלֵּם חֲצִי נֶזֶק. — **and for the second one** [lit., *the last*] **he pays half the damages.**

Since the animal did not break this vessel by contact with its body, but by its power, this is analogous to the case of pebbles discussed above, and it is governed by the halachah which requires payment of half the damages (*Rav; Rashi*).

Although the animal stepped on the vessel with such force that the fragments were able to break a second vessel, we do not consider this unusual, in which case it would be a *toladah* of *keren;* rather, it is a *toladah* of *regel* (*Tos. Yom Tov* from *Tos.* and *Nimmukei Yosef*).

Also, the *Tanna* wishes to teach us that there are cases in which one must pay both a full-damage payment and a half-damage payment (*Tos. Yom Tov* from *Nimmukei Yosef*).

הַתַּרְנְגוֹלִים מוּעָדִין לְהַלֵּךְ כְּדַרְכָּן וּלְשַׁבֵּר. — **Fowl are considered** *muadin* **to walk in their usual manner and break.**

Although Scripture deals with cattle and sheep in the cases of *shen* and *regel,* the law applies to beasts and fowl as well (*Tos. Yom Tov;* see 5:7).

הָיָה דְלִיל — **[If] a thread** [lit., *a string*] **was**

The word דְלִיל denotes anything attached to the foot of the fowl (*Rav; Rashi*).

Others (cited by *Rav, Rashi*) read: דְלִי, *a bucket.*

קָשׁוּר בְּרַגְלָיו, — **tied to its feet,**

[That is, to the feet of the fowl.]

אוֹ שֶׁהָיָה מְהַדֵּס, — **or [if] it was jumping,**

This translation follows *Rav* and *Rashi.* Others (*Rambam Commentary*) render: *digging,* which fowl are more accustomed to do than other birds.

וּמְשַׁבֵּר אֶת־הַכֵּלִים, — **and it broke vessels,**

If the fowl cast the strap [or the rope] on vessels, thereby breaking them, or jumped [or was digging] upon the vessels and caused pebbles to fly, thereby breaking them (*Rav*).

מְשַׁלֵּם — **he pays**

[The owner of the fowl pays.]

חֲצִי נֶזֶק. — **half the damages.**

Since the fowl cast off the strap or rope from its leg, it is analogous to the case of pebbles in which the halachah requires that only half the damages be paid. Should the fowl break the vessels while walking with the rope tied to its foot, it is regarded as though the damage

pays the full damages, and for the second one he pays half the damages.

Fowl are considered *muadin* to walk in their usual manner and break. [If] a thread was tied to its feet, or [if] it was jumping, and it broke vessels, he pays half the damages.

2.

In what way is *shen* [considered] *muad*? To eat

YAD AVRAHAM

was done with its body, and the owner must pay for the full damages (*Tif. Yis.; Rosh*).

Until this point, we have discussed the liability of the owner of the fowl. Should the strap belong to someone, the owner of the strap is liable for the damage inflicted by his strap. Since it is customary for a fowl to drag the strap and throw it, such a case would be comparable to a fire that is spread by a usual wind. It is therefore deemed a *toladah* of *eish* [fire], just as a stone, a knife, or a bundle, placed by someone on his own roof which was blown off by a normal wind and damaged something in its flight.

Consequently, if the strap was ownerless, or if its owner watched it adequately, the owner of the fowl is liable for half the damages. Should the owner of the strap neglect to watch it, or should he tie it to the foot of the fowl, then, if the fowl was ownerless, the owner of the strap is liable for the full damages. If the fowl had an owner, the latter is liable for one-fourth of the damages, and the owner of the strap is liable for three-fourths of the damages. This is because the owner of the fowl, whose maximum liability in this case is half the damages, shares that obligation with the owner of the strap; hence, he pays only one-fourth of the damages.

The strap's owner, however — whose maximum liability in this instance is the full damages — has a partner only in half the damages; consequently, he is liable for three-fourths of the total amount. (*Tos.; Rosh*).

Rashi, however, exempts the owner of the strap completely. He differentiates between this case and that of the stone falling from the roof. In the latter instance, although the wind carries the stone, it is the weight of the stone that inflicts the damage. In our case, however, it is the power of the fowl casting the strap that directly causes the damage. Therefore the owner of the strap is not responsible (*Levush Mordechai*, ch. 3).

If a man ties an ownerless strap to the fowl's foot, and the fowl walks with it, and while resting, a person or an animal stumble over the strap, the one who tied it is liable. Although the strap did not cause damage in the same place that it was tied, he is nevertheless liable, since such a case is included in the category of obstacles that are pushed about from place to place (*Gem.* 19b, *Rashi ad loc.*), for which one is liable, as deduced from the צַד הַשָׁוֶה, *common-feature interpretation* in 1:1; *it customarily causes damage, and you are responsible to watch it* (*Gem.* 6a).

Should the thread become attached by itself and cause damage while the fowl is resting, there is no liability whatever (*Gem. ad loc.*).

2.

כֵּיצַד הַשֵּׁן מוּעֶדֶת? — *In what way is shen [considered] muad?*

That is, in what cases of *shen* is the owner of the animal considered forewarned? (*Rav*).

לֶאֱכוֹל אֶת־הָרָאוּי לָהּ — *To eat what is fit for it.*

[31] THE MISHNAH/BAVA KAMMA — Chapter Two: *Keitzad HaRegel*

בבא קמא ב/ב

הַבְּהֵמָה מוּעֶדֶת לֶאֱכוֹל פֵּרוֹת וִירָקוֹת. אָכְלָה כְּסוּת אוֹ כֵלִים, מְשַׁלֵּם חֲצִי נֶזֶק. בַּמֶּה דְבָרִים אֲמוּרִים? בִּרְשׁוּת הַנִּזָּק; אֲבָל בִּרְשׁוּת הָרַבִּים, פָּטוּר. אִם־נֶהֱנֵית, מְשַׁלֵּם מַה־שֶּׁנֶּהֱנֵית. כֵּיצַד מְשַׁלֵּם מַה־שֶּׁנֶּהֱנֵית? אָכְלָה מִתּוֹךְ

יד אברהם

The translation follows *Rav* and *Rashi*, who construe this statement as the answer to the mishnah's question.

Tosafos, however, interpret it as part of the question: *In what way is shen [considered] muad to eat what is fit for it?* The question is a follow up to mishnah 1:4, which states: *Shen is muad to eat what is fit for it.*

הַבְּהֵמָה מוּעֶדֶת לֶאֱכוֹל פֵּרוֹת וִירָקוֹת — *The animal is muad to eat fruits and vegetables.*

Although the mishnah appears to be repetitious, [i.e., according to the explanation of *Rav* and *Rashi*, this sentence seems to be superfluous; according to *Tosafos*, it does not seem to answer the question] the *Gemara* (17b) explains that the first statement refers to a wild beast, whereas this statement refers to cattle. The latter category is placed second in the mishnah despite the fact that it is the subject of the verse (*Ex.* 22:4) upon which these laws are based, since the *Tanna* favors a law derived from a Rabbinical interpretation over one which is explicitly stated in the Torah. In the first mishnah, however, it would not make sense to place the *toladah* of *regel* before its *av*, although the former is derived exegetically, and the latter is stated in Scripture, since it is the *av* upon which the liability is based.

Another explanation why the first mishnah begins with the *av* of *regel* is that since the final mishnah of the first chapter uses the expression *regel*, it is fitting for the *Tanna* to begin with that expression in the first mishnah of the second chapter (*Tos. Yom Tov*).

אָכְלָה כְּסוּת אוֹ כֵלִים — [*If*] *it ate garments or vessels,*

These are things unfit for an animal's consumption (*Meiri*).

מְשַׁלֵּם חֲצִי נֶזֶק. — *he pays half the damages.*

Since it is unusual for an animal to eat garments or vessels, such an act is a *toladah* of *keren* and its owner pays only half the damages (*Rav*).

בַּמֶּה דְבָרִים אֲמוּרִים? — *In what [regard] were these words said?*

That is, the ruling that if the animal ate fruits or vegetables, its owner is liable for the full damages (*Rav* from *Gem.* 20a).

בִּרְשׁוּת הַנִּזָּק; — *On the premises of the damagee;*

[I.e., the animal's eating took place on the premises of the owner of the fruits and vegetables.]

As mentioned above [commentary to mishnah 1], this applies to *regel* as well; the *Tanna* states it here in the case of *shen* because of the ruling stated below that the animal's owner must pay for the benefit it derived from the fruit. Obviously, this applies only to *shen*, not to *regel* (*Tos. Yom Tov*).

אֲבָל בִּרְשׁוּת הָרַבִּים, פָּטוּר. — *but in a public domain, he is exempt.*

[If the animal ate them while on public property, its owner is exempt.] This is based on the verse (*Ex.* 22:4) which discusses *shen* — וּבִעֵר בִּשְׂדֵה אַחֵר, *and it grazes in another's field*, which is construed as excluding a public domain, in which the owner of the animal is exempt [as discussed above (1:2)]. If the animal ate garments or vessels there, however, the owner is liable. Although

what is fit for it. The animal is *muad* to eat fruits and vegetables. [If] it ate garments or vessels, he pays half the damages. In what [regard] were these words said? On the premises of the damagee; but in a public domain, he is exempt. If it benefited, he pays [for] what it benefited.

How does he pay [for] what it benefited? [If] it ate

YAD AVRAHAM

it is not proper for someone to leave his things in the public domain for any period of time, the damagee is not deemed as having committed an unlawful act, since one may leave his garments or vessels there for a short time when he wishes to rest. Because this act is unusual, it is regarded as *keren* in a public domain, and the owner is liable for half the damages *(Rav* from *Gem.* 20a).

אִם־נֶהֱנֵית, — *If it benefited,*

If the animal derived benefit from the fruits and vegetables it ate in the public domain, so that the owner need not feed it *(Meiri).*

מְשַׁלֵּם מַה־שֶׁנֶּהֱנֵית. — *he pays [for] what it benefited.*

[The owner of the animal must pay the owner of the fruits for the amount of benefit that it derived by eating.]

He does not always pay for what the animal ate. If it ate expensive food, we reckon the food as if it were barley, and the owner of the animal pays for it at the cheapest price for barley — i.e., two-thirds of the market price. If it ate something cheaper than barley, he must pay two-thirds of the market price of that food. If the animal ate wheat, however — since wheat is harmful for it — the owner is entirely exempt from paying *(Rav* from *Gem.* 20a).

In the *Gemara* (ibid.), we find a controversy between Rabbah and Rava. According to *Rashi's* interpretation, Rabbah's view is that since the animal is normally fed only straw, even if it eats barley belonging to someone else, its owner is liable only for the amount of straw he saved by virtue of the animal's eating. Rava rules that he must pay for that amount of barley at its cheapest price — viz., two-thirds of the market price. Since he would feed it barley if he could obtain it for that price, he must pay the cheapest price of barley *(Meiri).* According to *Rav, Ravad* and *Rosh* (§5) the halachah is according to Rava.

Rashi explains that, according to *Rava*, the owner of the animal must pay for the amount of barley he would have fed his animal had it not eaten the fruits and vegetables. *Rambam* (Commentary and *Hil. Nizkei Mamon* 3:2), however, maintains that he must pay for the amount of food the animal ate, judging it as though it were barley *(Tos. Yom Tov).*

Rambam (*Hil. Nizkei Mamon* loc. cit.), rules that he must pay for that amount of barley or bundled grain. According to *Maggid Mishneh, Rambam* interprets the term עָמִיר in the *Gemara* to mean *bundled grain,* unlike *Rashi's* translation: *straw.* He explains that because *Rambam* was in doubt whether the halachah is in accordance with Rabbah or Rava, he rules that the animal's owner must pay the smaller sum, be it barley or bundled grain. [See also *Lechem Mishneh* ad loc.]

כֵּיצַד מְשַׁלֵּם מַה־שֶׁנֶּהֱנֵית? — *How does he pay [for] what it benefited?*

That is, what place is regarded as the public domain so that the owner of an animal which eats another's food in it must pay only what it benefited? We will then know that anywhere less public than that is regarded as the premises of the damagee, in that the animal's owner must pay for the full damages, although it is not actually the damagee's property *(Meiri).*

אָכְלָה מִתּוֹךְ הָרְחָבָה, — *[If] it ate from the middle of the street,*

[33]   THE MISHNAH/BAVA KAMMA — Chapter Two: *Keitzad HaRegel*

בבא קמא ב/ג

הָרְחָבָה, מְשַׁלֵּם מַה־שֶּׁנֶּהֱנֵית; מִצִּדֵּי הָרְחָבָה, מְשַׁלֵּם מַה־שֶׁהִזִּיקָה. מִפֶּתַח הַחֲנוּת, מְשַׁלֵּם מַה־שֶּׁנֶּהֱנֵית; מִתּוֹךְ הַחֲנוּת, מְשַׁלֵּם מַה־שֶׁהִזִּיקָה.

[ג] **הַכֶּלֶב** וְהַגְּדִי שֶׁקָּפְצוּ מֵרֹאשׁ הַגַּג וְשִׁבְּרוּ אֶת־הַכֵּלִים, מְשַׁלֵּם נֶזֶק שָׁלֵם מִפְּנֵי שֶׁהֵן מוּעָדִין.

הַכֶּלֶב שֶׁנָּטַל חֲרָרָה וְהָלַךְ לַגָּדִישׁ, אָכַל אֶת־

יד אברהם

If the animal ate while it was in the middle of the street, regardless of whether it was walking or standing still (*Meiri*).

מְשַׁלֵּם מַה־שֶּׁנֶּהֱנֵית; — *he pays for what it benefited;*

According to Shmuel in the *Gemara* (21a) this hold true even if the fruits were on the sides of the street, and the animal was in the middle of the street and turned its head to eat from the sides of the street. The halachah follows this view (*Rambam, Hil. Nizkei Mamon* 3:10).

מִצִּדֵּי הָרְחָבָה, — *from the sides of the street,*

If the animal went from the middle of the street to the side of the street, where animals usually do not walk (*Rav*).

מְשַׁלֵּם מַה־שֶׁהִזִּיקָה. — *he pays for what it damaged.*

Since animals do not usually go there, it is not considered as the public domain, and the owner of the animal must pay the full damages [since the Torah only exempts him from paying for damages committed on public property, as explained above] (*Rav* from Shmuel's opinion in the *Gemara*).

מִפֶּתַח הַחֲנוּת, — *From the entrance of a store,*

[If the animal ate fruits which were at the entrance of a store.]

מְשַׁלֵּם מַה־שֶּׁנֶּהֱנֵית; — *he pays for what it benefited;*

Since the animal can eat from the fruits by turning its head when it stands in the public domain, it is considered as a damage committed there, and therefore, its owner need not pay for the complete damages, only for the benefit it derived (*Gemara* following Shmuel's opinion).

מִתּוֹךְ הַחֲנוּת, — *from inside the store,*

This is the premises of the damagee (*Tif. Yis.*).

מְשַׁלֵּם מַה־שֶׁהִזִּיקָה. — *he pays for what it damaged.*

The owner of the animal pays for the complete damages (*Tif. Yis.*) [as he does for every damage of the *shen* category committed on the damagee's property].

3.

Just as the *Tanna* above discusses *regel* and *shen* as they are applicable to cattle, he continues with a description of these *avos* as they apply to a dog (*Rabbeinu Yehonasan*, quoted by *Shitah Mekubetzes*).

הַכֶּלֶב וְהַגְּדִי שֶׁקָּפְצוּ מֵרֹאשׁ הַגַּג — *[If] a dog or a kid jumped off the top of a roof*

Its owner left it on the roof adjacent to his neighbor's yard, and it jumped off

[34] משניות / בבא קמא — פרק ב: **כיצד הרגל**

2 3 from the middle of the street, he pays for what it benefited; from the sides of the street, he pays for what it damaged. From the entrance of a store, he pays for what it benefited; from inside the store, he pays for what it damaged.

3. [If] a dog or a kid jumped off the top of a roof and broke vessels, [its owner] pays the full damages because they are *muadin*.

[If] a dog took a cake and went to a stack of grain,

YAD AVRAHAM

the roof into that yard *(Meiri)*.

וְשִׁבְּרוּ אֶת־הַכֵּלִים, — *and broke vessels*,
It did so by jumping on them (ibid.).

מְשַׁלֵּם נֶזֶק שָׁלֵם — [*its owner*] *pays the full damages*
He pays the full damages, since this is a *toladah* of *regel* (Rav).

מִפְּנֵי שֶׁהֵן מוּעָדִין. — *because they are muadin.*
Its owner is considered forewarned to prevent it from jumping. This is true only if the damage took place on the premises of the owner of the vessels, since it is a *toladah* of *regel* (Rav; Rashi). [If it took place in a public domain, he is exempt.]

The *Tanna* does not give a case in which the dog or kid fell from the roof and broke vessels that were lying near the wall, since that would be considered an accident, and the owner would not be liable. It is deemed an accident because, had the animal jumped, it would have landed past the vessels; since it fell, there was no negligence on the part of the owner.

If, however, the vessels were lying in such a position that if the dog or kid were to jump off the roof, it would break them, then even if it fell off the roof on them and broke them, its owner is liable. This is based on the rule that תְּחִלָּתוֹ בִּפְשִׁיעָה, וְסוֹפוֹ בְּאֹנֶס, חַיָּב, *if in the beginning there was negligence, and at the end there was an accident, he is*

liable. This means that if a person is negligent and could cause damage through his negligence, even if that damage is caused by accident, the person is liable. Our mishnah deals with a case in which the vessels are lying at a distance from the wall, and could easily be broken by the dog or kid if it jumps off the roof. Therefore, even if it subsequently falls off the roof, thereby breaking the vessels, its owner is liable, since the damage could have been caused through his negligence. The *Tanna* did not wish to state the case of falling, however, because in some cases — e.g., if the vessels lie near the wall — it would be considered an accident, as explained above *(Tos. Yom Tov* from *Nimmukei Yosef;* see *Lechem Shamayim).*

הַכֶּלֶב שֶׁנָּטַל חֲרָרָה — [*If*] *a dog took a cake*
That is, a cake that was baking on coals (Rav). In such cases, the burning coals sometimes adhere to the cake *(Tos. Yom Tov* from *Rambam*).

The mishnah deals with a case in which the owner of the coals locked the room in which they were burning and the dog dug its way in under the door. Otherwise, he would be liable for damages caused by the coals *(Tif. Yis.* from *Gem.* 23).

וְהָלַךְ לַגָּדִישׁ, — *and went to a stack of grain,*
The dog went with the cake to a stack

בבא קמא ב/ד

הַחֲרָרָה וְהִדְלִיק אֶת־הַגָּדִישׁ — עַל־הַחֲרָרָה, מְשַׁלֵּם נֶזֶק שָׁלֵם; וְעַל־הַגָּדִישׁ, מְשַׁלֵּם חֲצִי נֶזֶק.

[ד] אֵיזֶה הוּא תָם וְאֵיזֶה הוּא מוּעָד? מוּעָד — כָּל־שֶׁהֵעִידוּ בּוֹ שְׁלֹשָׁה יָמִים; וְתָם — מִשֶּׁיַּחֲזֹר בּוֹ שְׁלֹשָׁה יָמִים; דִּבְרֵי רַבִּי יְהוּדָה. רַבִּי מֵאִיר אוֹמֵר: מוּעָד — שֶׁהֵעִידוּ בּוֹ שְׁלֹשָׁה

יד אברהם

of grain belonging to the owner of the cake (*Tif. Yis.* from *Gem.* 23a).

אָכַל אֶת־הַחֲרָרָה — *ate the cake*

It did so on the premises of the cake's owner (*Tos. Yom Tov* from *Gem.* 23a). Should the dog take the cake and eat it elsewhere, the owner of the dog would be liable to pay only for the benefit derived, as explained in the previous mishnah (*Tos. Chadashim* from *Nimmukei Yosef*).

וְהִדְלִיק אֶת־הַגָּדִישׁ — *and ignited the stack of grain —*

Then, the dog ignited the stack of grain with the coal [that had adhered to the cake] (*Rambam Commentary*).

עַל־הַחֲרָרָה, מְשַׁלֵּם נֶזֶק שָׁלֵם; — *for the cake, [its owner] pays the full damages;*

[The owner of the dog pays the full value of the cake.]

This is a case of *shen* in the premises of the damagee (*Rav*).

Although a burning coal adhered to the cake, it is not considered unusual for the dog to have picked it up (*Meiri*).

וְעַל־הַגָּדִישׁ, מְשַׁלֵּם חֲצִי נֶזֶק. — *for the stack of grain, he pays half the damages.*

This is analogous to the case of pebbles (mishnah 1), in which the owner pays half the damages [i.e., just as pebbles damage through the power of the animal rather than its body, so, too, does the damage caused by the coals stem from the animal's power.] (*Rav* from *Gem.* 22a).

Rav alludes to the controversy between R' Yochanan and Resh Lakish concerning the halachic status of fire. R' Yochanan holds that when one ignites a fire and it spreads and burns the property of others, it is considered as though it had spread through his power, although, in fact, the wind had spread it. Resh Lakish maintains that since it is not his power that drives it, it is not deemed as if his power had spread it, but as if one of his belongings had done so.

R' Yochanan interprets our mishnah as referring to a case in which the dog placed the coal on the stack of grain. Since it is considered a usual occurrence for the dog to lay the coal on the stack, the damage is classified as *regel*, and therefore, the dog's owner is liable for the complete damages caused to the place where the dog laid the coal. When the fire spreads, it is considered as though the dog's power is spreading it, and like the case of pebbles, the owner is liable for half the damages.

Resh Lakish construes the mishnah as referring to a case in which the dog threw the coal into the stack. Since that act is similar to the case of pebbles, the owner is liable for half the damages even for the place where the coal lands. On damages to the remainder of the stack, however, he is totally exempt, since it is not deemed as having been caused by the dog's power, nor can it be said that the fire is considered one of the dog's belongings (*Tos. Yom Tov* from *Gem.* ibid.).

Tos. Yom Tov cites a controversy whether,

ate the cake and ignited the stack of grain — for the cake, [its owner] pays the full damages; for the stack of grain, he pays half the damages.

4. **W**hich is a *tam* and which is a *muad*? A *muad* is anyone that was warned three days; a *tam* — when it refrains [from goring] for three days. [These are] the words of R' Yehudah. R' Meir says: A *muad* is one that was warned three times; a *tam* — any one

YAD AVRAHAM

according to R' Yochanan — whose view is followed by the Halachah — the owner of the dog would be liable for the entire stack should the dog throw the coal thereon. He notes that *Tosafos* rule that he is liable only for the place where the coal lands, whereas *Rashba* rules that he is liable for the entire stack of grain. Since the fire spread only after the dog had thrown the coal onto the stack, this question hinges on the issue of whether indirect force is equal to direct force *(Tos. R' Akiva).*

4.

The following mishnah elaborates on the subject of the מוּעָד, *the muad animal,* mentioned above (1:4).

אֵיזֶה הוּא תָם וְאֵיזֶה הוּא מוּעָד? — *Which is a tam and which is a muad?*

That is, how does an animal become a *muad* and how is it restored to the status of a *tam*? *(Tos. Yom Tov from Nimmukei Yosef).*

This obviously deals with *keren (Tif. Yis.)* [because that is the only category in which an animal can change from one of these statuses to the other.]

מוּעָד — כָּל־שֶׁהֵעִידוּ בוֹ שְׁלֹשָׁה יָמִים; — *A muad is anyone that was warned three days;*

If the animal gored on three consecutive days, and after each goring the owner was notified and warned to watch it, he is then liable for the complete damages if it gores a fourth time *(Meiri; Tif. Yis.).*

This ruling is arrived at by expounding the verse *(Ex.* 21:36):אוֹ נוֹדַע כִּי שׁוֹר נַגָּח הוּא מִתְּמוֹל שִׁלְשֹׁם וְלֹא יִשְׁמְרֶנּוּ בְּעָלָיו, *But if it was known that the bull was a habitual gorer from yesterday and the day before, and its owner does not watch it.* The word מִתְּמוֹל, *from yesterday,* denotes one goring; שִׁלְשֹׁם, *the day before,* a second goring; וְלֹא יִשְׁמְרֶנּוּ בְּעָלָיו, *and its owner does not watch it* refers to a third goring *(Tos. Yom Tov from Gem.* 23b, following *Rava's* view).

וְתָם — *a tam* —

That is, how does a *muad* regain its previous status of a *tam,* for which the owner is liable only for half the damages if it gores? *(Meiri).*

מִשֶּׁיַּחֲזֹר בּוֹ שְׁלֹשָׁה יָמִים; דִּבְרֵי רַבִּי יְהוּדָה. — *when it refrains [from goring] for three days. [These are] the words of R' Yehudah.*

R' Yehudah contends that if the animal sees other animals on three days and refrains from goring them, it is restored to its original status of *tam (Rav; Rashi).*

רַבִּי מֵאִיר אוֹמֵר: מוּעָד — שֶׁהֵעִידוּ בוֹ שְׁלֹשָׁה פְעָמִים. — *R' Meir says: A muad is one that was warned three times;*

R' Meir disagrees with both definitions. He maintains that a *muad* is an animal that gored three times even in one day, and its owner was warned after each goring *(Rav; Rashi).*

בבא קמא ב/ה

פְּעָמִים; וְתָם — כָּל־שֶׁיְּהוּ הַתִּינוֹקוֹת מְמַשְׁמְשִׁין בּוֹ וְאֵינוֹ נוֹגֵחַ.

[ה] שׁוֹר הַמַּזִּיק בִּרְשׁוּת הַנִּזָּק — כֵּיצַד? נָגַח, נָגַף, נָשַׁךְ, רָבַץ, בָּעַט, בִּרְשׁוּת הָרַבִּים, מְשַׁלֵּם חֲצִי נֶזֶק; בִּרְשׁוּת הַנִּזָּק — רַבִּי טַרְפוֹן אוֹמֵר: נֶזֶק שָׁלֵם. וַחֲכָמִים אוֹמְרִים: חֲצִי נֶזֶק.

אָמַר לָהֶם רַבִּי טַרְפוֹן: וּמַה בִּמְקוֹם שֶׁהֵקֵל עַל

יד אברהם

R' Meir holds that a habit is formed more quickly by goring in short intervals. Therefore, since an animal is considered an habitual gorer by goring three animals in three days, it surely is considered to be in that category if it gores three animals in one day (Gem. 24a).

The halachah is in accordance with R' Yehudah's view, that the animal becomes a *muad* only if he gores three animals in three days (Rav; Rambam).

— וְתָם — a *tam* —

[According to R' Meir, which bull that has been deemed a *muad* is considered to have regained its status of *tam*?]

כָּל־שֶׁיְּהוּ הַתִּינוֹקוֹת מְמַשְׁמְשִׁין בּוֹ וְאֵינוֹ נוֹגֵחַ — any one that the children touch and it does not gore.

Although they pull the animal and play with it, it does not gore [Rav; Rambam] the children (Tos. R' Akiva from Rambam Commentary and Tos.). Tosefta (2:2) adds: They touch the animal between its horns (Meiri; Meleches Shlomo).

R' Meir agrees with R' Yehudah that if the animal sees other animals for three days and refrains from goring them, that it regains its status of *tam*. He only adds that the animal can also regain its status, even in one day, by refraining from goring the children who play with it (Tos. Yom Tov from Tos., Rosh). Tos. R' Akiva, however, deduces from Rav's wording that he interprets R' Meir's view to be that the only way for a *muad* to regain the status of *tam* is by not goring when children touch him; refraining from goring bulls for three days, however, does not change his status. Yam Shel Shlomo and Maggid Mishneh deduce the same from Rambam (Commentary and Hil. Nizkei Mamon 6:8).

Should the animal refrain from goring three other animals which it sees in one day, it does not regain the status of *tam* (Tos.; Tos. Yom Tov from Ritva, Nimmukei Yosef).

With regard to the question of regaining the status of *tam*, the halachah is in accordance with R' Meir's opinion (Rav, Rambam from Gem. 24a).

5.

The Mishnah now continues to explain the damagers classified in 1:4 as *muadin*.

שׁוֹר הַמַּזִּיק בִּרְשׁוּת הַנִּזָּק — The bull that damages [while] on the premises of the damagee —

[As explained in the commentary

[38] משניות / בבא קמא — פרק ב: כיצד הרגל

that the children touch and it does not gore.

5. The bull that damages [while] on the premises of the damagee — how is that? [If] it gored, pushed, bit, lay down, or kicked, in a public domain, he pays half the damages; on the premises of the damagee — R' Tarfon says: The full damages. The Sages, however, say: Half the damages.

R' Tarfon said to them: Seeing that where [the

YAD AVRAHAM

(ibid.), this refers to a *tam* that damages while on the damagee's property, which the mishnah adjudges as if it were a *muad*, whose owner must pay the complete damages.]

כֵּיצַד? — *how is that?*
[What damages are meant and according to whom is the bull a *muad*?]

נָגַח, נָגַף, נָשַׁךְ, — [*If*] *it gored, pushed, bit,*
The animal gored, pushed with its body, or bit another animal with intention to injure it *(Kehati)*.

רָבַץ, — *lay down,*
It lay down on vessels with the intent of breaking them *(Rashi* 2b; see commentary to 1:4, s.v. ולא לרבץ). [Others *(Tos.* 15b et al.) appear to hold that as long as the animal inflicts the damage in an unusual way, it is a *toladah* of *keren* even if it derives benefit thereby. See *Beis Aharon* (to 2b), where this matter is discussed at length.]

בָּעַט, — *or kicked,*
It kicked with the intent to damage *(Kehati)*.
All these are *tolados* of *keren (Rav)*, except goring, which is the *av* itself *(Tos. Yom Tov)*.

בִּרְשׁוּת הָרַבִּים — *in a public domain,*
[These damages occurred on public property.]

מְשַׁלֵּם חֲצִי נֶזֶק; — *he pays half the damages;*
[The damagee becomes a partner in the animal for the amount of half the damages, as stated in 1:4. Of course, this applies only if the animal is a *tam*.]

בִּרְשׁוּת הַנִּזָּק — *on the premises of the damagee —*
[The animal entered another person's premises and gored his animal ...]

רַבִּי טַרְפוֹן אוֹמֵר: נֶזֶק שָׁלֵם. — *R' Tarfon says: The full damages.*
Although the bull is a *tam*, since it damaged while on the premises of the damagee, its owner is liable for the full damages. The *Tanna* in 1:4 who adjudges the bull that damages while on the damagee's premises as a *muad* is R' Tarfon *(Gem.* 14a).

וַחֲכָמִים אוֹמְרִים: חֲצִי נֶזֶק. — *The Sages, however, say: Half the damages.*
[They maintain that regarding *keren*, there is no difference whether the damages are committed in the public domain or in the premises of the damagee.]

אָמַר לָהֶם רַבִּי טַרְפוֹן: — *R' Tarfon said to them:*
[That is, to the Sages. He wishes to prove by a קַל וָחֹמֶר, *kal vachomer*, that *keren* in the premises of the damagee is liable for the full damages even if the bull is a *tam*.]

[39] THE MISHNAH/BAVA KAMMA — Chapter Two: *Keitzad HaRegel*

בבא קמא ב/ה

הַשֵּׁן וְעַל הָרֶגֶל, בִּרְשׁוּת הָרַבִּים, שֶׁהוּא פָּטוּר, הֶחְמִיר עֲלֵיהֶם בִּרְשׁוּת הַנִּזָּק, לְשַׁלֵּם נֶזֶק שָׁלֵם — מָקוֹם שֶׁהֶחְמִיר עַל הַקֶּרֶן, בִּרְשׁוּת הָרַבִּים, לְשַׁלֵּם חֲצִי נֶזֶק, אֵינוֹ דִין שֶׁנַּחְמִיר עָלֶיהָ בִּרְשׁוּת הַנִּזָּק, לְשַׁלֵּם נֶזֶק שָׁלֵם?

אָמְרוּ לוֹ: דַּיּוֹ לַבָּא מִן־הַדִּין לִהְיוֹת כַּנִּדּוֹן: מַה בִּרְשׁוּת הָרַבִּים חֲצִי נֶזֶק, אַף בִּרְשׁוּת הַנִּזָּק חֲצִי נֶזֶק.

יד אברהם

קַל וָחֹמֶר / Kal Vachomer (The A Fortiori Argument)

[This is a hermeneutical principle which dictates that if a lenient case has a stringency, the same stringency certainly applies to a stricter case. (For a fuller exposition of the *kal vachomer* and the other hermeneutical principles, see *Gateway to the Talmud*, p. 121.)]

וּמַה בְּמָקוֹם שֶׁהֵקַל עַל הַשֵּׁן וְעַל הָרֶגֶל, בִּרְשׁוּת הָרַבִּים, שֶׁהוּא פָּטוּר — *Seeing that where [the Torah] was lenient regarding shen and regel [viz.] in the public domain, that exemption be granted.*

The verse (*Ex.* 22:4) specifies: וּבִעֵר בִּשְׂדֵה אַחֵר, *and it grazes in another's field* (Rashi), which is construed as exempting the animal's owner from damages of *shen* and *regel* committed on public property (see 1:2).

הֶחְמִיר עֲלֵיהֶם בִּרְשׁוּת הַנִּזָּק, לְשַׁלֵּם נֶזֶק שָׁלֵם — *it [nevertheless] dealt stringently regarding them in the premises of the damagee, that the full damages be paid* —

[As we learned in the commentaries to the first two mishnayos of this chapter, the Torah ordains that both *shen* and *regel*, when committed on the damagee's premises, incur liability for the full damages. See commentary to mishnah 2, s.v. בִּרְשׁוּת הַנִּזָּק.]

מָקוֹם שֶׁהֶחְמִיר עַל הַקֶּרֶן, בִּרְשׁוּת הָרַבִּים, לְשַׁלֵּם חֲצִי נֶזֶק — *where [the Torah] dealt stringently with keren [viz.] in the public domain, that half the damages be paid,*

[By not specifying where *keren* must take place in order to incur liability, the Torah indicates that for damages of *keren* committed even in the public domain, the animal's owner must pay half the damages, unlike *shen* and *regel* in a public domain, for which he is exempt.]

אֵינוֹ דִין שֶׁנַּחְמִיר עָלֶיהָ בִּרְשׁוּת הַנִּזָּק, לְשַׁלֵּם נֶזֶק שָׁלֵם? — *is it not right that we should deal stringently with it in the premises of the damagee, that the full damages be paid?*

[Is it not a *kal vachomer* that we should deal stringently with *keren* committed on the premises of the damagee by exacting the full damages from the animal's owner?]

אָמְרוּ לוֹ — *They said to him:*
[The Sages replied to R' Tarfon.]

דַּיּוֹ לַבָּא מִן־הַדִּין לִהְיוֹת כַּנִּדּוֹן — *It is enough for the inferred law to be [as strict] as that from which it is inferred:*

When a ruling is derived from a *kal vachomer*, it cannot be stricter than the ruling from which it is inferred (Rambam Commentary). [We will henceforth refer to this principle as דַּיּוֹ, *dayyo*.]

This principle is based on an incident in the Torah. Scripture states concern-

Torah] was lenient regarding *shen* and *regel* [viz.] in the public domain, that exemption be granted, it [nevertheless] dealt stringently regarding them in the premises of the damagee, that the full damages be paid — where [the Torah] dealt stringently with *keren* [viz.] in the public domain, that half the damages be paid, is it not right that we should deal stringently with it in the premises of the damagee, that the full damages be paid?

They said to him: It is enough for the inferred law to be [as strict] as that from which it is inferred: Just as in the public domain half the damages [must be paid], so [must] half the damages [be paid] in the premises of the damagee.

YAD AVRAHAM

ing Miriam *(Num. 12:14): If her father had but spit in her face, should she not hide in shame seven days?* [The allusion is to נְזִיפָה, *the minor ban*, incurred by unintentionally provoking one's superiors (see *Moed Kattan* 16a).]

Now [since the *Gemara* in *Niddah* 31a tells us that each parent of a person transmits five things to him — bones, skin, etc. — while God transmits ten things to him — soul, speech, etc. *(Tos. 25a, s.v. ק'ין; see ibid. and Tos. Yom Tov)*], the logic of *kal vachomer* would dictate that if God Himself is wroth with someone, that person should be separated from others for fourteen days. Yet, the Torah states: *Let her be shut out from the camp for seven days.* Hence, the law concerning God, which is inferred from the example of the father, is no more stringent than that of the father *(Rav; Rambam Commentary* from *Gem.* 25a).

מַה בִּרְשׁוּת הָרַבִּים חֲצִי נֶזֶק, אַף בִּרְשׁוּת הַנִּזָּק חֲצִי נֶזֶק. — *Just as in the public domain half the damages [must be paid], so [must] half the damages [be paid] in the premises of the damagee.*

The Sages reasoned with R' Tarfon:

Since you wish to deduce the law of *keren* in the premises of the damagee from that of *keren* in a public domain, the principle of *dayyo* dictates that the former cannot be more stringent than the latter, and *keren* in the premises of the damagee should be liable for no more than half the damages, just as in a public domain *(Rav; Rashi).*

Some commentators challenge this reasoning, since every *kal vachomer* is derived in this manner — namely: if case A, which is lenient, has a stringency, then certainly case B, which is stricter, also has this stringency.

For example, in the incident of Miriam [discussed above], the *kal vachomer* is: If the anger of a father — who transmits less to a person [see above] — causes him to separate for seven days, then the anger of God — Who transmits more to him — should cause him to separate for fourteen days. The principle of *dayyo*, however, dictates that the stringency of case B (involving God) cannot be more than that of case A (involving the father). Thus, even in the case involving God, the separation is limited to seven days.

In our case, however, the *kal vachomer* merely seeks to equate case B *(keren)* with case A *(shen* and *regel)* in that both should incur liability for full damages when committed on the premises of the damagee. This should not be affected by the principle

בבא קמא ב/ה

אָמַר לָהֶם: אֲנִי לֹא אָדוֹן קֶרֶן מִקֶּרֶן; אֲנִי אָדוֹן קֶרֶן מֵרֶגֶל: וּמַה בִּמְקוֹם שֶׁהֵקֵל עַל־הַשֵּׁן וְעַל־הָרֶגֶל, בִּרְשׁוּת הָרַבִּים, הֶחֱמִיר בַּקֶּרֶן — מְקוֹם שֶׁהֶחֱמִיר עַל־הַשֵּׁן וְעַל־הָרֶגֶל, בִּרְשׁוּת הַנִּזָּק, אֵינוֹ דִין שֶׁנַּחֲמִיר בַּקֶּרֶן?

אָמְרוּ לוֹ: דַּיּוֹ לַבָּא מִן־הַדִּין לִהְיוֹת כַּנִּדּוֹן: מַה בִּרְשׁוּת הָרַבִּים חֲצִי נֶזֶק, אַף בִּרְשׁוּת הַנִּזָּק חֲצִי נֶזֶק.

יד אברהם

apply the principle of *dayyo* in all cases — this *kal vachomer* should be valid, as explained below (*Tos. Yom Tov* from *Nimmukei Yosef*, quoting *Rosh*).

אֲנִי אָדוֹן קֶרֶן מֵרֶגֶל: — *I will derive* keren *from* regel:

I will derive *keren* in the premises of the damagee from *regel* in the premises of the damagee (*Tos. Yom Tov*).

[He actually uses the same *kal vachomer* as before, but restructures it to counter the Sages' refutation.]

וּמַה בִּמְקוֹם שֶׁהֵקֵל עַל־הַשֵּׁן וְעַל־הָרֶגֶל, בִּרְשׁוּת הָרַבִּים, הֶחֱמִיר בַּקֶּרֶן — *Seeing that where [the Torah] dealt leniently regarding* shen *and* regel, *[viz.] in the public domain, it dealt stringently regarding* keren —

This indicates that *shen* and *regel* are less stringent than *keren* (*Tos. Yom Tov*).

מְקוֹם שֶׁהֶחֱמִיר עַל־הַשֵּׁן וְעַל־הָרֶגֶל, בִּרְשׁוּת הַנִּזָּק, אֵינוֹ דִין שֶׁנַּחֲמִיר בַּקֶּרֶן? — *where [the Torah] dealt stringently with* shen *and* regel, *[viz.] in the premises of the damagee, is it not right that we should deal stringently with* keren?

That is, if in this case, Scripture dealt stringently with the less stringent cases of *shen* and *regel*, is it not a *kal vachomer* that we should deal stringently with the more stringent *keren*? Structuring the *kal vachomer* in this manner, we derive *keren* from *shen* and *regel*, not *keren* from *keren* (*Tos. Yom*

of *dayyo*.

They explain, however, that since, in our case, the stringency by which we demonstrated that case B *(keren)* is stricter than case A *(shen and regel)* — i.e., that it incurs liability for half the damages even if committed on public property — and the inference we wish to draw regarding case B — that it should incur liability for the full damages when committed on the damagee's premises — are closely related [they both involve payments for damages], the principle of *dayyo* applies in such an instance as well, dictating that the inference to case B cannot be more stringent than the stringency which demonstrated that case B is stricter than case A. This would mean that the *kal vachomer* cannot infer that *keren* in the damagee's property incurs greater liability than if it had been committed on public property, in which case the owner is only liable for half the damages (*Tos. Yom Tov* from *Tos., Nimmukei Yosef*).

אָמַר לָהֶם: — *He said to them:*

[R' Tarfon retorted to the Sages:]

אֲנִי לֹא אָדוֹן קֶרֶן מִקֶּרֶן; — *I will not derive* keren *from* keren;

I will not derive *keren* in the premises of the damagee from *keren* in a public domain as stated above (*Rav; Tos. Yom Tov*).

The truth is that R' Tarfon does indeed derive the *kal vachomer* as stated above, but he maintains — as will be explained — that in such cases the principle of *dayyo* does not apply. The intent of his reply to the Sages is that even according to their view — that we

משניות / בבא קמא — פרק ב: כיצד הרגל [42]

2 5 He said to them: I will not derive *keren* from *keren*; I will derive *keren* from *regel*: Seeing that where [the Torah] dealt leniently regarding *shen* and *regel* [viz.] in the public domain, it dealt stringently regarding *keren* — where [the Torah] dealt stringently with *shen* and *regel*, [viz.] in the premises of the damagee, is it not right that we should deal stringently with *keren*?

They said to him: It is enough for the inferred law to be [as strict] as that from which it is inferred: Just as in the public domain half the damages [must be paid], so [must] half the damages [be paid] in the premises of the damagee.

YAD AVRAHAM

Tov from *Nimmukei Yosef*).

אָמְרוּ לוֹ: — *They said to him:* [The Sages answered R' Tarfon.]

דַּיּוֹ לַבָּא מִן־הַדִּין לִהְיוֹת כַּנִּדּוֹן: — *It is enough for the inferred law to be [as strict] as that from which it is inferred:*

Even in this *kal vachomer*, we must resort to the fact that *keren* is liable in a public domain; otherwise, we would have no *kal vachomer*. Therefore, the principle of *dayyo* is to be applied [dictating that the liability for *keren* in the damagee's premises can be no greater than that of *keren* in a public domain — i.e., for half the damages] (*Rav*).

The commentators explain that it is easier to apply the principle of *dayyo* to the first *kal vachomer*, because in that instance it applies to the end of the *kal vachomer*, dictating that the inference to the stricter case cannot be more stringent than the stringency which demonstrated that it is indeed the stricter case. Nevertheless, the Sages maintain that this principle applies in the second case as well (*Tos. Yom Tov, Nimmukei Yosef* from *Rosh*).

מַה בִּרְשׁוּת הָרַבִּים חֲצִי נֶזֶק, אַף בִּרְשׁוּת הַנִּזָּק חֲצִי נֶזֶק. — *Just as in the public domain half the damages [must be paid], so [must] half the damages [be paid] in the premises of the damagee.*

In fact, R' Tarfon, too, subscribes to the principle of *dayyo*, which is derived from the Torah, as explained above. Nonetheless, he does not apply *dayyo* in our case, because he maintains that it is not applicable if it totally refutes the inference of the *kal vachomer*. In the case of Miriam, the *kal vachomer* teaches us that one with whom the Almighty is displeased is under a ban for seven days just as one whose father is displeased with him. The principle of *dayyo* limits the ban to seven days instead of fourteen. In the case of *keren* in the premises of the damagee, however, even without the *kal vachomer*, the owner would be liable for half the damages. Therefore, by applying the principle of *dayyo* — which dictates that he should not pay more than that amount — the *kal vachomer* is rendered totally ineffective. In such instances, maintains R' Tarfon, the principle of *dayyo* does not apply. The Sages, however, subscribe to the principle of *dayyo* in all cases (*Rav, Rambam Commentary* from *Gem.* 25a).

[43] THE MISHNAH/BAVA KAMMA — Chapter Two: *Keitzad HaRegel*

בבא קמא ב/ו

[ו] אָדָם מוּעָד לְעוֹלָם, בֵּין שׁוֹגֵג בֵּין מֵזִיד, בֵּין עֵר בֵּין יָשֵׁן. סִמֵּא אֶת עֵין חֲבֵרוֹ וְשִׁבֵּר אֶת־הַכֵּלִים, מְשַׁלֵּם נֶזֶק שָׁלֵם.

ג/א

[א] הַמַּנִּיחַ אֶת־הַכַּד בִּרְשׁוּת הָרַבִּים, וּבָא אַחֵר וְנִתְקַל בָּהּ וּשְׁבָרָהּ, פָּטוּר.

יד אברהם

6.

The following mishnah elaborates on *man*, one of the *muadin* in 1:4 *(Meiri)*.

אָדָם מוּעָד לְעוֹלָם — **Man is always muad,** That is, to pay the full damages for anything he damages *(Meiri)*.

בֵּין שׁוֹגֵג בֵּין מֵזִיד, — **whether unintentionally or intentionally,**

[I.e., whether he inflicts the damages unintentionally or intentionally.]

בֵּין עֵר בֵּין יָשֵׁן. — **whether awake or asleep.**

He is liable for unintentional damage not only if he inflicted it while being awake, but even if he did so while sleeping. We do not exempt him on the grounds that it was an unavoidable accident *(Tos. Yom Tov from Nimmukei Yosef)*.

If one person was sleeping, and another came along and lay down next to him, and the second one injured the first, the second one is liable [since he was aware that the first person was there]. If the first one injured the second one, however, he is exempt [since he was unaware of the other's presence]. Should they both lie down simultaneously, whoever injures the other is liable, since they are both considered forewarned against injuring each other *(Rav; Rambam, Hil. Chovel Umazzik 1:11, Nimmukei Yosef from Yerushalmi)*.

The first one is exempt if he injures the second one, since the latter was negligent [thereby causing his own injury] *(Tos. Yom Tov from Nimmukei*

Yosef). Tosafos (27b, s.v. שמואל) base this exemption on a distinction between אֹנֶס, **an accident,** and אֹנֶס גָּמוּר, **a complete accident.** Although the Torah regards man as forewarned to the extent that he is liable for accidental damages, it does not hold him accountable for those completely unavoidable. In this case, he had no way of knowing that his friend lay down beside him or placed vessels beside him. He is therefore exempt.

סִמֵּא אֶת עֵין חֲבֵרוֹ וְשִׁבֵּר אֶת־הַכֵּלִים, מְשַׁלֵּם נֶזֶק שָׁלֵם. — **[If] he blinded another's eye or broke vessels, he pays the full damages.**

If he blinded another's eye unintentionally, he is liable for the full payment of the damages — i.e., the depreciation of the other person's value if he were to be sold as a slave (see 8:1).

The other four obligations imposed by the Torah on one who injures another — namely: צַעַר, *pain*; רִפּוּי, *healing*; שֶׁבֶת, *time lost from work*; and בֹּשֶׁת, *disgrace* — do not apply in this case. The first three apply only if he injures intentionally or if his action borders on the intentional *(Rav from Gem. 26a, 27a)*. The injurer is liable to pay for embarrassment only if he intends to embarrass *(Tos. Yom Tov from Gem. 27a)* or if he intends to injure, in which case he is liable although he had no intention to embarrass *(Tos. R' Akiva from Gem. ad loc.)*.

משניות / בבא קמא — פרק ג: המניח [44]

2 6. Man is always *muad*, whether unintentionally
6 or intentionally, whether awake or asleep.
[If] he blinded another's eye or broke vessels, he pays
the full damages.

3 1. [If] one leaves a jug in a public domain, and
1 someone else comes along and stumbles over it
and breaks it, he is exempt. If he is injured by it, the

YAD AVRAHAM

The *Tanna* intimates this ruling by juxtaposing the case of blinding the eye with the case of breaking the vessels. Just as one who breaks vessels is liable only for the *damage*, since the other four charges do not apply, so is one who blinds another's eye liable only for the damages — i.e., in the case of unintentional injury *(Tos. Yom Tov from Gem. 26a).*

Chapter 3

1.

In this chapter, the Mishnah commences to elaborate on the unqualified statement in the preceding mishnah, that *Man is always muad.* This mishnah delineates the laws of one who places an obstacle in public property if it is the type of item people customarily place there *(Meiri).*

הַמַּנִּיחַ אֶת־הַכַּד בִּרְשׁוּת הָרַבִּים, — *[If] one leaves a jug in a public domain,*

[This may also be rendered: [If] one places ... See *Siddur Tzelosa D'Avraham*, pp. 27f., s.v. להניח, for an explanation of the vowelization of הַמַּנִּיחַ.]

The mishnah deals with one who becomes fatigued and, while resting, sets down his jug in the street *(Meiri).*

וּבָא אַחֵר וְנִתְקַל בָּהּ וּשְׁבָרָהּ, פָּטוּר. — *and someone else comes along and stumbles over it and breaks it, he is exempt.*

The one who broke the jug is exempt from paying for it, because people do not usually look at the road as they walk *(Rav from Gem. 27b).* Since they are engrossed in their thoughts, they normally do not take heed of what is lying on the road in front of them *(Meiri; Tos. Yom Tov from Nimmukei Yosef).*

Another reason given is that man walks upright and does not look down, unlike an animal, which, walking on all fours, looks down while walking. In fact, if a normal animal falls into a pit by day, the one who dug the pit is exempt, as explained in 5:6, because it should have watched where it was going *(Tos. Yom Tov from Tos. 27b).*

Although *Man is always muad* (2:6) and must pay the full damages even in cases of accidents, he is exempt if the damage he caused was a complete accident (see commentary ibid., s.v. בֵּין עֵר). Man's nature, being what it is, renders this case in the mishnah a complete accident (see *Tos.* 27b, s.v. ושמואל).

Accordingly, the one who broke the jug is exempt only if he stumbled and broke it inadvertently. Should he break it intentionally, he is liable, unless the street was filled with jugs, making it impossible to pass *(Tos. Yom Tov from Nimmukei Yosef).*

בבא קמא ג/א

וְאִם הֻזַּק בָּהּ, בַּעַל הֶחָבִית חַיָּב בְּנִזְקוֹ. נִשְׁבְּרָה כַדּוֹ בִּרְשׁוּת הָרַבִּים, וְהֻחְלַק אֶחָד בַּמַּיִם אוֹ שֶׁלָּקָה בַּחֲרָסֶיהָ, חַיָּב. רַבִּי יְהוּדָה אוֹמֵר: בְּמִתְכַּוֵּן, חַיָּב; בְּאֵינוֹ מִתְכַּוֵּן, פָּטוּר.

יד אברהם

Although the one who left the jug in the street committed an illegal act, that does not exempt the one who broke it. Such exemption was granted only in the case of an animal — which is not intelligent enough to avoid what is lying before it on the ground — not a human being (Tos. Yom Tov from Tos.).

וְאִם הֻזַּק בָּהּ, — If he is injured by it,

The one who was walking either tripped on the jug and hurt himself on the ground, or hurt himself on the shards of the broken jug (Kehati).

בַּעַל הֶחָבִית — the owner of the jug

It appears that the term חָבִית, chavis (jug), here is synonymous with כַּד, kad, in the beginning of the mishnah. The Tanna also uses them interchangeably in mishnah 5 and in 10:4. Common usage, however, distinguishes between them, using kad to denote a large jug. By using them interchangeably, the Mishnah teaches us that, in business transactions, the two terms are sometimes interchangeable — that is, in places where the majority of people use the term chavis for large jugs and a minority use the two terms interchangeably, the Mishnah applies the principle of אֵין הוֹלְכִין בְּמָמוֹן אַחַר הָרוֹב, We do not follow the majority in monetary matters. For example, should one agree to sell another a kad and he transferred its ownership to him with a kinyan (an act of acquisition) thereby obligating the purchaser to pay for it, the latter may withhold the money unless the former gives him a large jug, since he can claim that he calls a large jug a kad. Likewise, should one stipulate to sell a chavis, and the buyer has already paid for it, the seller may claim that he uses that term to refer to a small jug[1] (Tos. Yom Tov from Tos. 27a).

חַיָּב בְּנִזְקוֹ. — is liable for his injury.

[The owner of the jug is liable for the damage caused by it.]

Even if he had relinquished his ownership of the jug, he is nevertheless liable, because whoever relinquishes his ownership of something that causes damage in a situation that he had no right to create from the outset is adjudged as though he had not relinquished his ownership therefrom (Rav).

Although the verse (Ex. 21:33) וְנָפַל שָׁמָּה שׁוֹר, and a bull ... fall therein, is exegetically interpreted to exclude liability for a person falling into a pit or tripping over similar obstacles, this applies only if the person is killed by the fall; if he is merely injured, however, the owner of the pit or object is liable (Gem. 28b).

---

1. Although the majority factor is a determinant in matters dealing with a prohibition, it does not affect cases involving money in which one of the litigants is in possession of the money. In such cases, the majority factor is not a determinant to exact the money from him, and he may claim to be one of the minority (Tos. 27a, Gem. 46b).

   In deciding the verdict of a court, however, we follow the majority of the judges to obligate the defendant to pay. That is because the minority of the court is of no consequence, and the majority, representing the court, exacts the money from the litigant. In our case, however, in which there is a minority factor, and the defendant is in possession of the money, we cannot exact it from him by virtue of the majority factor (Tos. Yom Tov from Tos. 27b).

   Since the court has the power to exact money from the defendant, it is considered as if there were no possession of money involved, and therefore, the majority is the determinant factor. Likewise, if one finds a lost article in a city inhabited by both Jews and gentiles, as in Machshirin 2:8, since the finder has no definite possession of the object, the majority is the factor that determines who the loser was, and whether the finder may keep the article (Tif. Yis.).

3:1

owner of the jug is liable for his injury.

[If] one's jug broke in a public domain, and someone slipped on the water or was hurt by the shards, he is liable. R' Yehudah says: If he intended, he is liable; if he did not intend, he is exempt.

YAD AVRAHAM

נִשְׁבְּרָה כַדּוֹ בִּרְשׁוּת הָרַבִּים — [If] one's jug broke in a public domain,

A person stumbled while carrying a jug, and fell, breaking it (Tos. Yom Tov).

וְהֻחְלַק אֶחָד בַּמַּיִם — and someone slipped on the water

[Another person came along and slipped on the water that had been in the jug, and fell, injuring himself.]

אוֹ שֶׁלָּקָה בַחֲרָסֶיהָ — or was hurt by the shards,

[He bruised himself on the fragments of the broken jug.].

חַיָּב — he is liable.

[The owner of the jug is liable although the damage occurred due to his stumbling.]

This *Tanna* — identified by the *Gemara* as R' Meir — rules that if one stumbles, it is deemed negligence, and he is consequently liable for damage caused thereby *(Rav)*.

רַבִּי יְהוּדָה אוֹמֵר: בְּמִתְכַּוֵּן, חַיָּב — R' Yehudah says: If he intended, he is liable;

If the owner of the jug intended to retain ownership of the shards or the water after his jug broke, he is liable for the damage caused by his property. This is analogous to the case of a privately owned pit that caused damage *(Rav)*.

According to Shmuel's opinion in the *Gemara* (28b), this case is a *toladah* of *bor*, and the owner of the jug is therefore exempt for damages to utensils [see commentary to 1:1, s.v. *Bor*], including the garments of the person who falls. He is liable only for the latter's bodily injuries. According to Rav (ibid.), however, since he did not relinquish ownership of the shards or the water, this case is a *toladah* of *shor*, which includes damages committed by any of one's possessions, and he is therefore liable for damages to utensils. Rav maintains that if the person who fell injured himself on the ground, the owner of the jug is exempt from paying for the injury, since the ground is not his.

בְּאֵינוֹ מִתְכַּוֵּן, פָּטוּר — if he did not intend, he is exempt.

If he did not intend to retain the shards or the water, he is exempt. This is because — according to R' Yehudah — stumbling and falling are not considered acts of negligence, and since he abandoned the shards and the water, although he had time to clean them up, it is as though they were never his, and he is therefore not responsible for the damage they cause. The halachah is in accordance with R' Yehudah, that one who stumbles is not deemed guilty of negligence *(Rav)*.

The *Gemara* explains that the first, anonymous *Tanna* — identified as R' Meir — and R' Yehudah disagree on two points. One is the question of the negligence of one who stumbles where there is no obstacle. R' Meir rules that he is considered negligent; therefore, whether he had a chance to clean up the shards and water or not, he is liable for the damages.

R' Yehudah, however, rules that he is not considered negligent, because stumbling is an accident. Therefore, even if he did not relinquish ownership of the shards or the water as long as he has not had time to pick up the shards or mop up the water, he is not responsible for the damage caused by them. He is liable only if he intended to break the jug [i.e., if — according to *Rashi* — he threw it down with the intention of breaking it or — according to *Nimmukei Yosef* — he cast it away to avoid bruising himself on the shards when he falls], in which case he is analogous to one who digs a pit, and is liable for the damages caused by it.

Once he has had time to pick up the shards

[47]   THE MISHNAH/BAVA KAMMA – Chapter Three: *HaMeineach*

בבא קמא
ג/ב

[ב] **הַשּׁוֹפֵךְ** מַיִם בִּרְשׁוּת הָרַבִּים, וְהֻזַּק בָּהֶן אַחֵר, חַיָּב בְּנִזְקוֹ. הַמַּצְנִיעַ אֶת־הַקּוֹץ וְאֶת־הַזְּכוּכִית, וְהַגּוֹדֵר אֶת־גְּדֵרוֹ בְּקוֹצִים וְגָדֵר שֶׁנָּפַל לִרְשׁוּת הָרַבִּים, וְהֻזְּקוּ בָּהֶן אֲחֵרִים, חַיָּב בְּנִזְקָן.

יד אברהם

or mop up the water, all agree that if he did not relinquish ownership of them, he is liable for the damages. Even if he should abandon them, R' Meir rules that since the obstacle came about through his negligence, he is liable. This is tantamount to one digging a pit in a public place; although it does not belong to him, he is liable because he created an obstacle. R' Yehudah, however, rules that stumbling does not constitute negligence. Therefore, the owner of the jug never became responsible for damages caused by the shards or the water. He can become liable only if he leaves them in the street although he had time to pick them up. Since he abandoned them, however, thereby relinquishing his ownership, he is no longer responsible for damages caused by them.

According to *Tosafos* (28b), R' Yehudah rules that if one abandons an item that later causes damage, he is exempt in any case, even if he created the situation which caused the damage illegally — e.g., he placed the item deliberately or dropped it through negligence. This is because such cases are based on the pit, and R' Yehudah maintains that liability for a pit applies only if it has an owner. This applies if one digs a pit in his property and abandons the land around it, thus exposing an open pit to the public, or he digs one at the edge of his land, where passersby can easily fall into it. One is not liable, however, for damages caused by a pit in public property.

This ruling follows the view of Abaye. R' Yochanan, however, rules that the owner of the jug is exempt only if he fell accidentally, as above. Should he, instead, drop it intentionally or negligently, he is liable for damages that it causes as soon as he has time to pick it up, even if he abandons it (see *Tos. Yom Tov, Tos. R' Akiva*).

2.

הַשּׁוֹפֵךְ מַיִם בִּרְשׁוּת הָרַבִּים — [If] one spills water in a public domain,

This applies even at a time when it is permissible to spill water in the streets — namely, in the rainy season (*Rav* from *Gem.* 30a), and even if he abandoned the water, since the halachah follows R' Yochanan's view that although one abandons an obstacle that came about by intention or negligence, he is liable for the damages it causes (*Nimmukei Yosef*).

וְהֻזַּק בָּהֶן אַחֵר — and someone else is injured by it,

For example, someone slipped on the water and injured himself on the ground (*Gem.* 28b).

חַיָּב בְּנִזְקוֹ. — he is liable for his injury.

The liability applies only if the person himself is injured. Should he merely soil his garments or break vessels that he was carrying, the one who spilled the water is exempt, because this obstacle is adjudged as a pit, and [as discussed in the commentary to 1:1, s.v. *Bor*] the owner of a pit is exempt if vessels are damaged by it (*Tos. Yom Tov*). In this regard, all inanimate objects are classified as vessels. The owner of the pit is liable only if an animal is injured or killed because of it, or a person is injured — but not killed — because of it (*Gem.* 28b).

[As discussed in the commentary to the

משניות / בבא קמא — פרק ג: המניח   [48]

2. [If] one spills water in a public domain, and someone else is injured by it, he is liable for his injury.

[If] one hides thorns or glass, or [if] one makes a fence of thorns or a fence that fell into a public domain, and others are injured by them, he is liable for their injury.

YAD AVRAHAM

previous mishnah, Rav would hold the opposite: if a person slipped on the water and injured himself on the ground, the one who spilled the water is exempt, since the ground is not his. Rather, the mishnah is dealing with a case in which he did not abandon the water and therefore is responsible for the damages it causes as a *toladah* of *shor* — and the water damaged another person's clothes (see *Gem.* 30a).

הַמַּצְנִיעַ אֶת־הַקּוֹץ וְאֶת־הַזְּכוּכִית — [*If*] *one hides thorns or glass,*

In a public place (*Rav*). *Nimmukei Yosef* explains that he hid them in his wall, forgot about them, and later demolished the wall. Whether he abandons them or not, he is liable if they cause any damage.

וְהַגּוֹדֵר אֶת־גְּדֵרוֹ בְּקוֹצִים — *or* [*if*] *one makes a fence of thorns*

Although the term גָּדֵר usually refers to a stone fence, as in *Proverbs* 24:31, this fence was of thorns (*Rashi* 29b).

The mishnah's ruling applies only if the thorns protrude into the public domain. If they are within his own property, however, and someone leaned on the fence more than usual (*Tos. Yom Tov* from *Nimmukei Yosef*), the owner is not responsible if they cause damage, since it is not customary for people to rub against walls (*Rav* from *Gem.* 30a).

וּגְדֵר שֶׁנָּפַל לִרְשׁוּת הָרַבִּים, — *or a fence that fell into a public domain,*

Since there was no negligence involved in the fence falling into the public domain, we must qualify the mishnah as referring to a case in which the owner had time to remove the fallen fence and neglected to do so, yet he also did not abandon it. Had he abandoned the fence, he would not be liable if it caused damages, since it had fallen by accident, and by the time he was able to remove it, it was no longer his (*Tos. Yom Tov* from *Nimmukei Yosef*; see commentary to preceding mishnah, s.v. בְּאֵינוֹ מִתְכַּוֵּן).

This phrase may also refer to a flimsy wall which the court had warned him to demolish by a certain time, but he did not comply. Then it fell into the public domain and, while falling, injured someone (*Meiri*).

וְהֻזְּקוּ בָהֶן אֲחֵרִים, — *and others are injured by them,*

Since many types of damages are enumerated in this mishnah, the *Tanna* refers to those injured in the plural. Other editions read: וְהֻזַּק בָּהֶן אַחֵר, *and someone else is injured by them,* as in the beginning of the mishnah (*Tos. Yom Tov*).

חַיָּב בְּנִזְקָן. — *he is liable for their injury.*

[The owner is responsible for any damage sustained because of his wall, thorns, etc.]

Some rule that even if a strong wall fell, if the owner had time to clear away the debris, but neither did so, nor relinquished ownership therefrom, he is liable for the damages caused by it (*Tif. Yis.* from *Tur Choshen Mishpat* 416 and *Shulchan Aruch* ibid.).

בבא קמא ג/ג

[ג] **הַמּוֹצִיא** אֶת־תִּבְנוֹ וְאֶת־קַשּׁוֹ לִרְשׁוּת הָרַבִּים לִזְבָלִים, וְהֻזַּק בָּהֶן אַחֵר, חַיָּב בְּנִזְקוֹ; וְכָל־הַקּוֹדֵם בָּהֶן זָכָה. רַבָּן שִׁמְעוֹן בֶּן־גַּמְלִיאֵל אוֹמֵר: כָּל־הַמְקַלְקְלִין בִּרְשׁוּת הָרַבִּים וְהִזִּיקוּ חַיָּבִין לְשַׁלֵּם; וְכָל־הַקּוֹדֵם בָּהֶן זָכָה. הַהוֹפֵךְ אֶת־הַגָּלָל בִּרְשׁוּת הָרַבִּים, וְהֻזַּק בָּהֶן אַחֵר, חַיָּב בְּנִזְקוֹ.

יד אברהם

3.

הַמּוֹצִיא אֶת־תִּבְנוֹ וְאֶת־קַשּׁוֹ לִרְשׁוּת הָרַבִּים לִזְבָלִים — [If] one puts out his straw or his stubble into a public domain to [become] fertilizer,

The term תִּבְנוֹ from תֶּבֶן, straw, denotes what is cut off together with ears of grain and remains after the grain is threshed. קַשׁ, stubble, is what is left in the ground after the ears of grain have been cut off (*Bava Metzia* 9:1, quoted by *Meiri, Tos. Yom Tov*).

This is placed in the street to decay and become fertilizer to fertilize fields and vineyards (*Rav; Rashi*).

וְהֻזַּק בָּהֶן אַחֵר — and someone else is injured by it,

[Someone slipped on it and fell.]

חַיָּב בְּנִזְקוֹ; — he is liable for his injury;

[The owner of the straw is responsible for the injury.]

וְכָל־הַקּוֹדֵם בָּהֶן זָכָה. — and whoever seizes it first acquires [it].

The Rabbis thereby penalized the owner of the straw or stubble for placing it in public property (*Rav* from *Gem.* 30b), so that he should refrain from doing it again. If he did so at a time when it is permissible to put straw out in the public domain they did not penalize him (*Tif. Yis.* from *Choshen Mishpat* 414:2).

רַבָּן שִׁמְעוֹן בֶּן־גַּמְלִיאֵל אוֹמֵר: כָּל־הַמְקַלְקְלִין בִּרְשׁוּת הָרַבִּים וְהִזִּיקוּ — Rabban Shimon ben Gamliel says: All who litter the public domain and cause damage

That is, even if they do so when it is permissible — namely, during the season when people put out straw into the public domain for fertilizer (*Rav; Rashi*). During this season, a person may put his fertilizer in the public domain and heap it up there for thirty days so that it be crushed by the feet of men and animals, for with that condition [that people allow others to do this (*Rashi*)] did Joshua make Israel inherit the Land (*Gem.* 30a).

[This explanation follows *Rashi's* second interpretation of Rabban Shimon ben Gamliel's view. His first interpretation will be presented below.]

חַיָּבִין לְשַׁלֵּם; — are liable to pay;

They are liable although they put the straw out with permission (*Rav*).

וְכָל־הַקּוֹדֵם בָּהֶן זָכָה. — and whoever seizes them first acquires [them].

This does not refer to the case in which people are allowed to put the straw out into the public domain, for in that case there would be no reason to penalize them. It refers to the earlier case of the one who puts it out when he has no permission to do so (*Tos. R' Akiva* from *Tos.*).

According to *Rashi's* first interpretation, the controversy between the first, anonymous *Tanna* in the mishnah and

3. [I]f] one puts out his straw or his stubble into a public domain to [become] fertilizer, and someone else is injured by it, he is liable for his injury; and whoever seizes it first acquires [it]. Rabban Shimon ben Gamliel says: All who litter the public domain and cause damage are liable to pay; and whoever seizes them first acquires [them].

[If] one turns over dung in a public domain, and someone else is injured by it, he is liable for his injury.

YAD AVRAHAM

Rabban Shimon ben Gamliel is whether — in a case in which the straw increased in value while lying in the public domain — the Rabbis penalized the owner by permitting anyone to seize the straw and retain both the original value as well as the increase. The first *Tanna* rules that they may retain only the increase, but not the principal. Rabban Shimon ben Gamliel contends that they may retain even the principal. *Rambam* [*Hil. Nizkei Mamon* 13:14] rules according to Rabban Shimon ben Gamliel, since the halachah is always in accordance with his view throughout the Mishnah *(Tos. Yom Tov; Lechem Mishneh;* cf. commentary to 5:4, s.v. מִשֶּׁהָאֵשָׁה, and *Tos. Yom Tov* to *Eruvin* 8:7).

הַהוֹפֵךְ אֶת־הַגָּלָל — [If] one turns over dung

This refers to cattle dung (*Rav; Rambam*).

בִּרְשׁוּת הָרַבִּים, — in a public domain,

Since the dung is ownerless, and he picks it up with the intention of acquiring it, it becomes his property, and he is liable for any damage it causes (*Gem.* 29b).

וְהֻזַּק בָּהֶן אַחֵר, חַיָּב בְּנִזְקוֹ. — and someone else is injured by it, he is liable for his injury.

The *Gemara* (29b) explains that the expression *turns over* denotes picking up something to a height of less than three handbreadths, since — when taking possession of הֶפְקֵר, *ownerless property* — it is unnecessary to lift it to the height of three handbreadths. Therefore, if he intends to take possession of it, he is liable for any damages it causes. Should he pick it up to a height of three handbreadths, however, even if he does not intend to take possession of it, he is liable. Since he lifts it to this height, he has undone the deed of the one who originally placed it there. Hence, he is, in effect, doing the equivalent of digging a pit by replacing the dung on the ground in the public domain. Although he does not intend to acquire it, he is no less liable than one who abandons an obstacle that fell because of his negligence (*Tos. Yom Tov*).

In this case, the *Tanna* does not state: *whoever seizes it first acquires* [it]. Since it will not increase in value by lying in the public domain, the Rabbis did not penalize the one who placed it there (*Gem.* 29b). *Ran* explains that since he gains nothing from leaving it in the street, his only intention is to clean his yard, and he is not apt to leave it there for any length of time, but will remove it soon (*Tos. Yom Tov*).

בבא קמא
ג/ד-ה

[ד] **שְׁנֵי** קַדָּרִין שֶׁהָיוּ מְהַלְּכִין, זֶה אַחַר זֶה, וְנִתְקַל הָרִאשׁוֹן וְנָפַל, וְנִתְקַל הַשֵּׁנִי בָּרִאשׁוֹן, הָרִאשׁוֹן חַיָּב בְּנִזְקֵי הַשֵּׁנִי.

[ה] **זֶה** בָּא בְחָבִיתוֹ וְזֶה בָּא בְקוֹרָתוֹ, נִשְׁבְּרָה כַדּוֹ שֶׁל־זֶה בְּקוֹרָתוֹ שֶׁל־זֶה, פָּטוּר, שֶׁלָּזֶה רְשׁוּת לְהַלֵּךְ וְלָזֶה רְשׁוּת לְהַלֵּךְ. הָיָה בַעַל הַקּוֹרָה רִאשׁוֹן וּבַעַל הֶחָבִית אַחֲרוֹן, נִשְׁבְּרָה הֶחָבִית בַּקּוֹרָה, פָּטוּר בַּעַל הַקּוֹרָה; וְאִם

יד אברהם

4.

שְׁנֵי קַדָּרִין — [If] *two potters*
 The *Tanna* chooses a case of potters not necessarily because their wares — viz., the earthen pots — break easily, but because they stumble easily under the weight of their heavy load (*Meleches Shlomo*).

שֶׁהָיוּ מְהַלְּכִין, זֶה אַחַר זֶה, — *were walking, one after the other,*
 [They were walking in the street one behind the other.]

וְנִתְקַל הָרִאשׁוֹן וְנָפַל, וְנִתְקַל הַשֵּׁנִי בָּרִאשׁוֹן, — *and the first one stumbled and fell, and the second one stumbled over the first one,*
 [The second one was injured by his fall over the first one.]

הָרִאשׁוֹן חַיָּב בְּנִזְקֵי הַשֵּׁנִי. — *the first one is liable for the injuries of the second one.*
 This ruling is true only if the first one has time to pick himself up but fails to do so. Otherwise, he is exempt, since the halachah is in accordance with the view of R' Yehudah in mishnah 1, that stumbling does not constitute negligence (*Rav*, following R' Yochanan's view in the *Gem.* 31a).
 If he did not have time to stand up, he is exempt even if he had time to warn the one following him and failed to do so. This is because a person who is in the process of picking himself up is not expected to warn others, since he is busy with himself (*Tos. Yom Tov* from *Gem.*).
 As mentioned above, this follows R' Yochanan's view in the *Gemara*. R' Nachman bar Yitzchak, however, maintains that even if the first potter had no time to pick himself up, he was nevertheless required to warn the one following him. *Rif* and *Rambam* (Hil. Nizkei Mamon 13:8) rule according to R' Yochanan's opinion, whereas *Rosh* follows the view of R' Nachman bar Yitzchak (see *Tos. R' Akiva*).
 According to *Rambam* (loc. cit.) and *Rosh*, the potter lying on the ground is adjudged as a pit. Therefore, he is liable only for the bodily injuries sustained by the second potter, but not for the damages caused to the latter's pots, since a person is exempt from damages of vessels caused by his pit (see commentary to 1:1, s.v. *Bor*). According to *Rif*, however, although he inflicts damages passively, his body is adjudged as a man inflicting damage, and he is therefore liable even for the damages caused to the vessels (see *Sma* to *Choshen Mishpat* 413:2).

משניות / בבא קמא — פרק ג: המניח [52]

3
4-5

4. [If] two potters were walking, one after the other, and the first one stumbled and fell, and the second one stumbled over the first one, the first one is liable for the injuries of the second one.

5. [If] one came with his jug and another came with his beam, [and] this one's jug broke on that one's beam, he is exempt, since this one has the right to walk and that one has the right to walk.

[If] the owner of the beam was first and the owner of the jug second, [and] the jug broke on the beam, the owner of the beam is exempt; but if the owner of

YAD AVRAHAM

5.

זֶה בָּא בְחָבִיתוֹ וְזֶה בָּא בְקוֹרָתוֹ — [If] one came with his jug and another came with his beam,

And they collided into one another (Tos. Yom Tov, Tif. Yis. from Rashi).

[This is a new case and not a continuation of the previous mishnah.]

נִשְׁבְּרָה כַדוֹ שֶׁל-זֶה בְּקוֹרָתוֹ שֶׁל-זֶה — [and] this one's jug broke on that one's beam,

See commentary to mishnah 1, s.v. בַּעַל הֶחָבִית, for an explanation of the term כַּד as opposed to חָבִית (Tos. Yom Tov).

פָּטוּר, — he is exempt,

[The owner of the beam is exempt from paying for the damage to the jug.]

שֶׁלָּזֶה רְשׁוּת לְהַלֵּךְ וְלָזֶה רְשׁוּת לְהַלֵּךְ. — since this one has the right to walk and that one has the right to walk.

Because the one carrying the beam was permitted to walk there, the one holding the jug should have been careful to avoid colliding with him (Meiri).

The one carrying the beam is exempt only if both are walking, since — in that case — the one with the jug also contributes to the collision. Should the latter stand still, however, the one carrying the beam causes the entire damage by himself and is therefore liable (Tos. R' Akiva from Tos.).

הָיָה בַעַל הַקוֹרָה רִאשׁוֹן וּבַעַל הֶחָבִית אַחֲרוֹן, — [If] the owner of the beam was first and the owner of the jug second,

[They were walking one behind the other.]

נִשְׁבְּרָה הֶחָבִית בַּקוֹרָה, פָּטוּר בַּעַל הַקוֹרָה; — [and] the jug broke on the beam, the owner of the beam is exempt;

The owner of the beam is exempt, since he was walking normally, while the owner of the jug walked too fast (Rav; Rashi).

Since he sees the one carrying the beam in front of him walking at a normal pace, he too, should maintain that pace and not walk faster (Meiri).

וְאִם עָמַד בַּעַל הַקוֹרָה, חַיָּב. — but if the owner of the beam stopped, he is liable.

If the one carrying the beam stopped to rest from his heavy burden, and the one with the jug — unaware that the other had stopped — continued on his way, the one carrying the beam is liable. Since it is unusual for one to stop in the middle of the way to rest, the one with the jug did not realize that he should be careful. Should the one with the beam have stopped in order to adjust it on his

בבא קמא ג/ו

עָמַד בַּעַל הַקּוֹרָה, חַיָּב. וְאִם אָמַר לְבַעַל הֶחָבִית: ״עֲמֹד!״ פָּטוּר.

הָיָה בַעַל הֶחָבִית רִאשׁוֹן וּבַעַל הַקּוֹרָה אַחֲרוֹן, נִשְׁבְּרָה הֶחָבִית בַּקּוֹרָה, חַיָּב; וְאִם עָמַד בַּעַל הֶחָבִית, פָּטוּר. וְאִם אָמַר לְבַעַל הַקּוֹרָה: ״עֲמֹד!״ חַיָּב.

וְכֵן זֶה בָא בְנֵרוֹ, וְזֶה בְּפִשְׁתָּנוֹ.

[ו] **שְׁנַיִם** שֶׁהָיוּ מְהַלְּכִין בִּרְשׁוּת הָרַבִּים — אֶחָד רָץ וְאֶחָד מְהַלֵּךְ, אוֹ שֶׁהָיוּ

יד אברהם

shoulder, however, since this is customary, the one carrying the jug should have been careful, and therefore cannot sue for damages.

This is similar to the case of the preceding mishnah, in which the damager is liable only if he could have stood up and did not; but if he could not have gotten up, he is exempt, since this is considered a normal occurrence. So is it in this case — the owner of the beam is liable only if he stopped merely to rest; but if he stopped to adjust his load, which is a normal act, he is exempt (*Tos. Yom Tov* from *Gem.* 31a).

Although the beam broke the jug passively, we do not consider it to be in the category of *bor*, for which one is exempt from paying for damages it causes to vessels. Since [unlike the case of the previous mishnah] he is not lying on the ground, but rather is in full control of himself, it is as though he actively caused this damage, and is considered a man perpetrating a damage, who is liable for vessels as well (*Tos. Yom Tov* from *Nimmukei Yosef*).

וְאִם אָמַר לְבַעַל הֶחָבִית: ״עֲמֹד!״ — If, however, he said to the owner of the jug: 'Stop!'

[He had warned the owner of the jug while there was still time to avoid a collision.]

פָּטוּר. — he is exempt.

Even though the owner of the beam stopped to rest, since he had warned the owner of the jug to stop, he is exempt (*Tos. R' Akiva* from *Gem.* 31a).

According to R' Nachman bar Yitzchak, who holds that, in the case of the previous mishnah, if the potter had no time to pick himself up, he is exempt only if he warned the one behind him, the same applies here — that even if the owner of the beam stopped to merely adjust the beam on his shoulder, he is exempt from damages caused by it only if he warns the owner of the jug to stop.

According to R' Yochanan, however, since he is occupied with adjusting the beam, he is not required to warn the owner of the jug; only if he stops to rest is he required to warn him (*Gem.* ibid.).

[As in the case of the previous mishnah, *Rambam* (*Hil. Chovel* 6:8; see *Maggid Mishneh* ad loc.) rules in accordance with R' Yochanan's view.]

הָיָה בַעַל הֶחָבִית רִאשׁוֹן וּבַעַל הַקּוֹרָה אַחֲרוֹן, נִשְׁבְּרָה הֶחָבִית בַּקּוֹרָה, חַיָּב; — [If] the owner of the jug was first and the owner of the beam second, [and] the jug broke on the beam, he is liable;

The owner of the beam is liable, since

משניות / בבא קמא — פרק ג: המניח [54]

the beam stopped, he is liable. If, however, he said to the owner of the jug: 'Stop!' he is exempt.

[If] the owner of the jug was first and the owner of the beam second, [and] the jug broke on the beam, he is liable; but if the owner of the jug stopped, he is exempt. If, however, he said to the owner of the beam, 'Stop!' he is liable.

The same applies if one comes with his candle, and this one with his flax.

6. [If] two were going in a public domain — one was running and one was walking, or both

YAD AVRAHAM

the second one must always beware of walking too closely behind the first one (*Tif. Yis.; Meiri*).

וְאִם עָמַד בַּעַל הֶחָבִית, — *but if the owner of the jug stopped,*

He stopped to rest, as in the case above (*Meiri*).

פָּטוּר. — *he is exempt.*

He is exempt, since he had no reason to expect that the owner of the jug would stop to rest (*Meiri*).

וְאִם אָמַר לְבַעַל הַקּוֹרָה: "עֲמֹד!" חַיָּב. — *If, however, he said to the owner of the beam: 'Stop!' he is liable.*

[If he warned the owner of the beam to stop, the latter is liable. As explained above, had the owner of the jug stopped to adjust it on his shoulder, the halachah is the owner of the beam would be liable even if he were not warned.]

וְכֵן זֶה בָּא בְנֵרוֹ, וְזֶה בְּפִשְׁתָּנוֹ. — *The same applies if one comes with his candle, and another with his flax.*

This segment of the mishnah appears superfluous. *Tos. Yom Tov* suggests that we might think that since flax is highly flammable and will ignite if it but comes near a flame, the owner of the candle must beware of igniting the flax, and is therefore always liable. He suggests also that we may think that, on the contrary, the owner of the flax must be extremely cautious lest his flax catch fire, and, therefore, the owner of the candle should always be exempt. In view of the principle propounded by *Tosafos* 23a, that one must beware of damaging others more than he must beware of hurting himself, the first suggestion is more likely.

6.

שְׁנַיִם שֶׁהָיוּ מְהַלְּכִין בִּרְשׁוּת הָרַבִּים — — [If] *two were going in a public domain —*

They were going toward each other (*Meiri*).

אֶחָד רָץ וְאֶחָד מְהַלֵּךְ, אוֹ שֶׁהָיוּ שְׁנֵיהֶם רָצִים — — *one was running and one was walking, or both were running —*

The case of *one was running and one was walking* is to be qualified as taking place on the eve of the Sabbath and the eve of a festival; that of *both were running* is applicable any time of the year. As the mishnah concludes, in both cases both persons are exempt. On the eves of Sabbaths and festivals, one who runs is exempt if he injures another, since he is running to perform a *mitzvah*

[55]   THE MISHNAH/BAVA KAMMA — Chapter Three: *HaMeineach*

בבא קמא ג/ז

שְׁנֵיהֶם רָצִים — וְהִזִּיקוּ זֶה אֶת־זֶה, שְׁנֵיהֶם פְּטוּרִין.

[ז] הַמְבַקֵּעַ בִּרְשׁוּת הַיָּחִיד וְהִזִּיק בִּרְשׁוּת הָרַבִּים; בִּרְשׁוּת הָרַבִּים, וְהִזִּיק בִּרְשׁוּת הַיָּחִיד; בִּרְשׁוּת הַיָּחִיד, וְהִזִּיק בִּרְשׁוּת

יד אברהם

— namely, to prepare for the Sabbath or festival. [Otherwise, since he is not permitted to run, he would be liable to compensate for the injury.] At any other time, if both were running, since they both committed a breach of proper behavior, each is not liable for the other's injuries (*Rav, Rambam Commentary* from *Gem.* 32a).

The *Gemara* [and *Rambam, Hil. Chovel* 6:9] specifies that the exemption regarding the Sabbath and festival eve applies only during בֵּין הַשְּׁמָשׁוֹת, *twilight*[1] (*Tos. Yom Tov*).

Since — at this time — most people are running to prepare for the Sabbath, we can assume that this is the intention of the one who is running. Even if he has nothing in his hands, we can still assume that he is running home to fulfill the mishnah in *Shabbos* (2:7): *A man must say three things in his home on the eve of the Sabbath just before dark: 'Have you tithed? Have you prepared the eruv? Kindle the [Sabbath] light!'* He may also be running to wash his face, his hands, and his feet, or to change his clothes. If, however, we know definitely that he is running to take care of his own affairs, which are not related to the necessities of the Sabbath, the case is judged as if it were any weekday (*Nimmukei Yosef* from *Ramah*).

Rambam (loc. cit.), however, states that he has the right to run lest the Sabbath begin before he is free. It appears that *Rambam* holds that although he is running to take care of his own affairs, it is regarded as if he is doing so in honor of the Sabbath, since he is running in order to finish his business before then, and he therefore has the right to run. Accordingly, the statement of the mishnah needs less qualification, for anyone who runs at twilight on the eve of Sabbath is exempt from liability for any damages he may cause (*Tos. Yom Tov*).

Shulchan Aruch [*Choshen Mishpat* 378:8] quotes this ruling of *Rambam*, and *Rama* [ad loc.] quotes the comment of *Nimmukei Yosef* to explain that this is the intention of *Shulchan Aruch*. However, it seems certain that the second opinion is not a qualification of the first, but is a conflicting view (*Tos. Yom Tov*). *Sma* (378:11), on the other hand, supports *Rama* in his assertion that *Rambam* refers only to Sabbath preparations, and that his intention is that the damager is running to complete his Sabbath preparations and be free before the arrival of the Sabbath. See *Aruch Hashulchan* ibid. §18.

Hagahos Asheri, quoting *Or Zarua*, asserts that the mishnah's ruling applies from the time people commence to prepare for the Sabbath — to cook, bake, and roast — i.e., from midday on.

Should one run to perform any other *mitzvah*, for which he has more time, such as running to the synagogue or the study hall, and he causes damage, he is liable (*Mordechai* ad loc.; *Hagahos Maimonios, Hil. Chovel* 6:9).

וְהִזִּיקוּ זֶה אֶת־זֶה, — *and they injured one another*,

Since each one contributed to his own injury, they are both exempt. The intention is not that they injured one

---

1. The definition of this term is discussed in the ArtScroll commentary to *Shabbos* 2:7, p. 67.

were running — and they injured one another, both are exempt.

7. [If] one chops [wood] in a private domain and damages in a public domain; [or] in a public domain, and damages in a private domain; [or] in a private domain, and damages in another private

YAD AVRAHAM

another intentionally, but that each one was injured by the other *(Tos. Yom Tov from Tos.)*.

Others rule that since they both are equally active, it is as though one was injured by the other, and they are exempt even if they actively injured one another *(Nimmukei Yosef, Rosh, Gra, and Tur Choshen Mishpat 378, quoting Ramah)*.

שְׁנֵיהֶם פְּטוּרִין. — *both are exempt.*

Since, on the eve of the Sabbath, running — which is a deviation from proper behavior on weekdays — is permissible, it is immaterial whether they are going toward one another or one is behind the other; they are exempt. If both are running on a weekday, however, in which case both are exempt because they are committing the same deviation from proper behavior, we must differentiate — as in the case of the beam and the jug (see previous mishnah) — between going toward one another or one behind the other, and between the second one running too fast and the first one stopping *(Nimmukei Yosef)*.

7.

The following mishnah teaches us that if someone chops wood and the chips fly and cause damage, he is liable whether he chops it in his own property or in others' property, whether he causes damage in a place frequented by many people — namely, a public domain — or whether he causes damage in a place not frequented by many people — viz., private property. This is because *Man is always muad* [2:6] *(Rambam Commentary)*.

הַמְבַקֵּעַ בִּרְשׁוּת הַיָּחִיד — [If] one chops [wood] in a private domain

That is, in his own premises, although he has the right to do so there *(Tif. Yis. from Gem. 32b)*.

וְהִזִּיק בִּרְשׁוּת הָרַבִּים; — and damages in a public domain;

He damages with flying chips or with the ax handle which became detached and flew off, injuring someone *(Tos. Yom Tov from Nimmukei Yosef)*.

בִּרְשׁוּת הָרַבִּים, — [or] in a public domain,

He chopped wood in a place where he had no right to do so *(Gem. loc. cit.)*.

וְהִזִּיק בִּרְשׁוּת הַיָּחִיד — and damages in a private domain;

He damaged in a private domain belonging to someone else *(Rav; Rashi)*.

The ruling applies although the damage was done in a place that few people frequent, and he did not think anyone would be there *(Tif. Yis. from Gem.)*.

בִּרְשׁוּת הַיָּחִיד, — [or] in a private domain,

He chopped wood in his own premises *(Rav; Rashi)*.

וְהִזִּיק בִּרְשׁוּת הַיָּחִיד אַחֵר — and damages in another private domain —

[57] THE MISHNAH/BAVA KAMMA — Chapter Three: *HaMeineach*

בבא קמא ג/ח

הַיָּחִיד אַחֵר — חַיָּב.

[ח] **שְׁנֵי** שְׁוָרִים תַּמִּים שֶׁחָבְלוּ זֶה אֶת־זֶה, מְשַׁלְּמִים בַּמּוֹתָר חֲצִי נֶזֶק. שְׁנֵיהֶם מוּעָדִים, מְשַׁלְּמִים בַּמּוֹתָר נֶזֶק שָׁלֵם. אֶחָד תָּם וְאֶחָד מוּעָד, מוּעָד בְּתָם, מְשַׁלֵּם בַּמּוֹתָר נֶזֶק שָׁלֵם;

יד אברהם

I.e., in a place belonging to others (*Rav; Rashi*).

He is liable, as the mishnah concludes, although he had a right to chop wood in his own property, and the place where the chips flew was not one frequented by many people, which would necessitate that he exercise caution (*Rav from Gem.*).

חַיָּב. — *he is liable.*

He is liable to pay for the complete damage, since it was perpetrated by his power, which is tantamount to being perpetrated by his body. This ruling is based on the principle that *Man is always considered forewarned* (*Tos. Yom Tov from Nimmukei Yosef*).

8.

This mishnah deals with the method of reckoning the damages of two animals that wounded one another, two men that wounded one another, or a man and an animal that wounded one another. It elaborates on mishnah 1:3 (*Tos. Yom Tov*).

Meleches Shlomo explains that this mishnah is based on the final mishnah of the preceding chapter, which states that *Man is always muad*. This mishnah, too, equates him with the *muad* animal, stating that they pay equally.

שְׁנֵי שְׁוָרִים תַּמִּים שֶׁחָבְלוּ זֶה אֶת־זֶה, — [*If*] *two tam bulls wounded one another,*

[For example, Reuven's bull gored Shimon's bull, and vice versa; and both are *tamin* — i.e., they had not yet gored three times, as discussed in 2:4.]

מְשַׁלְּמִים בַּמּוֹתָר חֲצִי נֶזֶק. — [*their owners*] *pay half the excess* [lit., *of the excess, half the damages*].

If both damages are equal, neither one pays. Should one exceed the other, however, that one must pay half the excess (*Rav; Rashi*).

Since these animals are in the category of *tam*, each damagee becomes a partner in the other animal in the amount of half the damages (see preface to 4:1). Consequently, should one animal be worth less than half the damage it inflicted, only that amount is deducted from the damage done by the other (*Tos. Yom Tov from Nimmukei Yosef*).

[For example, if Reuven's bull wounded Shimon's bull to the extent of one hundred dollars, and Shimon's bull injured Reuven's to the extent of eighty dollars, we deduct forty dollars (half the damages inflicted by Shimon's bull) from fifty dollars (half the damages inflicted by Reuven's bull), giving us an excess of ten dollars.]

If the animal that inflicted the smaller damage is lost or dies, the owner of the animal that did the greater damage must nevertheless pay only half the difference, and we do not say that since the missing animal was a *tam*, in which the damagee becomes a partner as his compensation for the damage, the other owner should pay half the damages without any deduction (*Tif. Yis., Rama* 402, from *Nimmukei Yosef*). This is because, as soon as the animals injure each other, to the extent that the damages are equal they cancel each other out — as if they had never occured — and the owner of the animal that did the

משניות / בבא קמא — פרק ג: המניח [58]

domain — he is liable.

8. [If] two *tam* bulls wounded one another, [their owners] pay half the excess. [If] both are *muadin*, they pay the full excess. [If] one is *tam* and the other *muad*, [that which] the *muad* [injured] the *tam*, [its owner] pays the full excess; [that which] the

YAD AVRAHAM

greater damage becomes liable for only half the excess (*Sma* ad loc. from *Nimmukei Yosef*; see comment of *Rosh* cited below).

Rosh (§13) explains that the entire mishnah deals with two animals that began fighting simultaneously. Should one injure the other first, and the latter retaliate in anger, the second one is exempt. The same is true in a case of two men who injure one another. Should one provoke the other, the latter may injure the former in self-defense, but only to the extent required to defend himself (cf. *Rambam, Hil. Nizkei Mamon* 9:14).

שְׁנֵיהֶם מוּעָדִים — [If] both are muadin,

[Both animals had already gored three times; see 2:4.]

מְשַׁלְּמִים בַּמּוֹתָר נֶזֶק שָׁלֵם. — they pay the full excess.

The owner of the animal who did the greater damage pays the complete difference between the damage inflicted by his animal and the damage done by the other (*Tif. Yis.*).

אֶחָד תָּם וְאֶחָד מוּעָד, — [If] one is tam and the other muad,

[One of the two animals which wounded each other is a *tam*, and the other a *muad*.]

מוּעָד בְּתָם, מְשַׁלֵּם בַּמּוֹתָר נֶזֶק שָׁלֵם; — [that which] the muad [injured] the tam, [its owner] pays the full excess;

If the *muad* injured the *tam* more than the latter injured it, the owner of the *muad* pays the entire difference between the amounts of damages that the two animals caused (*Rav; Rashi*).

Rosh points out that, in effect, the owner of the *tam* pays for full damages in this case. For example, if the *muad* injured the *tam* to the extent of a hundred *zuz*, and the *tam* injured the *muad* to the extent of forty *zuz*, it would appear that the owner of the *muad* should pay eighty *zuz* — the difference between the hundred-*zuz* damage it inflicted and half the forty-*zuz* damage inflicted by the *tam*. Instead, the *Tanna* teaches us that he pays only sixty *zuz*, the excess over the damage that the *tam* caused to his animal.[1] The reason is that since the animals began fighting simultaneously, as explained above, to the extent that the two damages are equal, they cancel each other out as if they never occurred (see *Nimmukei Yosef*, cited above); thus, the entire injury — for purposes of payment — is only the excess. *Tos. Yom Tov* comments that this interpretation is borne out by the wording of the mishnah. Had the *Tanna* meant that the owner of the *muad* pays the excess over half the damages caused by the *tam*, he would have used the term מוֹתָר or הַמּוֹתָר, which implies that it refers to the excess in payments. The word בַּמּוֹתָר, however, implies that it refers only to the excess in damage and nothing more (*Tos. Yom Tov; Pilpula Charifta*).

Others (*Tos.; Rambam, Commentary and Hil. Nizkei Mamon* 9:14;

---

1. [Although *Rosh's* example uses different numbers, we have used the figures given in *Rambam's* example, cited below, so as to more easily juxtapose the two divergent opinions of the mishnah.]

[59]   THE MISHNAH/BAVA KAMMA — Chapter Three: *HaMeineach*

בבא קמא ג/ח

תָּם בְּמוּעָד, מְשַׁלֵּם בַּמּוֹתָר חֲצִי נֶזֶק. וְכֵן שְׁנֵי אֲנָשִׁים שֶׁחָבְלוּ זֶה בָּזֶה, מְשַׁלְּמִים בַּמּוֹתָר נֶזֶק שָׁלֵם. אָדָם בְּמוּעָד וּמוּעָד בְּאָדָם, מְשַׁלֵּם בַּמּוֹתָר נֶזֶק שָׁלֵם. אָדָם בְּתָם, וְתָם בְּאָדָם, אָדָם בְּתָם, מְשַׁלֵּם בַּמּוֹתָר נֶזֶק שָׁלֵם; תָּם בְּאָדָם, מְשַׁלֵּם בַּמּוֹתָר חֲצִי נֶזֶק. רַבִּי עֲקִיבָא אוֹמֵר: אַף תָּם שֶׁחָבַל בְּאָדָם מְשַׁלֵּם בַּמּוֹתָר נֶזֶק שָׁלֵם.

יד אברהם

Nimmukei Yosef), however, interpret the mishnah differently. They maintain that the excess consists of the difference between the damage of the *muad* and half the damage of the *tam*. Hence, they construe the above statement in the mishnah as follows: מוּעָד בְּתָם, if the amount of damage done by the *muad* to the *tam* exceeds half the damage done by the tam to the *muad*, then מְשַׁלֵּם בַּמּוֹתָר נֶזֶק שָׁלֵם, the owner of the *muad* pays the entire difference between the damage done by his animal and half of that done by the other. For example, if the *muad* injured the *tam* to the extent of one hundred zuz, and the *tam* injured the *muad* to the extent of forty zuz, the owner of the *muad* pays eighty zuz — the difference between the hundred-zuz damage it inflicted and half the forty-zuz damage done by the *tam*.

תָּם בְּמוּעָד, מְשַׁלֵּם בַּמּוֹתָר חֲצִי נֶזֶק — [that which] the tam [injured] the muad, [its owner] pays half the excess.

[As explained above, according to *Rav, Rashi,* and *Rosh,* as long as the *tam* injured the *muad* more than the latter injured it, its owner must pay half the excess. According to *Tosafos, Rambam,* and *Nimmukei Yosef,* the owner of the *tam* pays only if half the damage it did exceeds the entire damage inflicted by the *muad*; if it does, he pays that excess.]

וְכֵן שְׁנֵי אֲנָשִׁים שֶׁחָבְלוּ זֶה בָּזֶה, מְשַׁלְּמִים בַּמּוֹתָר נֶזֶק שָׁלֵם. — Likewise [if] two men wounded one another, they pay the full excess.

Just as the mishnah rules concerning two animals in the category of *muad*, so is the ruling concerning two people, since *Man is always muad* [2:6] *(Meiri).*

As explained above, this deals with two people who injured one another simultaneously. Should one provoke the other, the latter is exempt *(Rosh).*

אָדָם בְּמוּעָד וּמוּעָד בְּאָדָם, מְשַׁלֵּם בַּמּוֹתָר נֶזֶק שָׁלֵם. — [If] a man [injured] a muad [animal], and the muad [injured] the man, he pays the full excess.

This is analogous to two *muad* animals that injured one another *(Meiri).*

אָדָם בְּתָם וְתָם בְּאָדָם, — [If] a man [injured] a tam, and the tam [injured] the man,

This is analogous to the case of the *tam* and the *muad* (ibid.).

אָדָם בְּתָם, — [that which] the man [injured] the tam,

[That is, if the man injured the *tam* more than the latter injured him (according to *Rav, Rashi,* and *Rosh,*) or (according to *Tos., Rambam,* and *Nimmukei Yosef*) if the man injured the *tam* more than half the damage the latter caused.]

משניות / בבא קמא — פרק ג: המניח [60]

tam [injured] the *muad* [its owner] pays half the excess.

Likewise [if] two men wounded one another, they pay the full excess. [If] a man [injured] a *muad* [animal] and the *muad* [injured] the man, he pays the full excess. [If] a man [injured] a *tam*, and the *tam* [injured] the man, [that which] the man [injured] the *tam*, he pays the full excess; [that which] the *tam* [injured] the man, [its owner] pays half the excess. R' Akiva says: Also [if] a *tam* wounded a man, [its owner] pays the full excess.

YAD AVRAHAM

מְשַׁלֵּם בַּמּוֹתָר נֶזֶק שָׁלֵם; — *he pays the full excess*;
This is the same as the case of the *muad* wounding the *tam* (Meiri), since Man is always *muad* (Rav).

תָּם בְּאָדָם, מְשַׁלֵּם בַּמּוֹתָר חֲצִי נֶזֶק. — [*that which*] *the* tam [*injured*] *the man,* [*its owner*] *pays half the excess*.

[If the injuries inflicted by the *tam* exceeded those inflicted by the man, the owner of the *tam* pays half the excess according to Rav, Rashi, and Rosh. According to Tos., Rambam, and Nimmukei Yosef, if the half-damages for which the *tam* is liable exceeded the injuries inflicted by the man, the owner of the *tam* pays that excess.]

The Sages base this ruling on the verse (*Ex.* 21:31) אוֹ־בֵן יִגָּח אוֹ־בַת יִגָּח, כַּמִּשְׁפָּט הַזֶּה יֵעָשֶׂה לּוֹ, *Whether it gores a male child or it gores a female child, according to this judgment shall be done to it*. The intention is that the judgment of an animal that gores another animal is the same as the judgment of one that gores a man — viz., that a *tam* pays half the damages and a *muad* pays the full damages (*Rav* from *Gem.* 33a).

רַבִּי עֲקִיבָא אוֹמֵר: אַף תָּם שֶׁחָבַל בְּאָדָם, מְשַׁלֵּם בַּמּוֹתָר נֶזֶק שָׁלֵם. — *R' Akiva says: Also* [*if*] *a* tam *wounded a man,* [*its owner*] *pays the full excess*.

R' Akiva, too, bases his ruling on the aforementioned passage. He construes the phrase כַּמִּשְׁפָּט הַזֶּה, *according to this judgment*, as referring to the judgment mentioned immediately preceding this verse — namely, that of the *muad*. The implication is that if an animal gores a person, its owner must always pay the full damages, just as in the case of a *muad* that gores another animal (*Rav* from *Gem.* ad loc.).

The Rabbis, however, expound the word הַזֶּה, to mean that the owner of the animal pays only for the damage, not for the four other obligations, discussed in 8:1, that are imposed by the Torah upon one who injures another person (*Tos. Yom Tov* from *Gem.* 33a).

The halachah is not in accordance with R' Akiva's view (*Rav; Rambam*).

9.

The Torah states (*Ex.* 21:35): וְכִי־יִגֹּף שׁוֹר־אִישׁ אֶת־שׁוֹר רֵעֵהוּ וָמֵת וּמָכְרוּ אֶת־הַשּׁוֹר הַחַי וְחָצוּ אֶת־כַּסְפּוֹ וְגַם אֶת־הַמֵּת יֶחֱצוּן, *If a man's bull gores another's bull, and it dies, they shall sell the live bull and divide the money of it, and also divide the dead one.* This mishnah expounds on the procedure prescribed by the Torah.

בבא קמא ג/ט

[ט] שׁוֹר שָׁוֶה מָנֶה שֶׁנָּגַח שׁוֹר שָׁוֶה מָאתַיִם, וְאֵין הַנְּבֵלָה יָפָה כְלוּם, נוֹטֵל אֶת־הַשּׁוֹר.

שׁוֹר שָׁוֶה מָאתַיִם שֶׁנָּגַח שׁוֹר שָׁוֶה מָאתַיִם, וְאֵין הַנְּבֵלָה יָפָה כְלוּם — אָמַר רַבִּי מֵאִיר: עַל־זֶה נֶאֱמַר: "וּמָכְרוּ אֶת־הַשּׁוֹר הַחַי וְחָצוּ אֶת־כַּסְפּוֹ." אָמַר לוֹ רַבִּי יְהוּדָה: וְכֵן הֲלָכָה. קִיַּמְתָּ: "וּמָכְרוּ אֶת־הַשּׁוֹר הַחַי וְחָצוּ אֶת־כַּסְפּוֹ," וְלֹא קִיַּמְתָּ: "וְגַם אֶת־הַמֵּת יֶחֱצוּן." וְאֵיזֶה? זֶה שׁוֹר שָׁוֶה מָאתַיִם שֶׁנָּגַח שׁוֹר שָׁוֶה מָאתַיִם, וְהַנְּבֵלָה יָפָה חֲמִשִּׁים זוּז, שֶׁזֶּה נוֹטֵל חֲצִי הַחַי וַחֲצִי הַמֵּת, וְזֶה נוֹטֵל חֲצִי הַחַי וַחֲצִי הַמֵּת.

יד אברהם

שׁוֹר שָׁוֶה מָנֶה — [If] *a bull worth a maneh*

That is, a *tam* (Meiri; *Lechem Shamayim*).

[A *maneh* equals one hundred *zuz*.]

שֶׁנָּגַח שׁוֹר שָׁוֶה מָאתַיִם, וְאֵין הַנְּבֵלָה יָפָה כְּלוּם, — *gores a bull worth two hundred, and the carcass is worth nothing,*

[The gored animal died, and the carcass is of no value.]

נוֹטֵל אֶת־הַשּׁוֹר. — *he takes the bull.*

The owner of the dead animal takes the live *tam* which gored his bull, since its value equals half the damages. The mishnah follows the view of R' Akiva, who rules that the damaging animal is transferred to the damagee [see preface to 4:1]. R' Yishmael, however, maintains that the latter is merely a creditor who has a claim against the owner of the damaging animal, for the value of the dead animal (*Tos. Yom Tov* from *Gem.* 33a).

שׁוֹר שָׁוֶה מָאתַיִם שֶׁנָּגַח שׁוֹר שָׁוֶה מָאתַיִם — [If] *a bull worth two hundred gores a bull worth two hundred,*

[And it kills it.]

וְאֵין הַנְּבֵלָה יָפָה כְּלוּם — *and the carcass is worth nothing* —

Hence, half the damages equals half the value of the goring animal (*Meiri*).

אָמַר רַבִּי מֵאִיר: עַל־זֶה נֶאֱמַר: "וּמָכְרוּ אֶת־הַשּׁוֹר הַחַי וְחָצוּ אֶת־כַּסְפּוֹ." — *said R' Meir: Regarding this it is said* (Exodus 21:35): *'They shall sell the live bull and divide the money of it.'*

[This is the case referred to by the verse, in which the Torah ordains that the live animal be sold and the money divided, thus awarding half the damages to the owner of the dead animal.]

אָמַר לוֹ רַבִּי יְהוּדָה: וְכֵן הֲלָכָה. — *Said R' Yehudah to him: Indeed, so is the halachah.*

That is, the owner of the goring bull must pay one hundred *zuz*, which is half the damage. However, this is not the case referred to by the Torah (*Rav, Rashi*).

קִיַּמְתָּ: "וּמָכְרוּ אֶת־הַשּׁוֹר הַחַי וְחָצוּ אֶת־כַּסְפּוֹ," וְלֹא קִיַּמְתָּ: "וְגַם אֶת־הַמֵּת יֶחֱצוּן." — *You have fulfilled: 'They shall sell the live bull and divide the money of it,' but you have not fulfilled: 'and also divide the dead one.'*

9. [If] a bull worth a *maneh* gores a bull worth two hundred, and the carcass is worth nothing, he takes the bull.

[If] a bull worth two hundred gores a bull worth two hundred, and the carcass is worth nothing — said R' Meir: Regarding this it is said (*Exodus* 21:35): *They shall sell the live bull and divide the money of it.* Said R' Yehudah to him: Indeed, so is the halachah. You have fulfilled: *They shall sell the live bull and divide the money of it,* but you have not fulfilled: *and also divide the dead one.* Which one is that? That is a bull worth two hundred that gored a bull worth two hundred, and the carcass is worth fifty *zuz,* in which case this one takes half the live one and half the dead one, and that one takes half the live one and half the dead one.

YAD AVRAHAM

[Since the carcass is worth nothing, there is no point in dividing it. Scripture is surely referring to another case, in which the carcass is of some value.]

וְאֵיזֶה? — **Which one is that?**
[Which is the case referred to by the Torah?]

זֶה שׁוֹר שָׁוֶה מָאתַיִם שֶׁנָּגַח שׁוֹר שָׁוֶה מָאתַיִם, וְהַנְּבֵלָה יָפָה חֲמִשִּׁים זוּז, — **That is a bull worth two hundred that gored a bull worth two hundred, and the carcass is worth fifty zuz,**
The Torah is referring to a case in which both animals are worth the same, and the carcass is worth part of the damage — whether much of it or little of it — so that when you divide the money of the live one and the dead one between the damager and the damagee, each one sustains a loss of half the damage. For example, if an animal worth two hundred gores an animal worth two hundred, and the carcass is worth fifty, the entire damage is one hundred fifty [since the gored animal decreased in value from two hundred to fifty], and half the damage is seventy-five (*Meiri*).

שֶׁזֶּה נוֹטֵל חֲצִי הַחַי וַחֲצִי הַמֵּת, וְזֶה נוֹטֵל חֲצִי הַחַי וַחֲצִי הַמֵּת. — **in which case this one takes half the live one and half the dead one, and that one takes half the live one and half the dead one.**

When you divide the money of the live one, giving one hundred *zuz* to each one, and the money of the carcass, giving twenty-five *zuz* to each one, the result is that each one loses seventy-five *zuz,* which equals one-half of the damage (*ibid.*).

To resolve the difficulty posed by R' Yehudah, the *Gemara* tells us that R' Meir explains the passage in a figurative sense to mean that the depreciation caused by the death of the animal is divided by selling the living bull (*Tos. Yom Tov*).

The difference between R' Meir and R' Yehudah is in a case that the carcass increases in value — for example, it worth nothing at the time of death, but appreciated in value and can now be given to a dog or sold to a gentile. R'

בבא קמא ג/י

[י] **יֵשׁ** חַיָּב עַל־מַעֲשֵׂה שׁוֹרוֹ וּפָטוּר עַל־מַעֲשֵׂה עַצְמוֹ; פָּטוּר עַל־מַעֲשֵׂה שׁוֹרוֹ וְחַיָּב עַל־מַעֲשֵׂה עַצְמוֹ.

שׁוֹרוֹ שֶׁבִּיֵּשׁ, פָּטוּר; וְהוּא שֶׁבִּיֵּשׁ, חַיָּב. שׁוֹרוֹ שֶׁסִּמֵּא אֶת־עֵין עַבְדּוֹ וְהִפִּיל אֶת־שִׁנּוֹ, פָּטוּר; וְהוּא

יד אברהם

Meir rules that the increase of the value of the carcass belongs to the damagee, and the damager gains nothing by the increase of value, and must pay the complete amount of half the damages. This was R' Meir's intention when he said: *Regarding this it is said: They shall sell the live bull and divide the money of it.* That is to say that the damager must pay half the damages from the revenue of the sale of the live bull, and he may not deduct anything because of the increase in value of the carcass.

R' Yehudah, however, rules that the increase in the value of the carcass is shared by the damagee and the damager; hence, from the payment for half the damages, for which the latter is liable, he deducts half the increase in the value of the carcass from the time of death until the time of litigation. Accordingly, he questions R' Meir: *You have fulfilled: 'They shall sell the live bull and divide the money of it,' but you have not fulfilled: 'and also divide the dead one.'* That is, he must divide the increase of value of the carcass — and the damager takes half of it. The halachah is in accordance with R' Yehudah (*Rav* from *Gem.* 34b).

The *Gemara* points out that R' Meir and R' Yehudah agree that if the carcass depreciated, the damagee suffers that loss. Included in R' Meir's explanation of the verse is that the depreciation of the carcass caused by death is shared when dividing the revenue of the sale of the living animal. The intention is that the damager pays only for the depreciation caused by death; that which took place after the death of the animal is not his responsibility. R' Yehudah, too, concurs with this interpretation of the verse. He holds, however, that the Torah made the damager a partner with regard to receiving half the increase in value, but not with regard to the depreciation, since we find that the Torah was lenient with the damager in that he is not obligated to care for the carcass together with the damagee (*Nimmukei Yosef*, according to emendation of *Beis David*).

R' Yehudah does not say, however, that the damager shares the increase in value if that increase exceeds the value of the dead animal when it had been alive, for the Torah specifies that the owner of the damaging animal must *pay*; he does not *receive* payment (*Tos. Yom Tov* from *Gem.* 34b).

It would appear that if the dead animal had been worth two hundred when it was alive and one hundred after it was killed, and thereafter the carcass increased in value until it was worth one hundred twenty at the time of litigation, the owner of the *tam* that damaged should pay forty *zuz*. However, *Rambam* (*Hil. Nizkei Mamon* 7:9) and *Shulchan Aruch* (*Choshen Mishpat* 403:2) state that he pays forty-five *zuz*. *Yam Shel Shlomo* explains that since the owner of a *muad* in this case would pay ninety *zuz*, having deducted half the increase of the carcass, a *tam* must pay half what the *muad* pays — namely, forty-five *zuz* (*Tos. R' Akiva*).

10.

The following mishnah delineates several differences between damages inflicted by man and those inflicted by his animals.

10. Sometimes one is liable for the deed of his bull and exempt for his own deed; [sometimes he is] exempt for the deed of his bull and liable for his own deed.

[If] his bull embarrassed [someone], he is exempt; but if he embarrassed [someone], he is liable. [If] his bull blinded his slave's eye or knocked out his tooth,

YAD AVRAHAM

יֵשׁ חַיָּב עַל־מַעֲשֵׂה שׁוֹרוֹ וּפָטוּר עַל־מַעֲשֵׂה עַצְמוֹ; — *Sometimes one is liable for the deed of his bull and exempt for his own deed;*

[He is exempt if he himself commits the identical act.]

פָּטוּר עַל־מַעֲשֵׂה שׁוֹרוֹ וְחַיָּב עַל־מַעֲשֵׂה עַצְמוֹ. — *[sometimes he is] exempt for the deed of his bull and liable for his own deed.*

[He is exempt for a certain act committed by his animal, but liable if he himself does the identical act.]

שׁוֹרוֹ שֶׁבִּיֵּשׁ, — *[If] his bull embarrassed [someone],*

[The animal caused embarrassment to a person.]

פָּטוּר; — *he is exempt;*

In fact, if one's animal wounds a person, the owner is exempt from all four types of payment delineated in 8:1, as stated in 8:2. Nevertheless, the mishnah chooses the case of embarrassment to teach us that although one is not liable for the payment of בֹּשֶׁת, *shame,* unless he embarrasses someone intentionally, he is, however, liable to pay for embarrassment if he intends to harm someone bodily, although he does not intend to embarrass him. We learn this from the mishnah's comparison of the man to his animal. Just as an animal intends only to inflict bodily harm to a person, but not to embarrass him, so is this the case of the man that the mishnah is discussing, in which he is liable *(Tos. Yom Tov from Nimmukei Yosef, Tif. Yis., Meleches Shlomo, based on Gem. 35a).*

The exemption of the animal that embarrasses [or inflicts other harm such as pain, necessity of healing, or inability to work] is based on *Leviticus* 24:19, ... וְאִישׁ כִּי יִתֵּן מוּם בַּעֲמִיתוֹ, *If a man inflicts a blemish upon another ...,* which implies that only if a *man* inflicts a blemish on another person is he liable, but should an animal do so to a person, its owner is exempt *(Rav, Rashi* from *Gem.* 26a, 33a).

[We know that this exemption does not apply to payment for injury, since the *Gemara* (33a) interprets the phrase (*Ex.* 21:31) בַּמִּשְׁפָּט הַזֶּה יֵעָשֶׂה לּוֹ, *according to this judgment shall be done to it,* as equating the case of an animal injuring a man with that of an animal injuring another animal (see commentary to mishnah 8, s.v. תָּם בְּאָדָם).]

Another reason is that one is liable only if he embarrasses intentionally, which a bull does not do *(Rav* from *Rambam Commentary).*

Beis David and *Tosafos Chadashim* question this explanation, since the *Gemara* (35a), quoted above, explains that a man is liable for embarrassing another although his intention was only to harm him, not embarrass him. Obviously, the same would apply to an animal, unless we had a Scriptural implication to the contrary.

וְהוּא שֶׁבִּיֵּשׁ, חַיָּב. — *but if he embarrassed [someone], he is liable.*

As mentioned above, even if he has no intention to embarrass, only to inflict bodily injury, he is nevertheless liable for the embarrassment caused thereby *(Gem. ibid.).*

שׁוֹרוֹ שֶׁסִּמֵּא אֶת־עֵין עַבְדּוֹ וְהִפִּיל אֶת־שִׁנּוֹ, פָּטוּר; — *[If] his bull blinded his slave's*

בבא קמא ג/י

שֶׁסִּמֵּא אֶת־עֵין עַבְדּוֹ וְהִפִּיל אֶת־שִׁנּוֹ, חַיָּב. שׁוֹרוֹ שֶׁחָבַל בְּאָבִיו וּבְאִמּוֹ, חַיָּב; וְהוּא שֶׁחָבַל בְּאָבִיו וּבְאִמּוֹ, פָּטוּר. שׁוֹרוֹ שֶׁהִדְלִיק אֶת־הַגָּדִישׁ בַּשַּׁבָּת, חַיָּב; וְהוּא שֶׁהִדְלִיק אֶת־הַגָּדִישׁ בַּשַּׁבָּת, פָּטוּר, מִפְּנֵי שֶׁהוּא מִתְחַיֵּב בְּנַפְשׁוֹ.

יד אברהם

eye or knocked out his tooth, he is exempt;

That is, if one's animal blinded the eye or knocked out the tooth of his gentile slave, he is exempt from freeing the slave (Rav).

As explained below, Scripture requires the master to free his slave if he himself injures him, but not if his chattels do so (Nimmukei Yosef).

Even if the master incited the animal against his slave, he is exempt from freeing him (Tif. Yis.).

וְהוּא שֶׁסִּמֵּא אֶת־עֵין עַבְדּוֹ וְהִפִּיל אֶת־שִׁנּוֹ, חַיָּב. — but if he blinded his slave's eye or knocked out his tooth, he is liable.

I.e., he is obligated to free him (Tif. Yis.) as the Torah states [Ex. 21:26f.]: Should a man strike the eye of his male slave or the eye of his female slave and destroy it, he shall set him free in compensation for his eye. Or, if he knocks out the tooth of his male slave or the tooth of his female slave, he shall set him free in compensation for his tooth (Rav).

Vilna Gaon (Chiddushei Uveurei Rabbeinu HaGra) renders the mishnah: ... if he blinded ... and knocked out his tooth ..., meaning that if the master of the slave blinds him and then knocks out his tooth, he must free him due to the first injury and compensate him for the second one. The term liable applies only to monetary compensation, not to the obligation to free the slave. [Accordingly, the case dealing with the bull likewise refers to compensation for the second injury. The point is that since the slave is not freed in lieu of the first injury, the owner is also not liable for compensation for the second one.]

שׁוֹרוֹ שֶׁחָבַל בְּאָבִיו וּבְאִמּוֹ, — [If] his bull wounded his father or his mother,

That is, the father or mother of its owner (Tos. Yom Tov from Nimmukei Yosef).

Nimmukei Yosef states this lest we err and think that the intention is that the bull wounded his own father or mother. Compare our edition of Nimmukei Yosef (Lechem Shamayim).

חַיָּב; — he is liable;

The son is liable to pay for the damage inflicted upon his parents (Rav).

וְהוּא שֶׁחָבַל בְּאָבִיו וּבְאִמּוֹ, פָּטוּר. — but [if] he wounded his father or his mother, he is exempt.

Wounding one's parent is a capital offense, as the Torah states (Ex. 21:15): וּמַכֵּה אָבִיו וְאִמּוֹ מוֹת יוּמָת, One who strikes his father or his mother shall be put to death. Therefore, a person who does so is exempt from paying them for the damages, since one is not liable for monetary compensation for an act he committed simultaneously with a capital offense (Rav). [This follows the rule of קִים לֵיהּ בְּדְרַבָּה מִינֵיהּ, he suffers the more severe punishment — i.e., if one concurrently becomes liable for two punishments, he receives only the harsher one (see commentary to 6:5).]

In the case of one's bull wounding his parents, however, it is not considered a capital offense, because he himself did not do it, and it is as if a stranger had done it. Hence, he is liable to pay for the damage (Nimmukei Yosef).

שׁוֹרוֹ שֶׁהִדְלִיק אֶת־הַגָּדִישׁ בַּשַּׁבָּת, חַיָּב; — [If] his bull ignited a stack of grain on the Sabbath, he is liable;

If one's animal ignites a stack of

משניות / בבא קמא — פרק ג: המניח [66]

3 10 he is exempt; but if he blinded his slave's eye or knocked out his tooth, he is liable.

[If] his bull wounded his father or his mother, he is liable; but [if] he wounded his father or his mother, he is exempt. [If] his bull ignited a stack of grain on the Sabbath, he is liable; but [if] he ignited a stack of grain on the Sabbath, he is exempt, because he is liable for his life.

YAD AVRAHAM

grain, there is no difference whether it does so on the Sabbath or on a weekday; he is liable in any case. The mishnah's purpose in stating this case is to point out that the owner is exempt from paying for the grain in the same case that the animal is liable — namely, if he ignited it inadvertently, since — obviously — the animal is not aware of the Sabbath and its laws. Although the person in this case desecrates the Sabbath inadvertently — for which there is no death penalty — he is nevertheless exempt from monetary compensation [as explained below] (*Tos. Yom Tov* from *Gem.* 35a, *Nimmukei Yosef*).

Since it is unusual for a bull to ignite a stack of grain, this is a *toladah* of *keren* (see General Introduction, s.v. *Avos and Tolados*), and the owner is liable only for half the damages (*Rav; Rashi*).

In 2:3 the Mishnah discusses a similar case: If a dog took a cake to which coals had become attached and cast it onto a stack of grain, thereby igniting and destroying it, the dog's owner must pay half the value of the stack of grain. There, *Rav* and *Rashi* explain that this is because the damage is in the category of *tzeroros* (pebbles), since it was caused by the dog's power, not directly by his body.

The difference whether one pays half the damages because of *tzeroros*, as in that case, or because it is an unusual act, as in our case, is that in the former instance the animal's owner must pay from the best of his property, whereas in the latter case, the damagee becomes a partner in the animal that did the damage (see preface to 4:1).

The reason why *Rav* and *Rashi* do not explain the case in 2:3 to be an unusual damage is because, as explained there, it is usual for coals to adhere to the cake; therefore it is perfectly normal for the dog to carry the cake with the coals and place it onto the stack. Indeed, if the dog placed the cake on the stack rather than throwing it upon it, the dog's owner must pay for the full damage done to the spot where the cake was put down. It is only because the cake was cast onto the stack, rather than placed — a damage of *tzeroros* — that he pays half the damages (*Tos. Yom Tov*).

וְהוּא שֶׁהִדְלִיק אֶת־הַגָּדִישׁ בַּשַּׁבָּת, פָּטוּר — *but [if] he ignited a stack of grain on the Sabbath, he is exempt,*

[He is exempt from paying for the stack.]

מִפְּנֵי שֶׁהוּא מִתְחַיֵּיב בְּנַפְשׁוֹ — *because he is liable for his life.*

This follows the rule of ... קִים לֵיהּ, *he suffers the more severe punishment,* as discussed above. In our case, had the violator deliberately desecrated the Sabbath, he would be liable to the death penalty, and hence, exempt from paying the damages. The rule goes even further. Even if he commits the capital sin inadvertently — for which no death penalty is due him — he is nevertheless exempt from monetary payments (*Tos. Yom Tov* from *Nimmukei Yosef*). As mentioned above, the mishnah makes a contrast between the man and the bull to teach us that just as the bull commits the act with no knowledge of the Sabbath, so does the man in this case. Nevertheless, he is exempt from paying for the damages to the stack (*Tos.* 35a).

בבא קמא ג/יא

[יא] שׁוֹר שֶׁהָיָה רוֹדֵף אַחַר שׁוֹר אַחֵר וְהֻזַּק — זֶה אוֹמֵר: "שׁוֹרְךָ הִזִּיק," וְזֶה אוֹמֵר: "לֹא כִי, אֶלָּא בְּסֶלַע לָקָה," הַמּוֹצִיא מֵחֲבֵרוֹ עָלָיו הָרְאָיָה.

הָיוּ שְׁנַיִם רוֹדְפִים אַחַר אֶחָד — זֶה אוֹמֵר: "שׁוֹרְךָ הִזִּיק," וְזֶה אוֹמֵר: "שׁוֹרְךָ הִזִּיק," שְׁנֵיהֶם פְּטוּרִין. אִם הָיוּ שְׁנֵיהֶן שֶׁל־אִישׁ אֶחָד, שְׁנֵיהֶן

יד אברהם

11.

This mishnah is based on the principle of הַמּוֹצִיא מֵחֲבֵרוֹ עָלָיו הָרְאָיָה, *the [burden of] proof lies on the one who seeks to exact [something] from the other.* Whenever there is a doubt if the latter is liable, the item remains in his possession until witnesses or conclusive evidence of his liability is brought. See General Introduction.

שׁוֹר שֶׁהָיָה רוֹדֵף אַחַר שׁוֹר אַחֵר — [If] one bull was chasing another bull,

[For example, Reuven's bull was chasing Shimon's bull.]

וְהֻזַּק; — and it was injured;

The one which was chased [Shimon's bull] was injured (*Rashi*).

זֶה אוֹמֵר: "שׁוֹרְךָ הִזִּיק," — [and] this one says: 'Your bull injured [it],'

[Shimon claims to Reuven that the latter's bull injured his bull, and that Reuven is therefore liable for the damages.]

וְזֶה אוֹמֵר: "לֹא כִי, אֶלָּא בְּסֶלַע לָקָה," — and that one says: 'Not so; it hurt itself on a rock,'

Reuven replies that Shimon's bull scraped itself against a rock and was injured (*Rav; Rashi*).

הַמּוֹצִיא מֵחֲבֵרוֹ עָלָיו הָרְאָיָה. — the [burden of] proof lies on the one who seeks to exact [something] from the other.

[Therefore, if Shimon does not bring proof that it was Reuven's bull that injured his, Reuven is entirely exempt.] The *Gemara* adds that even if Shimon claims that Reuven's bull definitely gored his bull, and Reuven retorts that perhaps it hurt itself on a rock, he is nevertheless exempt. This is because, even in such a case, we apply the above rule, and Shimon must bring proof to support his claim. We also learn from this mishnah that although there is circumstantial evidence that the bull caused the injury, Shimon must nevertheless bring witnesses to prove it. Furthermore, although Reuven admits that it was his bull's pursuit that drove Shimon's bull against the rock where it was injured, he is nevertheless exempt. This is classified as גְּרָמָא בִּנְזָקִין, *an indirect cause of damages*, for which one is not liable (*Tos. Yom Tov* from *Nimmukei Yosef*, quoting *Ramah*).

Should Shimon claim that Reuven is aware that the latter's bull gored his bull, Reuven must swear a שְׁבוּעַת הֶיסֵת, *a Rabbinical oath*, that he is unaware that his bull did it. This is true only in the case of a *muad*. In the case of a *tam*, however, no such oath is required, since even if he admits that his bull had gored Shimon's bull, he is exempt. This is because the half-damage payment of the *tam* is a fine, and one who admits to a fine is exempt from paying it (*Tif. Yis.* from *Choshen Mishpat* 400:1).

הָיוּ שְׁנַיִם רוֹדְפִים אַחַר אֶחָד — [If] two were chasing one —

משניות / בבא קמא — פרק ג: המניח [68]

11. [If] one bull was chasing another bull, and it was injured; [and] this one says: 'Your bull injured [it],' and that one says: 'Not so; it hurt itself on a rock,' the [burden of] proof lies on the one who seeks to exact [something] from the other.

[If] two were chasing one — this one says: 'Your bull injured [it],' and that one says: 'Your bull injured [it],' both are exempt. If both belonged to one man, both

YAD AVRAHAM

Two bulls belonging to two people [e.g., Reuven and Levi] were chasing Shimon's bull *(Rav; Rashi)*.

זֶה אוֹמֵר: "שׁוֹרְךָ הִזִּיק„ — *this one says: 'Your bull injured [it],'*

[Reuven claims to Levi that the latter's bull injured Shimon's.]

וְזֶה אוֹמֵר: "שׁוֹרְךָ הִזִּיק„ — *and that one says: 'Your bull injured [it],'*

[Levi claims that Reuven's bull is the one that injured Shimon's.]

שְׁנֵיהֶם פְּטוּרִין. — *both are exempt.*

Both are exempt, since each one can send Shimon to the other *(Rav; Rashi)*.

This is true even if there are witnesses that one of their bulls injured Shimon's bull *(Tif. Yis.; Nimmukei Yosef)*.

Nimmukei Yosef adds that even if Shimon claims with certainty that Reuven's bull injured his, and Reuven replies that perhaps it was Levi's bull, they are both exempt, because of the principle of ... הַמּוֹצִיא, *the burden of proof* ....

אִם הָיוּ שְׁנֵיהֶן שֶׁל־אִישׁ אֶחָד, — *If both belonged to one man,*

[Both bulls pursuing Shimon's bull belonged to Reuven.]

שְׁנֵיהֶן חַיָּבִים. — *both are liable.*

From the wording of the mishnah,[1] the *Gemara* (36a) deduces that Reuven's two bulls in this case were *tamin*, and therefore Shimon collects half the damages from both of them *(Rav)*. This means that he collects by becoming a partner in the less valuable bull *(Tif. Yis.* from *Rambam, Hil. Nizkei Mamon* 9:7), because the above principle also dictates that in such cases involving a question of which one of two amounts someone must pay, he pays the lesser amount unless it is proven that he owes more *(Maggid Mishneh ad loc.)*.

This rule applies only if there are witnesses that one of Reuven's two bulls inflicted the damage. Should there be no witnesses, even if Reuven admits that his bull did it, he is exempt. Since the bull is a *tam*, and the half-damage payment for damages caused by a *tam* is a fine, he cannot become liable by dint of his own admission, as explained above *(Tos. Yom Tov)*.

If one of Reuven's bulls is lost following the incident involving the damage, Reuven can claim that perhaps the lost bull is the one who did the damage, and — since it was a *tam*, in which the latter becomes a partner as his payment — he need not pay Shimon, unless the latter proves that it was the other bull that injured his *(Rav; Rosh; Rambam* loc. cit. §8). R' *Yehudah Barceloni*, however, quotes one of the

---

1. Had Reuven's two bulls been *muadin*, the statement *both are liable* — referring to the animals themselves, and implying that the damage is paid by becoming a partner in the animals that did the damage — would not be appropriate *(Gem.* 36a). In such a case, even if both bulls are subsequently lost, their owner must pay the full damages from the best of his property *(Tif. Yis.)*.

בבא קמא ג/יא

חַיָּבִים. הָיָה אֶחָד גָּדוֹל וְאֶחָד קָטָן, הַנִּזָּק אוֹמֵר: "הַגָּדוֹל הִזִּיק," וְהַמַּזִּיק אוֹמֵר: "לֹא כִי, אֶלָּא הַקָּטָן הִזִּיק"; אֶחָד תָּם וְאֶחָד מוּעָד, הַנִּזָּק אוֹמֵר: "הַמּוּעָד הִזִּיק," וְהַמַּזִּיק אוֹמֵר: "לֹא כִי, אֶלָּא הַתָּם הִזִּיק," הַמּוֹצִיא מֵחֲבֵרוֹ עָלָיו הָרְאָיָה. הָיוּ הַנִּזּוֹקִין שְׁנַיִם — אֶחָד גָּדוֹל וְאֶחָד קָטָן — וְהַמַּזִּיקִים שְׁנַיִם — אֶחָד גָּדוֹל וְאֶחָד קָטָן — הַנִּזָּק אוֹמֵר: "הַגָּדוֹל הִזִּיק אֶת־הַגָּדוֹל, וְהַקָּטָן אֶת־

יד אברהם

Geonim, who maintains that Shimon collects one-fourth of the damages by becoming a partner for that amount in the remaining bull.

הָיָה אֶחָד גָּדוֹל — [If] one was large
That is, in the case of the two pursuing bulls belonging to one man (Tos. Yom Tov from Nimmukei Yosef), if one of the two was sufficiently large so that its value equals the entire half-damage payment (Tif. Yis.).

וְאֶחָד קָטָן, — and one small,
I.e., its value is less than the half-damage payment (Tif. Yis.).

הַנִּזָּק אוֹמֵר: "הַגָּדוֹל הִזִּיק," — [and] the damagee says: 'The large one injured [it],'
'And it is valuable enough to be able to pay for the entire half-damage payment' (Rav; Rashi).

וְהַמַּזִּיק אוֹמֵר: "לֹא כִי, אֶלָּא הַקָּטָן הִזִּיק"; — and the damager says: 'Not so; the small one injured [it]';
'And therefore, you should receive only the value of the small bull, and lose the remainder of the half-damage payment' (Rav; Rashi).

אֶחָד תָּם וְאֶחָד מוּעָד, — [or if] one was a tam and one a muad,
[One of Reuven's bulls that had pursued Shimon's was a tam, and one was a muad.]

הַנִּזָּק אוֹמֵר: "הַמּוּעָד הִזִּיק," — [and] the damagee says: 'The muad injured [it],'
[Accordingly, its owner must pay full damages from the best of his property.]

וְהַמַּזִּיק אוֹמֵר: "לֹא כִי אֶלָּא הַתָּם הִזִּיק" — and the damager says: 'Not so; the tam injured [it]' —
[Accordingly, he is liable for only half the damages] and the damagee collects only by becoming a partner in the damaging bull, and not from his other property (Meiri).

הַמּוֹצִיא מֵחֲבֵרוֹ עָלָיו הָרְאָיָה. — the [burden of] proof lies on the one who seeks to exact [something] from the other.
Although it is more likely that the muad gored the damaged bull, since it is more accustomed to goring, the damagee cannot collect full damages unless he produces witnesses who testify that it was indeed the muad who had gored (Tos. Yom Tov from Tos.).
Should the damagee fail to bring witnesses, he collects nothing, not even the half-damage payment the damager admits to owing, or the half-damage payment of the small bull in the previous case. This is analogous to the classic case of one who claims that another owes him wheat and the other person admits to owing barley (Bava Metzia 5a), in which case the latter is exempt from paying even the barley that he admits to. [This is because by claiming only wheat, the claiment relinquishes, his claim to barley (Rashi,

משניות / בבא קמא — פרק ג: המניח [70]

3 11 are liable. [If] one was large and one small, [and] the damagee says: 'The large one injured [it],' and the damager says: 'Not so; the small one injured [it]'; [or if] one was a *tam* and one a *muad*, [and] the damagee says: 'The *muad* injured [it],' and the damager says: 'Not so; the *tam* injured [it],' the [burden of] proof lies on the one who seeks to exact [something] from the other.

[If] the injured ones were two — one large and one small — and the damagers were two — one large and one small — [and] the damagee says: 'The large one injured the large one, and the small one [injured] the

YAD AVRAHAM

Tos. 35b; see *Rosh*).] If the claimant seizes the smaller amount, however, we do not take it back from him *(Rav* from *Gem.* 35b).

This follows *Tos. Yom Tov's* explanation of *Rav*. According to *Tosafos* and *Rosh*, however, the damagee's seizure avails only in the mishnah's next case, in which there is a claim on both bulls. In this case, however, since the damagee admits that he has no claim on the small bull, he cannot seize it.

In the case of one being a *tam* or both of them being of that category, their owner is exempt even if he admits his obligation, since the half-damage payment for damage caused by a *tam* is a fine, and one who admits to it is exempt from paying it, as explained above *(Tos. Yom Tov)*.

In cases of a fine, should the one to whom it is due seize the money, he must return it, since the obligation is not in force until the verdict is handed down by the court. Many authorities hold, however, that the half-damage payment for the *tam's* damages is an exception. Therefore, if the damagee seizes the amount admitted by the damager, we do not take it back from him *(Tos. Yom Tov* from *Maggid Mishneh, Hil. Nizkei Mamon* 9:11).

Tos. Yom Tov qualifies this statement as applying only if the one to whom the fine is due seizes the money in the presence of witnesses. Otherwise, even if he seizes as much as he claims, we do not take it from him since he can deny that he has seized it.[1]

הָיוּ הַנִּזּוֹקִין שְׁנַיִם — אֶחָד גָּדוֹל וְאֶחָד קָטָן — וְהַמַּזִּיקִים שְׁנַיִם — אֶחָד גָּדוֹל וְאֶחָד קָטָן — [*If*] *the injured ones were two — one large and one small — and the damagers were two — one large and one small —*

[For example, if two bulls — one large and one small — belonging to Reuven gored two bulls — one large and one small — belonging to Shimon, and it is not known which bull gored the large one and which gored the small one.]

הַנִּזָּק אוֹמֵר: ,,הַגָּדוֹל הִזִּיק אֶת־הַגָּדוֹל, וְהַקָּטָן אֶת־הַקָּטָן״ — [*and*] *the damagee says: 'The large one injured the large one, and the small one [injured] the small one.'*

[Accordingly, each one suffices for its

---

1. [This reasoning is known as a מִיגּוֹ, *miggo* (lit., *because*): Because a deponent — had he wished to lie — could have invented a statement more advantageous to him, the fact that he instead says the less advantageous statement indicates that he is telling the truth. In our case, had the one to whom the fine is due been lying, he could have denied his seizure. Since he admits it, we believe that it is indeed due him.]

בבא קמא ד/א

הַקָּטָן," וְהַמַּזִּיק אוֹמֵר: "לֹא כִי; אֶלָּא הַקָּטָן אֶת־הַגָּדוֹל, וְהַגָּדוֹל אֶת־הַקָּטָן"; אֶחָד תָּם וְאֶחָד מוּעָד, הַנִּזָּק אוֹמֵר: "הַמּוּעָד הִזִּיק אֶת־הַגָּדוֹל, וְהַתָּם אֶת־הַקָּטָן," וְהַמַּזִּיק אוֹמֵר: "לֹא כִי; אֶלָּא הַתָּם אֶת־הַגָּדוֹל, וְהַמּוּעָד אֶת־הַקָּטָן" — הַמּוֹצִיא מֵחֲבֵרוֹ עָלָיו הָרְאָיָה.

[א] **שׁוֹר** שֶׁנָּגַח אַרְבָּעָה וַחֲמִשָּׁה שְׁוָורִים — זֶה אַחַר זֶה — יְשַׁלֵּם לָאַחֲרוֹן שֶׁבָּהֶם.

יד אברהם

owner to pay half the damages it caused.]

וְהַמַּזִּיק אוֹמֵר: "לֹא כִי; אֶלָּא הַקָּטָן אֶת־הַגָּדוֹל, וְהַגָּדוֹל אֶת־הַקָּטָן" — *and the damager says: 'Not so; the small one [injured] the large one, and the large one the small one';*

[Therefore, the small one does not suffice to pay for the damage inflicted upon the large one, and the damagee has no other recourse to get the money for it.]

אֶחָד תָּם וְאֶחָד מוּעָד, — *[or if] one was a tam and one was a muad,*

[One of the two bulls that gored was a *tam*, and the other was a *muad*.]

הַנִּזָּק אוֹמֵר: "הַמּוּעָד הִזִּיק אֶת־הַגָּדוֹל, וְהַתָּם אֶת־הַקָּטָן," — *[and] the damagee says: 'The muad injured the large one, and the tam the small one,'*

[Accordingly, the damager must pay for the full damage of the large bull, which exceeds the full damage of the small one.]

וְהַמַּזִּיק אוֹמֵר: "לֹא כִי; אֶלָּא הַתָּם אֶת־הַגָּדוֹל, וְהַמּוּעָד אֶת־הַקָּטָן" — *and the damager says: "Not so; the tam [injured] the large one, and the muad the small one' —*

[Accordingly, he must pay the full damages for the small one and only half the damages for the large one.]

הַמּוֹצִיא מֵחֲבֵרוֹ עָלָיו הָרְאָיָה. — *the [burden of] proof lies on the one who seeks to exact [something] from the other.*

As in the previous cases, if the damagee brings no evidence, he collects nothing, not even what the damager admits, since it is analogous to one claiming wheat and the other admitting barley, in which case the latter is exempt from paying even the value of the barley. If the damagee seizes what the damager admits, however, we do not take it back from him *(Rav)*.

Chapter 4

1.

The following mishnah deals with an animal that is a *tam* and gores numerous animals while still being a *tam*. The variant views in this mishnah are based upon the dispute between R' Akiva and R' Yishmael concerning the half-damage payment. Regarding the *tam*, Scripture (21:35) states: וּמָכְרוּ אֶת־הַשּׁוֹר הַחַי וְחָצוּ אֶת־כַּסְפּוֹ, *they shall sell the live bull and divide the money of it.* R' Akiva interprets this as meaning that the damagee becomes a partner in the animal that gored for half

משניות / בבא קמא — פרק ד: שור שנגח ארבעה וחמשה   [72]

4 1 small one,' and the damager says: 'Not so; the small one [injured] the large one, and the large one the small one'; [or if] one was a *tam* and one was a *muad*, [and] the damagee says: 'The *muad* injured the large one, and the *tam* the small one,' and the damager says: 'Not so; the *tam* [injured] the large one, and the *muad* the small one' — the [burden of] proof lies on the one who seeks to exact [something] from the other.

1. [If] a bull gores four or five bulls — one after the other — [its owner] shall pay the last of them.

YAD AVRAHAM

the damages done to his bull. If half the damages equals or exceeds the entire value of the damaging animal, the damagee assumes ownership of the animal. Even in the latter case, however, he cannot recover the balance of the damages. R' Yishmael contends that the bull that gored is appraised and, then, its owner pays the damagee with money. According to his opinion, the Torah's intention is that the damagee is a creditor, and the animal is pledged to pay the debt. He does not gain possession of it, nor can he collect more than its value (*Gem.* 33a). [Both opinions agree that if the damaging animal is lost, the damagee can no longer collect the damage.]

שׁוֹר — [If] *a bull*
That is, a *tam* (Rambam Commentary).

שֶׁנָּגַח אַרְבָּעָה וַחֲמִשָּׁה שְׁוָרִים — זֶה אַחַר זֶה — — *gores four or five bulls — one after the other —*
It gored four or five animals, yet remained a *tam* throughout all these gorings, as explained below. Therefore, the restitution for these damages is taken from the sale of the goring bull (Rav; Rashi).

[Although the *Tanna* — who wishes to demonstrate that the animal in this case remains a *tam* even after it has gored three times — could have chosen any number higher than three, he uses the standard example of *four or five* that is found throughout the mishnah.] *Tos. Yom Tov* (*Shabbos* 18:1, quoted in ArtScroll commentary ad loc.) conjectures that this choice of numbers stems from תַּשְׁלוּמֵי אַרְבָּעָה וַחֲמִשָּׁה, *the fourfold and fivefold payments* (see 7:1), which are specified by the Torah (*Ex.* 21:37).

The commentators give several examples of such cases in which the animal would still be deemed a *tam*. One is the case in which the owner is not warned by the court after each goring (Ravad; Meiri; Tos. Yom Tov).

Another example is the animal that gores three times in one day, which — according to R' Yehudah [2:4] — does not become a *muad* (Meiri).

A third case is that of the animal that gores at irregular intervals. For example, it saw an animal and gored it, then saw another animal and gored it, then saw two animals and gored neither of them, and then saw another one and gored it. An animal becomes a *muad* only by consecutively goring three animals that it sees, or by goring alternately with the same interval between one goring and the other. In this case, however, since it gored at irregular intervals, it does not become a *muad* (Rashi).

[For simplification, let us say that Reuven's bull gored bulls belonging to Shimon, Levi, Yehudah, Yissachar, and Zevulun in that order.]

יְשַׁלֵּם לָאַחֲרוֹן שֶׁבָּהֶם. — [its owner] *shall pay the last of them.*
He pays half the damages to the owner of the bull that was gored last (Rav; Rashi).

בבא קמא ד/א

וְאִם יֵשׁ בּוֹ מוֹתָר, יַחֲזִיר לְשֶׁלְּפָנָיו; וְאִם יֵשׁ בּוֹ מוֹתָר, יַחֲזִיר לְשֶׁלִּפְנֵי פָנָיו. וְהָאַחֲרוֹן נִשְׂכָּר — דִּבְרֵי רַבִּי מֵאִיר.

יד אברהם

The *Gemara* (36b) qualifies the mishnah as referring to a case in which Shimon seized Reuven's bull to collect the damages due him, and attributes this view to R' Yishmael, who rules that the damagee is merely a creditor having a lien on the bull. Therefore, by seizing the bull, Shimon becomes a שׁוֹמֵר שָׂכָר, *paid guardian* (see mishnah 9), who is responsible to watch the bull and prevent it from doing any further damage (*Rav, Rashi, Tos. Yom Tov*). He is considered 'paid' because, by having seized the bull, he benefits in that its owner cannot hide it, making it impossible for him to collect the damages due him (*Rashi*). Following Shimon's seizure of the bull, it gored Levi's bull. Levi then seized it from Shimon to collect *his* debt, and, in turn, became responsible for its subsequent damages (*Rav; Rashi*). [The same was done by Yehudah and Yissachar, and then, the bull gored Zevulun's bull.]

In this instance, the damages done to all the animals were equal to each other — e.g., two hundred *zuz*. When Reuven's bull gores Shimon's, Shimon is now owed a hundred *zuz*, and has a lien on the bull for that amount. However, when — after Shimon's seizure of the bull — it does the same amount of damage to Levi's bull, since Shimon is liable for the damages it causes, he forfeits the lien to Levi. The same subsequently occurs with Yehudah, Yissachar, and Zevulun. Consequently, Zevulun — *the last of them* — is the only one who receives half the damages done to his animal (*Tos.; Talmid Rabbeinu Peretz*, quoted by *Shitah Mekubetzes*).

וְאִם יֵשׁ בּוֹ מוֹתָר, יַחֲזִיר לְשֶׁלְּפָנָיו — *If there is an excess in it, he shall return [it] to the one before him;*

That is, if the half-damage payment due the penultimate damagee [Yissachar] exceeds the half-damage payment due the last damagee [Zevulun], the difference between those two amounts is given to the penultimate damagee (*Rav* from *Gem.* 36b).

In this instance, all the damages were equal [e.g., two hundred] except for the last one, which was less [e.g., fifty] (*Talmid Rabbeinu Peretz* loc. cit.). [Thus, in our example, the difference between the half-damage payment due Yissachar (one-hundred) and that due Zevulun (twenty-five) is seventy-five, which would be given to Yissachar.]

וְאִם יֵשׁ בּוֹ מוֹתָר, יַחֲזִיר לְשֶׁלִּפְנֵי פָנָיו — *if there is an excess in it, he shall return [it] to the one before that one.*

[If there is an excess in the half-damage payment due Yehudah, the third from the last damagee, over the half-damage payment due Yissachar, it is given to Yehudah.]

In this case, the first three damages were equal [e.g., two hundred], and the last two were progressively less [e.g., to Yissachar's: one hundred; to Zevulun's fifty] (ibid.). [Thus, in our example, the difference between the half-damage payment due Yissachar (fifty) and that due Zevulun (twenty-five) is twenty-five, which is given to Yissachar. The difference between the half-damage payment due Yehudah (one hundred) and that due Yissachar (fifty) is fifty, which is awarded to Yehudah.

Note that throughout this entire sequence of events, the original owner (Reuven) retains his ownership of the goring bull and is liable for only half the

4 1 If there is an excess in it, he shall return [it] to the one before him; if there is an excess in it, he shall return [it] to the one before that one. The later the injury, the more the advantage — [these are] the words of R' Meir.

YAD AVRAHAM

damage done to Shimon's bull, even if this amount is divided among others, as described above. This is because once Shimon seized the bull, Reuven is no longer responsible for the damages it causes.

Note also that the half-damage payment awarded to any of the damagees cannot exceed the amount of the lien on the bull held by the person who is now responsible for it. Although he is considered a paid guardian, who is liable for the damages caused by the animal, his liability cannot be greater than that of an owner, who never needs to pay more than the value of the animal. Similarly, the liability of the person in this case is limited to the amount of the lien he has on the bull.]

וְהָאַחֲרוֹן אַחֲרוֹן נִשְׂכָּר — *The later the injury, the more the advantage* —

In each of the instances above, the last one of those who have suffered equal damages is the only one to receive payment (ibid.). [As explained above, this is because each of the others forfeits his lien on the bull to the owner of the one it gores while in the former's custody. In the first example given, in which all the bulls were damaged to the extent of two hundred *zuz*, only Zevulun, the last one, receives payment. In the second example, in which the bulls of Shimon, Levi, Yehudah and Yissachar were damaged equally, only Yissachar is awarded half the damages. The same is true of the final example, in which only the last of the equal damagees, Yehudah, is paid.]

דִּבְרֵי רַבִּי מֵאִיר — [*these are*] *the words of R' Meir.*

As stated above, R' Meir follows R' Yishmael's view that the owner of the damaged bull [Shimon] becomes a creditor of the owner of the bull that gored [Reuven], and the latter bull is pledged to pay the debt. Therefore, if Shimon seizes Reuven's bull, he becomes responsible for its damagees. According to R' Akiva, however, both Reuven and Shimon become partners in the goring bull; hence, both are responsible for its subsequent damages. Even if Shimon seizes it, it is an article jointly owned by two partners which is sometimes watched by one owner and sometimes by the other. Therefore, the responsibility lies on both *(Tos. Yom Tov* from *Tos.,* as explained by *Rosh; Rabbeinu Ephraim* quoted by *Nimmukei Yosef).*

Rashi, however, holds that the reason R' Meir could not possibly be following the view of R' Akiva is that according to the latter, it would be obvious that the last damagee has the advantage, even if the earlier ones did not seize the bull to collect their debts. [This is because, while each of the earlier damagees is a partner in the bull and thus is responsible for the damages it caused, the bull had not gored since the last damagee became a partner on it.].

According to *Rashi,* R' Akiva maintains that if a damagee seizes the goring bull, although he jointly owns it with others, only he is responsible for its subsequent damages. *Rif, Rambam* [*Commentary* and *Hil. Nizkei Mamon* 9:13], and *Ramban* concur with this view (*Nimmukei Yosef;* see *Hamaor Hagadol*).

בבא קמא ד/ב

רַבִּי שִׁמְעוֹן אוֹמֵר: שׁוֹר שָׁוֶה מָאתַיִם שֶׁנָּגַח שׁוֹר שָׁוֶה מָאתַיִם, וְאֵין הַנְּבֵלָה יָפָה כְלוּם, זֶה נוֹטֵל מָנֶה, וְזֶה נוֹטֵל מָנֶה. חָזַר וְנָגַח שׁוֹר אַחֵר שָׁוֶה מָאתַיִם, הָאַחֲרוֹן נוֹטֵל מָנֶה; וְשֶׁלְּפָנָיו, זֶה נוֹטֵל חֲמִשִּׁים זוּז, וְזֶה נוֹטֵל חֲמִשִּׁים זוּז. חָזַר וְנָגַח שׁוֹר אַחֵר שָׁוֶה מָאתַיִם, הָאַחֲרוֹן נוֹטֵל מָנֶה; וְשֶׁלְּפָנָיו, חֲמִשִּׁים זוּז; וּשְׁנַיִם הָרִאשׁוֹנִים, דִּינַר זָהָב.

[ב] **שׁוֹר** שֶׁהוּא מוּעָד לְמִינוֹ, וְאֵינוֹ מוּעָד

יד אברהם

רַבִּי שִׁמְעוֹן אוֹמֵר: שׁוֹר שָׁוֶה מָאתַיִם שֶׁנָּגַח שׁוֹר שָׁוֶה מָאתַיִם, וְאֵין הַנְּבֵלָה יָפָה כְלוּם — R' Shimon says: [If] a bull worth two hundred gores a bull worth two hundred, and the carcass is worth nothing,

[As in the case above, the mishnah is dealing with a *tam*.]

R' Shimon follows R' Akiva's view that the damagee becomes a partner with the damager in the bull, and both are equally liable for its subsequent damages (*Rav*).

According to R' Akiva, if the bull depreciates or gains value following the goring, both the damagee and the damager share that loss or gain, since the animal belongs to both of them. For this same reason, the liability of each one of them is limited to their share — i.e., they are responsible for half of its damages.

According to R' Yishmael, however, since the damagee has no definite portion of the bull, but only has a lien on it, if he seizes the bull to collect his debt, he is responsible for the entire damage it causes. This is analogous to the case of Reuven, who owes Shimon a hundred *zuz*, and Shimon seizes an article worth two hundred from which to exact payment. Obviously, Shimon is responsible for the entire article. According to R' Akiva, on the other hand, our case is analogous to a jointly owned article, which is sometimes watched by one partner and sometimes by the other partner. Consequently, the damagee's seizure of the bull does not alter his status of responsibility; rather, both he and the damager continue to be equally responsible for the damages it causes (*Tos. Yom Tov* from *Rosh*).

The halachah is in accordance with R' Shimon, who follows R' Akiva's view (*Tos. Yom Tov*).

זֶה נוֹטֵל מָנֶה, וְזֶה נוֹטֵל מָנֶה — this one takes a maneh, and that one takes a maneh.

[The damagee (Shimon) is awarded a hundred-*zuz* share in the bull and the original owner (Reuven) retains a hundred-*zuz* share, making them partners in the animal.]

חָזַר וְנָגַח שׁוֹר אַחֵר שָׁוֶה מָאתַיִם — [If] it goes and gores another bull worth two hundred,

[For example, a bull originally belonging to Reuven first gored Shimon's bull and now gores Levi's bull which is worth two hundred *zuz*.]

הָאַחֲרוֹן נוֹטֵל מָנֶה; — the last one takes a hundred;

[Levi, whose bull was gored last, receives a hundred-*zuz* share in the goring bull.]

וְשֶׁלְּפָנָיו, — [as for] those preceding him,

That is, Reuven, the original owner, and Shimon, the first damagee (*Rav*).

משניות / בבא קמא — פרק ד: שור שנגח ארבעה וחמשה [76]

R' Shimon says: [If] a bull worth two hundred gores a bull worth two hundred, and the carcass is worth nothing, this one takes a *maneh*, and this one takes a *maneh*. [If] it goes and gores another bull worth two hundred, the last one takes a hundred; [as for] those preceding him, this one takes fifty *zuz*, and this one takes fifty *zuz*. [If] it goes and gores another bull worth two hundred, the last one takes a *maneh*; the one before him, fifty *zuz*; and the first two, a golden dinar [each].

2. [If] a bull is a *muad* toward its kind, but not a

YAD AVRAHAM

זֶה נוֹטֵל חֲמִשִׁים זוּז, וְזֶה נוֹטֵל חֲמִשִׁים זוּז. — *this one takes fifty zuz, and that one takes fifty zuz.*
Shimon — whose bull was the first one to be gored — and Reuven each retain a fifty-zuz share in the goring bull. Since Shimon owns half the bull, he is liable for half of the half-damage payment owed to Levi (*Rav*).

חָזַר וְנָגַח שׁוֹר אַחֵר שָׁוֶה מָאתַיִם, — [If] *it goes and gores another bull worth two hundred,*
[After goring the bulls of Shimon and Levi, it gores Yehudah's bull, which is worth two hundred zuz.]

הָאַחֲרוֹן נוֹטֵל מָנֶה; — *the last one takes a maneh;*
Yehudah, the last damagee, is awarded a hundred-zuz share in the animal, since each of the other owners is liable for the damages caused by the bull in proportion to his share (*Rav; Rashi*).

וְשֶׁלְּפָנָיו, — *the one before him,*

That is, the penultimate damagee [Levi] (*Tif. Yis.*).

חֲמִשִׁים זוּז; — *fifty zuz;*
Since half the bull belonged to him, he is obligated to pay for half the damages done to Yehudah's bull — i.e., fifty *zuz* from his hundred-zuz share in the goring bull; hence, he retains fifty zuz (*Rav; Rashi*).

וּשְׁנַיִם הָרִאשׁוֹנִים, — *and the first two,*
I.e., Reuven, the original owner; and Shimon, the first damagee (*Rav*).

דִּינַר זָהָב. — *a golden dinar* [each].
A golden dinar equals twenty-five silver dinars (*Rav*). [A silver dinar is equivalent to a *zuz*.]
Since each one owns one-fourth of the bull, he is liable for one-fourth of the total liability — i.e., twenty-five *zuz* from his fifty-zuz share in the bull, leaving him with a share of twenty-five zuz (*Rav*).

2.

This mishnah deals with an animal that has a tendency to gore certain species and not others, or to gore on certain days and not others.

שׁוֹר שֶׁהוּא מוּעָד לְמִינוֹ, — [If] *a bull is a muad toward its kind,*
[It became accustomed to goring other bulls.]

וְאֵינוֹ מוּעָד לְשֶׁאֵינוֹ מִינוֹ; — *but not a muad toward those not of its kind;*

בבא קמא ד/ב

לְשֶׁאֵינוֹ מִינוֹ; מוּעָד לְאָדָם, וְאֵינוֹ מוּעָד לִבְהֵמָה; מוּעָד לִקְטַנִּים, וְאֵינוֹ מוּעָד לִגְדוֹלִים — אֶת־שֶׁהוּא מוּעָד לוֹ, מְשַׁלֵּם נֶזֶק שָׁלֵם; וְאֶת־שֶׁאֵינוֹ מוּעָד לוֹ, מְשַׁלֵּם חֲצִי נֶזֶק.

אָמְרוּ לִפְנֵי רַבִּי יְהוּדָה: הֲרֵי שֶׁהָיָה מוּעָד לְשַׁבָּתוֹת, וְאֵינוֹ מוּעָד לְחֹל? אָמַר לָהֶם: לְשַׁבָּתוֹת

יד אברהם

For example, it has been seen standing among horses and camels, and not goring them (Meiri).

מוּעָד לְאָדָם — *a muad toward man*,
[It became accustomed to goring humans.]

וְאֵינוֹ מוּעָד לִבְהֵמָה — *but not a muad toward beasts;*
[It has been seen standing among animals and not goring them.]

מוּעָד לִקְטַנִּים — [or] *a muad toward small ones,*
It is accustomed to goring calves (Rav; Rashi; Meiri; Nimmukei Yosef).
Lest we think that the mishnah refers to *small cattle* — viz., sheep and goats — Rashi states that it means the small ones of its kind — viz., calves.
The same is true regarding humans: if a certain bull is a *muad* toward children, it is not necessarily a *muad* toward adults. This is so obvious that the mishnah did not find it necessary to state it (Tos. Yom Tov).
Lechem Shamayim points out that *Rashi* explains the mishnah in this manner, since small cattle and large cattle are two distinct species, and this case is included in the category stated above of *a muad toward its kind, but not a muad toward those not of its kind.*

וְאֵינוֹ מוּעָד לִגְדוֹלִים — *but not a muad toward large ones* —
It does not gore the large ones of that species. We do not say that since the bull has become accustomed to goring this species, it makes no distinction between the large ones and the small ones (Tos. Yom Tov from Gem. 37a).

אֶת־שֶׁהוּא מוּעָד לוֹ, מְשַׁלֵּם נֶזֶק שָׁלֵם; — [for] *those toward which it is a muad, [its owner] pays the full damages;*
[If it gores those species which it has become accustomed to goring, it owner pays the full damages in accordance with the law of a *muad*.]

וְאֶת־שֶׁאֵינוֹ מוּעָד לוֹ, — [for] *those toward which it is not a muad,*
[I.e., for those species that it does not habitually gore.]

מְשַׁלֵּם חֲצִי נֶזֶק. — *he pays half the damages.*
[In accordance with the law of a *tam*.]

We have explained the mishnah until this point according to R' Zevid in the *Gemara,* whose reading of the mishnah coincides with our editions — that the Tanna depicts various cases in which a bulls a *muad* for one species, which he has gored three times, and has abstained from goring another species although he has seen members of this species and come in contact with them. Should the bull not have come in contact with other species, however, it is adjudged a *muad* for other species as well, as long as we have no indication to the contrary.

R' Papa, however, reads: אֵינוֹ מוּעָד, *it is not a muad,* instead of our version — וְאֵינוֹ מוּעָד, *but not a muad* — meaning that, in each of these cases, if we have no indication whether the bull will gore other species, we assume that it is not a *muad,* toward the other species and its owner pays only half the damages if it gores one of the latter. Accordingly, the mishnah is to be translated as follows:

[If] *a bull is a muad toward its kind, it*

muad toward those not of its kind; a *muad* toward man, but not a *muad* toward beasts; [or] a *muad* toward small ones, but not a *muad* toward large ones — [for] those toward which it is a *muad*, [its owner] pays the full damages; [for] those toward which it is not a *muad*, he pays half the damages.

They said before R' Yehudah: [What] if it was a *muad* for Sabbaths, and not a *muad* for weekdays?

YAD AVRAHAM

is not a muad toward those not of its kind. [If it] is a muad against man, it is not a muad toward beasts. [If] it is a muad toward small ones, it is not a muad toward large ones. [Therefore] for those toward which it is a muad, he pays the full damages; [for] those toward which it is not a muad, he pays half the damages.

Although R' Papa's version presents a number of difficulties, *Rambam* (Commentary and *Hil. Nizkei Mamon* 6:8), *Rif* and *Nimmukei Yosef* rule in accordance with it.

אָמְרוּ לִפְנֵי רַבִּי יְהוּדָה: — *They said before R' Yehudah:*

I.e., R' Yehudah's disciples asked him (Rav).

הֲרֵי שֶׁהָיָה מוּעָד לְשַׁבָּתוֹת, — *[What] if it was a muad for Sabbaths,*

The bull became accustomed to goring on the Sabbath, because it was idle from work and became overbearing [Rashi], or because it saw people dressed in their Sabbath finery and it does not recognize them [Yerushalmi] (Rav).[1]

The second explanation applies only to a *muad* toward man, not toward beasts, whereas the first explanation applies to any *muad*. Consequently, according to the second explanation, the mishnah follows the first *Tanna* in 3:8, who rules that a *tam* that wounds a man pays half the damages. According to R' Akiva, however, even a *tam* that wounds a man pays the full damages, and there would be no question what kind of payment it should make *(Lechem Shamayim).*

Pnei Moshe interprets *Yerushalmi* differently. He explains that the bull became a *muad* on the Sabbath, because the appearance of the Sabbath garments excites it and drives it mad.

[Accordingly, this applies also to a bull that is a *muad* toward animals on the Sabbath.]

וְאֵינוֹ מוּעָד לְחֹל? — *and not a muad for weekdays?*

It is definite that between the three Sabbaths — i.e., during the weekdays — the bull saw those whom he was accustomed to gore, and he did not gore them *(Nimmukei Yosef).*

R' Yehudah's disciples asked him what the ruling is in such a case *(Rashi).*

Nimmukei Yosef explains that the students of the yeshivah heard that R' Yehudah had ruled (2:4) that if a *muad* refrains from goring for three days, it returns to its status of *tam*. They therefore asked R' Yehudah what he would rule in the case of a *muad* for Sabbaths, since there is an interval of

1. A woman once came to *R' Yoseif Rosen*, the *Rogatchover Gaon*, with a serious problem: her infant son strangely refused to nurse on the Sabbath and festivals! She was at a loss as to what to do, since formula was out of the question for the impoverished family, and the long Succos holiday was approaching.

Without a moment's hesitation, the *Rogatchover* suggested that when nursing on the Sabbath or festivals, the mother change from her Sabbath clothes into her weekday attire. She did so, and the baby began nursing!

R' Rosen explained: *Yerushalmi* tells us that a bull can become a *muad* to gore on the

בבא קמא ד/ג

מְשַׁלֵּם נֶזֶק שָׁלֵם; לִימוֹת הַחֹל מְשַׁלֵּם חֲצִי נֶזֶק. אֵימָתַי הוּא תָם? מִשֶּׁיַּחֲזֹר בּוֹ שְׁלֹשָׁה יְמֵי שַׁבָּתוֹת.

[ג] **שׁוֹר** שֶׁל־יִשְׂרָאֵל שֶׁנָּגַח שׁוֹר שֶׁל־הֶקְדֵּשׁ, וְשֶׁל־הֶקְדֵּשׁ שֶׁנָּגַח לְשׁוֹר שֶׁל־יִשְׂרָאֵל, פָּטוּר, שֶׁנֶּאֱמַר: "שׁוֹר רֵעֵהוּ", וְלֹא שׁוֹר שֶׁל־הֶקְדֵּשׁ.

יד אברהם

more than three days between one Sabbath and the next.

אָמַר לָהֶם: — **He said to them:**
[R' Yehudah replied to his disciples:]

לְשַׁבָּתוֹת מְשַׁלֵּם נֶזֶק שָׁלֵם; — **For Sabbaths he pays the full damages;**
[If it gores on the Sabbath, its owner pays the full damages, as he does for a *muad*.]

לִימוֹת הַחֹל מְשַׁלֵּם חֲצִי נֶזֶק. — **for weekdays he pays half the damages.**
[If it gores on weekdays, its owner pays half the damages, as for a *tam*.]

אֵימָתַי הוּא תָם? — **When does it become a tam?**
[When is it restored to its previous state of *tam*?]

מִשֶּׁיַּחֲזֹר בּוֹ שְׁלֹשָׁה יְמֵי שַׁבָּתוֹת. — **When it refrains for three Sabbath days.**
If, after it became a *muad* for Sabbaths, they led other bulls before it on three consecutive Sabbaths, and it did not gore them, it is restored to its previous state of a *tam*, and if it gores on any subsequent Sabbath, its owner pays only half the damages (*Rav; Rashi*).

This is in accordance with *Rashi's* explanation that the bull becomes accustomed to goring on the Sabbath because it does not work. Therefore, the mishnah may be dealing with a bull that is a *muad* toward animals. According to *Yerushalmi's* explanation, however, the case deals only with a bull that gores people. Such a bull is obviously not affected by leading other bulls before it. Accordingly, we must say that people walked past it attired in their Sabbath finery, and it did not gore them (*Tos. Yom Tov*). According to *Pnei Moshe's* interpretation of *Yerushalmi*, on the other hand, the mishnah may be dealing even with a *muad* toward animals, which goes mad when it sees people attired in their Sabbath finery.

Nimmukei Yosef states that, according to the halachah, which follows R' Meir's view in 2:4, the criterion for giving the bull the status of a *tam* once again is if children play with the bull on three Sabbaths and it does not gore.

Tos. R' Akiva is puzzled by this explanation, since *Nimmukei Yosef* himself states above (2:4) that if the children play with the bull only once, and it does not gore, it is no longer a *muad*. Our case should be no different: either three Sabbaths when animals pass before it or one Sabbath when children play with it should suffice to transform it into a *tam* again.

Although R' Yehudah already stated above [ibid.] that a bull reverts to the status of a *tam* by refraining from goring for three days, he must nevertheless repeat this ruling as regards a bull that is a *muad* for Sabbaths, since we may think that a partial *muad* requires a shorter time of refraining from goring in order to revert to its former state. According to *Rashi*, who explains that the cessation of work causes the bull to gore, R' Yehudah teaches us that even if the bull is allowed to rest during the week and it does not gore, it remains a *muad* until it refrains from goring on three consecutive Sabbaths (*Tos. Yom Tov* from *Tos.* 37a).

Sabbath, because it does not recognize the people in their Sabbath finery. We see from this that intelligence at its simplest stages identifies people by outer factors, such as colors and shape. In this situation, too, the infant did not recognize his mother because she was attired differently, and he therefore refused to nurse from this 'strange' woman! (*R' Yaakov Feitman*, quoting *R' Shemaryahu Shulman* and *R' Tovia Preschel*, in *The Torah Personality*, p. 121).

משניות / בבא קמא — פרק ד: שור שנגח ארבעה וחמשה   [80]

4
3

He said to them: For Sabbaths he pays the full damages; for weekdays he pays half the damages. When does it become a *tam*? When it refrains for three Sabbath days.

3. [If] a bull of a Jew gores a bull consecrated to the Temple, or [if] a bull consecrated to the Temple gores a bull of a Jew, [its owner] is exempt, as it is said (*Exodus* 21:35): *another's bull,* but not a bull consecrated to the Temple.

YAD AVRAHAM

3.

The following mishnah is related to 1:2, which specifies that one is liable only for damaging *property that is not subject to me'ilah* and *property of Jews.*

שׁוֹר שֶׁל־יִשְׂרָאֵל — [If] *a bull of a Jew*

Some editions read: שׁוֹר שֶׁל־הֶדְיוֹט, *a bull of a common man* (Meiri; Bach; Rome Ms.; Paris Ms.). [This is the usual term used in contrast to הֶקְדֵּשׁ, *hekdesh* (consecrated property).]

The following applies whether the bull is a *tam* or a *muad* (Tif. Yis.).

שֶׁנָּגַח שׁוֹר שֶׁל־הֶקְדֵּשׁ, — *gores a bull consecrated to the Temple,*

In 1:2 the *Tanna* specifies that the only type of consecrated property for which one is exempt from the liability of damages is that which is subject to the rules of *me'ilah* (Tos. Yom Tov).

Beis David questions this very strongly, since we never find an early mishnah explaining a later mishnah; on the contrary, the opposite is always the case. He contends, therefore, that this mishnah does not concur with the earlier one. That mishnah is in accordance with the view of R' Yose the Galilean, who rules that קָדְשִׁים קַלִּים, *offerings of lesser holiness* (see commentary to 1:2) are considered the property of their owners, and if someone damages them, he must pay the owner. This mishnah, however, which does not distinguish between *hekdesh* subject to the rules of *me'ilah* and *hekdesh* not subject to it, follows the opinion of the Sages, who rule that offerings of lesser holiness are not regarded as the property of their owners, and one is therefore exempt if he damages them.

Although our mishnah is the later one, Rambam (Hil. Nizkei Mamon 8:1) rules in accordance with the earlier mishnah. The reason is that the rulings of the *Gemara* in Chapter 1 all follow the view of R' Yose the Galilean.

Kol HaRemez claims that this mishnah does indeed concur with the earlier one. It was repeated here because it quotes the Scriptural source of the ruling.

וְשֶׁל־הֶקְדֵּשׁ שֶׁנָּגַח לְשׁוֹר שֶׁל־יִשְׂרָאֵל, — *or [if] a bull consecrated to the Temple gores a bull of a Jew,*

In this instance, too, it makes no difference whether the goring bull be a *tam* or a *muad* (Tif. Yis.).

פָּטוּר, שֶׁנֶּאֱמַר; — [its owner] *is exempt, as it is said (Exodus 21:35):*

[In each of these cases, the owner of the damaging bull is exempt as stated in the Biblical passage dealing with damages.]

"שׁוֹר רֵעֵהוּ,, — '*another's bull,*'

The verse begins: וְכִי־יִגֹּף שׁוֹר־אִישׁ אֶת־שׁוֹר רֵעֵהוּ, *If a man's bull gores another's bull,* which is interpreted as meaning:

וְלֹא שׁוֹר שֶׁל־הֶקְדֵּשׁ. — *but not a bull consecrated to the Temple.*

Although this verse deals with a *tam* — since Scripture begins discussing the

בבא קמא ד/ד

שׁוֹר שֶׁל־יִשְׂרָאֵל שֶׁנָּגַח לְשׁוֹר שֶׁל־נָכְרִי, פָּטוּר; וְשֶׁל־נָכְרִי שֶׁנָּגַח לְשׁוֹר שֶׁל־יִשְׂרָאֵל — בֵּין תָּם בֵּין מוּעָד — מְשַׁלֵּם נֶזֶק שָׁלֵם.

[ד] **שׁוֹר** שֶׁל־פִּקֵּחַ שֶׁנָּגַח שׁוֹר שֶׁל־חֵרֵשׁ, שׁוֹטֶה, וְקָטָן, חַיָּב. וְשֶׁל־חֵרֵשׁ, שׁוֹטֶה,

יד אברהם

muad only in the next verse — the owner of a *muad*, too, would be exempt, because the latter is liable for full damages only when a *tam* in the same case would be liable for half the damages, as stated in the *Gemara*.

The Torah's intention is that wherever the damaging bull and the bull it damages are different [in that one is consecrated, and the other is not], there is no liability (*Tos. Yom Tov* from *Nimmukei Yosef*).

שׁוֹר שֶׁל־יִשְׂרָאֵל שֶׁנָּגַח לְשׁוֹר שֶׁל־נָכְרִי, — [*If*] *a bull of a Jew gores a bull of a gentile*,

[Whether the goring bull is a *tam* or a *muad*.]

פָּטוּר; — [*the Jew*] *is exempt*;

Some explain that, just as the word רֵעֵהוּ, *another man*, in the verse quoted above, excludes a consecrated bull, it excludes also the bull of a gentile, who is not regarded as the רֵעַ [lit., *friend*] of the Jew (*Meiri; Nimmukei Yosef; Yam Shel Shlomo; Lechem Mishneh, Hil. Nizkei Mamon* 8:5).

Rambam (ibid.) explains that the gentiles do not hold one another accountable for damage caused by one's animals, and we therefore judge them according to their own laws.

Rav quotes the *Gemara* (38a), which cites two verses as the basis for this ruling: (1) עָמַד וַיְמֹדֶד אֶרֶץ רָאָה וַיַּתֵּר גּוֹיִם, *He stood and shook the earth; He saw, and made the nations tremble* (Habakkuk 3:6), which is interpreted as meaning that because God saw the seven Noachide commandments[1] which the gentiles had accepted but did not observe, He permitted their money to the Jews [in this case of an animal belonging to a Jew goring an animal of a gentile (*Tos.*)]; (2) הוֹפִיעַ מֵהַר פָּארָן, *He shone forth from Mount Paran* (Deut. 33:2), which is interpreted to mean that because of what occurred at Paran — where God had offered the Torah to all the nations, and they rejected it [*Rashi*] — He permitted their money to the Jews [in this case]. (See *Tos. Yom Tov*.)

Apparently, *Rav* — unlike *Meiri* and the others cited above — holds that רֵעֵהוּ, *another man*, does not exclude a gentile, since he, too, is a mortal of flesh and blood. This theory is also suggested by *Tos. Rabbeinu Peretz* and *Maharam*.

וְשֶׁל־נָכְרִי שֶׁנָּגַח לְשׁוֹר שֶׁל־יִשְׂרָאֵל — בֵּין תָּם בֵּין מוּעָד — מְשַׁלֵּם נֶזֶק שָׁלֵם. — *but* [*if a bull*] *of a gentile gores a bull of a Jew — whether* [*it be*] *a tam or a muad —* [*the gentile*] *pays the full damages.*

Rambam (*Hil. Nizkei Mamon* 8:5) explains that this is a fine imposed on the gentiles, who — heedless of the commandments — do not eliminate sources of damage. Were we not to make them liable for the damages inflicted by their animals, they would not watch them, and the animals would cause losses to other people. (See *Lechem Mishneh* ad loc.; *Rambam Commentary*, quoted by *Tos. Yom Tov*.)

---

1. They are: the prohibitions of (1) idolatry, (2) cursing God's Name, (3) murder, (4) illicit sexual relations, (5) theft, (6) eating the limb of a live animal; and (7) the responsibility to establish a judicial system (*Rambam, Hil. Melachim* 9:1ff.; cf. *Ramban* to Gen. 34:11).

[If] a bull of a Jew gores a bull of a gentile, [the Jew] is exempt; but [if a bull] of a gentile gores a bull of a Jew — whether [it be] a *tam* or a *muad* — [the gentile] pays the full damages.

4. [If] the bull of a person of sound mind gores the bull of a deaf-mute, a mentally deranged person, or a minor, [its owner] is liable. But [if the

YAD AVRAHAM

Meiri explains in a manner similar to that of *Rambam*, concluding: According to what is stated in the *Gemara*, this applies only to nations that are not restrained by laws and regulations. If, however, they do keep the seven Noachide commandments, their status to us is the same as our status to them, and we do not show favoritism to ourselves in litigation.

4.

שׁוֹר שֶׁל־פִּקֵּחַ — [If] the bull of a person of sound mind

[That is, one who is neither a deaf-mute, a mentally deranged person, or a minor.]

שֶׁנָּגַח שׁוֹר שֶׁל־חֵרֵשׁ, — gores the bull of a deaf-mute,

The word חֵרֵשׁ here, as usual, denotes one who can neither hear nor speak because he was born deaf. If, however, one was born with these faculties, but became deaf later on, he is considered a perfectly normal person and is obligated by all the laws of the Torah *(Tos. Yom Tov* from *Nimmukei Yosef).*

[Technically, the term חֵרֵשׁ signifies a deaf person. But throughout the Talmud (see *Terumos* 1:2, *Chagigah* 2b-3a), wherever the term is juxtaposed with the terms שׁוֹטֶה וְקָטָן, a mentally deranged person and a minor, it refers to a deaf person who is deemed mentally incompetent. As the *Gemara* (ibid.) makes clear, this refers to a deaf-mute who, because of his condition, lacks the ability to communicate and is therefore not obligated in the performance of the commandments[1].]

שׁוֹטֶה, — a mentally deranged person,

[This refers to one who is wont to commit senseless acts. Such a person is considered deranged to the extent that he is no longer obligated to observe the *mitzvos* because he is not considered responsible for his actions. The exact criteria for judging a deranged person are discussed in *Chagigah* (3b) and at length by the halachic authorities, and do not lend themselves to synopsis (see *Rambam, Hil. Eidus* 9:9f., *Even Haezer* 121; *Yoreh Deah* 1:5, *Choshen Mishpat* 35:8-10). *Rambam* adds that the very feeble-minded are included in the category of deranged.]

וְקָטָן, — or a minor,

[This refers to children who are legally not yet considered responsible and competent, either because they have not reached the necessary age — in the case of a boy, thirteen; of a girl, twelve — or because they have not shown signs of puberty.]

חַיָּב. — [its owner] is liable.

The owner of a bull which gored the bull of one of these types of individuals is liable for the damage, since he is a normal person and is obligated to

---

1. [The halachic status of a deaf-mute who has been taught to talk by modern methods is extensively discussed in the responsa of later authorities. See *Teshuvos Divrei Chaim (Even Haezer* 72), *Maharam Schick* (ibid. §79a), *Igros Moshe* (ibid. §3:33), *Maharsham* (2:140); *Teshuvos HaGri Steif* (23a).]

בבא קמא ד/ד

וְקָטָן שֶׁנָּגַח שׁוֹר שֶׁל־פִּקֵּחַ, פָּטוּר. שׁוֹר שֶׁל־חֵרֵשׁ, שׁוֹטֶה, וְקָטָן שֶׁנָּגַח, בֵּית־דִּין מַעֲמִידִין לָהֶן אַפּוֹטְרוֹפּוֹס, וּמְעִידִין לָהֶן בִּפְנֵי אַפּוֹטְרוֹפּוֹס.

נִתְפַּקַּח הַחֵרֵשׁ, נִשְׁתַּפָּה הַשּׁוֹטֶה, וְהִגְדִּיל הַקָּטָן, חָזַר לְתַמּוּתוֹ; דִּבְרֵי רַבִּי מֵאִיר. רַבִּי יוֹסֵי אוֹמֵר: הֲרֵי הוּא בְחֶזְקָתוֹ.

יד אברהם

prevent his bull from doing damage (*Meiri*).

וְשֶׁל־חֵרֵשׁ, שׁוֹטֶה, וְקָטָן שֶׁנָּגַח שׁוֹר שֶׁל־פִּקֵּחַ, פָּטוּר. — But [if the bull] of a deaf-mute, a mentally deranged person, or a minor gores the bull of a person of sound mind, [its owner] is exempt.

[These individuals are not mentally competent, and therefore cannot be held liable for their own actions, and certainly not for those of their property.]

Even if the court appoints an administrator to guard the bull so that it should not gore, he does not become a representative of the owners with regard to the half-damage payment, since it is a fine (*Gem.* 15b), and these individuals are not fined (*Meiri* from *Gem.* 39a).

The reason for this — according to *Rav* and *Rashi* — is that the bull is a chattel, and chattels belonging to orphans are not pledged to pay a debt, as stated above (commentary to 1:3, s.v. וְשֶׁוֶה), that the court does not collect movables of orphans for damages they or their property have done. The same applies to deaf-mutes and mentally deranged persons (*Tos. Yom Tov*).

Tosafos, however, object to this reasoning, since the rule that chattels are not collected applies only for damages committed during their father's lifetime, not after his death. They therefore conclude that the reason these individuals are not liable if their animal did damage is that since the Torah was lenient with payment for damages committed by a *tam*, making its owner liable for only half the damages, the Rabbis were also lenient in this case, which deals with a *tam*, not to hold orphans [or other mentally incompetent persons (*Tif. Yis.*)] liable for damages caused by their animals, even if an administrator had been appointed (*Tos. Yom Tov*).

שׁוֹר שֶׁל־חֵרֵשׁ, שׁוֹטֶה, וְקָטָן שֶׁנָּגַח — [If] the bull of a deaf-mute, a mentally deranged person, or a minor gores,

That is, it becomes a habitual gorer (*Rav* from *Gem.* 39a).

This does not mean that it becomes a *muad*, because that happens only after its owner has been warned after each of three times that it has gored. In this case, however, warning these individuals accomplishes nothing, and no administrator has yet been appointed to represent them. Rather, it means that the bull became extremely wild and obsessed with goring (*Tos.* ibid.).

בֵּית־דִּין מַעֲמִידִין לָהֶן אַפּוֹטְרוֹפּוֹס, — the court appoints for them an administrator,

I.e., to watch it (*Tif. Yis.*).

They appoint an administrator, not for the purpose of making the orphans liable for the half-damage payment [as explained above], but for the purpose of representing them in being warned after each goring (*Rav*; *Rashi*).

Although it is categorically stated in 8:4 that a deaf-mute, a mentally incompetent person, and a minor are exempt from paying for damages they do, implying that we do not appoint an

4. bull] of a deaf-mute, a mentally deranged person, or a minor gores the bull of a person of sound mind, [its owner] is exempt.

[If] the bull of a deaf-mute, a mentally deranged person, or a minor gores, the court appoints for them an administrator, and they forewarn them in the presence of the administrator.

[If] the deaf-mute gains his senses, the mentally deranged person becomes sane, or the minor becomes of age, [the bull] reverts to its status of *tam;* this is R' Meir's view. R' Yose says: It remains in its present state.

YAD AVRAHAM

administrator in order to make collection from their properties possible, that is only because they themselves may become uncontrollable, and if we appoint an administrator so as to be able to collect from them, their property will become depleted. An animal, however, is possible to control, and once we appoint an administrator to watch it, there is no danger of this occurring *(Tos. Yom Tov* from *Nimmukei Yosef).*

וּמַעֲמִידִין לָהֶן בִּפְנֵי אֲפּוֹטְרוֹפּוֹס. — *and they forewarn them in the presence of the administrator.*

That is, if the bull gores three times while under the jurisdiction of the administrator, it becomes a *muad,* and each time it gores thereafter, he must pay the complete damages from the best of the orphans' property *(Rav, Tos. Yom Tov* from *Tos.).*

According to the opinion *(Gem.* 24a) which maintains that the method necessary to make an animal a *muad* is not for the purpose of warning the owner each time it gores, but to demonstrate that it has become accustomed to goring, even if the witnesses testify that the animal gored three times while under the jurisdiction of the deaf-mute, the mentally deranged person, or the minor, if it gores a fourth time while under the jurisdiction of the administrator, he must pay the full damages from their property *(Tos.,*

Meiri).

נִתְפַּקַּח הַחֵרֵשׁ, נִשְׁתַּפָּה הַשּׁוֹטֶה, וְהִגְדִּיל הַקָּטָן, — [If] *the deaf-mute gains his senses, the mentally deranged person becomes sane, or the minor becomes of age,*

[And hence, responsibility for the animal shifts from the administrator back to him.]

חָזַר לְתַמּוּתוֹ; דִּבְרֵי רַבִּי מֵאִיר. — [*the bull] reverts to its status of tam; this is R' Meir's view.*

R' Meir subscribes to the principle that, upon a change in the jurisdiction over the animal, it reverts to the status of a *tam (Rav* from *Gem.* 39b). This is because the orphan or one of the others who was not previously capable of watching the animal may claim that had it been in his jurisdiction, he would have watched it better. Therefore, it becomes a *tam* again until it gores three times and its 'new' owner is warned *(Tos. Yom Tov* from *Nimmukei Yosef).*

Meiri contends that, according to R' Meir, the very change in ownership actually changes the future and nature of the animal.

רַבִּי יוֹסֵי אוֹמֵר: הֲרֵי הוּא בְּחֶזְקָתוֹ. — *R' Yose says: It remains in its present state.*

That is, it remains a *muad.* R' Yose disagrees with the above principle; rather, he maintains that the animal remains in its present state although its jurisdiction is transferred to the

בבא קמא ד/ה

שׁוֹר הָאִצְטָדִין אֵינוֹ חַיָּב מִיתָה, שֶׁנֶּאֱמַר: ״כִּי יִגַּח,״ וְלֹא שֶׁיְגִיחוּהוּ.

[ה] **שׁוֹר** שֶׁנָּגַח אֶת־הָאָדָם, וָמֵת — מוּעָד, מְשַׁלֵּם כֹּפֶר; וְתָם, פָּטוּר מִן־הַכֹּפֶר.

יד אברהם

erstwhile deaf-mute, mentally deranged person, or minor.

Rambam (Hil. Nizkei Mamon 6:6) differentiates between an animal that was sold or given as a gift — in which case he rules that the change of possession does change its status — and the animal that had been under the jurisdiction of the administrator and was then returned to its rightful owner, in which case there is no real transfer, and it remains a *muad*.

Others rule contrarily: only in our case involving the administrator does the principle apply, since the rightful owner can claim that the administrator had no right to make his animal a *muad*; therefore, it reverts to its original status of *tam*. If one purchases an animal or receives one as a gift, however, it retains the status of *muad* that it had when in the possession of its former owner (*Meiri* from *Sefer Hahashlamah*).

שׁוֹר הָאִצְטָדִין — *A bull from the arena*

I.e., a bull that is trained to gore (*Rav; Rashi*).

These are bulls that are trained to fight each other in the arena. Two owners send in their bulls, and each one signals to his animal with his voice. The bulls have been trained to incite their opponents in order to see which one will win. This is not the nature of the bull but the desire of its owner. Many foolish people do this with certain species of beasts and fowl (*Rambam Commentary*).

Nimmukei Yosef describes the bullfights in which men torment the bull and incite it to gore. This was the entertainment of royalty.

אֵינוֹ חַיָּב מִיתָה, — *is not liable to death,*

If the bull killed a man through being incited in this manner, it is not put to death (*Meiri*).

שֶׁנֶּאֱמַר: ״כִּי יִגַּח,״ — *as it is said (Exodus 21:28): 'If [a bull] gores,'*

[In the passage dealing with an animal that kills a person, the Torah states: ... וְכִי יִגַּח שׁוֹר אֶת־אִישׁ, *If a bull gores a man or a woman and he dies, the bull shall surely be stoned.*

וְלֹא שֶׁיְגִיחוּהוּ. — *but not that it should be made to gore.*

Such an animal is regarded as having been forced to gore and is therefore not liable to the death penalty prescribed by Scripture (*Nimmukei Yosef* from *Gem.* 40b).

Meiri adds that neither is the one who incites it liable to the death penalty, since he was only an indirect cause of the killing.

Rambam (Hil. Nizkei Mamon 6:5) rules that even should an animal gore other animals three times after being incited, it does not become a *muad*; *Ravad* (ad loc.) disagrees.

Whether or not the one who incited the bull must pay damages or כֹּפֶר, *ransom* [to redeem himself from the sin of having killed a man (see next mishnah)] is controversial (*Meiri*).

5.

After mentioning the law of a bull from the arena which kills a man, the mishnah proceeds to delineate all the laws dealing with a bull that kills a man as regards stoning, ransom, and the fine imposed on the owner of a bull that kills a gentile slave.

משניות / בבא קמא — פרק ד: שור שנגח ארבעה וחמשה [86]

4 A bull from the arena is not liable to death, as it is
5 said *(Exodus* 21:28): *If [a bull] gores,* but not that it
should be made to gore.

5. [**I**f] a bull gores a man, and he dies — [if the bull
is] a *muad,* [its owner] pays ransom; if a *tam,*
he is exempt from ransom. Both are liable to death.

YAD AVRAHAM

שׁוֹר שֶׁנָּגַח אֶת־הָאָדָם, וָמֵת — *[If] a bull gores a man, and he dies —*
[I.e., the man dies.]

מוּעָד, — *[if the bull is] a muad,*
That is, it became a *muad* by virtue of having killed three people prior to this goring. The *Gemara* asks how it is possible for an animal to become a *muad* in this respect, since Scripture *(Ex.* 21:28) prescribes that it be stoned the first time it kills a person. One answer is that it becomes a *muad* if it kills three gentiles, for which it is not stoned. Another is that it killed three Jews stricken with fatal organic diseases. Since these people, in this regard, are considered already dead, the animal that kills them is not sentenced to death, but — after the third such incident — is nevertheless deemed a *muad (Rav).*

Rav's comment here follows the interpretation of *Rambam (Commentary* and *Hil. Nizkei Mamon* 10:3). *Rambam's* reading of the *Gemara* (41a) differs from ours. According to our version, the *Gemara* rejects the two answers given above, maintaining that even if an animal kills three gentiles or persons suffering from fatal organic diseases, it still does not become a *muad* toward killing healthy Jewish people. In *Rambam's* version however, the *Gemara* accepts these answers *(Tos. Yom Tov* from *Nimmukei Yosef* and *Maggid Mishneh* ad loc.).

According to his version of the *Gemara, Rambam* states also the case of the bull having gored three animals, by virtue of which it becomes a *muad* toward man as well *(Hil. Nizkei Mamon* 10:3).

Other answers given by the *Gemara* are:

The bull gored and then fled three consecutive times, thus making it impossible to stone it *(Rav; Tos. Yom Tov).*

The bull wounded three men mortally, but they all died only after the third goring *(Tif. Yis.).*

The witnesses who testified that the bull gored the first three times recognized the owner but not the bull. Therefore, the bull could not be stoned, but the owner was warned that he had a habitual gorer in his herd and that he should watch his entire herd. When the bull gored the fourth time, it was recognized, and is therefore liable to death.

מְשַׁלֵּם כֹּפֶר; — *[its owner] pays ransom;*
[If the bull is a *muad,* the owner pays ransom.]

This is based on *Exodus* 21:29f.: *But if the bull was a habitual gorer from yesterday and the day before, and its owner was warned, but he did not watch it, and it kills a man or a woman, the bull shall be stoned, and also its owner shall be put to death. A ransom shall be imposed upon him; he shall give the redemption of his soul according to whatever be imposed upon him.*

Tradition teaches us that the death sentence imposed upon the owner referred to in the verse is death at the hands of Heaven; but if the owner pays ransom for the slain person, his sin is expiated *(Rambam* loc. cit. §4).

The intention is that the amount of ransom is determined according to the value of the one slain by the animal *(Tos. Yom Tov; Meiri; Rav* to *Arachin* 3:3). The ransom is not considered a monetary obligation, but an atonement for the sin of neglecting to watch one's animal *(Rambam* ibid.).

וְתָם, — *if a tam,*
[That is, if one's *tam* killed a man.]

פָּטוּר מִן־הַכֹּפֶר. — *he is exempt from ransom.*

This is based on *Exodus* 21:28: *If a*

[87] THE MISHNAH/BAVA KAMMA — Chapter Four: *Shor SheNagach*

בבא קמא ד/ו

וְזֶה וָזֶה חַיָּבִים מִיתָה. וְכֵן בְּבֵן וְכֵן בְּבַת. נָגַח עֶבֶד אוֹ אָמָה, נוֹתֵן שְׁלֹשִׁים סְלָעִים, בֵּין שֶׁהוּא יָפֶה מֵאָה מָנֶה וּבֵין שֶׁאֵינוֹ יָפֶה אֶלָּא דִינָר אֶחָד.

[ו] **שׁוֹר** שֶׁהָיָה מִתְחַכֵּךְ בְּכֹתֶל, וְנָפַל עַל־

יד אברהם

bull gores a man or a woman, and he dies, the bull shall surely be stoned, and its flesh shall not be eaten, and the owner of the bull is quit.

The intention is that he is exempt from ransom *(Meiri)*.

Alternatively, since ransom is mentioned only in reference to *muad*, we deduce that the owner of a *tam* is exempt from paying it *(Tif. Yis.)*.

וְזֶה וָזֶה — *Both* [lit., *and this and this*] [I.e., both a *tam* and a *muad*.]

חַיָּבִים מִיתָה. — *are liable to death.*

Since the bull being put to death is stated in reference to a *tam* as well as a *muad* *(Tos. Yom Tov* from *Rashi* 41a*)*.

וְכֵן בְּבֵן וְכֵן בְּבַת. — *The same applies to a male child, and the same applies to a female child* [lit., *and so with a son and so with a daughter*].

For killing young children, the bull is liable to stoning, and — in the case of a *muad* — the owner must pay ransom *(Rav)*.

This is based on *Exodus* 21:31: אוֹ־בֵן יִגָּח אוֹ־בַת יִגָּח כַּמִּשְׁפָּט הַזֶּה יֵעָשֶׂה לּוֹ, *Whether it gores a male child or it gores a female child, according to this judgment shall be done to it.* The superfluous expressions *it gores ... it gores* indicate that both a *tam* and a *muad* are liable for goring minors, whether the victims die or are merely injured *(Gem.* 44a*)*.

Both of these expressions are superfluous — since it is already known from the previous verses in the passage that Scripture is discussing cases of bulls that gored — and are meant to teach us that this law applies to a *tam* as well as a *muad*, and to injury as well as death *(Talmid Rabbeinu Peretz* quoted by *Shitah Mekubetzes)*.

Since minors are not obligated to perform *mitzvos*, we need a specific verse to teach us that the stoning of the animal and the ransom payment apply even when a child is killed by an animal.

The above is applicable only to viable infants. If an animal kills an infant that was born after eight months of pregnancy [and has definite signs of immaturity (see ArtScroll *Shabbos,* p. 319)], however, it is exempt, since such an infant is not viable. Also, if it kills an infant less than one month old, since at that age it is not yet certain that the child will live, no money can be exacted from the defendant [see following mishnah] *(Tos. Yom Tov* from *Nimmukei Yosef)*.

נָגַח עֶבֶד אוֹ אָמָה, — *[If] it gores a male slave or a female slave,*

That is, gentile slaves who were immersed in a *mikveh* [ritual pool] upon becoming slaves of a Jew — as is the standard procedure — at which time they become obligated to perform the commandments applicable to Jewish women. Therefore, the Torah imposed the death penalty upon the animal that kills them, just as the owner of the animal is liable to death should he kill the slaves (ibid.; see there).

נוֹתֵן שְׁלֹשִׁים סְלָעִים, — *[its owner] pays thirty selaim,*

[A סֶלַע, *sela* (pl. *selaim*), is the Mishnaic term for the Biblical shekel. A

[88]

The same applies to a male child and the same applies to a female child. [If] it gores a male slave or a female slave, [its owner] pays thirty *selaim*, whether it was worth a hundred *maneh* or whether it was worth no more than one dinar.

6. [**I**f] a bull was rubbing itself against a wall, and

YAD AVRAHAM

sela equals four *zuz*, or four silver dinars (see Appendix I to ArtScroll *Shekalim* p. 161, and *Gateway to the Talmud*, p. 119).]

This is based on *Exodus* 21:32: אִם־עֶבֶד יִגַּח הַשּׁוֹר אוֹ אָמָה כֶּסֶף שְׁלֹשִׁים שְׁקָלִים יִתֵּן לַאדֹנָיו וְהַשּׁוֹר יִסָּקֵל, *If the bull gores a male slave or a female slave, he shall give his master thirty silver shekels, and the bull shall be stoned.*

[The payment is a fine imposed by the Torah for neglecting to watch a *muad*, allowing it to kill a male slave or female slave *(see Kesubos* 3:9 and ArtScroll commentary there).]

בֵּין שֶׁהוּא יָפֶה מֵאָה מָנֶה — *whether it was worth a hundred maneh*

[That is, whether the slave was worth a hundred *maneh*. A *maneh* is equivalent to one hundred dinars (or *zuz);* a hundred *maneh* equals ten thousand dinars].

Although many editions read: יָפֶה מָנֶה, *worth a maneh*, we have followed the version of the Mishnah printed with the *Gemara*, as well as those of *Rif*, *Meiri*, and *Rambam Commentary* (ed. *Kaffich*).

[This is undoubtedly the correct reading, since a *maneh* — which equals twenty-five *selaim* — is less than the thirty-*selaim* payment discussed in the mishnah. According to that version, the implication would be that the owner of the bull must pay thirty *selaim* regardless of how much *less* the slave was worth. The mishnah would not be telling us, however, that even if the slave was worth more, the fine is only thirty *selaim*, and that the owner of the bull does not have to pay more. Yet the Mishnah in *Arachin* (3:1,3) states explicitly that the fine of thirty *selaim* is sometimes a leniency and sometimes a stringency, implying that if the slave was worth more, the Torah was lenient in imposing the uniform fine of thirty *selaim*. Mishnah 3 (ibid.) states that no matter whether the animal killed the most handsome slave or the most ugly one, its owner must pay thirty *selaim*, whereas if it killed a freeman, he pays the latter's value. *Mechilta* (*Ex.* 21:32) states explicitly that even if the victim was worth ten thousand dinars, the payment is only thirty *selaim*. *Rambam* (*Hil. Nizkei Mamon* 11:1) and *Smag* rule likewise. *Lekach Tov* (*Ex.* loc. cit.) states מָאתַיִם מָנֶה, *two hundred maneh*, and *Rashi* (ibid.) states אֶלֶף זוּז, *one thousand zuz*. In any case, all these sources unanimously agree that the uniform fine of thirty *selaim* applies even if the value of the slave exceeded that amount. Obviously, the reading מֵאָה מָנֶה, *a hundred maneh*, is the correct one.

R' Yoel Chasid of Amchislav also notes this error in the mishnah.]

וּבֵין שֶׁאֵינוֹ יָפֶה אֶלָּא דִּינָר אֶחָד. — *or whether it was worth no more than one dinar.*

Various editions of the mishnah (*Yerushalmi; Rambam Commentary*, ed. *Kaffich*) read: דִּינָר זָהָב, *a gold dinar*. [As mentioned in the commentary to mishnah 1, a gold dinar is worth twenty-five silver dinars, or twenty-five *zuz*.] *Meleches Shlomo*, however, deems that reading an error.

6.

שׁוֹר שֶׁהָיָה מִתְחַכֵּךְ בְּכֹתֶל — [*If*] *a bull was rubbing itself against a wall,*

It did so for its own pleasure *(Tos. Yom Tov* from *Gem.* 44a).

[89]   THE MISHNAH/BAVA KAMMA — Chapter Four: *Shor SheNagach*

בבא קמא ד/ז

הָאָדָם; נִתְכַּוֵּן לַהֲרֹג אֶת־הַבְּהֵמָה וְהָרַג אֶת־הָאָדָם; לְנָכְרִי, וְהָרַג בֶּן־יִשְׂרָאֵל; לִנְפָלִים, וְהָרַג בֶּן־קַיָּמָא — פָּטוּר.

[ז] שׁוֹר הָאִשָּׁה, שׁוֹר הַיְתוֹמִים, שׁוֹר

יד אברהם

וְנָפַל — *and it fell*
[The wall fell.]

עַל־הָאָדָם; — *upon a man;*
And the man died (Tif. Yis.).

In this case, as the mishnah concludes, the animal is not liable to the death penalty. Scripture states (Ex. 21:29): הַשּׁוֹר יִסָּקֵל וְגַם־בְּעָלָיו יוּמָת, *the bull shall be stoned, and also its owner shall be put to death*; the death penalty of the animal is compared to that of the owner. Just as the latter is not put to death unless he kills intentionally, neither is the animal. Since the animal is a *tam*, its owner need not pay ransom, as stated in the preceding mishnah.

If, however, the animal was a *muad* to do such things — e.g., it was accustomed to rubbing itself against walls, in order to fell them upon people, and this time it rubbed against the wall for its pleasure, thereby causing it to fall on a man and kill him, although the animal is not put to death, its owner is liable for ransom. This is derived from the verse (ibid., 30): אִם כֹּפֶר יוּשַׁת עָלָיו, *A ransom shall be imposed upon him*, in which the word אִם is superfluous [since the statement is unconditional (*Rashi* ad loc.)] and is intended to include the payment of ransom even if the animal kills a person unintentionally (*Rav; Rashi* 44a, s.v. וחייב).

The reason the animal was not stoned after it had intentionally felled a wall upon a person is that it ran off to the fields after each time that it had done so. The fourth time, however, it killed unintentionally. Since it is slightly unusual for an animal to rub against a wall for its own pleasure and push it down, it is a *muad* only by dint of the three previous killings. [Therefore, the animal is not stoned, but its owner must pay ransom] (*Tos. Yom Tov* from *Tos.* 48b, s.v. רחזא).

Tiferes Yisrael and *Shoshannim LeDavid* challenge this interpretation, since the animal should be liable to stoning for the first killing, which was intentional. *Tiferes Yisrael* therefore explains that the first three times, too, it had killed unintentionally. *Shoshannim LeDavid* suggests that the witnesses testified that a bull belonging to this owner had gored, but they did not recognize the animal, and therefore, could not sentence it to death. They could, however, obligate the owner to watch his herd since he has a habitual gorer among his cattle [as mentioned in the commentary to the previous mishnah, s.v. מוּעָד].

Tosafos (44a), however, object to this reasoning. Since the animal rubbed against the wall for its own pleasure, it should not be considered an unusual act. They object also to the reasoning that the animal should become a *muad* with regard to the fourth time, when the killing was unintentional, by dint of the first three times, when they were intentional. Instead, they explain that this was the first time the animal had killed a person. Since it had rubbed against the wall for its own pleasure and killed the person unintentionally, it is not liable to the death penalty. However, since such an act is a *toladah* of *shen* (see General Introduction, s.v. *Avos and Tolados*), regarding which the animal is considered a *muad* from the outset, the owner is liable to pay ransom.

Rambam, according to *Maggid Mishneh* (Hil. Nizkei Mamon 10:10), concurs with *Rashi's* interpretation of the Gemara.

The Gemara (44b) explains that the owner is liable only if the animal kills a

4 7 it fell upon a man; [or if] it aimed to kill a beast and killed a man; a gentile, and killed a Jew; [or] nonviable infants, and killed a viable child — it is exempt.

7. A bull of a woman, a bull of orphans, a bull of

YAD AVRAHAM

man with its body, in a manner similar to the goring mentioned in Scripture. Should it push a wall upon its victim, however, the owner is exempt from paying ransom unless the wall was tilted toward the ground and ready to fall, and the animal placed its weight on the wall, and both it and the wall fell upon the person and killed him. Otherwise, if the animal pushes the wall down, and the wall falls by itself, it is analogous to an animal damaging with *tzeroros* [pebbles], regarding which its owner is liable only for damages, not ransom *(Tos. Yom Tov* from *Nimmukei Yosef).*

The only indication we have that the bull rubbed against the wall for its own pleasure is the fact that after the wall fell down, it continued to rub against it *(Tos. Yom Tov* from *Gem.* 44b).

נִתְכַּוֵּן לַהֲרֹג אֶת־הַבְּהֵמָה וְהָרַג אֶת־הָאָדָם — [*or if*] *it aimed to kill a beast and killed a man;*

[This is a new case: An animal intended to kill another animal, for which there is no death penalty, but unintentionally killed a man, an act which — if done intentionally — makes the killer liable to stoning.]

לְנָכְרִי, וְהָרַג בֶּן־יִשְׂרָאֵל; — *a gentile, and killed a Jew;*

The animal intended to kill a gentile, for whose death it would not be liable to stoning, but instead killed a Jew, for whose death it is stoned.]

לִנְפָלִים, וְהָרַג בֶּן־קַיָּמָא — — [*or*] *nonviable infants, and killed a viable child —*

[An animal aimed to kill prematurely born infants who are unable to live, and instead killed a child — an act for which it is liable to the death penalty, as stated in the previous mishnah.]

פָּטוּר. — *it is exempt.*

[In each of these instances, the animal is exempt from the death penalty by stoning, since they are all deemed unintentional.]

7.

The following mishnah enumerates various animals, who — because of the types of owner which they have, or because they have no owner — would give us reason to believe that they are exempt from the death penalty should they kill a person. Nevertheless, we deduce from Scripture that they are liable.

שׁוֹר הָאִשָּׁה, — *A bull of a woman,*

Although she is not as skilled as a man in watching her animal that it not kill, the animal is nevertheless liable to stoning should it kill a person *(Meiri).*

Rashi explains that the Torah must tell us this lest we think that, since it speaks of בַּעַל הַשּׁוֹר, *the master of the bull* (Ex. 21:28), a masculine expression, an animal belonging to a woman would be exempt.

Tosafos object to this reasoning since it is customary for Scripture to speak in masculine terms. They reason instead that, since — in the section dealing with damages — the Torah uses the expression, שׁוֹר־אִישׁ, *a man's bull* (ibid., v. 35), we would think that the same should apply to the death penalty of an animal that kills a person, since the two subjects are compared to each other (see commentary to mishnah 5, s.v. וְכֵן). The Torah must therefore tell us that a woman's animal is also liable to death.

בבא קמא ד/ח

הָאֲפּוֹטְרוֹפּוֹס, שׁוֹר הַמִּדְבָּר, שׁוֹר הַהֶקְדֵּשׁ, שׁוֹר הַגֵּר שֶׁמֵּת וְאֵין לוֹ יוֹרְשִׁים — הֲרֵי אֵלּוּ חַיָּבִים מִיתָה. רַבִּי יְהוּדָה אוֹמֵר: שׁוֹר הַמִּדְבָּר, שׁוֹר הַהֶקְדֵּשׁ, שׁוֹר הַגֵּר שֶׁמֵּת פְּטוּרִים מִן־הַמִּיתָה, לְפִי שֶׁאֵין לָהֶם בְּעָלִים.

[ח] **שׁוֹר** שֶׁהוּא יוֹצֵא לְהִסָּקֵל, וְהִקְדִּישׁוֹ

יד אברהם

Consequently, we deduce that she is liable for the damages it causes as well (Tos. Yom Tov).

שׁוֹר הַיְתוֹמִים — *a bull of orphans*,

That is, minor orphans who have no administrator (Rav; Rashi).

We should not think that, since they are not of mature intelligence, the Torah was lenient with an animal belonging to them (Tos. Yom Tov from Nimmukei Yosef).

שׁוֹר הָאֲפּוֹטְרוֹפּוֹס — *a bull of an administrator*,

This, too, refers to an animal belonging to orphans, but, in this case, an administrator was appointed to watch it (Rav; Rashi).

We shoul not think that, since the animal has an administrator to watch it, and therefore will probably not do too much damage in the future, the Torah was lenient with it so that the orphans should not lose their money (Tos. Yom Tov from Nimmukei Yosef).

שׁוֹר הַמִּדְבָּר — *a bull of the wilderness*,

I.e., a bull that has no owner (Tif. Yis.). We may have thought that, since it has no owner, it is exempt (Tos. Yom Tov from Nimmukei Yosef).

This is not a wild bull, which is called שׁוֹר הַבָּר, but an ordinary domesticated bull, whose owner has abandoned it (Lechem Shamayim).

שׁוֹר הַהֶקְדֵּשׁ — *a bull consecrated to the Temple*,

The mishnah concludes that such an animal is liable to the death penalty, although the Temple would thereby suffer a loss (Tos. Yom Tov from Nimmukei Yosef).

שׁוֹר הַגֵּר שֶׁמֵּת וְאֵין לוֹ יוֹרְשִׁים — *a bull of a proselyte who died and left no heirs* —

[When a gentile converts, he is considered as having been newly born, hence having no relationship to those previously related to him. If, subsequently, no children are born to him, his property becomes ownerless upon his death.]

Nimmukei Yosef comments that it was unnecessary for the mishnah to tell us that such an animal is stoned; but, since a verse is required from which to learn this, the mishnah, too, listed it with the others.

Tos. Yom Tov, however, challenges this reasoning: if the law that such an animal is liable to death is so obvious that the mishnah does not have to tell it to us, why is it necessary for the Torah to do so? He suggests that the verse is necessary lest we believe that only if the animal gores while it has an owner — e.g., it gores and then the owner consecrates it or abandons it — is it liable to death. But if he consecrates it or abandons it, and then it gores and kills a person, we would think that it is exempt. The verse is therefore necessary to teach us that the animal is liable even in that case. The mishnah illustrates this with the case of an animal belonging to a proselyte, which is liable to stoning

משניות / בבא קמא — פרק ד: שור שנגח ארבעה וחמשה [92]

4
8

an administrator, a bull of the wilderness, a bull consecrated to the Temple, a bull of a proselyte who died and left no heirs—these are liable to death. R' Yehudah says: A bull of the wilderness, a bull consecrated to the Temple, [and] a bull of a proselyte who died are exempt from death, since they have no owners.

8. [I]f] a bull was condemned to be stoned, and its

YAD AVRAHAM

even if it gored after the proselyte's death, when it is ownerless *(Tos. Yom Tov).*

הֲרֵי אֵלוּ חַיָּבִים מִיתָה — *these are liable to death.*

[If any of the aforementioned animals kill a person, it is liable to death by stoning, just as an animal that is owned by a man.] The *Gemara* deduces this from the fact that the word שׁוֹר, bull, appears seven times in the section dealing with an animal that killed a person. One is necessary for the understanding of the text itself; the other six represent the six types of animal mentioned in the mishnah *(Rav from Gem.* 44b).

רַבִּי יְהוּדָה אוֹמֵר: שׁוֹר הַמִּדְבָּר, שׁוֹר הַהֶקְדֵּשׁ, שׁוֹר הַגֵּר שֶׁמֵּת — *R' Yehudah says: A bull of the wilderness, a bull consecrated to the Temple, [and] a bull of a proselyte who died*

[That is, who died and left no heirs. In the *Naples* edition of the Mishnah and those of *Rav, Meiri* and *Kaffich,* this is stated explicitly, as above.]

פְּטוּרִים מִן־הַמִּיתָה, לְפִי שֶׁאֵין לָהֶם בְּעָלִים — *are exempt from death, since they have no owners.*

Even if the animal gored and then the owner abandoned it or consecrated it, or if the proselyte died after the animal gored, it is nevertheless exempt *(Rav from Gem.* 44b).

The repetition of *a bull of the wilderness* and *a bull of the proselyte who died* — which are in essence the same, since both are ownerless — leads the Rabbis to believe that the final case is stated to teach us that R' Yehudah declares them exempt even if the goring took place when the animal had an owner *(Tos. Yom Tov from Gem.).*

The halachah is not in accordance with R' Yehudah *(Rav; Rambam Commentary).*

8.

The following mishnah delineates the laws dealing with an animal that killed a person and was subsequently sentenced to death for it, and those related to such an animal that has not yet been sentenced.

שׁוֹר שֶׁהוּא יוֹצֵא לְהִסָּקֵל — *[If] a bull was condemned* [lit., *that is going out]* to *be stoned,*

The present tense of the literal definition intimates that although it has not yet gone out to be stoned, as long as the sentence has been passed, the following rules apply *(Tos. Yom Tov from Nimmukei Yosef,* as explained by *Hon Ashir, Shoshannim LeDavid).*

וְהִקְדִּישׁוּ בְעָלָיו — *and its owner*[1]

---

1. It is common for Scripture to use the plural form when referring to a בַּעַל, owner — e.g., Exodus 21:36: וְלֹא יִשְׁמְרֶנּוּ בְּעָלָיו, *and its owner does not watch it* (Rashi to Gen. 20:13). [The same is true of the Mishnah.]

[93]   THE MISHNAH/BAVA KAMMA — Chapter Four: *Shor SheNagach*

בְּעָלָיו, אֵינוֹ מֻקְדָּשׁ; שְׁחָטוֹ, בְּשָׂרוֹ אָסוּר. וְאִם, עַד שֶׁלֹּא נִגְמַר דִּינוֹ, הִקְדִּישׁוֹ בְּעָלָיו, מֻקְדָּשׁ; וְאִם שְׁחָטוֹ, בְּשָׂרוֹ מֻתָּר.

[ט] מְסָרוֹ לְשׁוֹמֵר חִנָּם, וּלְשׁוֹאֵל, לְנוֹשֵׂא שָׂכָר, וּלְשׂוֹכֵר, נִכְנְסוּ תַחַת

יד אברהם

consecrated it,
[He consecrated it to the Temple.]

אֵינוֹ מֻקְדָּשׁ — *it is not consecrated;*
It is no longer in the possession of the owner with respect to consecrating it (Rashi 45a).

שְׁחָטוֹ, — [*if*] *he slaughtered it,*
[The owner slaughtered it before it was stoned by the court.]

בְּשָׂרוֹ אָסוּר. — *its flesh is prohibited.*
Its flesh is prohibited to be eaten, as the Torah states (*Ex.* 21:28): סָקוֹל יִסָּקֵל הַשּׁוֹר וְלֹא יֵאָכֵל אֶת־בְּשָׂרוֹ, *the bull shall surely be stoned, and its flesh shall not be eaten.* Since the bull is stoned, it is obvious that it has the law of a נְבֵלָה, *an animal which died before it was slaughtered,* and may not be eaten. Rather, the verse teaches us that if he slaughtered it before it was stoned, but after it was condemned to death, it is prohibited to be eaten (*Rav* from *Gem.* ibid.).
The intention is that even if it is made and prepared like other flesh, it is still prohibited (*Tos. Yom Tov* from *Gem.* 41a).
Rishon LeZion points out that, in fact, the flesh is not only prohibited for consumption, but also for any benefit. This is discussed by the *Gemara* (41a).

וְאִם, עַד שֶׁלֹּא נִגְמַר דִּינוֹ, הִקְדִּישׁוֹ בְּעָלָיו, — *If, before its sentence was passed, its owner*

consecrated it,
[The owner of an animal that killed a man consecrated it before it was sentenced to death.]

מֻקְדָּשׁ; — *it is consecrated;*
Although it is stoned in any case, the consecration is effective that, if one derives benefit from the animal, he is obligated by the laws of *me'ilah* — i.e., he must pay the value to the Temple and an additional one-fifth of that amount, and bring an אֲשַׁם מְעִילוֹת, *a guilt-offering* for using consecrated objects (*Rav; Rashi*).
Meiri states that the court coerces the owner to redeem that animal, and then the sentence is passed and it is stoned. Since an animal that has killed a person is disqualified to be used as an offering, its consecration cannot be for the purpose of being offered upon the Altar, in which case it could not be redeemed unless it developed a disqualifying blemish, but for בֶּדֶק הַבַּיִת, *the repairs of the Temple* — i.e., it is to be sold, and the money used for the Temple. Therefore, it may be redeemed.

וְאִם שְׁחָטוֹ, — *if he slaughtered it,*
[The owner slaughtered the animal before the sentence was passed.]

בְּשָׂרוֹ מֻתָּר. — *its flesh is permissible.*
It may be eaten (*Rambam, Hil. Nizkei Mamon* 11:9).

9.

The following mishnah begins a new case (*Rashi*).

מְסָרוֹ — [*If*] *he gave it over*
Before an animal gored, the owner had given it over (*Tos. Yom Tov* from *Rashi*.)

4 owner consecrated it, it is not consecrated; [if] he
9 slaughtered it, its flesh is prohibited. If, before its sentence was passed, its owner consecrated it, it is consecrated; if he slaughtered it, its flesh is permissible.

9. [I]f] he gave it over to an unpaid guardian, to a borrower, to a paid guardian, or to a renter, [the latter] is responsible in lieu of the owner: [for] a

YAD AVRAHAM

לְשׁוֹמֵר חִנָּם, — *to an unpaid guardian,*
[That is, to one who undertook to watch it without remuneration.]

וּלְשׁוֹאֵל, — *to a borrower,*
[The owner of the animal lent it to someone gratis.]

לְנוֹשֵׂא שָׂכָר, — *to a paid guardian* [lit., one who receives payment],
[I.e., one who is paid for watching the animal.]

The mishnah often uses this term instead of the more explicit expression, שׁוֹמֵר שָׂכָר, to indicate that even if one accepts an article merely as a broker, who earns a commission only if he can sell it, he has the same responsibility to watch the article as does a paid guardian because of the benefit he expects to derive from it *(Tif. Yis. to Bava Metzia 7:8).*

וּלְשׂוֹכֵר, — *or to a renter,*
[That is, one who pays for the privilege of using the animal.]

This order of listing the four types of guardians which is also found in 7:6, in *Bava Metzia* 7:8, and in *Shevuos* 8:1, requires explanation since the Torah [*Ex.* 22:6-14] lists them in another order: (1) the unpaid guardian (2) the paid guardian (3) the borrower, and (4) the renter.

Tosafos (4b) explain that the Mishnah's order reflects the contrasts between the responsibilities of the various categories of guardians. The unpaid guardian — who is responsible only for damages to the item resulting from negligence — is contrasted to the borrower — who is responsible for anything that happens to it, including theft, loss, or accidents. The borrower is exempt only if the item breaks — or, if he had borrowed an animal, and it dies — because of its work. The paid guardian is listed next, since he is responsible for some types of losses — viz., if it is stolen or lost — but is exempt from accidental damages, such as fracture or death. [According to R' Yehudah (*Gem.* 45b), the renter's liability is identical to that of the paid guardian, and that is why one is listed after the other.]

Another reason for this order is that the laws of the unpaid guardian and the borrower are related in that neither one pays for his privileges: the owner does not pay the guardian for his services, nor does the borrower pay the owner for the right to use the item. Next follow the paid guardian and the renter, each of whom pays for his privilege: the owner pays the guardian for his services, and the renter pays for the use of the item (*Tos. Yom Tov*).

נִכְנְסוּ תַּחַת הַבְּעָלִים: — *[the latter] is responsible* [lit., enters] *in lieu of the owner:*
[The guardian assumes the liability for damages done by the animal while it is in his custody.]

This statement is not to be construed as an unqualified rule that a guardian is always responsible in lieu of the owner. This is because — as discussed in the second half of the mishnah — all agree that the owner of a *tam* is liable for half the damages caused by it unless he took adequate precautions to prevent the animal from doing damage (e.g., it was locked in a stall with a door that can withstand even an unusually strong wind). An unpaid guardian, however, is required only to take precautions of an inferior nature (e.g., locking it in a stall with a door that can withstand only an ordinary wind) to prevent the animal from doing damage. Consequently, if

[95]

בבא קמא ד/ט

הַבְּעָלִים: מוּעָד, מְשַׁלֵּם נֶזֶק שָׁלֵם; וְתָם, מְשַׁלֵּם חֲצִי נֶזֶק.

קְשָׁרוֹ בְעָלָיו בְּמוֹסֵרָה, וְנָעַל בְּפָנָיו כָּרָאוּי, וְיָצָא וְהִזִּיק, אֶחָד תָּם וְאֶחָד מוּעָד, חַיָּב; דִּבְרֵי רַבִּי מֵאִיר. רַבִּי יְהוּדָה אוֹמֵר: תָּם חַיָּב; וּמוּעָד פָּטוּר, שֶׁנֶּאֱמַר: ״וְלֹא יִשְׁמְרֶנּוּ בְּעָלָיו״, וְשָׁמוּר הוּא זֶה.

יד אברהם

the owner entrusts the *tam* to an unpaid guardian, and the latter takes only inferior precautions in watching it, the guardian is exempt, since he fulfilled his task; but the owner is liable for half the damages, since it is his responsibility to see to it that the proper precautions are taken.

Rather, the mishnah refers only to a case in which the watcher was completely negligent in guarding the animal. In that case, he must pay for the damage in lieu of the owner *(Tos. Yom Tov* from *Nimmukei Yosef).*

מוּעָד, מְשַׁלֵּם נֶזֶק שָׁלֵם — [for] a *muad*, he pays the full damages;

If the animal is a *muad*, the guardian is liable for the full damages, and the owner is exempt. Even if the guardian had not specified what he agrees to be responsible for, he is liable both for damages sustained by the animal while in his trust, as well as for the damages that the animal does during that time *(Meiri).*

וְתָם, מְשַׁלֵּם חֲצִי נֶזֶק. — [for] a *tam*, he pays half the damages.

If the animal is a *tam*, the guardian must pay half the damages, and the owner is exempt *(Tif. Yis.).*

The following is a new case, dealing with the owner of the animal, not a guardian.

קְשָׁרוֹ בְעָלָיו בְּמוֹסֵרָה, וְנָעַל בְּפָנָיו כָּרָאוּי, — [*If*] *its owner tied it with a rein, or locked* [*the stall*] *before it properly,*

That is, the door of the stall could stand up only against an ordinary wind.

This is considered guarding the animal in an inferior manner *(Rav, Rashi* from *Gem.* 55b).

וְיָצָא — *and it went out*

[The animal went out of the stall.]

וְהִזִּיק, אֶחָד תָּם וְאֶחָד מוּעָד, חַיָּב; — *and damaged, whether it is a tam or a muad, he is liable;*

[Whether the animal is a *tam* or a *muad*, the owner is liable for the damages.]

דִּבְרֵי רַבִּי מֵאִיר. — [*these are*] *the words of R' Meir.*

R' Meir rules that both a *tam* and a *muad* require a superior method of guarding — viz., to tie it with an iron chain, or to lock it in a stall behind a door that can withstand even an unusually strong wind *(Meiri* explaining *Gem.* 45b).

The *Gemara* expounds R' Meir's reasoning. He maintains that a normal bull is not regarded as being under control. Therefore, the Torah would require a *tam* to be watched with at least an inferior method of guarding. When Scripture *(Ex.* 21:36) writes, regarding a *muad:* וְלֹא יִשְׁמְרֶנּוּ בְּעָלָיו, *and its owner does not watch it,* implying that it must be watched more carefully, it obviously refers to a superior method of guarding. Through an exegetical interpretation comparing the *tam* to the *muad* (see commentary to mishnah 5, s.v. וְכֵן), R' Meir deduces that a *tam*, too, must be watched with a superior method of guarding. If it is not, and it damages, the owner is liable *(Tos. Yom Tov).*

משניות / בבא קמא — פרק ד: שור שנגח ארבעה וחמשה [96]

4 9 *muad*, he pays the full damages; [for] a *tam*, he pays half the damages.

[If] its owner tied it with a rein, or locked [the stall] before it properly, and it went out and damaged, whether it is a *tam* or a *muad*, he is liable; [these are] the words of R' Meir. R' Yehudah says: [The owner of] a *tam* is liable; [the owner of] a *muad* is exempt, as it is said (*Exodus* 21:36): *and its owner does not watch it,* and this one is watched. R' Eliezer says: No

YAD AVRAHAM

רַבִּי יְהוּדָה אוֹמֵר: תָּם חַיָּב; — *R' Yehudah says: [The owner of] a tam is liable;*
[If the animal is a *tam*, its owner is liable for half the damages.]
וּמוּעָד פָּטוּר, שֶׁנֶּאֱמַר: "וְלֹא יִשְׁמְרֶנּוּ בְעָלָיו", וְשָׁמוּר הוּא זֶה. — *[the owner of] a muad is exempt, as it is said (Exodus 21:36): 'and its owner does not watch it,' and this one is watched.*

This verse, stated regarding a *muad*, implies that as long as the owner watches it, even inferiorly, he is exempt. The intention is that he is exempt from the extra half of the damages, for which the owner of a *muad* is usually liable over the owner of a *tam*. He is, however, liable for the first half of the damages for which the owner of a *tam* would also be liable *(Rav from Gem.* 45b).

R' Yehudah reasons that the liability of a *muad* cannot be more lenient than that of a *tam*. We cannot say that when the animal becomes a *muad*, its owner should no longer be obligated to pay when it is watched inferiorly. Therefore, we must say that the lenient ruling for *muad* applies only to the other half of the damages. Since the full damages usually paid by the owner of a *muad* consists of a combination of the half damages of the *tam* and the additional half of the *muad* — in our case, the *muad's* owner must pay half the damages, just as one pays for damage done by a *tam (Tos. Yom Tov* from *Tos.* 45b).

Unlike R' Meir, R' Yehudah maintains that even had the Torah not instructed us concerning the guarding of a bull, the average bull would be watched by its owner in any case. Therefore, when Scripture requires a *tam* to be watched, the intention is that this be done in a superior manner. When the Torah requires a *muad* to be watched, a still more superior guarding is meant. This is known as רִבּוּי אַחַר רִבּוּי, *an amplification after an amplification,* and the rule is that such a sequence is actually intended to limit the details of the law being discussed. Therefore, the watching required for the *muad* — i.e., in order to exempt its owner from being liable for the second half of damages — is limited to an inferior method of guarding. Although we should exegetically compare the watching required of the *tam* to that required of the *muad,* as discussed above, and require an inferior guarding for the *tam* as well as for the *muad*, R' Yehudah holds that the phrase וְלֹא יִשְׁמְרֶנּוּ בְעָלָיו, *and its owner does not watch it,* is a limitation, telling us that this inferior method of guarding suffices only for a *muad*. This is implied by the suffix נּוּ, *it,* limiting the implication of the verse to a *muad.* [As explained above, the *muad's* owner is still liable for half the damages unless he watches the animal superiorly.] A *tam,* however, requires a superior method of guarding [in order to exempt its owner from liability for half the damages] *(Tos. Yom Tov* from *Gem.* 45b).

בבא קמא ה/א

רַבִּי אֱלִיעֶזֶר אוֹמֵר: אֵין לוֹ שְׁמִירָה אֶלָּא סַכִּין.

[א] **שׁוֹר** שֶׁנָּגַח אֶת־הַפָּרָה וְנִמְצָא עֻבָּרָהּ בְּצִדָּהּ, וְאֵין יָדוּעַ אִם־עַד שֶׁלֹּא נְגָחָהּ יָלָדָה, אִם־מִשֶּׁנְּגָחָהּ יָלָדָה מְשַׁלֵּם חֲצִי נֶזֶק לַפָּרָה וּרְבִיעַ נֶזֶק לַוָּלָד.

יד אברהם

— רַבִּי אֱלִיעֶזֶר אוֹמֵר: אֵין לוֹ שְׁמִירָה אֶלָּא סַכִּין. R' Eliezer says: No guarding it is sufficient [lit., it has no guarding] except the knife.

The only method of properly guarding a *muad* is by slaughtering it (Rav).

Even if the owner watched it in a superior manner — e.g., locking it in a stall with a strong door — and it knocked down the wall and went out and damaged, he is liable (Rashi).

Accordingly, we have three variant views: R' Meir rules that with an inferior guarding, the owner is always liable; with a superior guarding, he is always exempt. R' Yehudah contends that with an inferior guarding of a *muad*, the owner is exempt from the second half of the damages, but is liable for the first half. Only if he watches it superiorly is he exempt from the first half as well. The same applies to the half-damage payment of the *tam*. R' Eliezer rules that, even with a superior-type guarding of a *muad*, its owner is liable for its damages.

The halachah is in accordance with the view of R' Yehudah. Nevertheless, as soon as an animal becomes a *muad* it is a *mitzvah* to slaughter it in order to prevent it from damaging (Rav, based on Rashi and Rambam Commentary).

Meiri, too, writes that, as regards payment, the halachah is in accordance with R' Yehudah's opinion; but, as regards fulfilling one's obligation to Heaven, the halachah follows the view of R' Eliezer.

The *Gemara* (46a) explains that R' Eliezer considers having a *muad* in one's possession similar to raising a vicious dog or standing a shaky ladder in his house, which are prohibited by the verse (*Deut.* 22:8): וְלֹא תָשִׂים דָּמִים בְּבֵיתֶךָ, *You shall not place blood in your house.*

Although — for the same reason — it would seem that if one digs a pit, it should not be sufficient for him merely to cover it; he should be required to eliminate it completely by filling it with earth, the law is not so. This is because covering a pit is a better safeguard than any method of guarding an animal that is a *muad*. Alternatively, R' Eliezer's statement was not said with regard to the payment for damages. He meant only that it is a *mitzvah* upon the owner of the *muad* to rid himself of the animal. The same would apply to one who digs a pit. It is a *mitzvah* for him to fill the pit with earth and eliminate it completely. However, even if he merely covers it in a proper manner, and an animal falls into the pit, he is not liable (*Tos. Yom Tov*).

Chapter 5

1.

The following mishnah continues to elaborate on the laws of the *tam*.

שׁוֹר — [If] *a bull* [That is, *a tam*, whose owner normally pays half the damages it causes.]

משניות / בבא קמא — פרק ה: שור שנגח את הפרה [98]

5
1

guarding it is sufficient except the knife.

1. [If] a bull gores a cow and its fetus is found at its side, and it is not known whether it gave birth before it was gored, [or] whether it gave birth after it was gored, [the owner of the bull] pays for half the damage [done] to the cow and for one-fourth of the damage [done] to the young.

YAD AVRAHAM

שֶׁנָּגַח אֶת־הַפָּרָה — *gores a cow*
And the cow was pregnant (*Rav*).

וְנִמְצָא עֻבָּרָהּ בְּצִדָּהּ, — *and its fetus is found at its side*,
The cow's fetus was found dead at its side (*Rav; Rashi*).

וְאֵין יָדוּעַ אִם־עַד שֶׁלֹּא נְגָחָהּ יָלָדָה, — *and it is not known whether it gave birth before it was gored,*
In which case the calf did not die because of the goring (ibid.), and the owner of the bull need not pay for the fetus (*Meiri*).

אִם־מִשֶּׁנְּגָחָהּ יָלָדָה. — [*or*] *whether it gave birth after it was gored,*
In which case the cow aborted its fetus because of the goring (*Rav; Rashi*), and, therefore, the owner of the bull must pay for the fetus (*Meiri*).

The mishnah deals with a case in which witnesses had seen the goring from a distance. Later, they approached the cow and found it dead with a dead calf at its side, and they do not know if the cow died before or after giving birth (ibid.).

מְשַׁלֵּם חֲצִי נֶזֶק לַפָּרָה — [*the owner of the bull*] *pays for half the damage* [*done*] *to the cow*
The owner of the bull pays half the damages for the cow in accordance with the laws governing a *tam* (ibid.).

וּרְבִיעַ נֶזֶק לַוָּלָד. — *and for one-fourth of the damage* [*done*] *to the young.*
Since the owner of a *tam* pays half the damages, and in this case, it is doubtful whether there is any liability for the young, he is liable only for half that amount — i.e., one-fourth of the value of the fetus. This mishnah follows the view of Sumchos, who maintains that in any dispute involving money in which neither of the disputants can prove conclusively that he is in the right, the money is divided equally between them. The Sages, however, contend that such cases are subject to a כְּלָל גָּדוֹל, an all-inclusive principle: הַמּוֹצִיא מֵחֲבֵרוֹ עָלָיו הָרְאָיָה, *the burden of proof lies on the one who seeks to exact something from the other* (3:11). The expression, *all-inclusive principle,* alludes to the case in which the damagee claims with certainty that the money is owed him, and the damager replies only that perhaps it is not so. Even in such a case, the damagee must bring proof that his claim is true. Consequently, the owner of the bull is liable only for the cow — which we are certain was injured — not for the calf, regarding whose injury we are in doubt (*Rav* from *Gem.* 46a; see *Tif. Yis.*).

Tiferes Yisrael adds that even Sumchos, who holds that the half-damage payment is to be shared, rules so only if the calf is known to have been born dead, since such a situation prompts the obvious question of when the calf was born, and hence, if the owner of the bull is liable for it. Should there be any doubt concerning that, even Sumchos concurs with the Sages that the burden of proof lies on the damagee, because the question of liability is not an obvious one (see *Bava Metzia* 2b, *Tos.* ad loc.).

[99]   THE MISHNAH/BAVA KAMMA — Chapter Five: *Shor SheNagach*

בבא קמא
ה/ב

וְכֵן, פָּרָה שֶׁנָּגְחָה אֶת־הַשּׁוֹר וְנִמְצָא וְלָדָהּ בְּצִדָּהּ, וְאֵין יָדוּעַ אִם־עַד שֶׁלֹּא נָגְחָה יָלְדָה אִם־מִשֶּׁנָּגְחָה יָלְדָה, מְשַׁלֵּם חֲצִי נֶזֶק מִן־הַפָּרָה וּרְבִיעַ נֶזֶק מִן־הַוָּלָד.

[ב] **הַקָּדָר** שֶׁהִכְנִיס קְדֵרוֹתָיו לַחֲצַר בַּעַל

יד אברהם

וְכֵן, פָּרָה — Likewise, [if] a cow
That was known to have been pregnant (Meiri).

שֶׁנָּגְחָה אֶת־הַשּׁוֹר וְנִמְצָא וְלָדָהּ בְּצִדָּהּ, — gores a bull and its young is found at its side,
Witnesses saw the goring from a distance and then approached the cow and found a live calf at its side (ibid.).
Since the calf was born alive, the term וָלָד, young, is used rather than the term עֻבָּר, fetus, as in the first part of the mishnah (Tos. Yom Tov). Although the mishnah states רְבִיעַ נֶזֶק לַוָּלָד, one-fourth of the damages [done] to the young even in the first case, the intention there is: the fetus that could possibly have been born as a viable calf (Tif. Yis.).

וְאֵין יָדוּעַ אִם־עַד שֶׁלֹּא נָגְחָה יָלְדָה — and it is not known whether it gored before it gave birth
In which case the cow was pregnant at the time of the goring, and the fetus — as part of the goring cow — is pledged to pay for the damage if the mother is not available (Rav).

אִם־מִשֶּׁנָּגְחָה יָלְדָה, — or whether it gored after it had given birth,
In which case the calf did not participate in goring, and is not pledged to pay for the damage (ibid.).

מְשַׁלֵּם חֲצִי נֶזֶק מִן־הַפָּרָה — the [owner of the cow] pays half the damages from the cow
If the cow is available, the owner must pay half the damages, in accordance to the law of *tam*, whose owner pays 'from the body' of the animal that did the damage [see preface to 4:1] (Rav from Gem. 46b).

וּרְבִיעַ נֶזֶק מִן־הַוָּלָד. — or a fourth of the damages from the young.
If the cow is not available, the damagee cannot collect his full half-damage payment 'from the body' of the young, since it is not known definitely that the latter participated in the goring. He therefore collects — according to Sumchos' view — one-fourth of the damages 'from the body' of the young (Rav from Gem. 47a).

The same applies if the cow does not suffice to pay half the damages inflicted on the bull. If it is known definitely that the cow had not yet given birth when it gored, the damagee collects the balance from the calf. In our case, however, since there is doubt whether the calf was born before or after the goring, he collects only half the balance from the calf, following the opinion of Sumchos (Tos. Yom Tov).

Accordingly, the mishnah does not follow R' Akiva's view [see preface to 4:1] that the damagee and the damager become partners in the body of the goring animal, for, according to him, they both share any increase or depreciation in its value. Hence, the damagee, too, would suffer a loss if the cow is not available, even if the calf is. Rather, the mishnah follows R' Yishmael's opinion that the damagee is a creditor to whom the body of the goring animal is pledged. Consequently, in this case, if the cow gored before giving birth, the calf is pledged to pay the debt as well as the cow (Tos. 47a, as explained by Tos. R' Akiva, Kol Haremez, and Beis David).

We have heretofore explained the mishnah according to Rava. Abaye, however, interprets it as referring to a case in which the cow belongs to one

5:2

Likewise, [if] a cow gores a bull and its young is found at its side, and it is not known whether it gored before it gave birth or whether it gored after it had given birth, [the owner of the cow] pays half the damages from the cow or a fourth of the damages from the young.

2. [If] a potter brings his pots into another's yard

YAD AVRAHAM

person and the fetus to another. [This can occur, for example, if someone sells another his cow, but does not include the fetus in the sale *(Rashi)*.] Consequently, were we to know definitely that the goring took place before the birth, the damagee — who is entitled to half the damages, as in every case in which a *tam* gored — could collect one-fourth of the damages from the owner of the cow and one-fourth from the owner of the fetus, since the two animals were partners in the goring. However, because we do not know definitely when the goring occurred, the damagee can collect only one-eighth of the damage from the owner of the fetus, in keeping with Sumchos' ruling. Hence, the mishnah is construed as meaning that the damagee collects a fourth of the damages [which is *one-half* of what he is entitled to] from the owner of the cow, and one-eighth of the damages [which is *one-fourth* of what he is entitled to] from the owner of the calf *(Gem.* 46b).

According to Abaye, the mishnah does not mean literally that the owner of the calf would pay one-fourth of the damages if we know definitely that it was born after the goring, and one-eighth in this case in which we are unsure, since the calf — which was then a fetus — obviously did not participate

in the goring in the same measure as its mother. Rather, the mishnah means that the owner of the calf must pay one-fourth of the damages done by it. The cow and calf are each considered to have done the part of the damage proportionate to its value. For example, if the cow is worth eighty *zuz* without the fetus, and was worth one hundred *zuz* with the fetus [so that the latter's value is twenty percent of the total], and the damage done was two hundred *zuz* — making the half-damage payment one hundred — were the calf definitely born after the goring, the damagee would take the entire cow and the calf. Since there is a doubt, however, the damagee takes the entire cow and one-half the calf, a share equaling ten *zuz (Tos.* 46b, s.v. ורביע).

This ruling, that the damagee can collect from something no longer part of the gorer, applies only to the case of the fetus. Should a ram butt and cause damage, however, the damagee cannot collect from the wool which will eventually be shorn, since that is not deemed part of the ram's body. The same applies to the fourfold and fivefold payments for stealing and slaughtering or selling, discussed in chapter 7: the thief pays fourfold the value of the sheep without its wool *(Tif. Yis.).*

2.

הַקַּדָּר שֶׁהִכְנִיס קְדֵרוֹתָיו לַחֲצַר בַּעַל הַבַּיִת שֶׁלֹּא בִרְשׁוּת, וּשְׁבָרָתַן בְּהֶמְתּוֹ שֶׁל-בַּעַל הַבַּיִת — פָּטוּר; — [If] *a potter brings his pots into another's* [lit., *a householder's*] *yard without permission, and the other person's animal breaks them, he is exempt;*

The owner of the yard claims, 'Who

בבא קמא ה/ג

הַבַּיִת שֶׁלֹּא בִרְשׁוּת, וּשְׁבָרָתַן בְּהֶמְתּוֹ שֶׁל־בַּעַל הַבַּיִת, פָּטוּר; וְאִם־הֻזְּקָה בָּהֶן, בַּעַל הַקְּדֵרוֹת חַיָּב. וְאִם־הִכְנִיס בִּרְשׁוּת, בַּעַל הֶחָצֵר חַיָּב.

הִכְנִיס פֵּרוֹתָיו לַחָצֵר בַּעַל הַבַּיִת שֶׁלֹּא בִרְשׁוּת, וַאֲכָלָתַן בְּהֶמְתּוֹ שֶׁל־בַּעַל הַבַּיִת, פָּטוּר; וְאִם־הֻזְּקָה בָּהֶן, בַּעַל הַפֵּרוֹת חַיָּב. וְאִם־הִכְנִיס בִּרְשׁוּת, בַּעַל הֶחָצֵר חַיָּב.

[ג] **הִכְנִיס** שׁוֹרוֹ לַחֲצַר בַּעַל הַבַּיִת שֶׁלֹּא בִרְשׁוּת, וּנְגָחוֹ שׁוֹרוֹ שֶׁל־בַּעַל הַבַּיִת, אוֹ שֶׁנְּשָׁכוֹ כַּלְבּוֹ שֶׁל־בַּעַל הַבַּיִת, פָּטוּר. נָגַח הוּא שׁוֹרוֹ שֶׁל־בַּעַל הַבַּיִת, חַיָּב. נָפַל לְבוֹרוֹ

יד אברהם

permitted you to enter and bring your pots into my yard?' (Meiri).

וְאִם־הֻזְּקָה בָּהֶן — if it is injured by them,
An animal belonging to the owner of the yard is injured by the pots (ibid.).

בַּעַל הַקְּדֵרוֹת חַיָּב — the owner of the pots is liable.
He must pay for the damage done to the animal, because the pots are a *toladah* of *bor* [pit] as are all obstacles (ibid.).

וְאִם־הִכְנִיס בִּרְשׁוּת — If he brings [them] in with permission,
[The owner of the yard permitted the potter to bring pots into his yard.]

בַּעַל הֶחָצֵר חַיָּב — the owner of the yard is liable.
He is responsible if the pots are damaged while they are in the yard. Since he permits the potter to bring in his pots, it is tantamount to accepting responsibility to watch them even from being damaged by the wind, and surely from being damaged by his own animals. The potter, however, accepts no responsibility, and is therefore exempt if the animal belonging to the

owner of the yard is injured by his pots. Only if he enters without permission is he liable (*Tos. Yom Tov* from *Gem.*, following the view of *Rava*).

The mishnah continues by telling us that these same laws apply also to a case involving produce instead of pots.

הכניס פרותיו לחצר בעל הבית שלא ברשות, ואכלתן בהמתו של בעל הבית, פטור. — [If] one brings his produce into another's yard without permission, and the other person's animal eats them, he is exempt;
[The owner of the yard is exempt from paying for the produce his animal consumed.]

ואם־הזקה בהן — if it is injured by them,
[An animal belonging to the owner of the yard is injured by the produce.]

בַּעַל הַפֵּרוֹת חַיָּב — the owner of the produce is liable.
This applies only if the animal slipped on the produce and fell. However, should the animal continue eating the fruit until it dies [from overeating (*Rashi*)], the owner of the fruit is exempt, since it should not have eaten them (*Rav* from *Gem.* 47b).

משניות / בבא קמא — פרק ה: **שור שנגח את הפרה** [102]

without permission, and the other person's animal breaks them, he is exempt; if it is injured by them, the owner of the pots is liable. If he brings [them] in with permission, the owner of the yard is liable.

[If] one brings his produce into another's yard without permission, and the other person's animal eats them, he is exempt; if it is injured by them, the owner of the produce is liable. If he brings [them] in with permission, the owner of the yard is liable.

3. [I]f] one brings his bull into another's yard without permission, and the other person's bull gores it, or the other person's dog bites it, he is exempt. [If] it gores the other person's bull, [the owner of the goring bull] is liable. [If] it falls into his

YAD AVRAHAM

The intention is that since the animal knowingly brought harm to itself, the owner is not liable (*Tos. Yom Tov* from *Tos.*).

Since the owner of the yard is frequently there, he should have prevented his animal from overeating (*Rosh*).

ואם־הכניס ברשות, — *If he brings [them] in with permission,*

[He brings in the produce with permission of the owner of the yard.]

בַּעַל הֶחָצֵר חַיָּב. — *the owner of the yard is liable.*

[He is responsible for any damage done to the produce while they are in the yard.]

The mishnah gives us this additional example of a case involving fruits to teach us that not only in the case of the pots, which are very fragile and easily broken, do we assume that if the owner of the yard allowed the potter to bring them in, he is thereby accepting responsibility for any damage done to them [otherwise, he would not have agreed to let them in], but even in the case of the fruits, which are not so easily broken, we assume the same (*Tos. Yom Tov* from *Tos.* 47a).

3.

הַכְנִיס שׁוֹרוֹ לַחֲצַר בַּעַל הַבַּיִת שֶׁלֹּא בִרְשׁוּת, וּנְגָחוֹ שׁוֹרוֹ שֶׁל־בַּעַל הַבַּיִת, אוֹ שֶׁנְּשָׁכוֹ כַּלְבּוֹ שֶׁל־בַּעַל הַבַּיִת, פָּטוּר. — *[If] one brings his bull into another's yard without permission, and the other person's bull gores it, or the other person's dog bites it, he is exempt.*

Although the dog is wont to bite any stranger entering the yard, the owner is not required to take him away when someone enters without permission (*Tif. Yis.*).

[The same ruling applies if the dog bites a man who enters without permission (see *Gem.* 33a).]

נָגַח הוּא שׁוֹרוֹ שֶׁל־בַּעַל הַבַּיִת, חַיָּב. — *[If] it gores the other person's bull, [the owner*

בבא קמא ה/ג

וְהִבְאִישׁ מֵימָיו, חַיָּב. הָיָה אָבִיו אוֹ בְנוֹ לְתוֹכוֹ, מְשַׁלֵּם אֶת־הַכֹּפֶר. וְאִם־הִכְנִיס בִּרְשׁוּת, בַּעַל הֶחָצֵר חַיָּב.

רַבִּי אוֹמֵר: בְּכֻלָּן אֵינוֹ חַיָּב עַד־שֶׁיְּקַבֵּל עָלָיו לִשְׁמֹר.

יד אברהם

of the goring bull] is liable.

That is, if the outsider's animal gores the one belonging to the owner of the yard, the outsider is liable for the damages — if his bull is a *tam*, for half the damages; if a *muad*, for the full damages. According to R' Tarfon, even the owner of a *tam* pays for the full damage if it was done in the premises of the damagee [see 2:5] *(Tos. Yom Tov).*

נָפַל לְבוֹרוֹ — [*If] it falls into his pit*
[The intruding animal falls into a pit or cistern in the yard.]

וְהִבְאִישׁ מֵימָיו — *and makes its water foul,*
The animal's body is soiled with mud or dung, and it makes the water foul immediately upon falling in *(Meiri from Gem. 48b).*

חַיָּב. — *he is liable.*
[The animal's owner is liable for the damage done to the water.]
This is considered a direct damage, falling under the category of *regel* [see General Introduction], and the owner of the animal is therefore liable. However, should it die in the pit and make the water foul with its odor, its owner is exempt. This is because the carcass, lying in its place, is then analogous to a *bor* [pit], and the water — being inanimate — is analogous to vessels, as are all inanimate objects, and *bor* is exempt for damages to vessels, as discussed in the commentary to 3:2 *(Tif. Yis. from Gem.).*

Meiri points out that even if the animal makes the water foul with the mud or dung on its body, if it does not do so immediately upon falling, it is deemed a *bor*, and the owner is not liable for making the water foul.

הָיָה אָבִיו אוֹ בְנוֹ לְתוֹכוֹ, — [*If] his father or his son was in it,*
The father or the son of the owner of the yard was in the pit [and the animal fell on him and killed him *(Meiri)*]. The same applies to strangers, but the mishnah chooses to speak of a usual case *(Rav from Gem. 48b).*

מְשַׁלֵּם אֶת־הַכֹּפֶר. — *he pays ransom.*
This animal had become a *muad* by casting itself upon people in pits three times. This time it saw an herb growing at the mouth of the pit and, in an attempt to obtain it, fell upon the person there and killed him. The animal is not liable to death since it killed its victim unintentionally, but the owner is liable for the payment of ransom, as explained in the commentary to 4:6 *(Rav).*

Just as in 4:6, this case, too, must be qualified as referring to an animal which had killed three gentiles or three people suffering from fatal organic ailments. Otherwise, it would have been liable to stoning after the first time it killed a person. However, unlike the earlier mishnah, we cannot qualify this case as referring to an animal that fled to the fields after each killing, since, in this case, it had to be lifted out of the pit each time. We must also explain this mishnah to mean that the bull saw the herb only the fourth time, but not the first three, similar to *Rav's* explanation in 4:6, so that the first three times were done with the intention to kill, and the fourth time for its own pleasure. The difficulties involved in this explanation

5 3 pit and makes its water foul, he is liable. [If] his father or his son was in it, he pays ransom. But if he brings [it] in with permission, the owner of the yard is liable.

Rabbi says: In no case is he liable unless he accepts to watch.

YAD AVRAHAM

were discussed in the commentary to that mishnah. A simpler interpretation is that of *Tosafos* — that the animal did not become a *muad* by killing three people, but that this act of attempting to obtain an herb growing at the mouth of a pit belongs under the category of *shen* [tooth] for which an animal is considered a *muad* from the outset [see 1:4] *(Tos. Yom Tov).*

The above qualification follows Rav [the Talmudic sage]. Shmuel, however, qualifies the mishnah as referring to a *tam*, and is following the view of R' Yose the Galilean, who rules that a *tam* pays half-ransom. Ulla goes further, maintaining that the mishnah follows the views of both R' Yose the Galilean and R' Tarfon, who rules that the owner of a *tam* pays in full for damages done in the premises of the damagee. Consequently, if a *tam* kills the owner of the premises, its owner is liable for the full ransom *(Gem. 48b).*

וְאִם־הִכְנִיס בִּרְשׁוּת, — *But if he brings [it] in with permission,*

[The outsider brings his animal into the other person's yard with the latter's permission.]

בַּעַל הֶחָצֵר חַיָּב — *the owner of the yard is liable.*

He is liable both for injuries to the animal, and for ransom if the animal should kill anyone *(Tif. Yis.).*

The *Tanna* gives us this example involving a bull, although it is similar to the two cases in the previous mishnah which dealt with pottery and produce, to illustrate that if the owner gives permission to bring something into his yard, it means that he accepts responsibility for it — not only in the case of vessels, which break easily, and produce which spoils easily, but even in the case of an animal *(Tos. Yom Tov from Tos.).*

רַבִּי אוֹמֵר: — *Rabbi says:*

[This refers to R' Yehudah HaNassi — R' Judah the Prince — (135-219 C.E.), redactor of the Mishnah, who was reverently referred to as רַבִּי, *Rabbi* — i.e., the teacher par excellence, and *Rabbeinu Hakadosh* (our Holy Teacher).]

בְּכֻלָּן אֵינוֹ חַיָּב — *In no case is he liable*

In none of the three cases discussed in this mishnah and the previous one is the owner of the yard responsible for what the outsider brings in even if he gives him permission to enter *(Meiri).*

עַד־שֶׁיְּקַבֵּל עָלָיו — *unless he accepts*

[That is, unless he explicitly accepts upon himself the responsibility to watch what is being brought in.]

לִשְׁמֹר. — *to watch.*

Therefore, if one brings in his animal with the permission of the owner of the yard, but without his explicit acceptance of responsibility, each of them is exempt from paying the other for any damages — the owner of the yard is exempt, since he did not accept responsibility; the outsider, since he brought in his articles with permission *(Rav).*

Although the outsider should be liable if his animal gored the one belonging to the owner of the yard, in which case each one is liable for damages of *keren* (horn; see General Introduction) — in this case, when the owner of the yard grants the other

בבא קמא ה/ד

[ד] **שׁוֹר** שֶׁהָיָה מִתְכַּוֵּן לַחֲבֵרוֹ וְהִכָּה אֶת־הָאִשָּׁה, וְיָצְאוּ יְלָדֶיהָ, פָּטוּר מִדְּמֵי וְלָדוֹת. וְאָדָם שֶׁהָיָה מִתְכַּוֵּן לַחֲבֵרוֹ וְהִכָּה אֶת־הָאִשָּׁה, וְיָצְאוּ יְלָדֶיהָ, מְשַׁלֵּם דְּמֵי וְלָדוֹת. כֵּיצַד מְשַׁלֵּם דְּמֵי וְלָדוֹת? שָׁמִין אֶת־הָאִשָּׁה כַּמָּה הִיא יָפָה עַד־שֶׁלֹּא יָלְדָה וְכַמָּה הִיא יָפָה מִשֶּׁיָּלְדָה. אָמַר רַבָּן שִׁמְעוֹן בֶּן־גַּמְלִיאֵל: אִם־כֵּן, מִשֶּׁהָאִשָּׁה יוֹלֶדֶת, מַשְׁבַּחַת! אֶלָּא, שָׁמִין אֶת־

יד אברהם

person permission to bring in his animal, it is as though each one exempts the other from any liability (*Tos. Yom Tov* from *Maggid Mishneh*, quoting *Tos.*).

Rosh, however, rules that, according to Rabbi, if the outsider enters with permission, he is liable for the damages caused by his pots, produce, or animals. *Maharsha* maintains that *Tosafos* concur with this ruling. *Tos. R' Akiva*, however, contends that *Tosafos* rule that the outsider is liable only for damages caused but not for those caused passively by his pots or produce, since he did not accept responsibility for the animal belonging to the owner of the yard.

The halachah is in accordance with Rabbi's view (*Rav; Rambam, Commentary* and *Hil. Nizkei Mamon* 7:5; *Rif; Rosh*).

4.

The following mishnah deals with one who strikes a pregnant woman, causing her to abort her child, and delineates the damages for which the perpetrator is liable. It is based on *Exodus* 21:22: *If men quarrel and strike a pregnant woman, and her children come out, and there is no harm, he shall surely be punished as the husband of the woman imposes upon him, and he shall give by the sentence of the judges.*

שׁוֹר שֶׁהָיָה מִתְכַּוֵּן לַחֲבֵרוֹ וְהִכָּה אֶת־הָאִשָּׁה, — [*If*] *a bull aims for another bull and strikes a woman,*

[It intended to gore another animal, but instead struck a pregnant woman.]

וְיָצְאוּ יְלָדֶיהָ, — *causing her to abort* [lit., *and her children come out*],

[Because of the blow, she miscarried.]

פָּטוּר — [*its owner*] *is exempt*

[The owner of the bull is exempt.]

מִדְּמֵי וְלָדוֹת. — *from* [*paying*] *the value of the fetus.*

In fact, even if the animal intended to strike the woman, the owner is still exempt from paying for the fetus, because the Torah did not impose such a payment on the owner of an animal that causes a woman to miscarry, only upon a human being that does so. Nevertheless, the mishnah states the case of one animal aiming for another in order to contrast it with the case of the man who aims for another man, but instead strikes a pregnant woman, in which case he *is* liable for the value of the fetus (*Rav* from *Gem.* 49a).

In the *Gemara* (42a), we find a dispute between two *Tannaim* regarding the origin of this ruling. R' Akiva derives it from the beginning of the verse cited in the preface: וְכִי יִנָּצוּ אֲנָשִׁים, *If men quarrel.* This denotes that the liability discussed in the verse deals only

4. [I]f] a bull aims for another bull and strikes a woman, causing her to abort, [its owner] is exempt from [paying] the value of the fetus. But [if] a person aims for another person and strikes a woman, causing her to abort, he pays the value of the fetus.

How does one pay the value of the fetus? We appraise how much the woman was worth before giving birth and how much she is worth since she gave birth. Said Rabban Shimon ben Gamliel: If so, when the woman gives birth, she increases in value!

YAD AVRAHAM

with men, not animals. Should an animal gore a woman and cause her to miscarry, the owner is exempt. R' Yose the Galilean, however, derives this from a phrase in verse 28: וּבַעַל הַשּׁוֹר נָקִי, *and the owner of the bull is quit.* He explains this to mean that the owner of the bull is quit from paying the value of the fetus (see *Tos. Yom Tov* and *Tos. R' Akiva*).

וְאָדָם שֶׁהָיָה מִתְכַּוֵּן לַחֲבֵרוֹ וְהִכָּה אֶת־הָאִשָּׁה, וְיָצְאוּ יְלָדֶיהָ, מְשַׁלֵּם דְּמֵי וְלָדוֹת — *But [if] a person aims for another person and strikes a woman, causing her to abort, he pays the value of the fetus.*

[If he intends to strike another person, but instead strikes a pregnant woman, he pays the value of the fetus to the husband, as stated in verse 22.]

כֵּיצַד מְשַׁלֵּם דְּמֵי וְלָדוֹת? — *How does one pay the value of the fetus?*

[How do we compute its value?]

The *Gemara* [49a] explains this to mean: How do we compute the value of the fetus and the enhancement of her body due to the pregnancy? (*Tos. Yom Tov*). [Until very recently, stout women were considered healthier and more attractive than thin women.]

שָׁמִין אֶת־הָאִשָּׁה כַּמָּה הִיא יָפָה עַד־שֶׁלֹּא יָלְדָה — *We appraise how much the woman was worth before giving birth*

This appraisal includes both the value of the fetus and the enhanced value of the woman, who looks bigger and stouter because of her pregnancy (*Tos. Yom Tov* from *Rashi* 49a).

וְכַמָּה הִיא יָפָה מִשֶּׁיָּלְדָה — *and how much she is worth since she gave birth.*

That is, had she given birth normally, without being wounded. The injury inflicted upon her body, however, is a damage which, according to R' Yehudah ben Beseirah [*Kesubos* 6:1], is shared by the husband and wife. When the injury is in a hidden place, two-thirds of the payment belongs to her, and one-third to him; when it is in a revealed place, two thirds belong to him; and one third to her (*Rashi*). *Rambam* [*Hil. Chovel* 4:1] differentiates between the two cases. He rules that only in the case in which a woman is maimed in one of her limbs and her ability to work is impaired does the husband receive a share of the payment. In our case, however, in which the injury she sustains does not impair her ability to work, she receives the entire payment, with the exception of the payment for her inability to work during the time she is laid up after her injury (*Tos. Yom Tov* from *Sma, Choshen Mishpat* 423:2).

אָמַר רַבָּן שִׁמְעוֹן בֶּן־גַּמְלִיאֵל: אִם־כֵּן — *Said Rabban Shimon ben Gamliel: If so,*

If we appraise the woman in this manner, the perpetrator will pay nothing (*Rav*).

מִשֶּׁהָאִשָּׁה יוֹלֶדֶת, מַשְׁבַּחַת! — *when the woman gives birth, she increases in value!*

[107]   THE MISHNAH/BAVA KAMMA – Chapter Five: *Shor SheNagach*

בבא קמא ה/ד

הַוְּלָדוֹת כַּמָּה הֵן יָפִין, וְנוֹתֵן לַבַּעַל; וְאִם אֵין לָהּ בַּעַל, נוֹתֵן לְיוֹרְשָׁיו. הָיְתָה שִׁפְחָה וְנִשְׁתַּחְרְרָה, אוֹ גִיּוֹרֶת, פָּטוּר.

יד אברהם

Since a pregnant woman is in danger of dying in childbirth, her value [which is determined by how much she could be sold for as a bondwoman] is decreased. When she gives birth and is no longer subject to that danger, her value increases. [These changes in her value balance each other out.] Therefore, there should be no payment (Rav). The Gemara explains that Rabban Shimon ben Gamliel's contention applies only to a woman expecting her first child. In subsequent pregnancies, however [when she is less likely to die of childbirth], Rabban Shimon ben Gamliel agrees that her value is increased by her pregnancy. He rules that the husband and wife share the increase (Tos. Yom Tov from Gem. 49a). The halachah is not in accordance with the view of Rabban Shimon ben Gamliel (Rambam Commentary; Tur 423; see Tos. Yom Tov to Eruvin 8:7).

אֶלָּא, שָׁמִין אֶת־הַוְּלָדוֹת כַּמָּה הֵן יָפִין — Rather, we appraise how much the fetus was worth.

[It is appraised independently of the woman.]

We compute its value by determining how much a person would pay for it prior to birth. Others maintain that the amount is reckoned by determining how much one would be willing to pay — were this woman his slave — that she not abort her fetus (Meiri). Rambam (Hil. Chovel Umazzik 4:2) and Chiddushei HaRavad (p. 134) rule that its value is the difference between the value of the woman before the miscarriage and after it. [The intention probably is: How much one would pay for her as a slave with the prospect of acquiring her child as a slave as well.]

וְנוֹתֵן לַבַּעַל — and he gives [it] to the husband;

This is in accordance with the phrase (Exodus 21:22): בַּאֲשֶׁר יָשִׁית עָלָיו בַּעַל הָאִשָּׁה, as the husband of the woman imposes upon him. The intention is that the husband is awarded the value of the fetus (Rashi).

This sentence is not part of Rabban Shimon ben Gamliel's statement; it is an anonymous opinion in the mishnah which maintains that the value of the fetus is awarded to the husband. As stated above, the first, anonymous Tanna rules that the increase in the value of the woman, too, is awarded to the husband. He bases his ruling on the Torah's wording (ibid.) וְנָגְפוּ אִשָּׁה הָרָה, and strike a pregnant woman. From the words that follow this phrase — וְיָצְאוּ יְלָדֶיהָ, and her children come out — it is obvious that the woman was pregnant. We therefore construe the verse to be telling us that the increase in the woman's value because of the pregnancy is awarded to the husband. Rabban Shimon ben Gamliel, however, maintains that since the pregnancy was caused by both the husband and the wife, they share the increase it caused in her value. He interprets the superfluous word הָרָה, pregnant, as teaching us that the one who struck her is liable only if he strikes her on a part of the body which affects the fetus, not on the hand or foot, which does not (Tos. Yom Tov from Gem.).

וְאִם אֵין לָהּ בַּעַל, נוֹתֵן לְיוֹרְשָׁיו — if she has no husband, he gives [it] to his heirs.

The one who injured the woman must pay her husband's heirs (Tif. Yis.). Should the husband have died prior to the incident, Rambam (Hil. Chovel 4:2) rules that the woman is awarded the value of the fetus. Tosafos (49a) and Ravad (loc. cit.) rule that, even in that case, the husband's heirs are awarded

5 4

Rather, we appraise how much the fetus was worth, and he gives [it] to the husband; if she has no husband, he gives [it] to his heirs. [If] she had been a slave who was freed, or a proselyte, he is exempt.

YAD AVRAHAM

the value of the fetus.

הָיְתָה שִׁפְחָה וְנִשְׁתַּחְרְרָה — [If] she had been a slave who was freed,

The injured woman had been a gentile slave who belonged to a Jew and was freed [thereby attaining the status of a full-fledged Jewess]. She was married to a proselyte or to a gentile slave who belonged to a Jew and was freed [who likewise becomes a full-fledged Jew], and the husband died [after the injury to his wife] (Rav).

אוֹ גִיּוֹרֶת, — or a proselyte,

She was a proselyte woman married to a freed slave or to another proselyte, and her husband died (Rav from Gem. 49a).

פָּטוּר. — he is exempt.

The one who caused the miscarriage is exempt from paying for the fetus, because it belongs to the husband, and the latter has no heirs.[1]

Actually, the same applies to a natively Jewish woman married to a proselyte or to a freed slave. The Tanna, however, chooses the usual case of a female freed slave or a proselyte because the women normally marry their male counterparts (Rav; Tos. 42b; Rashi 49a).

The mishnah's use of the expression, שִׁפְחָה וְנִשְׁתַּחְרְרָה, a slave who was freed, rather than מְשֻׁחְרֶרֶת, a freed slave, indicates that she was recently freed or proselytized and had no children born to her as a Jewess (Rashi 49a; Tos. 42b). [Should she have children born to her and this husband when they were already Jews, the children would be her husband's heirs and inherit the value of the fetus.]

If she was a slave at the time of the pregnancy and miscarriage, the value of the fetus belongs to her owner, since the child would have belonged to him had it been born (Tos. from Riva 42b).

Rambam (Hil. Chovel 4:4) adds that if the woman had been a Jewish-owned slave or a free gentile at the time of the fetus' conception, but had been freed or proselytized before the miscarriage, the value of the fetus belongs to her.

Should the husband die before the miscarriage, there is a controversy in the Gemara whether the perpetrator is exempt — as in the case that the miscarriage took place during the husband's lifetime — or whether the woman is entitled to the value of the child. The halachah is in accordance with the latter view (Rambam ibid., §3), which is Rabbah's opinion in the Gemara. Rosh, however, follows R' Chisda's view, that the perpetrator is exempt. Rambam (ibid. §2) extends this ruling to include a case in which the husband was a native Jew who died prior to the miscarriage. He rules that the woman is entitled to the value of the child although the husband left heirs, because the Torah states: כַּאֲשֶׁר יָשִׁית עָלָיו בַּעַל הָאִשָּׁה, as the husband of the woman imposes upon him, which implies that the husband has rights to the fetus only if he was alive at the time of the miscarriage (Maggid Mishneh). Ravad disagrees.

---

1. A proselyte is considered completely severed from his gentile relatives and, consequently, has no heirs other than his children (Yevamos 22a). In this case he had no children, as explained below. A wife does not inherit her husband's estate (Rambam, Hil. Nachalos 1:8). The only method to ensure that she acquires his property following his death is by the husband giving it to her as a gift while he is still alive (see there 6:5).

בבא קמא
ה/ה

[ה] הַחוֹפֵר בּוֹר בִּרְשׁוּת הַיָּחִיד וּפְתָחוֹ לִרְשׁוּת הָרַבִּים, אוֹ בִּרְשׁוּת הָרַבִּים וּפְתָחוֹ לִרְשׁוּת הַיָּחִיד, בִּרְשׁוּת הַיָּחִיד וּפְתָחוֹ לִרְשׁוּת הַיָּחִיד אַחֵר, חַיָּב.

יד אברהם

5.

From here until the end of the chapter, the *Tanna* elaborates on the laws of בּוֹר, *bor* (the pit) — for which pits one is liable, and under what circumstances.

הַחוֹפֵר בּוֹר בִּרְשׁוּת הַיָּחִיד וּפְתָחוֹ לִרְשׁוּת הָרַבִּים, — [If] one digs a pit in a private domain and opens it into a public domain,

He dug a hole in a public domain and extended it on a downward slant until it ended under his property, or he dug a pit in his property and then dug a passageway into it from the public domain, and subsequently closed the opening in his property. In either case, the opening is in the public domain, and the pit itself is in a private domain (*Meiri*).

The mishnah's ruling — that he is liable — surely applies if he digs a pit in a public domain and opens it into a public domain. It cannot be that the *Tanna* rules that the one who digs the pit is liable only if the pit is in his own domain, but not if it is completely in a public domain, since the latter part of the mishnah states: [If] *one digs a pit in a public domain ... he is liable* (*Tos. Yom Tov from Rashi*).

The rule is that we view the pit according to its opening. It is deemed as though that is the site of the pit (*Tos. Yom Tov from Tos.* 49b).

אוֹ בִּרְשׁוּת הָרַבִּים וּפְתָחוֹ לִרְשׁוּת הַיָּחִיד, — or [if he digs it] in a public domain and opens it into a private domain,

The description of this pit is exactly the opposite of the one in the first case. In this instance, the passersby cannot fall into the pit unless they enter his property (*Meiri*).

As mentioned above, this is deemed a pit in a private domain. The digger is liable only if he abandons his ownership of the area surrounding the pit, allowing the public to walk in close proximity to it. Otherwise, the owner of the pit can say to the damagee: 'What were you doing in my property?' (*Rashi*).

Tosafos comment that if the owner of the land digs a pit abutting the public domain, although the pit is in his own property, he is liable just as if he had abandoned his property surrounding the pit. *Rashi*, however, specifies that the owner abandoned his property, since he explains the case to be that the opening of the pit was in the middle of the private domain. Consequently, he is liable only if he abandons his property surrounding the pit (*Tos. Yom Tov*).

בִּרְשׁוּת הַיָּחִיד וּפְתָחוֹ לִרְשׁוּת הַיָּחִיד אַחֵר, — [or if he digs it] in a private domain and opens it into another private domain,

Although neither the pit nor the opening is in a public domain, the digger is nevertheless liable if he abandons his ownership of the property surrounding the opening of the pit (*Rav*; *Rashi*).

Accordingly, we render: into another private domain, not: into another's private domain, although that would be more correct grammatically. [The correct grammatical form for this meaning would be אַחֶרֶת, *another*, since it is an adjective modifying רְשׁוּת, *domain*. Indeed, this is *Rav's* version.] The intention is that he opens the pit into another part of his own property

משניות / בבא קמא — פרק ה: שור שנגח את הפרה   [110]

5. [If] one digs a pit in a private domain and opens it into a public domain, or [if he digs it] in a public domain and opens it into a private domain, [or if he digs it] in a private domain and opens it into another private domain, he is liable.

YAD AVRAHAM

and abandons the surrounding area. Although the mishnah could have expressed the same idea in brief by stating: *If he digs in a private domain*, the *Tanna* chooses this expression to conform with the other instances mentioned in the mishnah, in which the base of the pit is in one domain and the opening in another.

Another interpretation of our version of the mishnah is possible: he dug the pit in his property and opened it into another person's property. This teaches us that although the property is closed to the public, the digger is nevertheless liable for endangering the owner of the other property and his livestock *(Tos. Yom Tov* from *Tos.).*

Nimmukei Yosef comments that the digger is liable only until the owner of the other property discovers the pit. Once he discovers it, however, the digger is liable only for the damage done to the property. The owner is then required to fill up the hole; if he does not, he is liable for any damages it causes *(Tos. Yom Tov).*

חַיָּב. — *he is liable.*

[The *Tanna* of the mishnah maintains that the Torah holds the digger of a pit liable for any damages it causes whether it is in his property or in the public domain.] As long as it opens into a place accessible to the damagee.

הַחוֹפֵר בּוֹר בִּרְשׁוּת הָרַבִּים, וְנָפַל לְתוֹכוֹ שׁוֹר אוֹ חֲמוֹר וָמֵת, חַיָּב. — [If] *one digs a pit in a public domain, and a bull or a donkey falls into it and dies, he is liable.*

[As stated in mishnah 7, the same applies to any animal. The mishnah is merely using the examples given in the Torah *(Ex.* 21:33), which mentions only the most common cases.]

Unlike one's chattels, a pit that he digs in public property does not belong to him. He is liable for it — not because it is his property — but because he created it. The *Gemara* (49b) derives this from a superfluous expression in the section dealing with pits. The Torah (loc. cit.) states: וְכִי־יִפְתַּח אִישׁ בּוֹר אוֹ כִּי־יִכְרֶה אִישׁ בֹּר, *If a man opens a pit or if a man digs a pit* .... The Rabbis reason: If he is liable for opening a covered pit which someone else dug, is it not obvious that he is liable for digging a pit himself? Rather, Scripture teaches us that he is liable for a pit he dug, even if it is not in his property, because he created an obstacle in the public domain by digging or opening it *(Tos. Yom Tov).*

This is one of the two cases in which the Torah regarded something that is not owned by a person as if it were. The other instance is that of one's *chametz* on the afternoon of Erev Pesach, the fourteenth of Nissan, which — although benefit may not be derived from it, thereby rendering it ownerless — he is responsible to destroy [see *Pesachim* 1:4] *(Gem.* 29b, *Rashi* ad loc.).

⇃§ Liability for a Pit

When one digs a deep pit, he creates two types of damagers. By lowering the base of the pit, he creates the potential for a death-dealing blow to anyone who falls into his pit. He also creates foul air which is capable of killing anyone that falls into it. In the *Gemara* (50b), we find a controversy between Rav and Shmuel. Rav's view is that the Torah imposed liability upon one who creates a pit in public property only if the victim is injured by the foul air caused by it. If, however, he was injured by

בבא קמא ה/ה

הַחוֹפֵר בּוֹר בִּרְשׁוּת הָרַבִּים, וְנָפַל לְתוֹכוֹ שׁוֹר אוֹ חֲמוֹר וָמֵת, חַיָּב. אֶחָד הַחוֹפֵר בּוֹר, שִׁיחַ, וּמְעָרָה, חֲרִיצִין, וּנְעִיצִין, חַיָּב. אִם־כֵּן, לָמָּה נֶאֱמַר ,,בּוֹר"? מַה־בּוֹר שֶׁיֵּשׁ בּוֹ כְּדֵי לְהָמִית — עֲשָׂרָה טְפָחִים, אַף כָּל־

יד אברהם

the blow of the fall, the digger is not liable since it is considered that the publicly owned ground caused the damage.

Shmuel contends that the Torah imposed liability for the foul air — although it forms by itself — and surely for the blow, which the digger creates directly.

The *Gemara* explains that, in practical law, the opinions of Rav and Shmuel would differ in the case of one who makes a mound on public property, and an animal walks up the mound and falls from it, killing or injuring itself.[1] According to Shmuel, he is liable for the damage; according to Rav, he is exempt. We will explain the following segment of the mishnah according to both opinions.

אֶחָד הַחוֹפֵר בּוֹר, — Whether one digs a pit,

The *Gemara* (50b) defines בּוֹר as a round and narrow pit (*Rav*). In such a pit, the air is very foul and capable of killing its victim (*Tos. Yom Tov* from *Gem.*).

שִׁיחַ, — a trench,

That is, a long and narrow pit (*Rav; Rashi*).

Although it is long, there is still foul air in it (*Gem.* loc. cit.).

וּמְעָרָה, — a cave,

Although it is quadrangular [and, consequently more airy than the first two], it still has foul air (*Tos. Yom Tov* from *Gem.*).

חֲרִיצִין, — quadrangular pits,

These are wide and square like caves, but completely open, without a cover (*Rav; Rashi*).

Although they are wide and uncovered, they still have foul air that can asphyxiate one who falls into them (*Tos. Yom Tov* from *Gem.*).

Others define חֲרִיצִין as pits narrow at the top and wide at the bottom (*Rabbeinu Chananel; Aruch*).

וּנְעִיצִין — or wedge-like ditches,

That is, narrow at the base and wide at the top (*Rav, Rashi* from *Gem.*).

Although they are wider at the top, such ditches — which are ten handbreadths deep — have in them air foul enough to asphyxiate those who fall into them (*Tos. Yom Tov* from *Gem.*).

חַיָּב. — he is liable.

[The one who dug or opened any of these types of pit is liable for the damages caused by it.]

We have explained the mishnah's reason for listing the various types of pits into which one may fall and be killed or injured. This reasoning follows the view of Rav, who rules that the Torah imposed liability on the creator of a pit for the foul air generated by it. According to Shmuel, however, who

---

1. [The *Gemara* does not give the case of an animal falling into the pit and breaking its neck, because — as explained by *Talmid Rabbeinu Peretz* (quoted by *Shitah Mekubetzes*) and *Ravad* see below) — even in such an instance, it is not obvious that it was solely the blow that caused the injury. Had there been no foul air in the pit, the animal would have been able to position itself and fall in a manner in which it would not have been harmed. The foul air, however, caused it to be dizzy, and it therefore broke its neck.]

משניות / בבא קמא — פרק ה: שור שנגח את הפרה   [112]

5 [If] one digs a pit in a public domain, and a bull or a donkey falls into it and dies, he is liable.

Whether one digs a pit, a trench, a cave, quadrangular pits, or wedge-like ditches, he is liable. If so, why is *pit* stated? [To teach us that] just as a pit is deep enough to cause death — [being] ten

YAD AVRAHAM

rules that the Torah imposed liability for the foul air, and surely for the blow of falling, it is obvious that one is liable for any type of pit into which an animal can fall and be injured or killed by the blow. Why, then, did the *Tanna* enumerate all these types of pits?

One solution suggested is that Shmuel qualifies the mishnah as dealing with a pit full of pads of wool, in which the victim cannot be injured by the blow, but only by the foul air. Therefore, the same reasons for listing the various types of pits according to Rav apply according to Shmuel as well *(Ravad; Rashba).*

Ravad suggests further that were it not for the foul air of the pit, an animal falling with its legs downward would be able to protect itself by its abdomen and its legs, and would not fracture its spine or burst its belly. However, since the foul air makes it dizzy and sick, it cannot gain its balance. Hence, the mishnah must tell us that, among the various types of pits, even the airier ones have air foul enough to accomplish this. [Other explanations will be discussed further in the mishnah.]

אִם־כֵּן, לָמָה נֶאֱמַר ,,בּוֹר"? — *If so, why is 'pit' stated?*

Since one is liable for all types of excavations — trenches, ditches, etc. — why did the Torah [*Ex.* 21:33] specify only *pit*? *(Beis David).*

Others explain that this does not present any difficulty, since, in the language of the Scripture, all these excavations are included in the word בּוֹר. Rather, the mishnah's question is why the word בּוֹר is repeated in the verse *(Shoshannim LeDavid; Kol Haremez).*

מַה־בּוֹר שֶׁיֵּשׁ בּוֹ כְּדֵי לְהָמִית — עֲשָׂרָה טְפָחִים, — [*To teach us that*] *just as a pit is deep enough to cause death* — [*being*] *ten handbreadths,*

That is, the usual pit is ten handbreadths deep [the amount required to cause death] *(Rav; Rashi).*

This is measured from the base of the pit to its opening *(Tos. Yom Tov).*

Tosafos (Sanhedrin 45a) question this in light of the various pits mentioned in Scripture — e.g., the pit into which Joseph was cast (*Gen.* 37:24); the pit into which Jeremiah was cast (*Jer.* 38:6); and the pit that Ishmael, the son of Nethaniah, filled with corpses (ibid. 41:7). All these were probably much deeper than ten handbreadths. [In the first two instances, because if not, they could have easily climbed out; in the last instance, because so many corpses would not have fit into less.] Rashi *(Sanhedrin* ad loc.) explains that a pit is *at least* ten handbreadths deep *(Tos. Yom Tov).*

Rabbeinu Tam suggests that the word בּוֹר usually denotes a very deep pit, one from which it is virtually impossible to emerge alive. We would therefore think that one is liable only for such a pit. To avoid this misimpression the Torah states (*Ex.* 21:34): וְהַמֵּת יִהְיֶה־לּוֹ, *and the dead one shall be his,* implying that the minimum depth of a pit for which the digger is liable is one that can be expected to cause death, although it *is* possible for the victim to escape death — that is, a pit of ten handbreadths *(Tos.* 3a and to *Sanhedrin* loc. cit.).

[113] THE MISHNAH/BAVA KAMMA — Chapter Five: *Shor SheNagach*

בבא קמא ה/ו שֶׁיֵּשׁ בּוֹ כְּדֵי לְהָמִית — עֲשָׂרָה טְפָחִים. הָיוּ פְּחוּתִין מֵעֲשָׂרָה טְפָחִים, וְנָפַל לְתוֹכוֹ שׁוֹר אוֹ חֲמוֹר וָמֵת, פָּטוּר; וְאִם־הֻזַּק בּוֹ, חַיָּב.

[ו] בּוֹר שֶׁל־שְׁנֵי שֻׁתָּפִין, עָבַר עָלָיו הָרִאשׁוֹן וְלֹא כִסָּהוּ, וְהַשֵּׁנִי וְלֹא כִסָּהוּ, הַשֵּׁנִי

יד אברהם

אַף כָּל — *so is everything*
That is, so is every type of excavation.
According to Shmuel, this refers to a mound in the public domain (*Gem.* 50b).

שֶׁיֵּשׁ בּוֹ כְּדֵי לְהָמִית — עֲשָׂרָה טְפָחִים. — *that is deep enough to bring about death —* [being] *ten handbreadths.*

[I.e., all these excavations must be ten handbreadths deep for liability; according to Shmuel, the mound must be ten handbreadths high for liability.]

Shmuel maintains that all types of excavations ten handbreadths deep can be derived from the word בּוֹר, *a pit*, since they all have the same properties to kill those who fall into it because of the impact of the fall. Accordingly, the mishnah merely wishes to list the various types of excavations; it is listing not because we would believe that one type is liable and another is exempt. According to Rav, however, since certain types of excavations have less foul air, they are not included in the word בּוֹר; rather we must derive them from it through a בִּנְיָן אָב, *general principle*.[1] The *Gemara* therefore seeks reasons for the mishnah's stating all types of excavations, since one would apparently suffice to teach us all of them (*Tos. Rabbeinu Peretz*).

הָיוּ פְּחוּתִין מֵעֲשָׂרָה טְפָחִים, וְנָפַל לְתוֹכוֹ שׁוֹר אוֹ חֲמוֹר וָמֵת, פָּטוּר; — [*If*] *they are less than ten handbreadths* [*deep*], *and a bull or a donkey fell into it and died, he is exempt;*

According to Rav, the mishnah needs no explanation, since there is no deadly air in a pit less than ten handbreadths deep. According to Shmuel, however, the mishnah is construed as referring to an animal rolling into the pit. There must therefore be a depth of ten handbreadths for it to die (see below). Should the animal be walking, however, and then fall into the pit, we measure the distance from the animal's belly when it was standing above the pit to the bottom of the pit. If there are ten handbreadths, the blow would have been sufficient to kill it (*Gem.* 51a; *Ramah*, cited by *Tur Choshen Mishpat* 410; see also *Rif, Ravad, Tur, Beis Yosef, Rosh, Meiri*).

According to *Tur, Rosh* follows the view of Rav. *Shulchan Aruch* (ibid. §17), however, following *Rambam* (*Hil. Nizkei Mamon* 12:14), rules in accordance with Shmuel's opinion. They do not, however, quote the conclusion of the *Gemara*, that if the animal is standing when it falls into the pit, we measure from its belly to the bottom of the pit.

The Torah exempts the digger of a pit less than ten handbreadths deep if an animal dies in it, since it is considered a freak accident. The digger was not required to think that perhaps an animal would die by falling into his pit (*Rambam, Hil. Nizkei Mamon* 12:15; *Sma* 410:16; *Tif. Yis.*). *Rabbeinu Yehonasan* (quoted in *Shitah Mekube-*

---

1. [This is one of the thirteen hermeneutical rules by which the Torah is expounded: A general principle derived from one case is applied to all cases that logically appear to be similar (see *ArtScroll Siddur, Ashkenaz* ed., p. 50; and *Gateway to the Talmud*, p. 136).]

משניות / בבא קמא — פרק ה: שור שנגח את הפרה [114]

5
6

handbreadths, so is everything that is deep enough to bring about death — [being] ten handbreadths. [If] they are less than ten handbreadths [deep], and a bull or a donkey fell into it and died, he is exempt; if it is injured, he is liable.

6. [I]f] a pit belongs to two partners [and] the first one passes by it and does not cover it, and the second one [passes by] and does not cover it, the

YAD AVRAHAM

tzes) explains that the pit could not have caused the death of the animal. It must have been the misfortune of the animal's owner that caused it to die suddenly.

Should the depth of the pit not exceed its width, in which case there is no foul air, then, even if the pit is ten handbreadths deep and the animal dies, he is exempt. Should it die because of the blow, however, he is liable [according to Shmuel] (*Tif. Yis.* from *Shulchan Aruch* 410:17).

וְאִם הֻזַּק בּוֹ, חַיָּב. — *if it is injured, he is liable.*

Injuries are common in pits of any depth or mounds of any height (*Tos. Yom Tov* from *Rambam, Hil. Nizkei Mamon* 12:15).

Should the animal die, some authorities rule that the digger of the pit is liable for damages up to the point of death. *Meiri*, however, rules that he is completely exempt. *Rabbeinu Yehonasan* (quoted by *Shitah Mekubetzes*) rules that if the animal breaks a leg and dies from the fracture, the perpetrator is liable for the fracture but not for the death. Likewise, if the animal suffers no fractures but is slowly dying, he is liable for the damages up to the point of death.

6.

בּוֹר שֶׁל־שְׁנֵי שֻׁתָּפִין — [*If*] *a pit belongs to two partners*

This law is applicable if two partners own a yard in which there is a pit, and they make the yard ownerless but retain the pit (*Gem.* 51a). Should they make the pit ownerless as well, there is no liability, since they dug it when it was in the midst of their property and not exposed to the public, and now it is no longer theirs (*Tos. Yom Tov*).

It is also applicable in the case of a pit in a public domain, which had been nine handbreadths deep, and two men dug out another handbreadth, thereby making it ten handbreadths deep. In this case, both become partners in the pit and share the liability for the death or injury of an animal that falls into it.

This is true according to the Sages, who maintain that whether the animal which fell into such a pit died or merely injured itself, the one who dug the first nine handbreadths is exempt. According to Rabbi, however, who contends that, in the case of injury, all who participated in the digging of the pit are liable, the mishnah could be qualified as dealing with a pit which was partially dug by one person and completed by another; both are liable for the injury of a bull that falls therein (*Gem.* ibid.).

This law is not applicable, however, if two people appoint a third person to dig a pit for them, since in such a case it is the agent — and not they — who is liable for it in accordance with the principle of אֵין שָׁלִיחַ לִדְבַר עֲבֵרָה, *there is no agent in matters of sin* (*Tos. R' Akiva* from *Gem.*).

עָבַר עָלָיו הָרִאשׁוֹן וְלֹא כִסָּהוּ, וְהַשֵּׁנִי וְלֹא

[115]   THE MISHNAH/BAVA KAMMA — Chapter Five: *Shor SheNagach*

בבא קמא ה/ו

חַיָּב. כִּסָּהוּ הָרִאשׁוֹן, וּבָא הַשֵּׁנִי וּמְצָאוֹ מְגֻלֶּה וְלֹא כִסָּהוּ, הַשֵּׁנִי חַיָּב.

כִּסָּהוּ כָּרָאוּי, וְנָפַל לְתוֹכוֹ שׁוֹר אוֹ חֲמוֹר וָמֵת, פָּטוּר. לֹא כִסָּהוּ כָּרָאוּי, וְנָפַל לְתוֹכוֹ שׁוֹר אוֹ חֲמוֹר וָמֵת, חַיָּב.

נָפַל לְפָנָיו מִקּוֹל הַכְּרִיָה, חַיָּב; לְאַחֲרָיו מִקּוֹל

יד אברהם

כִּסָּהוּ, הַשֵּׁנִי חַיָּב. — [and] the first one passes by it and does not cover it, and the second one [passes by] and does not cover it, the second one is liable.

This ruling applies only if the first partner hands over the cover of the pit to the second one when he leaves, and then the second partner does not cover the pit (Rav from Gem. 51b Rashi ad loc.).

Should the first partner leave the second one using the pit, and not give him the cover, they are both responsible. This ruling is based on the principle of בְּרֵרָה, selection, which dictates that when jointly owned property is used by one of the partners, it is considered as if the part that he is using belongs entirely to him at that time. It is not considered as if he is borrowing the partner's share of that part. Consequently — in our case — if the partner does not cover the pit, he is responsible only for his own share, not for his partner's. However, if he had been given the cover by the first partner, it is as if he had undertaken to watch the partner's share as well, and, if he does not cover the pit, he is liable for the entire damages (Tos. Yom Tov from Rashi ibid.; see Nedarim 5:1 and ArtScroll commentary ad loc., p. 101).

כִּסָּהוּ הָרִאשׁוֹן — [If] the first one covers it,

The first partner covered the pit after using it (Rashi).

וּבָא הַשֵּׁנִי — and the second one comes

The second partner comes to use it (ibid.).

וּמְצָאוֹ מְגֻלֶּה — and finds it uncovered

For example, the cover became worm-eaten and broke (ibid.).

וְלֹא כִסָּהוּ, הַשֵּׁנִי חַיָּב. — and does not cover it, the second one is liable.

The second partner alone is liable until the first one learns of the deterioration of the cover and has time to hire workers and to cut trees and make a new one. From then on, if an animal is killed by falling into the pit, both partners are liable (Tos. Yom Tov from Gem. 52a).

This follows the view of Rambam (Hil. Nizkei Mamon 12:7) Ravad (ad loc.), however, rules that the time limit is as long as it usually takes the first partner to learn of the deterioration by returning to the pit and to hire workers and make a new cover. According to Tosafos, the limit is until he is actually notified and given time to hire workers, etc.

The second partner — who finds the pit uncovered — however, is not given that period of time to cover it; rather, he should arrange for someone to watch the pit until he can have a new cover made (Rashi). Others contend that the second partner is given the same period of time as the first, except — of course — that he need not be notified, since he sees the pit uncovered (Tos.).

כִּסָּהוּ כָּרָאוּי — [If] he covers it properly,

[This is a new case, and applies to any pit, not only one belonging to two partners.]

וְנָפַל לְתוֹכוֹ שׁוֹר אוֹ חֲמוֹר וָמֵת — and a bull or a donkey falls into it and dies,

5 6 second one is liable. [If] the first one covers it, and the second one comes and finds it uncovered and does not cover it, the second one is liable.

[If] he covers it properly, and a bull or a donkey falls into it and dies, he is exempt. [If] he does not cover it properly, and a bull or a donkey falls into it and dies, he is liable.

[If] it fell forward because of the sound of digging,

YAD AVRAHAM

For example, the cover of the pit became rotten from the inside [so that the owner was unaware of it (*Tif. Yis.*)], and a bull or a donkey fell into the pit (*Rav* from *Gem.* 52a).

Tos. Yom Tov adds that, according to the conclusion of the *Gemara*, even if he used a cover sufficiently strong to support bulls, but not camels, although camels were common in that section, we do not say that because he was negligent as regards camels, he is also considered negligent with regard to the decay of the cover. This is because the cover would have decayed even if it had been strong enough to support camels. Therefore, if a bull or donkey fell in, he is exempt. Since the mishap did not occur because of his negligence, we do not apply the rule of תְּחִלָּתוֹ בִּפְשִׁיעָה וְסוֹפוֹ בְּאֹנֶס, חַיָּב, *if in the beginning there was negligence, and at the end there was an accident, he is liable* [see commentary to 2:3, s.v. מִפְּנֵי]. This is *Rambam's* view (*Hil. Nizkei Mamon* 12:5). Some construe the *Gemara* as meaning that he covered it with a weak cover — one that would give way should camels step on it. This is, however, not considered negligence as regards bulls, since, if it caves in, a bull with his full faculties will not go there, as discussed at the end of this mishnah. However, should he cover it with a cover that will not fall in when trodden by camels, but will merely become weakened, so that it will fall in if bulls tread on it, this is considered negligence as regards bulls, and if it decays from the inside and a bull falls in, he is liable (*Tos. Yom Tov, Tif. Yis.* from *Tur* 410).

פָּטוּר — *he is exempt.*

Since the Torah (*Ex.* 21:33), with regard to a pit, specifies: וְלֹא יְכַסֶּנּוּ, *and he does not cover it,* the implication is that if one covers it properly, he is exempt from damages caused by it (*Tos. Yom Tov* from *Gem.* 55b).

לֹא כִסָּהוּ כָּרָאוּי, וְנָפַל לְתוֹכוֹ שׁוֹר אוֹ חֲמוֹר וָמֵת, חַיָּב. — [*If*] *he does not cover it properly, and a bull or a donkey falls into it and dies, he is liable.*

As explained above, this refers to the case in which he used a cover that can support bulls but not camels, although the latter are common in that area. Then, camels trod on the cover and weakened it, making it vulnerable for bulls. Later, a bull passed on the weakened cover and fell in. According to the opinion of *Tur,* mentioned above, even if the cover had also been weakened by worms, and then a bull walked over it and fell in, he is liable since he was guilty of negligence as regards bulls, because they could have fallen in after it was weakened by the camels (*Tif. Yis.*).

נָפַל לְפָנָיו — [*If*] *it fell forward*

The animal fell into the pit (*Rav* from *Gem.* 53a).

This is in accordance with *Shmuel,* who rules that the Torah imposed liability upon the digger of a pit both for its foul air and for the blow of falling into it. Therefore, as long as the animal fell *forward* — i.e., into the pit — and was injured or killed, the digger is liable. According to *Rav,* however, the intention is that the animal fell head first, thus becoming asphyxiated by the foul air in the pit (*Gem.* 52b-53a).

מִקּוֹל הַכְּרִיָּה, — *because of the sound of digging,*

בבא קמא ה/ו

הַבְּרִיָה, פָּטוּר. נָפַל לְתוֹכוֹ שׁוֹר וְכֵלָיו וְנִשְׁתַּבְּרוּ, חֲמוֹר וְכֵלָיו וְנִתְקָרְעוּ, חַיָּב עַל־הַבְּהֵמָה, וּפָטוּר עַל־הַכֵּלִים. נָפַל לְתוֹכוֹ שׁוֹר חֵרֵשׁ, שׁוֹטֶה, וְקָטָן, חַיָּב. בֵּן אוֹ בַת, עֶבֶד אוֹ אָמָה, פָּטוּר.

יד אברהם

The pit had already been dug out, and someone entered it to widen it or deepen it. The animal, standing on the edge of the pit, heard the noise of the digging, became startled, and fell into the pit (*Rashi; Meiri*).

חַיָּב — **he is liable;**

Since it fell because of the noise of the digging, we might think that the liability no longer lies on the original digger of the pit, but that it is considered the negligence of the one whose digging startled the animal, and that even he should be exempt, since he, too, was only an indirect cause of the injury. The mishnah therefore teaches us that since the animal is found in the pit belonging to the original digger, he is liable (*Rav* from *Rashi*).

The *Gemara* attributes this ruling to R' Nassan, who maintains that when two persons commit a damage, if one cannot be made liable for it, the other must pay the damages (*Tos. Yom Tov*).

לְאַחֲרָיו מִקּוֹל הַכְּרִיָה, — **backward because of the sound of digging,**

The animal, while standing at the edge of the pit, stumbled because of the noise made by the digger and fell backwards, outside the pit (*Rav*).

פָּטוּר. — **he is exempt.**

Since the injured animal did not fall into the pit, and the digger was only an indirect cause of the damage, no one is liable (*Rav*). As mentioned above, this follows the view of Shmuel, who rules that the Torah imposed liability upon the digger of a pit both for its foul air and for the blow of falling into it. Accordingly, there is no difference how the bull falls into the pit — there is liability in either case. The mishnah's exemption applies only if the bull fell outside of the pit. Rav, however, explains that even if the animal fell into the pit, if it fell backwards — i.e., with its head up, so that it did not become asphyxiated by the foul air — no one is liable for the damages (*Gem.* 52b-53a).

נָפַל לְתוֹכוֹ שׁוֹר וְכֵלָיו וְנִשְׁתַּבְּרוּ, — **[If] an ox**[1] **with its trappings falls into it and they break,**

An ox with its yoke and plowshare falls into the pit, and the implements break (*Rav; Rashi*).

חֲמוֹר וְכֵלָיו וְנִתְקָרְעוּ, — **or a donkey with its trappings and they tear,**

This refers to the donkey's packsaddle or the bundle of clothes it is carrying (*Rav; Rashi*).

Alternatively, it refers to the reins (*Tif. Yis.*).

חַיָּב עַל־הַבְּהֵמָה, וּפָטוּר עַל־הַכֵּלִים. — **he is liable for the animal, but exempt for the trappings.**

[Should the animal die or be injured, the digger of the pit is liable for the damages, as discussed above. Regardless of what happens to the animal, however, he is exempt for the trappings that are broken or torn.]

The *Gemara* (53b) derives this from the words (*Ex.* 21:33), וְנָפַל שָׁמָּה שׁוֹר אוֹ חֲמוֹר, **and a bull or a donkey falls therein.** The implication is that he is liable for *a bull* [i.e., an animal], but not

---

1. [Since the subject here is obviously a draft animal, we have translated שׁוֹר as *ox*.]

משניות / בבא קמא — פרק ה: **שור שנגח את הפרה** [118]

5, 6

he is liable; backward because of the sound of digging, he is exempt.

[If] an ox with its trappings falls into it and they break, or a donkey with its trappings and they tear, he is liable for the animal, but exempt for the trappings.

[If] a bull that was deaf, foolish, or young falls into it, he is liable; a male child or a female child, a male slave or a female slave, he is exempt.

YAD AVRAHAM

for a man; or for a *donkey*, but not for vessels *(Rav)*.

This derivation is based on the fact that the verse could have merely stated: *and someone falls therein*. Since the Torah chooses to elaborate, it is apparent that the intention is to exclude certain things, for which the digger of the pit is exempt. In the case of man, he is exempt only if the person dies, since Scripture's case deals with an animal that dies, as specified in verse 34. Should a person be injured, however, the digger of the pit is liable. In the case of vessels, on the other hand, even if they are damaged and not completely broken, he is exempt, since even the partial breakage of vessels is analogous to death. Therefore, that damage is excluded from the liability of a pit *(Tos. Yom Tov* from *Gem.* 53b, 54a).

נָפַל לְתוֹכוֹ שׁוֹר חֵרֵשׁ, שׁוֹטֶה, וְקָטָן — [If] *a bull that was deaf, foolish, or young falls into it,*

The same would apply to a blind bull, or one walking at night *(Tif. Yis.* from *Gem.* 54b).

חַיָּב — *he is liable;*

However, should a bull in full possession of its senses, walking by day, fall into a pit, the digger of the pit is exempt, since he can claim that the animal should have watched where it was going (Rav, Tos. Yom Tov from Gem. ad loc.).

בֵּן אוֹ בַת, עֶבֶד אוֹ אָמָה, פָּטוּר — *a male child or a female child, a male slave or a female slave, he is exempt.*

[These, too, are included by the term שׁוֹר, *a bull,* in the verse cited above.]

Although children are incapable of being cautious not to fall into pits, the digger of the pit is nevertheless exempt for damages to them; surely, if an adult fell into the pit and died, the owner is exempt *(Rashi)*.

Since gentile slaves are considered chattels of their owners, we would think that they are not excluded from the liability of a pit as are other humans. Indeed, we find that, although the owner of an animal is exempt from paying the value of the fetus should it cause a woman to abort (mishnah 4), it is nevertheless liable for the value of the fetus whose mother is a gentile slave, since she is a chattel *(Tos. R' Akiva)*.

Another reason for thinking that one should be liable for a slave is that slaves are called עַם הַדּוֹמֶה לַחֲמוֹר, *the people that are like donkeys (Gem.* 49a, based on *Gen.* 22:5), as regards their pedigree. Therefore, we would think that they are not excluded by the word *bull* in *Exodus* 21:33 *(Tif. Yis.; Lechem Shamayim; Shoshannim LeDavid).*

Since the following mishnah teaches us that all creatures owned by masters are included in the law of a pit, we would think that this applies to slaves as well, although they are human *(Tos. Yom Tov).*

To refute these theories, the mishnah tells us that the digger of a pit is exempt if a slave dies by falling into it, since this

[119] THE MISHNAH/BAVA KAMMA — Chapter Five: *Shor SheNagach*

בבא קמא ה/ז

[ז] אֶחָד שׁוֹר וְאֶחָד כָּל־בְּהֵמָה לִנְפִילַת הַבּוֹר, וּלְהַפְרָשַׁת הַר סִינַי, וּלְתַשְׁלוּמֵי כֶפֶל, וְלַהֲשָׁבַת אֲבֵדָה, לִפְרִיקָה, לַחֲסִימָה, לְכִלְאַיִם,

יד אברהם

is indeed included in the interpretation of verse 33. The probable reason that slaves are not included in the next mishnah's categorization of creatures with masters is that the mishnah refers only to animals whose masters are called בְּעָלִים, as alluded to in the verse (loc. cit., v. 34) concerning pit. The master of a slave, however, is referred to as אָדוֹן (ibid.).

The *Gemara* (9b) states that should a man die in a pit, the one who dug it is exempt from ransom. *Tosafos* (ad loc.) derive this from the phrase (ibid., v. 30)

אִם־כֹּפֶר יוּשַׁת עָלָיו, *A ransom shall be imposed upon him*, referring to the case of a goring bull, not that of a pit. Nevertheless, the interpretation of the word *bull*, which excludes man, is required to exempt the owner of a pit if a gentile slave is killed by it. *Rashba* (ibid.) suggests that since there are instances in which one is liable for the value of the slave although he is exempt from paying ransom, two verses are necessary: one to exempt him for the ransom, and the other to exempt him for paying for the slave's value.

7.

The following mishnah illustrates that, although Scripture (*Ex.* 21:33) states only that the owner of a pit is liable if a bull or a donkey falls into it, this liability actually applies to all animals. The same is true of many other passages which specify bulls, oxen, donkeys or cattle.

This is based mainly on two Biblical passages, both in the Decalogue, concerning the commandments to abstain from work on the Sabbath. The Torah interdicts not only personally performing labor on the Sabbath, but also leading an animal to perform labor, such as guiding an ox pulling a plowshare. This prohibition is first stated in *Exodus* 20:10: ... לֹא־תַעֲשֶׂה כָל־מְלָאכָה אַתָּה וּבִנְךָ וּבִתֶּךָ עַבְדְּךָ וַאֲמָתְךָ וּבְהֶמְתֶּךָ, *You shall do no work — neither you, your son, your daughter, your male slave, your female slave, nor your cattle*....

It is also stated in *Deuteronomy* 5:14. There it is worded: וְשׁוֹרְךָ וַחֲמֹרְךָ וְכָל־ בְּהֶמְתֶּךָ, *nor your ox, your donkey, nor any of your cattle*.

The *Gemara* comments that the term בְּהֵמָה, *cattle*, often includes beasts as well. The word וְכָל, *any*, serves to include fowl in this interdict. We find that the words, וְשׁוֹרְךָ וַחֲמֹרְךָ, *your ox, your donkey*, in the second Decalogue as well as the word וּבְהֶמְתֶּךָ, *your cattle*, in the first Decalogue, are superfluous. From these words, we derive that, in certain other instances mentioned in the Torah, all animals are included although they are not stated specifically.

אֶחָד שׁוֹר וְאֶחָד כָּל־בְּהֵמָה לִנְפִילַת הַבּוֹר, — *A bull and all other animals are alike as regards falling into a pit*,

Although the Torah states (*Ex.* 21:33): וְנָפַל שָׁמָּה שׁוֹר אוֹ חֲמוֹר, *and a bull or a donkey fall therein*, it also says (v. 34): כֶּסֶף יָשִׁיב לִבְעָלָיו, *he shall give money to its owner*, which is interpreted to mean that any creature that has an owner is included in these laws — i.e., the owner of a pit is liable if one of them is killed by falling into it (*Rav* from *Gem.* 54b).

וּלְהַפְרָשַׁת הַר סִינַי, — *separation from Mt. Sinai*,

When the Torah was given, people and animals were forbidden to approach

7. A bull and all other animals are alike as regards falling into a pit, separation from Mt. Sinai, the twofold payments, returning a loss, unloading, muzzling, *kilayim*, and the Sabbath. The same

YAD AVRAHAM

the mountain *(Tif. Yis.)*. Scripture *(Ex. 19:13)* warns that anyone who does so — אִם־בְּהֵמָה אִם־אִישׁ לֹא יִחְיֶה, *whether cattle or man, he shall not live.* בְּהֵמָה, *cattle*, includes wild beasts as well. The word אִם, *whether*, includes fowl *(Rav from Gem. 54b).*

Although the law of approaching the mountain is irrelevant today, we find in *Sanhedrin* (15b) that the *Gemara* asks how many judges were required to judge a bull that approached the mountain, although this, too, is obviously not relevant *(Tos. Yom Tov).*

Tiferes Yisrael suggests an example in which this law would be relevant: If a person consecrates all the creatures in his possession that would have been separated from Mt. Sinai, it is necessary to know that all creatures were separated. A similar instance is found in *Chagigah* (6b).

וּלְתַשְׁלוּמֵי כֶפֶל, — *the twofold payments*,

This is the penalty for a thief — he must pay double the value of the item he stole to the owner *(Ex. 22:3).*

Although Scripture (ibid.) specifies: מִשּׁוֹר עַד־חֲמוֹר עַד־שֶׂה *whether a bull, a donkey, or a lamb*, the liability actually extends to all animals, as stated further in the passage (v. 8): עַל־כָּל־דְּבַר־פֶּשַׁע, *for every matter of trespass* — i.e., for anything with which one commits a transgression *(Rav from Gem. 54b).*

[אַרְבָּעָה וַחֲמִשָּׁה, *the fourfold and fivefold payments*, however, apply exclusively to a lamb and an ox, respectively (see 7:1 and commentary ad loc.).]

וּלְהָשְׁבַת אֲבֵדָה, — *returning a loss*,

Although the passage concerning this subject (*Deut.* 22:1ff.) speaks explicitly of a bull, a donkey, and a lamb, it adds (v. 3): וְכֵן תַּעֲשֶׂה לְכָל־אֲבֵדַת אָחִיךָ, *and so shall you do to any loss of your brother* *(Rav from Gem.).*

לִפְרִיקָה, — *unloading,*

The Torah states *(Ex. 23:5)*: כִּי־תִרְאֶה חֲמוֹר שֹׂנַאֲךָ רֹבֵץ תַּחַת מַשָּׂאוֹ וְחָדַלְתָּ מֵעֲזֹב לוֹ עָזֹב תַּעֲזֹב עִמּוֹ, *Should you see your enemy's donkey lying under its load, and refrain from helping him? You shall surely help him.*

Although *donkey* is specified, the intention is that one must help unload any animal belonging to a Jew that he sees lying under its load. [Of course, the intention of *your enemy* means *even your enemy.*] We derive this through a גְּזֵרָה שָׁוָה, *gezeirah shavah* [an analogous wording; see *Gateway to the Talmud*, p. 129], from the passage regarding the Sabbath in the second Decalogue, as discussed in the preface to this mishnah. The superfluous word וַחֲמוֹרֶךָ, *and your donkey*, is written to teach us that, just as — regarding the Sabbath — all animals are included in the interdict, so is it as regards unloading *(Rav from Gem. 54b).*

לַחֲסִימָה, — *muzzling,*

The reference is to the prohibition stated in *Deuteronomy* 25:4: לֹא־תַחְסֹם שׁוֹר בְּדִישׁוֹ, *You shall not muzzle the ox when it is threshing.* This, too, is derived by means of a *gezeirah shavah* from the passage regarding Sabbath, stated below, in which all animals are included. The superfluous word, שׁוֹרְךָ, *your ox*, in the second Decalogue is meant to teach us that, in the case of muzzling, all animals are included in the interdict *(Rav from Gem. ad loc.).*

לִכְלָאַיִם, — *kilayim,*

The Torah prohibits mingling species by mating them. This prohibition is found in *Leviticus* 19:19: בְּהֶמְתְּךָ לֹא תַרְבִּיעַ כִּלְאַיִם, *You shall not couple your cattle with a diverse kind.* Plowing or

[121] THE MISHNAH/BAVA KAMMA — Chapter Five: *Shor SheNagach*

בבא קמא א/ו

וְלַשַּׁבָּת. וְכֵן חַיָּה וָעוֹף כַּיּוֹצֵא בָהֶן. אִם־כֵּן, לָמָה נֶאֱמַר שׁוֹר אוֹ חֲמוֹר? אֶלָּא שֶׁדִּבֶּר הַכָּתוּב בַּהֹוֶה.

[א] **הַכּוֹנֵס** צֹאן לַדִּיר וְנָעַל בִּפְנֵיהֶם כָּרָאוּי, וְיָצְאָה וְהִזִּיקָה, פָּטוּר. לֹא נָעַל

יד אברהם

leading diverse species is forbidden by the Torah as well [*Deut.* 22:10, *Rashi* ad loc.]: לֹא־תַחֲרֹשׁ בְּשׁוֹר־וּבַחֲמֹר יַחְדָּו, *You shall not plow with an ox and a donkey together.*

Although the first verse specifies cattle, we learn from the same word — mentioned in the Decalogue [*Ex.* 20:10], where the implication is that one may not work with any creature on the Sabbath — that the same applies to the prohibition of mating diverse kinds.

The second verse specifies plowing with an ox and a donkey. The Rabbis derive from the word שׁוֹרְךָ, *your ox*, which is mentioned in the second Decalogue [*Deut.* 5:14] as regards working with animals on the Sabbath, and is interpreted as including all living creatures, that the same applies to plowing with diverse species (*Rav* from *Gem.* 54b).

Tos. Yom Tov maintains that, according to the conclusion of the *Gemara*, we do not compare the law of plowing with mixed species to the law of the Sabbath, but that one type of *kilayim* (law of mixed species) is derived from the other — i.e., just as the prohibition of mating diverse kinds includes even wild beasts and fowl — as derived from the law of Sabbath — so does the prohibition of leading or plowing with mixed species include any two kinds, even wild beasts and fowl.

Rav continues to expound the subject of *kilayim*, stating that, according to the Torah, the prohibition of plowing with two species applies only to doing so with one ritually clean animal and one ritually unclean animal, parallel to Scripture's example of the ox and the donkey, one of which is a clean animal and one of which is an unclean animal. Leading or plowing with two clean animals or two unclean animals is prohibited Rabbinically. This follows *Rambam* (*Commentary* and *Hil. Kilayim* 9:7). *Rosh* (*Hil. Kilayim* §5) does not differentiate, but rules that even plowing with or leading any two species — even two clean or two unclean animals — is Biblically prohibited (see *Tos. Yom Tov* to *Kilayim* 8:2).

It seems difficult to reconcile *Tos. Yom Tov's* interpretation of the *Gemara* — that the two types of *kilayim* are exegetically compared to each other — with the opinion of *Rambam*, who differentiates between them in this regard (*Rashash*).

וְלַשַּׁבָּת. — *and the Sabbath.*

In the second Decalogue, the Torah prohibits working with animals on the Sabbath, and states: וְכָל־בְּהֶמְתֶּךָ, *nor any of your cattle.* As mentioned above, the word בְּהֵמָה is broadly defined to include wild beasts as well as cattle. The word וְכָל, *nor any,* is added in order to include fowl (*Rav* from *Gem.*).

וְכֵן חַיָּה וָעוֹף כַּיּוֹצֵא בָהֶן. — *The same applies to wild beasts and fowl.*

[As explained in each case, these laws include wild beasts and fowl.]

This applies to fish as well (*Tif. Yis., Lechem Shamayim* from *Gem.* 55a).

אִם־כֵּן, לָמָה נֶאֱמַר שׁוֹר אוֹ חֲמוֹר — *If so, why is ox or donkey stated?*

That is, why is the ox mentioned in certain places, such as the interdict of muzzling, and the donkey in other places, such as the obligation to unload it? (*Shoshannim LeDavid*). [Since a person uses these animals more often

applies to wild beasts and fowl. If so, why is ox or donkey stated? Because Scripture speaks of the usual.

1. [If] one brings a sheep into a fold and locks [the door] before it properly, but it gets out and damages, he is exempt. [If] he does not lock [the

YAD AVRAHAM

than others, Scripture uses them as examples regarding the other laws as well.]

אֶלָּא שֶׁדִּבֶּר הַכָּתוּב בַּהוֹוֶה. — *Because Scripture speaks of the usual.*

It is usual to thresh grain with an ox and to use a donkey as a beast of burden (ibid.).

Although the *Tanna* mentions only the above laws, there are several others which include all species of living creatures. As discussed above, one is liable for the damages inflicted by his animals, no matter what species they are (see *Tur Choshen Mishpat* 38a). Also, the prohibition of castrating an animal applies to all species. The precept to help load one's fellow's animal when the load falls off applies also to all types of animals. *Tiferes Yisrael* suggests that the *Tanna* omits this last example since one is not required to do so unless the owner of the merchandise is willing to remunerate him for it. Unloading, however, is obligatory even if the owner of the animal refuses to pay, since cruelty to animals is involved.

Chapter 6

1.

After delineating the obligation to watch a bull lest it gore (4:9), the *Tanna* proceeds to discuss the obligations of watching sheep lest they go out and damage by trampling neighboring fields or devouring their produce. The laws of a pit (5:5-7) were interpolated because a pit was mentioned incidentally in 5:3.

Another theory is that the laws regarding a pit were intended to precede the laws of watching. Indeed, even those regarding a fire (mishnah 4ff.) would have preceded the latter. Since, however, the laws of a pit include the obligation to cover it properly, the *Tanna* continues with the laws of locking up an animal properly *(Tos. Yom Tov* from *Tos.).*

הַכּוֹנֵס צֹאן לַדִּיר — [*If*] *one brings a sheep into a fold*

דִּיר, *a fold,* is an enclosure where the farmers would leave the sheep overnight to fertilize the field. A gate would be made to prevent them from scattering until that enclosure is adequately fertilized. Then they would be moved to another area for the same purpose *(Meiri).*

וְנָעַל בְּפָנֶיהָ כָּרָאוּי. — *and locks [the door]* *before it properly,*

He locks the fold with a door that can withstand a wind of usual velocity *(Tos. Yom Tov* from *Gem.* 55b).

וְיָצְאָה וְהִזִּיקָה, — *but it gets out and damages,*

The animal tramples or devours someone else's property *(Gem.* 55b).

פָּטוּר. — *he is exempt.*

As regards the damages of devouring

[123]   THE MISHNAH/BAVA KAMMA – Chapter Six: *HaKoneis*

בבא קמא ו/א

בְּפָנֶיהָ כָּרָאוּי, וְיָצְאָה וְהִזִּיקָה, חַיָּב. נִפְרְצָה בַּלַּיְלָה, אוֹ שֶׁפְּרָצוּהָ לִסְטִים, וְיָצְאָה וְהִזִּיקָה, פָּטוּר. הוֹצִיאוּהָ לִסְטִים, הַלִּסְטִים חַיָּבִים.

יד אברהם

— which is in the category of *shen* (tooth) — or trampling, which is *regel* (foot) [see commentary to 1:1], even an inferior type of watching suffices. The Gemara derives this from the wording of the verse (22:4) imposing liability for these types of damages. In the case of *regel*, Scripture states: ... וְשִׁלַּח [lit., *and he sends* ...], indicating that the owner of the animal is not liable unless he commits an act of negligence tantamount to sending his animal to trample another person's field. Regarding *shen*, it is written: וּבִעֵר, *and it grazes*, which is interpreted to mean that the owner of the animal is liable only if his negligence is tantamount to deliberately feeding his animal from another person's field (*Tos. Yom Tov* from *Gem.*). This is implied by Scriptures use of the masculine form וּבִעֵר, which obviously refers to the owner, rather than the feminine וּבִעֲרָה, which would refer to the animal (*R' Yeshayah*, and *Talmid Rabbeinu Peretz*, quoted in *Shitah Mekubetzes*).

Even R' Meir — who rules that an animal that is a *muad* requires superior watching (4:9) — concurs here that regarding *shen* and *regel* only an inferior type of watching is required, as indicated by the above verse (*Gem.* loc. cit.).

לֹא נָעַל בְּפָנֶיהָ כָּרָאוּי — [If] *he does not lock [the door] before it properly,*

[The door to the fold is unable to withstand a wind of usual velocity.]

וְיָצְאָה וְהִזִּיקָה — *and it gets out and damages,*

[By trampling or devouring another's property.]

חַיָּב — *he is liable.*

[He is liable to pay the complete damages, since he neglected to watch the sheep adequately.]

נִפְרְצָה בַּלַּיְלָה — [If] *it breaks at night,*

The wall breaks. Alternatively, this refers to the sheep: *it breaks out at night* (*Tif. Yis.*).

If the owner locks the door properly, but the wall is broken at night, and the sheep gets out, he is exempt from paying for any damages it causes. Should the wall become broken by day, however, the news will spread, and the owner will soon learn what has happened. He is therefore responsible to go after his sheep and stop it from doing damage. It is also possible that, at night, even if the owner discovers that the wall has become broken and the sheep have escaped, he is not required to look for them while it is dark (*Tos. Yom Tov* from *Tos.*). This is, in fact, the accepted halachah (*Choshen Mishpat* 396:2).

If the wall remains intact, but the door breaks open, the owner is exempt even if this occurs by day, since there is nothing sensational about a door opening, and the news does not spread (*Tif. Yis.; Beis David* from *Maharsha*).

אוֹ שֶׁפְּרָצוּהָ לִסְטִים, וְיָצְאָה וְהִזִּיקָה, פָּטוּר. — *or if robbers break it, and it goes out and damages, he is exempt.*

If robbers break down the wall at night, not only is the owner exempt, as explained above, but even the robbers are not liable for damages done by the sheep, since they did not actually take the animal out and are considered only an indirect cause of the damages (*Tos. Yom Tov* from *Tos.*).

הוֹצִיאוּהָ לִסְטִים, הַלִּסְטִים חַיָּבִים. — *Should robbers take it out, the robbers are*

משניות / בבא קמא — פרק ו: הכונס [124]

6 1

door] before it properly, and it gets out and damages, he is liable.

[If] it breaks at night, or if robbers break it, and it goes out and damages, he is exempt. Should robbers take it out, the robbers are liable.

YAD AVRAHAM

liable.

The mishnah teaches us that robbers, who take over the responsibility for the animal they steal, are responsible for the damages it commits. Although one cannot acquire any article by performing an act of acquisition without the explicit permission of its owner, in this case, since the robber performed מְשִׁיכָה, *pulling*, by taking the animal — an act which is a valid means of acquisition when purchasing an item — and it is now in his possession, the act results in his being responsible for watching it (*Rosh*).

The *Gemara* (56b) considers the mishnah's statement to be obvious and wonders why it is necessary to tell us this. *Tosafos* (56b, s.v. פשיטא) explain that since the robbers took it out of the owner's domain and into theirs, thus making it impossible for the owner to watch it, it is obviously adjudged as belonging to the robbers with regard to liability for the damages it causes.

Two alternate interpretations of the mishnah are therefore offered in the *Gemara*. Rabbah's view is that the robbers stood in front of the animal at all sides except one, thereby compelling it to leave the fold and go to the field to graze. [Since they induced the animal to commit the damage, they are considered as its owner in this respect. It is tantamount to one who burns another person's flax with the latter's fire (*Tos.* ibid., s.v. המעמיד).] R' Yosef interprets the mishnah to mean that the robbers struck the animal with a rod, thus causing it to walk.

The point of the mishnah is that this is considered an act of *meshichah*, and the robbers thereby assume responsibility for the animal, both for the accidents that occur to it, and the damages it commits.

Tos. Yom Tov explains that, as long as the robbers urge the animal to leave the fold, regardless of the method they use, they are liable for the damages it causes. This is a Rabbinic fine imposed on robbers who take out the animal with the intention of stealing it. Should they take it out with the intention of losing it, however (e.g., for spite or revenge), they are not liable. Since it is unusual for robbers to intend to lose or destroy what they steal, the Rabbis saw no necessity to institute a fine for such a rare case. This distinction is found in *Yerushalmi*, where it is deduced from the mishnah's use of the word לסטים, *robbers*, referring to people who take an animal in the usual manner of robbers — i.e., with the intention of stealing it.

Rav and *Rambam* [*Commentary*] rule in accordance with R' Yosef's interpretation, but explain that he does not mean literally that the robbers struck the sheep; rather, that he includes any method the robbers employ to get the sheep out of the fold, even merely calling to it (*Tos. Yom Tov*).

Shoshannim LeDavid, contends, on the other hand, that *Rav* and *Rambam* follow Rabbah's interpretation. Therefore, as long as the robbers stand in the animal's path and compel it to go in the direction of the field, they are liable. In *Hilchos Nizkei Mamon* (4:3), however, *Rambam* retracts this decision and rules in accordance with a strict interpretation of R' Yosef's opinion — i.e., the robbers are liable only if they actually take the sheep out of the fold or if they cause it to walk by striking it with a rod.

בבא קמא ו/ב

[ב] **הִנִּיחָהּ** בַּחַמָּה, אוֹ שֶׁמְּסָרָהּ לְחֵרֵשׁ, שׁוֹטֶה, וְקָטָן, וְיָצְאָה וְהִזִּיקָה, חַיָּב. מְסָרָהּ לְרוֹעֶה, נִכְנַס הָרוֹעֶה תַּחְתָּיו. נָפְלָה לְגִנָּה וְנֶהֱנֵית, מְשַׁלֶּמֶת מַה־שֶּׁנֶּהֱנֵית. יָרְדָה כְדַרְכָּהּ וְהִזִּיקָה, מְשַׁלֶּמֶת מַה־שֶּׁהִזִּיקָה. כֵּיצַד מְשַׁלֶּמֶת מַה־שֶּׁהִזִּיקָה? שָׁמִין בֵּית סְאָה

יד אברהם

2.

הִנִּיחָהּ בַּחַמָּה — [If] he leaves it in the sun,

If the owner of the sheep leaves it in the sun, the heat causes it so much discomfort that it will resort to all means to avoid the discomfort, even to the extent of digging under the wall. Therefore, watching it in the normal manner is insufficient and is considered negligence (Rav from Gem. 56a).

אוֹ שֶׁמְּסָרָהּ לְחֵרֵשׁ, שׁוֹטֶה, וְקָטָן, — or gives it over to a deaf-mute, a mentally deranged person, or a minor,

[If he gave the animal over to any of these people, who are considered irresponsible (see commentary to 4:4), it is deemed that the animal was left unwatched. If, subsequently, the animal gets out and damages vegetation either by trampling or grazing, the owner is liable.]

וְיָצְאָה וְהִזִּיקָה, חַיָּב. — and it goes out and damages, he is liable.

[In all of these instances, if the animal gets out and damages vegetation either by trampling or grazing, the owner is liable since he was negligent in watching it.]

מְסָרָהּ לְרוֹעֶה, נִכְנַס הָרוֹעֶה תַּחְתָּיו. — [If] he gives it over to a shepherd, the shepherd assumes the responsibility [lit., enters] in his stead.

The apparent intention is that the owner entrusts his sheep to a shepherd, who assumes responsibility for the damages the sheep does. The owner is not deemed negligent for giving the animal to a shepherd, since the shepherd is in full possession of his senses. However, this law has already been stated above (4:9) and it would be unnecessary to repeat it here. The Gemara (56b), therefore, interprets our mishnah to mean that the owner gives the sheep over to a shepherd, who, in turn, gives it over to his apprentice. The Tanna is telling us that, although a watcher who gives over the object he was entrusted with to another person is liable, in this case he is not, since it is customary for a shepherd to entrust sheep to his apprentice. It is therefore only the apprentice who is liable (Rav).

Since the mishnah does not state: [If] he (i.e., the shepherd) gives it over to another, but rather: [If] he gives it over to a shepherd, the intention is that the shepherd gives it to his apprentice. Should he give it over to another person, however, the shepherd is still responsible, since the owner can claim that he does not trust the second person, even if the latter swears that the damages were the result of an accident (Gem. 56b, Rashi).

Tos. Yom Tov explains the mishnah to mean: If he gives it over to a shepherd, the shepherd under him assumes the responsibility.

By the same token, a שׁוֹמֵר, guardian, may give over the article he was entrusted with to his family members (Tif. Yis.).

משניות / בבא קמא — פרק ו: הכונס [126]

2. [If] he leaves it in the sun, or gives it over to a deaf-mute, a mentally deranged person, or a minor, and it goes out and damages, he is liable. [If] he gives it over to a shepherd, the shepherd assumes the responsibility in his stead.

[If] it falls into a garden and derives benefit, [its owner] pays [for] what it benefited. Should it go down in its usual manner and damage, he pays [for] what it damaged. How does he pay [for] what it damaged? We appraise how much a *seah's* space in

YAD AVRAHAM

נָפְלָה לַגִּנָּה — [If] it falls into a garden [This is a new case.]
The sheep fell by accident from its owner's roof abutting another's property. Alternatively, the public domain was higher than a private person's property, and the sheep slipped from the public domain and fell into that property (*Tos. Yom Tov* from *Rashi*).

וְנֶהֱנִית, — and derives benefit,
It fell on the produce growing in the field and was thereby saved from injury, or, after it fell into the field, it ate the produce growing there (*Gem.* 48a).

מְשַׁלֶּמֶת מַה־שֶּׁנֶּהֱנִית. — [its owner (lit., she)] pays [for] what it benefited.
The owner of the sheep is liable only for the amount of benefit that it derived from the produce, not for the amount that it damaged (*Rav; Rashi*).
In the case that the produce saved the animal from injury, the owner is liable for the amount of money he would be willing to pay for produce to cushion his animal's fall and save it from injury. Regarding the case that the animal benefited by eating the produce, thereby saving the owner the price of a meal to feed it, this is explained at length in the commentary to 2:2 (*Meiri*).
This ruling applies only if the sheep slipped on a stone or the like and fell into the field. Since it was an accident, the sheep's owner is exempt from paying for the damage, and is liable only for the amount of benefit derived. If, however, the owner's other sheep pushed this one and caused it to fall, there is a controversy in the *Gemara* whether he is guilty of negligence for not leading his sheep in single file. *Rav,* following *Rif* and *Rambam,* rules that it is deemed negligence, and the owner is liable. *Rosh,* on the other hand, contends that since an animal's owner is required to watch it only in an inferior manner with regard to preventing it from committing damages of the *shen* and *regel* categories, this amount of caution suffices.

יָרְדָה כְּדַרְכָּהּ וְהִזִּיקָה, — Should it go down in its usual manner and damage,
[The animal went down in a usual manner to the other person's garden, and caused damage by either eating his produce or trampling it.]

מְשַׁלֶּמֶת מַה־שֶּׁהִזִּיקָה. — he pays [for] what it damaged.
Since this is not an accident, the owner is liable for the complete damages (*Meiri*).

כֵּיצַד מְשַׁלֶּמֶת מַה־שֶּׁהִזִּיקָה? שָׁמִין בֵּית סְאָה בְּאוֹתָהּ שָׂדֶה כַּמָּה הָיְתָה יָפָה וְכַמָּה הִיא יָפָה. — How does he pay [for] what it damaged? We appraise how much a *seah's* space in that field was worth and how much it is worth.
That is, how much a *seah's* space in that field was worth before this garden

בָּאוֹתָהּ שָׂדֶה כַּמָּה הָיְתָה יָפָה וְכַמָּה הִיא יָפָה. רַבִּי שִׁמְעוֹן אוֹמֵר: אָכְלָה פֵּרוֹת גְּמוּרִים, מְשַׁלֶּמֶת פֵּרוֹת גְּמוּרִים; אִם־סְאָה סְאָה; אִם־סָאתַיִם סָאתַיִם.

[ג] הַמַּגְדִּישׁ בְּתוֹךְ שָׂדֶה שֶׁל־חֲבֵרוֹ שֶׁלֹּא בִרְשׁוּת, וַאֲכָלָתַן בְּהֶמְתּוֹ שֶׁל־בַּעַל הַשָּׂדֶה, פָּטוּר. וְאִם־הֻזְּקָה בָהֶן, בַּעַל הַגָּדִישׁ חַיָּב. וְאִם הִגְדִּישׁ בִּרְשׁוּת, בַּעַל הַשָּׂדֶה חַיָּב.

[ד] הַשּׁוֹלֵחַ אֶת־הַבְּעֵרָה בְּיַד חֵרֵשׁ, שׁוֹטֶה,

יד אברהם

bed was consumed.

A בֵּית סְאָה, *a seah's space* [lit., *the house of a seah*], is the area in which a *seah* [a measure of volume] of barley seeds is planted. The standard tract of land in which a *seah* of barley seeds is planted is fifty cubits square. [The U.S. equivalent for this amount is disputed by the authorities, opinions ranging from 1378-2006 square yards (see *Gateway to the Talmud, p. 117f.*).]

We do not impose upon the damager the full value of the bed that the animal ate or damaged, by appraising it alone, since that would be an undue stringency. Rather, the phrase in *Exodus 22:4*, בשדה אחר, *in another's field*, is exegetically interpreted to mean that we must compute how much a much larger field would be depreciated by the loss of the produce consumed by this animal. When someone purchases a *seah's* space of field covered with grain, he deducts very little from the price because of the absence of one bed (*Rav; Rashi*).

Others explain the mishnah to mean that the animal consumed a *seah* of produce (*Tos. Yom Tov from Tos. 58b*). [According to this interpretation, a *seah's* space is not where a *seah* of grain is sown, but where a *seah* of produce grows. This is obviously a much smaller area.]

רַבִּי שִׁמְעוֹן אוֹמֵר: אָכְלָה פֵּרוֹת גְּמוּרִים, — R' Shimon says: [If] it eats ripe fruit,

The animal eats completely ripe fruit that no longer needs the earth to which it is attached (*Rav, Tos. Yom Tov from Gem. 59b*).

מְשַׁלֶּמֶת פֵּרוֹת גְּמוּרִים; — he pays for ripe fruit:

He must pay for the complete value of the fruit the animal ate [as though it were detached from the earth] (*Rav; Rashi*).

אִם־סְאָה סְאָה; אִם־סָאתַיִם, סָאתַיִם. — if a seah, a seah; if two seahs, two seahs.

R' Shimon rules that the principle set down by the Torah — that the appraisal must be made 'in another field' as discussed above — applies only if the produce eaten requires the ground to which it is attached in order to fully ripen. However, ripe produce, which no longer requires the ground, is appraised independently, like produce that has already been harvested. The halachah is in accordance with R' Shimon (*Rav, Tos. Yom Tov from Gem. 59b*).

6
3-4
that field was worth and how much it is worth. R' Shimon says: [If] it eats ripe fruit, he pays for ripe fruit; if a *seah*, a *seah*; if two *seahs*, two *seahs*.

3. [If] one makes stacks of grain in another's field without permission, and the animal belonging to the owner of the field eats them, he is exempt. If it is injured by them, the owner of the stack is liable. Should he make the stacks with permission, the owner of the field is liable.

4. [If] one causes a fire through a deaf-mute, a mentally deranged person, or a minor, he is

YAD AVRAHAM

13.

הַמַּגְדִּישׁ בְּתוֹךְ שָׂדֵה שֶׁל־חֲבֵרוֹ שֶׁלֹּא בִרְשׁוּת, [If] — וַאֲכָלָתַן בְּהֶמְתּוֹ שֶׁל־בַּעַל הַשָּׂדֶה, פָּטוּר. *one makes stacks of grain in another's field without permission, and the animal belonging to the owner of the field eats them, he is exempt.*

The owner of the animal is exempt because he can claim, 'What are your stacks doing in my property?' (*Meiri*).

וְאִם־הֻזְּקָה בָּהֶן, — *If it is injured by them,*

The animal belonging to the owner of the field slips on the stack of grain and is injured thereby (*Tos. Yom Tov*).

בַּעַל הַגָּדִישׁ חַיָּב. — *the owner of the stack is liable.*

Even in an open field that has no walls or fences around it, one must have permission to enter and stack up his grain (*Tif. Yis.*).

Should the animal eat the grain and become ill and die, however, the owner of the stack is exempt, as explained in the commentary to 5:2, s.v. בַּעַל הַפֵּרוֹת (*Tos. Yom Tov* from *Beis Yosef*, end of ch. 393).

וְאִם־הִגְדִּישׁ בִּרְשׁוּת, — *Should he make the stacks with permission,*

[He had permission from the owner of the field before stacking his grain, and the owner's animal ate the grain.]

בַּעַל הַשָּׂדֶה חַיָּב. — *the owner of the field is liable.*

The *Gemara* qualifies the mishnah as referring to a valley where many farmers stack their grain on one threshing-floor and appoint someone to guard all the stacks. When the latter permits a farmer to bring in his grain and put up his stacks, it is tantamount to accepting the responsibility of watching them. In other cases, however, even if the owner of the field allows the farmer to bring in his grain, he does not accept responsibility for it unless he says so explicitly (*Rav* from *Gem.* 59b).

Thus, the mishnah is no contradiction to the view of Rabbi in 5:3. For this reason, the *Tanna* chose this case to teach us that, in such an instance, even according to Rabbi, allowing the farmer to bring in his grain amounts to accepting responsibility (*Tos. Yom Tov* from *Tos.*).

4.

הַשּׁוֹלֵחַ אֶת־הַבְּעֵרָה בְּיַד חֵרֵשׁ, שׁוֹטֶה, וְקָטָן, — [If] *one causes a fire through a deaf-mute, a mentally deranged person, or a minor,*

בבא קמא ו/ד

וְקָטָן, פָּטוּר בְּדִינֵי אָדָם, וְחַיָּב בְּדִינֵי שָׁמָיִם. שָׁלַח בְּיַד־פִּקֵּחַ, הַפִּקֵּחַ חַיָּב. אֶחָד הֵבִיא אֶת־הָאוּר וְאֶחָד הֵבִיא אֶת־הָעֵצִים, הַמֵּבִיא אֶת־הָעֵצִים חַיָּב; אֶחָד הֵבִיא אֶת־הָעֵצִים, וְאֶחָד הֵבִיא אֶת־הָאוּר, הַמֵּבִיא אֶת־הָאוּר חַיָּב. בָּא אַחֵר וְלִבָּה, הַמְלַבֶּה חַיָּב; לִבַּתָּה הָרוּחַ, כֻּלָּן פְּטוּרִין.

יד אברהם

Someone gave a glowing coal to one of these types of individuals, who fanned it into a flame and caused a fire which damaged property (*Tif. Yis.* from *Gem.* 59b).

פָּטוּר בְּדִינֵי אָדָם, — *he is exempt by the laws of man*,

Since such individuals are not capable of being agents, the one who gave them the coal is exempt (*Tos. Yom Tov* from *Tos.* to *Bava Metzia* 10b). Should he give them a flame, however, he is liable. Since he gave them a fire that is capable of burning property, his deeds are regarded as having caused the fire (*Tif. Yis.* from *Choshen Mishpat* 418:7). This is in accordance with the view of Resh Lakish in the *Gemara*, and is followed by *Rif*, *Rambam* (*Hil. Nizkei Mamon* 14:5), and *Rosh*.

וְחַיָּב בְּדִינֵי שָׁמָיִם. — *but liable by the laws of Heaven.*

The one who gave the coal is liable by the laws of Heaven. The individual whom he sent, however, is exempt in any case, since these types of people are not deemed responsible (*Meiri*).

שָׁלַח בְּיַד־פִּקֵּחַ, — [*If*] *he causes it through one of sound mind,*

[He gives the fire to a person of sound mind, who, in turn, takes it and causes a fire in another's property.]

הַפִּקֵּחַ חַיָּב. — *the one of sound mind is liable.*

[He is liable for any damages caused by the fire.]

Although, as regards all transactions, one can appoint an agent whose act is effective in behalf of the appointer, this does not apply if the agent was commissioned to do a sin. In such an instance, the rule is: אֵין שָׁלִיחַ לִדְבַר עֲבֵרָה, *there is no agent in matters of sin.* Since the agent is expected to ignore the directive of his appointer when it contradicts a Divine command, which they are both obligated to obey, the appointer does not expect the agent to fulfill his wishes. Consequently, if the agent does commit the sin, he is doing it on his own and is held accountable for it. In the case of the deaf-mute, the mentally deranged person, and the minor, on the other hand, since they are not considered responsible for their actions, this reasoning does not apply, and the appointer should be held accountable. However, since these types of individuals cannot be made agents, he, too is not liable for their actions (*Tos. Yom Tov* from *Tos.* loc. cit. 10b).

Should the agent be unaware that he is committing a sin, some authorities rule that the appointer is liable, since he relies on the agent to perform the act (*Tos.* 79a, s.v. נתנו).

Others contend, however, that even in such cases, there is no agency in matters of sin (*Tif. Yis.* from *Choshen Mishpat* 182:1). [This will be discussed in more detail in the commentary to 7:6.]

Should the one who ignited the fire ask someone to watch it, the latter is liable if it causes damage (*Tif. Yis.* from

משניות / בבא קמא — פרק ו: הכונס   [130]

6:4

exempt by the laws of man, but liable by the laws of Heaven. [If] he causes it through one of sound mind, the one of sound mind is liable.

[If] one brings the fire and one brings the wood, the one who brings the wood is liable; [if] one brings the wood and one brings the fire, the one who brings the fire is liable. [If] another one comes along and fans it, the one who fans it is liable; should the wind fan it, all are exempt.

YAD AVRAHAM

Rambam, Hil. Nizkei Mamon 14:6, Choshen Mishpat 418:8).

אֶחָד הֵבִיא אֶת־הָאוּר וְאֶחָד הֵבִיא אֶת־הָעֵצִים, — [If] one brings the fire and one brings the wood,

[This is a new case. One person brings a fire and another one brings wood and ignites it with that fire, and the fire spreads and causes damage.]

הַמֵּבִיא אֶת־הָעֵצִים חַיָּב; — the one who brings the wood is liable;

Were it not for the second one, who brought the wood, the fire would have gone out and would not have spread to do the damage it did (Tos. Yom Tov from Rashi).

אֶחָד הֵבִיא אֶת־הָעֵצִים — [if] one brings the wood

[One person brought wood that had not been ignited.]

וְאֶחָד הֵבִיא אֶת־הָאוּר, — and one brings the fire,

[Subsequently, someone else brought fire and ignited the wood.]

הַמֵּבִיא אֶת־הָאוּר חַיָּב. — the one who brings the fire is liable.

[In this case, it is even more apparent that the latter is liable, since the former brought wood that had not been ignited.]

בָּא אַחֵר וְלִבָּה, — [If] another comes along and fans it,

The fire required fanning and did not respond to the fanning of a usual wind; then, another person came along and fanned it into a flame (Meiri).

The expression לִבָּה, fanned, stems from the verse (Ex. 3:2): בְּלַבַּת אֵשׁ, in a flame of fire. That is, the third person in our mishnah blew on the fire until it became a flame. The Gemara (60a) relates that some would read this word as נִבָּה, an expression stemming from (Isa. 57:19): בּוֹרֵא נִיב שְׂפָתָיִם, [I] create the speech of the lips. When one speaks, he moves his lips and wind comes out of his mouth (Rashi).

הַמְלַבֶּה חַיָּב; — the one who fans it is liable;

[Since the fire would have gone out had this person not fanned it into a flame, he is liable, and any others who contributed to it previously are exempt.]

לִבְּתָה הָרוּחַ, — should the wind fan it,

An unusual wind fanned the fire into a flame (Tif. Yis. from Tos. 59b).

כֻּלָּן פְּטוּרִין. — all are exempt.

All those who contribute to the fire by bringing wood or fire are exempt from liability for the damages it causes. Since the fire would have gone out were it not for the fanning of the wind, they are exempt. As mentioned above, the mishnah refers to an unusual wind — i.e., one that does not come often, although it does come occasionally. Surely, if a wind of exceptional velocity — such as a hurricane — fans the flames, all the participants in making the flame are exempt (Tos. Yom Tov from Maggid Mishneh, Hil. Nizkei Mamon

בבא קמא ו/ד

הַשּׁוֹלֵחַ אֶת־הַבְּעֵרָה וְאָכְלָה עֵצִים, אוֹ אֲבָנִים, אוֹ עָפָר, חַיָּב, שֶׁנֶּאֱמַר: "כִּי תֵצֵא אֵשׁ וּמָצְאָה קוֹצִים וְנֶאֱכַל גָּדִישׁ אוֹ הַקָּמָה אוֹ הַשָּׂדֶה, שַׁלֵּם יְשַׁלֵּם הַמַּבְעִר אֶת־הַבְּעֵרָה". עָבְרָה גָּדֵר שֶׁהוּא גָּבוֹהַּ אַרְבַּע אַמּוֹת, אוֹ דֶּרֶךְ הָרַבִּים, אוֹ נָהָר, פָּטוּר.

הַמַּדְלִיק בְּתוֹךְ שֶׁלּוֹ, עַד־כַּמָּה תַעֲבֹר הַדְּלֵקָה?

יד אברהם

14:7; Tos. 59b).

Should a usual wind fan the fire into a flame, the last one who contributed to the fire is liable. Just as one is liable if a usual wind transports a fire that he made, thereby causing it to do damage, so is one liable if a usual wind fans his fire into a flame, which then causes damage (Tos. 59b). Indeed, the cases above in the mishnah, in which the last contributor to the fire is liable, refer even to an instance that the fanning of a usual wind is required for the flame to spread (Tif. Yis.).

הַשּׁוֹלֵחַ אֶת־הַבְּעֵרָה וְאָכְלָה עֵצִים — [If] one sets a fire and it consumes wood,

The mishnah uses the term שׁוֹלֵחַ (lit., sends) rather than מַבְעִיר, ignites, to conform with the first case of the mishnah. It is also possible that the mishnah uses this wording to indicate that, although one ignites a fire in his own premises without intending to damage the property of others, if he is guilty of negligence in watching it, it is as though he set fire to the others' property. This principle is expressed by the verse quoted in the mishnah, which concludes with the words, הַמַּבְעִר אֶת־הַבְּעֵרָה, the one who ignited the fire, which indicates that although the fire spreads by itself, the one who neglected it is as guilty as if he had started the fire where the damage occurred (Meleches Shlomo).

אוֹ אֲבָנִים, אוֹ עָפָר — stones, or earth,
The fire singed stones or the upper surface of a newly plowed field (Rav; Rashi) [thereby spoiling it and necessitating that the field be replowed].

חַיָּב — he is liable,
[He must pay the complete damages.]

שֶׁנֶּאֱמַר: "כִּי תֵצֵא אֵשׁ וּמָצְאָה קוֹצִים וְנֶאֱכַל גָּדִישׁ אוֹ הַקָּמָה אוֹ הַשָּׂדֶה שַׁלֵּם יְשַׁלֵּם הַמַּבְעִר אֶת־הַבְּעֵרָה." — as it says (Exodus 22:5): 'If a fire goes forth and comes across thorns, and a stack of grain, or standing grain, or a field is consumed, the one who ignited the fire shall surely pay.'

Since all types of flammable objects, as well as vegetation, both growing and harvested, are included in this verse, the words, אוֹ הַשָּׂדֶה, or a field, are superfluous. The Gemara therefore construes this as referring to the earth itself — i.e., if the fire singes a plowed field, necessitating another plowing, the one who ignited the fire is liable for the damages.

עָבְרָה גָדֵר — [If] it crosses a fence
The fire from the burning wood crosses a stone fence (Lechem Shamayim).

שֶׁהוּא גָּבוֹהַ אַרְבַּע אַמּוֹת — four cubits high,

That is, four cubits higher than the wood. This is implied by the expression, it crosses, indicating that the wall is higher than the burning wood, and the flames went over the wall (Tos. Yom Tov from Tos., Nimmukei Yosef).

אוֹ דֶּרֶךְ הָרַבִּים — or a public road,

6 [If] one sets a fire and it consumes wood, stones, or
4 earth, he is liable, as it says (*Exodus* 22:5): *If a fire goes forth and comes across thorns, and a stack of grain, or standing grain, or a field, is consumed, the one who ignited the fire shall surely pay.* [If] it crosses a fence four cubits high, or a public road, or a river, he is exempt.

[If] one ignites a fire within his own property, how

YAD AVRAHAM

That is, a road at least sixteen cubits wide. This dimension is based on the width of the wagons used to transport the parts of the Tabernacle when the Jews traveled in the Wilderness. As regards the Sabbath, in order for a street, a highway, or a public square to be considered a public domain, it must be at least sixteen cubits wide (*Rav; Rashi; Tos. Yom Tov*). [The U.S. equivalent of this measurement is disputed by the authorities, opinions varying from twenty-four to thirty-two feet (see *ArtScroll Shabbos* pp. 11f.).

This part of the mishnah follows R' Eliezer's view — stated below — that there must be a space of sixteen cubits between the fire one sets and the neighboring property in order for the one who set the fire to be exempt from paying the damages (*Tos. Yom Tov* from *Gem.* 61a).

אוֹ נָהָר, — *or a river,*
The river referred to here is a ditch at least eight cubits wide, which is half that of the public road mentioned above. According to *Rambam* (*Hil. Nizkei Mamon* 14:2), there must be water running through it; otherwise, if the fire crosses it, he is liable. This view is followed by *Shulchan Aruch* (*Choshen Mishpat* 418:4) and *Yam Shel Shlomo.*

Rosh and *Tur*, however, contend that a ditch eight cubits wide is included in this category even if there is no water running through it. *Tosafos*, too, concur with this opinion, adding that although — as discussed above — a

public road requires sixteen cubits, a riverbed, even without water, requires no more than eight.

Because it is deep, and has the chill of the water which usually runs through it, eight cubits suffice to keep fire from crossing it (*Tos. Yom Tov*). According to this opinion, should there be any water in the ditch, even if it is shallow and narrow, it will prevent the fire from crossing (*Tur; Rama* 418:4; *Tif. Yis.*).

פָּטוּר. — *he is exempt.*
Since a fire cannot normally cross these barriers, if it does, the incident is deemed an act of God, and the one who started the fire is liable for the damages it caused after crossing the barrier (*Rambam, Hil. Nizkei Mamon* 14:2).

הַמַּדְלִיק בְּתוֹךְ שֶׁלוֹ, — [*If*] *one ignites a fire within his own property,*
To be sure, the previous case of the mishnah, too, deals with one who ignites a fire within his own property. Should he do so within another's property, since he does so unlawfully, he is always liable, regardless of how far the fire spreads or how far it crosses over obstacles. This is stated by *Tur* (*Choshen Mishpat* 418) and is implied by *Rambam* (loc. cit. §1 ibid.). Moreover, the *Gemara's* statement, that the previous part of the mishnah follows the view of R' Eliezer, which is cited below regarding this case, proves that both segments of the mishnah deal with the same situation. Therefore, it is likely that the reason the *Tanna* began this case by specifying that the fire was

[133] THE MISHNAH/BAVA KAMMA — Chapter Six: *HaKoneis*

בבא קמא ו/ה

רַבִּי אֶלְעָזָר בֶּן־עֲזַרְיָה אוֹמֵר: רוֹאִין אוֹתָהּ כְּאִלּוּ הִיא בְּאֶמְצַע בֵּית כּוֹר. רַבִּי אֱלִיעֶזֶר אוֹמֵר: שֵׁשׁ־עֶשְׂרֵה אַמּוֹת, כְּדֶרֶךְ רְשׁוּת הָרַבִּים. רַבִּי עֲקִיבָא אוֹמֵר: חֲמִשִּׁים אַמָּה. רַבִּי שִׁמְעוֹן אוֹמֵר: ,,שַׁלֵּם יְשַׁלֵּם הַמַּבְעִר אֶת־הַבְּעֵרָה'' — הַכֹּל לְפִי הַדְּלֵקָה.

[ה] **הַמַּדְלִיק** אֶת הַגָּדִישׁ, וְהָיוּ בוֹ כֵלִים, וְדָלְקוּ — רַבִּי יְהוּדָה אוֹמֵר: יְשַׁלֵּם מַה־שֶּׁבְּתוֹכוֹ; וַחֲכָמִים אוֹמְרִים: אֵינוֹ מְשַׁלֵּם אֶלָּא גָדִישׁ שֶׁל־חִטִּין אוֹ שֶׁל־שְׂעוֹרִים.

יד אברהם

ignited in one's own property is to indicate that the person did so in a place without walls which would stop the fire from spreading, and that the only vindicating factor is that he ignited it within his own property. The question is: how much empty space must there be between the fire and the property of the nearest neighbor, so that, if the fire spreads, it should not be considered a result of his negligence and he should be exempt from liability? *(Tos. Yom Tov).*

עַד־כַּמָּה תַעֲבֹר הַדְּלֵקָה? — *how far can the fire cross?*

How far can the fire travel along an empty space with nothing combustible to feed it? If there would be a larger space between the fire and the other's property, one may start it, and should it happen to cross that space, he is exempt, as stated above *(Rambam Commentary).*

רַבִּי אֶלְעָזָר בֶּן־עֲזַרְיָה אוֹמֵר: רוֹאִין אוֹתָהּ כְּאִלּוּ הִיא בְּאֶמְצַע בֵּית כּוֹר — *R' Elazar ben Azariah says: We view it as though it were in the middle of a kor's space of land.*

[According to R' Elazar ben Azariah, the one who sets the fire is exempt only if the space between it and the neighboring property is as least as much as if his property were a *kor's* space and the fire was in middle of it.]

A *kor* is thirty *se'in* [sing. *seah*], a measure of volume [67.5-120 gallons (see *Gateway to the Talmud* p. 118)]. A *kor's space* is the area required to sow a *kor* of seed — approximately 274 cubits by 274 cubits [4.3-6.2 acres (ibid., p. 119)]. Hence, if the fire has 137 cubits on all sides between it and another property, that is considered the maximum distance that the fire can travel with nothing flammable to feed it *(Tif. Yis.).*

רַבִּי אֱלִיעֶזֶר אוֹמֵר: שֵׁשׁ־עֶשְׂרֵה אַמּוֹת, כְּדֶרֶךְ רְשׁוּת הָרַבִּים — *R' Eliezer says: Sixteen cubits, like a public highway.*

That is, a distance of sixteen cubits — the width of a public highway — as mentioned above in the mishnah. Since the *Gemara* deduces from here that the previous part of the mishnah follows R' Eliezer's view, it is apparent that the intention is that the fire can travel sixteen cubits, not that we view the fire as being in the middle of sixteen cubits. The same applies to R' Akiva's opinion below *(Tos. Yom Tov).*

Since the *Tanna* teaches us that the

משניות / בבא קמא — פרק ו: הכונס [134]

far can the fire cross? R' Elazar ben Azariah says: We view it as though it were in the middle of a *kor's* space of land. R' Eliezer says: Sixteen cubits, like a public highway. R' Akiva says: Fifty cubits. R' Shimon says: *The one who ignited the fire shall pay — all is according to the fire.*

5. [If] one ignites a stack of grain, and utensils were in it, and they burned — R' Yehudah says: He must pay for what was inside it; the Sages, however, say: He pays only for a stack of wheat or of barley.

YAD AVRAHAM

previous part of the mishnah follows R' Eliezer's view, it does not have the status of an anonymous mishnah — in which case the halachah would follow it — but that of an anonymous mishnah followed by a controversy; in which case the halachah is not necessarily in accordance with it *(Tos. Yom Tov from Tos.).*

רַבִּי עֲקִיבָא אוֹמֵר: חֲמִשִּׁים אַמָּה. — R' *Akiva says: Fifty cubits.*

[There must be a distance of fifty cubits between the fire and the neighboring property in order for the one who set it to be exempt from liability.]

רַבִּי שִׁמְעוֹן אוֹמֵר: ״יְשַׁלֵּם הַמַּבְעִיר אֶת־הַבְּעֵרָה״ — הַכֹּל לְפִי הַדְּלֵקָה. — R' *Shimon says: 'The one who ignited the fire shall pay' — all is according to the fire.*

The seemingly superfluous term אֶת־הַבְּעֵרָה, *the fire,* indicates that it all depends on the size of the fire *(Meleches Shlomo* quoting *Lekach Tov).* If the flames are high, the fire spreads further, and a larger space is required around it. The halachah is in accordance with R' Shimon's view *(Rav, Tos. Yom Tov from Gem. 61b).*

5.

The following mishnah deals primarily with the exemption from liability for hidden things that are burnt in a fire, and the various details involved.

הַמַּדְלִיק אֶת־הַגָּדִישׁ, — [If] *one ignites a stack of grain,*

He sets a fire on his own premises and it spreads to another person's property and burns a stack of grain *(Rav from Gem.).*

[The case of one setting a fire in the other's premises is discussed below.]

וְהָיוּ בוֹ כֵלִים, — *and utensils were in it,*

[They were hidden in the stack of grain.]

וְדָלְקוּ — *and they burned —*

[The utensils were burned along with the grain.]

רַבִּי יְהוּדָה אוֹמֵר: יְשַׁלֵּם מַה־שֶּׁבְּתוֹכוֹ, — R' *Yehudah says: He must pay for what was inside it;*

R' Yehudah makes no distinction between things that are hidden and those out in the open; he maintains that the one who set the fire is liable for everything that is burnt (ibid.).

וַחֲכָמִים אוֹמְרִים: אֵינוֹ מְשַׁלֵּם אֶלָּא גָּדִישׁ שֶׁל־חִטִּין אוֹ שֶׁל־שְׂעוֹרִים. — *the Sages,*

בבא קמא ו/ה

הָיָה גְדִי כָפוּת לוֹ וְעֶבֶד סָמוּךְ לוֹ, וְנִשְׂרַף עִמּוֹ, חַיָּב; עֶבֶד כָּפוּת לוֹ וּגְדִי סָמוּךְ לוֹ, וְנִשְׂרַף עִמּוֹ, פָּטוּר.

וּמוֹדִים חֲכָמִים לְרַבִּי יְהוּדָה בְּמַדְלִיק אֶת־

יד אברהם

however say: He pays [lit., need not pay] only for a stack of wheat or of barley.

If it is a stack of wheat, he must pay as though the entire stack were wheat; if it is a stack of barley, he must pay as though the entire stack were barley. But he does not pay for the utensils (Rashi).

The Sages maintain that one is liable only for objects that are visible, not for those that are hidden. This is derived from the words (Ex. 22:5) אוֹ הַקָּמָה, or standing grain, from which we interpret that, just as standing grain is visible, so is the liability for a fire applicable only to visible things, but not to those which are hidden. R' Yehudah, however, does not interpret the verse in this manner and therefore rules that the perpetrator is liable for everything that was burnt (Rav from Gem. 60a).

Although the inner part of the stack is not presently visible, it is not considered 'hidden,' since everyone knows that there is wheat or barley there. Consequently, he is liable for it even according to the Sages (Tos. Yom Tov from Nimmukei Yosef).

Should one set fire in someone else's premises, R' Yehudah rules that he is liable for anything there, even a purse in a stack of grain. The Sages, however, rule that he is liable only for articles usually found in a stack of grain, such as threshing sledges and cattle harnesses. For purses and other such things not usually found in stacks of grain, however, he is exempt, since it does not enter one's mind that a purse should be found in a stack of grain (Tos. 61b, s.v. אלא).

◆§ קִים לֵיהּ... / **Receiving Only the More Severe Punishment**

The following segment of the mishnah deals with the principle of קִים לֵיהּ בְּדְרַבָּה מִינֵיהּ, he suffers only the more severe punishment: should one commit two sins simultaneously, one bearing the death penalty and one bearing monetary charges, he receives the more severe penalty and is exempt from the more lenient one. We have already mentioned this principle in 3:10. Just as in that case, if one is liable for desecrating the Sabbath by igniting a stack of grain, he is exempt from the monetary liability thereby incurred, so it is in the case of murder: if one is liable for murder by igniting a stack of grain — e.g., because a person is bound to it and is killed by the fire — he is exempt from any monetary liability incurred by that act.

הָיָה גְדִי כָּפוּת לוֹ — [If] there was a kid bound to it;

A young goat was bound to the stack of grain (Rav).

וְעֶבֶד סָמוּךְ לוֹ. — and a slave near it;

The slave was not bound and was able to escape (Rav; Rashi).

וְנִשְׂרַף עִמּוֹ. — and it was burned with it;

[The kid was burned with the stack of grain.]

חַיָּב; — he is liable;

The one who set the fire is liable for the stack of grain, as explicitly stated in the Torah (Ex. 22:5), and is also liable for the kid. This we derive from the phrase (ad loc.) אוֹ הַקָּמָה, or the standing grain, which is construed as including all things possessing stature, such as trees and living creatures (Gem. 60a).

Even if the slave, too, is killed by the fire, the perpetrator is not guilty of a

[136] משניות / בבא קמא — פרק ו: הכונס

6. [If] there was a kid bound to it and a slave near it, and it was burned with it, he is liable; a slave bound to it and a kid near it, and it was burned with it, he is exempt.

The Sages concur with R' Yehudah in [the case of]

YAD AVRAHAM

capital offense, since the slave was not tied and was therefore able to flee. If he did not flee, he is to blame for his own death *(Rav; Rashi).*

עֶבֶד כָּפוּת לוֹ — *a slave bound to it*
[There was a slave tied to the stack of grain.]

וּגְדִי סָמוּךְ לוֹ, — *and a kid near it,*
[A kid was standing near the stack of grain, but was not bound.]

וְנִשְׂרַף עִמּוֹ, — *and it was burned with it,*
[The kid was burned with the stack, as well as the slave.]

פָּטוּר. — *he is exempt.*
The one who set the fire is exempt from paying for the kid and the stack. This is because he is liable for the slave, since the slave was bound and could not escape, and the Torah *(Ex.* 21:20) imposes the death penalty for killing a slave. Consequently, we apply the principle that *he suffers only the more severe punishment,* which — in our case — dictates that he is exempt for paying the damages because he is liable to death for having killed the slave *(Rav; Rashi).*

Even if he was not forewarned before igniting the grain, and therefore is not subject to the death penalty, he is nevertheless exempt from other liabilities, because the very fact that he committed an offense of the gravity that warrants such a punishment frees him from the monetary payment *(Rashi from Kesubos* 34b).

As far as the kid is concerned, although it was not bound, the perpetrator should be liable for it, since it has no sense to escape from the fire. In this case, however, since he is liable for the slave's death, he is exempt from paying for the kid *(Rav; Rashi).*

Rashi cites others who rule that if the kid were untied, the perpetrator would not be liable for its death, since we expect it to escape from a fire. Rather, the meaning of the mishnah is: *a slave bound to it* or *a kid near it ... he is exempt* — i.e., he is exempt for the kid either if there was also a slave bound to the stack, thereby making him guilty of a capital offense, or if there is a kid *near* the stack of grain, for which he is not liable, since it could have run away.

Tosafos (22b) cite this explanation in the name of *Rashbam.* He explains the mishnah to mean that only if there is a kid bound to the stack of grain and a slave near it is the perpetrator liable, since the kid could not escape and there is no penalty for the slave. Should there be both a slave and a kid bound to it, or both a kid and a slave near it, he is exempt.

This mishnah, which imposes the death penalty upon one who commits murder by fire, seems to subscribe to the principle of אִשּׁוֹ מִשּׁוּם חִצָּיו, *one is as liable for his fire as he is for his arrows* — i.e., it is as though he had performed the deed with his own power, and, in this case, it is therefore a capital offense. Resh Lakish, however, who rules that אִשּׁוֹ מִשּׁוּם מָמוֹנוֹ, *one is as liable for his fire as he is for his chattels,* qualifies the mishnah as referring to an instance in which the arsonist ignited the body of the slave directly. In that case, he is a direct murderer *(Gem.* 22b).

וּמוֹדִים חֲכָמִים לְרַבִּי יְהוּדָה — *The Sages concur with R' Yehudah*
[The Sages, who disagree with R' Yehudah concerning the matter of hidden articles burned in a fire, nevertheless concur with him in the following instance.]

[137] THE MISHNAH/BAVA KAMMA — Chapter Six: *HaKoneis*

בבא קמא ו/ו

הַבִּירָה, שֶׁהוּא מְשַׁלֵּם כָּל־מַה־שֶּׁבְּתוֹכָהּ, שֶׁכֵּן דֶּרֶךְ בְּנֵי אָדָם לְהַנִּיחַ בְּבָתִּים.

[ו] **גֵּץ** שֶׁיָּצָא מִתַּחַת הַפַּטִּישׁ וְהִזִּיק, חַיָּב. גָּמָל שֶׁהָיָה טָעוּן פִּשְׁתָּן וְעָבַר בִּרְשׁוּת הָרַבִּים, וְנִכְנַס פִּשְׁתָּנוֹ לְתוֹךְ הַחֲנוּת, וְדָלְקוּ בְּנֵרוֹ שֶׁל־חֶנְוָנִי, וְהִדְלִיק אֶת־הַבִּירָה, בַּעַל הַגָּמָל חַיָּב. הִנִּיחַ חֶנְוָנִי נֵרוֹ מִבַּחוּץ, הַחֶנְוָנִי חַיָּב. רַבִּי יְהוּדָה אוֹמֵר: בְּנֵר חֲנֻכָּה, פָּטוּר.

יד אברהם

בְּמַדְלִיק אֶת־הַבִּירָה — *in [the case of] one igniting a large tower,*

This translation follows *Rashi* here. In 22a, however, he defines בִּירָה as *a large house.* In I Chronicles 29:1, it is defined [by *Targum* et al.] as *a palace* (*Tos. Yom Tov*). [*Rashi* in 22a appears to fit our mishnah better than *Rashi* here.]

In this case, he sets fire to another person's property, which makes him a direct damager (*Rav*).

שֶׁהוּא מְשַׁלֵּם כָּל־מַה־שֶּׁבְּתוֹכָהּ — *that he pays for all that was inside it,*

[He must pay for all the things in the tower that were burned.]

שֶׁכֵּן דֶּרֶךְ בְּנֵי אָדָם לְהַנִּיחַ בְּבָתִּים — *for it is customary for people to place [things] in houses.*

Although the arsonist in this case is a direct damager, he is liable only because it is customary to place all sorts of things in houses. In a stack of grain, however, he is liable only for threshing sledges or cattle harnesses, which are generally found in stacks of grain. For purses, on the other hand, since they are not usually found there, he is exempt [as explained above] (*Rav*).

Hence, we deduce that the Sages require two stipulations to be liable for hidden articles burned in a fire. The first is that he set fire directly to another's property, and the second is that the articles burned are usually found in such places (*Tif. Yis.*).

6.

גֵּץ — *[If] a spark*

This translation follows *Rav* and *Rashi*. *Aruch*, however, defines it as a fine particle of metal (*Tif. Yis.*).

שֶׁיָּצָא מִתַּחַת הַפַּטִּישׁ — *flies out from under a hammer*

It flew out from under the hammer wielded by a blacksmith (*Rambam, Hil. Chovel Umazzik* 6:11).

וְהִזִּיק — *and damages,*

For example, it ignites a load of flax passing by in the street (*Meiri*).

חַיָּב — *he is liable.*

This is tantamount to one shooting an arrow or throwing a stone (*Tos. Yom Tov* from *Rambam* loc. cit.).

He should have stayed well within his shop to avoid causing such damage (*Meiri*).

גָּמָל שֶׁהָיָה טָעוּן פִּשְׁתָּן וְעָבַר בִּרְשׁוּת הָרַבִּים, וְנִכְנַס פִּשְׁתָּנוֹ לְתוֹךְ הַחֲנוּת, וְדָלְקוּ בְּנֵרוֹ שֶׁל־חֶנְוָנִי — *[If] a camel that is laden with flax stands in the public domain, and its flax protrudes [lit., enters] into a*

one igniting a large tower, that he pays for all that was inside it, for it is customary for people to place [things] in houses.

6. [If] a spark flies out from under a hammer and damages, he is liable. [If] a camel that is laden with flax stands in the public domain, and its flax protrudes into a shop, catches fire from the shopkeeper's lamp and ignites a large tower, the owner of the camel is liable. [If] the shopkeeper leaves his lamp outside, the shopkeeper is liable. R' Yehudah says: In [the case of] a Chanukah light, he is exempt.

YAD AVRAHAM

shop, catches fire from the shopkeeper's lamp,

Because of the length of the load, it protruded into the entrance of the shop and caught fire on a lamp burning there (*Meiri*).

וְהִדְלִיק אֶת־הַבִּירָה. — *and ignites a large tower,*

[The burning flax ignites a large tower (see mishnah 5).]

בַּעַל הַגָּמָל חַיָּב. — *the owner of the camel is liable.*

He is liable because he overloaded the camel (*Rambam, Hil. Nizkei Mamon* 14:13). The extent of his liability is identical to that described in 2:3, regarding the owner of a dog which takes a burning cake and ignites a stack with it. In that case, the dog's owner is liable for complete damages only for the place where the dog put down the cake, and only if it does so in a normal manner. Here, too, the owner of the camel is liable for the entire tower only if the entire tower is ignited at once. Otherwise, he is liable for full damages only for the place it ignites; for the rest of the tower, however, he is liable only for half the damages (*Tos. Yom Tov.* from *Tur* 418).

The intention is that when the fire spreads, it is considered a direct result of the camel's power, according to the principle of אִשּׁוֹ מִשּׁוּם חִצָּיו, *one is as liable for his fire as he is for his arrows* [see commentary to previous mishnah], and is tantamount to the case of *pebbles* (see 2:1,3 and commentary there) for which the owner is liable only for half the damages.

הִנִּיחַ חֶנְוָנִי נֵרוֹ מִבַּחוּץ, — [If] *the shopkeeper leaves his lamp outside,*

[And the camel passes by, the flax on it catches fire, and ignites the tower.]

הַחֶנְוָנִי חַיָּב. — *the shopkeeper is liable.*

He is liable not only for the tower, but even for the flax (*Rambam* loc. cit.).

רַבִּי יְהוּדָה אוֹמֵר: בְּנֵר חֲנֻכָּה, — *R' Yehudah says: In [the case of] a Chanukah light,*

[The shopkeeper had placed a Chanukah light outside his shop on one of the nights of Chanukah.]

פָּטוּר. — *he is exempt.*

[The shopkeeper is exempt from liability for the damages caused by the fire.]

Since it is a *mitzvah* to place the light in the street within ten handbreadths from the ground, he could not place it higher than the camel and its rider. He therefore has permission to place it there

[139] THE MISHNAH/BAVA KAMMA – Chapter Six: *HaKoneis*

בבא קמא ז/א

[א] מְרֻבָּה מִדַּת תַּשְׁלוּמֵי כֶפֶל מִמִּדַּת תַּשְׁלוּמֵי אַרְבָּעָה וַחֲמִשָּׁה, שֶׁמִּדַּת תַּשְׁלוּמֵי כֶפֶל נוֹהֶגֶת בֵּין בְּדָבָר שֶׁיֵּשׁ בּוֹ רוּחַ חַיִּים וּבֵין בְּדָבָר שֶׁאֵין בּוֹ רוּחַ חַיִּים, וּמִדַּת תַּשְׁלוּמֵי אַרְבָּעָה וַחֲמִשָּׁה אֵינָהּ נוֹהֶגֶת אֶלָּא בְשׁוֹר וָשֶׂה בִּלְבָד, שֶׁנֶּאֱמַר: "כִּי יִגְנֹב־אִישׁ שׁוֹר אוֹ־שֶׂה וּטְבָחוֹ אוֹ מְכָרוֹ וְגוֹ'."

יד אברהם

and is exempt for the damages it causes. Unlike those who have permission to litter the public domain [3:2f.], since the permission in this case is the result of a *mitzvah*, he is exempt (*Tif. Yis.* from *Gem.* 30a, 62b).

The Sages, however, differ with R' Yehudah and rule that, even in the case of the Chanukah light, the owner is liable because he should have remained there and guarded it. The halachah follows this view (*Rav; Rambam Commentary; Tos. Yom Tov* from *Rambam* loc. cit.).

This differs from the case of 3:6, in which the one who runs on the eve of the Sabbath is exempt for the damages he commits, since it is impossible to be totally careful while running. In the case of the Chanukah light, however, he can stay and watch the light (*Tif. Yis.*).

Chapter 7

After delineating the laws of damages, in which people are liable in certain cases although they had no intention of damaging, the Mishnah proceeds to discuss the laws of a thief, who intends to deprive his victim of his property in order to profit thereby. Following this are the laws of one person wounding another (chapter 8), in which the perpetrator — similar to the thief — intends to injure his victim, and, finally, the laws of the robber (see below) [chapters 9, 10]. The *Tanna* does not combine the laws of the thief and the robber, but rather discusses the subjects in descending order of their stringency: A thief may be liable to a twofold, fourfold, or fivefold payment, as discussed below; one who wounds is liable for five items (8:1); a robber, however, pays only the principal [*Lev.* 5:23] (*Tif. Yis.*).

כֶּפֶל / The Twofold Payment

The following chapter deals with the laws of theft. A גַּנָּב, *thief*, is one who stealthily takes a person's property without the owner's knowledge, such as a pickpocket. A גַּזְלָן, *robber*, on the other hand, takes it openly and in public by force (*Gem.* 79b; *Rambam, Hil. Geneivah* 1:3).

If qualified witnesses testified that a thief stole something, he is liable to pay twice that amount to the owner of the stolen property. If he stole a dinar, he pays two; if he stole a donkey, a garment, or a camel, he pays twice its value. He thus loses an amount equal to that which he wished to deprive another of (*Rambam* ibid. §4).

A robber, however, is liable only for the value of the item he stole. This is because a thief, who commits his crime clandestinely so as not to be seen by people,

[140]

7
1

1. The rule of twofold payment is more inclusive than the rule of fourfold and fivefold payments, for the rule of twofold payment applies both to living things and to inanimate things, whereas the rule of fourfold and fivefold payments applies exclusively with regard to an ox or a lamb, as it is said (*Exodus* 21:37): *If a man steals an ox or a lamb and slaughters it or sells it ...*

YAD AVRAHAM

obviously is not concerned that God sees him, and, in effect, denies God's knowledge of his deeds. The robber, in contrast, takes his plunder by force, disregarding both God and man. The Torah therefore imposes a fine only on the thief, not the robber (*Gem.* loc. cit.).

⊷§ אַרְבָּעָה וַחֲמִשָּׁה / **The Fourfold and Fivefold Payments**

If one steals a lamb and slaughters or sells it, he pays fourfold its value; if he does the same to an ox, he pays fivefold its value (*Rambam* ibid. §6).

The reason that the payment for stealing a lamb is less is that since it is not a draft animal, he is not taking it away from doing work. One who steals an ox, however, is interfering with its work. R' Meir said: See how great is the importance of work!

Alternatively, since a lamb is usually carried by the thief on his shoulders, and he thereby belittles himself, the Torah dealt with him more leniently than with one who steals an ox, which walks on its own. R' Yochanan ben Zakkai said: See how great is the importance of human dignity! (*Gem.* loc. cit., *Rashi* ad loc.).

1.

מְרֻבָּה מִדַּת תַּשְׁלוּמֵי כֶפֶל מִמִּדַּת תַּשְׁלוּמֵי אַרְבָּעָה וַחֲמִשָּׁה. — *The rule of twofold payment is more inclusive than the rule of fourfold and fivefold payments,*

[The rule of כֶּפֶל, *the twofold payment,* which a thief pays for stealing, applies to more items than the rule of the fourfold and fivefold payments, which a thief who has slaughtered or sold the stolen animal must pay.]

שֶׁמִּדַּת תַּשְׁלוּמֵי כֶפֶל נוֹהֶגֶת בֵּין בְּדָבָר שֶׁיֵּשׁ בּוֹ רוּחַ חַיִּים וּבֵין בְּדָבָר שֶׁאֵין בּוֹ רוּחַ חַיִּים — *for the rule of twofold payment applies both to living things and to inanimate things,*

This is based on *Exodus* 22:8: *For any article of trespass, for an ox, for a donkey, for a lamb, for a garment, for any lost article ... he shall pay twofold to the other person.* This includes all types of articles, whether living or inanimate (*Rav* from *Gem.* 62b-64b).

וּמִדַּת תַּשְׁלוּמֵי אַרְבָּעָה וַחֲמִשָּׁה אֵינָה נוֹהֶגֶת אֶלָּא בְּשׁוֹר וָשֶׂה בִּלְבָד, שֶׁנֶּאֱמַר: ,,כִּי יִגְנֹב אִישׁ שׁוֹר אוֹ שֶׂה וּטְבָחוֹ אוֹ מְכָרוֹ וגו'". — *whereas the rule of fourfold and fivefold payments applies exclusively to an ox or a lamb, as it is said (Exodus 21:37): If a man steals an ox or a lamb and slaughters it or sells it ...*

The verse concludes: *He shall pay five cattle instead of the ox and four sheep instead of the lamb.* Although other references to *ox* include all species of cattle, beasts, and fowl, as discussed in 5:7, here the verse refers exclusively to an ox and a lamb. This is derived from the repetition of *ox* and *lamb* (*Tif. Yis.* from *Gem.* 67b).

[141]   THE MISHNAH/BAVA KAMMA — Chapter Seven: *Merubah*

בבא קמא ז/ב

אֵין הַגּוֹנֵב אַחַר הַגַּנָּב מְשַׁלֵּם תַּשְׁלוּמֵי כֶפֶל, וְלֹא הַטּוֹבֵחַ וְלֹא הַמּוֹכֵר אַחַר הַגַּנָּב מְשַׁלֵּם תַּשְׁלוּמֵי אַרְבָּעָה וַחֲמִשָּׁה.

[ב] **גָּנַב** עַל-פִּי שְׁנַיִם, וְטָבַח וּמָכַר עַל-פִּיהֶם, אוֹ עַל-פִּי שְׁנַיִם אֲחֵרִים, מְשַׁלֵּם תַּשְׁלוּמֵי אַרְבָּעָה וַחֲמִשָּׁה. גָּנַב וּמָכַר בַּשַּׁבָּת; גָּנַב וּמָכַר לַעֲבוֹדָה זָרָה; גָּנַב וְטָבַח בְּיוֹם הַכִּפּוּרִים; גָּנַב מִשֶּׁל-אָבִיו, וְטָבַח

יד אברהם

— אֵין הַגּוֹנֵב אַחַר הַגַּנָּב מְשַׁלֵּם תַּשְׁלוּמֵי כֶפֶל, *One who steals after a thief does not pay the twofold payment,*

This is derived from Exodus 22:6: וְגֻנַּב מִבֵּית הָאִישׁ, *and it is stolen from the house of the man,* which is interpreted to mean that the thief pays twofold only if the article is stolen from its owner or a שׁוֹמֵר, *guardian,* to whom it was entrusted, but not if it was stolen from a thief, who was holding the article for himself, not for the owner (Rav, Rashi from Gem. 79b).

Tos. R' Akiva explains that the ownership of an article is considered impaired if it is not in its owner's possession, but in the possession of a thief, who is keeping it for himself. This is evidenced by the fact that in such a situation the owner has no power to consecrate the article. An article entrusted to a guardian, however, who is keeping the article for the owner, is regarded as being in the owner's possession. Therefore, one who steals such an object is liable to pay the twofold payment. [In fact, the verse mentioned above, from where we derive the law of the double payment, deals with a thief who steals from a guardian.]

וְלֹא הַטּוֹבֵחַ וְלֹא הַמּוֹכֵר אַחַר הַגַּנָּב מְשַׁלֵּם תַּשְׁלוּמֵי אַרְבָּעָה וַחֲמִשָּׁה. — *nor does one who slaughters or sells after a thief pay the fourfold or fivefold payment.*

If someone steals a lamb or an ox from a thief and slaughters it or sells it, since he makes no twofold payment, as explained above, there would remain only a threefold payment for the lamb and a fourfold payment for the ox. Since the Torah did not prescribe any such payments, he does not pay them either (*Tos. Chadashim*).

Moreover, since — when the animal is in the first thief's possession — it is not considered as being in the possession of its owner, for which reason the Torah exempts the second thief from the twofold payment, so does it exempt him from the fourfold and fivefold payments (*Rambam, Hil. Geneivah* 1:17).

2.

The following mishnah enumerates instances in which a thief pays fourfold or fivefold payments.

גָּנַב עַל-פִּי שְׁנַיִם, וְטָבַח וּמָכַר עַל-פִּיהֶם, אוֹ עַל-פִּי שְׁנַיִם אֲחֵרִים, — *[If] according to two [witnesses, a person] stole, and — according to them or according to two others — he slaughtered or sold,*

Two witnesses testify that a person

7 One who steals after a thief does not pay the two-
2 fold payment, nor does one who slaughters or sells
after a thief pay the fourfold or fivefold payment.

2. [If] according to two [witnesses, a person] stole, and — according to them or according to two others — he slaughtered or sold, he pays the fourfold or fivefold payment.

[If] one stole and sold on the Sabbath; stole and sold for idolatry; stole and slaughtered on Yom Kippur; stole from his father, slaughtered or sold it,

YAD AVRAHAM

stole a lamb or an ox *(Rav; Rashi)* [and the same two, or another pair, testify that he slaughtered or sold it].

מְשַׁלֵּם תַּשְׁלוּמֵי אַרְבָּעָה וַחֲמִשָּׁה — *he pays the fourfold or fivefold payment.*

Although the testimony of the first pair of witnesses is necessary to make the testimony of the second pair relevant — for if the animal was not stolen, there is obviously nothing wrong with selling or slaughtering it — the latter testimony is not regarded as one concerning 'half a matter' and is acceptable even according to R' Akiva, who disallows testimony concerning 'half a matter.'[1] Because the testimony of the first pair — that the thief stole — is relevant even without the testimony of the second pair, since it causes the thief to pay the twofold payment, both testimonies are regarded as concerning a complete matter *(Tos. Yom Tov from Gem. 70b).*

גָּנַב וּמָכַר בְּשַׁבָּת; — [*If*] *one stole and sold on the Sabbath;*

Since selling on the Sabbath is a Rabbinical prohibition and therefore

not punishable by death, the perpetrator in this case is liable to the fourfold or fivefold payment *(Rambam, Hil. Geneivah* 3:5). However, if after stealing an animal, the thief *slaughters* it on the Sabbath — a capital crime — he is exempt from the fourfold or fivefold payment, because of the principle of קִים לֵיהּ בְּדְרַבָּה מִינֵּיהּ, *he suffers only the more severe punishment* [see commentary to 6:5] *(Rav; Rashi).*

גָּנַב וּמָכַר לַעֲבוֹדָה זָרָה; — *stole and sold for idolatry;*

[If one stole a lamb or an ox and sold it for idolatrous purposes, he is liable for the four/fivefold payment. This is because he did not perform the idolatrous worship, and is therefore not guilty of a capital crime.] Should he slaughter the animal as a sacrifice to the idol, however, he is exempt from the four/fivefold payment, since *he suffers only the more severe punishment:* death [see mishnah 4] *(Tif. Yis.).*

גָּנַב וְטָבַח בְּיוֹם הַכִּפּוּרִים; — *stole and slaughtered on Yom Kippur;*

The deliberate desecration of Yom

---

1. R' Akiva interprets the verse *(Deut.* 19:15) עַל־פִּי שְׁנֵי עֵדִים ... יָקוּם דָּבָר, *By the testimony of two witnesses ... shall a matter be established,* as applying only to *a matter,* but not *half a matter.* For example, when a person uses the fact that he enjoyed the undisturbed use of property for three years as proof that he owns it *(Bava Basra* 3:1), R' Akiva requires that the same set of witnesses testify regarding all three years. If, however, one set can testify only with regard to one or two years, this is considered testimony concerning 'half a matter' and is not valid (ibid. 56b).

בבא קמא ז/ב

וּמָכַר, וְאַחַר־כָּךְ מֵת אָבִיו; גָּנַב וְטָבַח, וְאַחַר־כָּךְ הִקְדִּישׁ — מְשַׁלֵּם תַּשְׁלוּמֵי אַרְבָּעָה וַחֲמִשָּׁה. גָּנַב וְטָבַח לִרְפוּאָה אוֹ לִכְלָבִים, הַשּׁוֹחֵט וְנִמְצָא טְרֵפָה, הַשּׁוֹחֵט חֻלִּין בָּעֲזָרָה, מְשַׁלֵּם תַּשְׁלוּמֵי

יד אברהם

Kippur is punishable by כָּרֵת, *kares* [spiritual excision, premature death], decreed by the Heavenly Tribunal [*Lev.* 23:29f.*]*. Since the rule of *he suffers only the more severe punishment* applies only to penalties meted out by a court, the perpetrator in this case is not exempt from the four/fivefold payment. Although, under certain conditions, such a person would be liable to lashes — a punishment by the court which does exempt one from monetary payment — the mishnah is dealing with an instance in which he would not be subject to lashes; e.g., he was not properly warned. However, should one commit a capital offense even inadvertently or without being warned, he is exempt from monetary liabilities incurred simultaneously (*Rav; Rashi*).

If the thief gives the animal to another person to slaughter for him on Yom Kippur, since the latter is the one who is liable for lashes if he does it, the thief must pay the four/fivefold payment. Although the general rule is that אֵין שָׁלִיחַ לִדְבַר עֲבֵרָה, *there is no agent in matters of sin*, as discussed in 6:4, the verse which teaches us the laws of the four/fivefold payment (*Ex.* 21:37) is exegetically interpreted as indicating that they are an exception (*Rambam Commentary* from *Gem.* 71a).

Surprisingly, the commentators do not quote the conclusion of the *Gemara*, that the mishnah is attributed to R' Meir, who rules that one is liable to monetary payment although he receives lashes. *Shoshannim LeDavid* explains that the *Gemara* follows Resh Lakish, who rules that if one is guilty of a sin for which the penalty is lashes, even if he is not actually liable for that punishment — e.g., he was not warned — he is nevertheless exempt from monetary liabilities [see commentary to 3:10, s.v. מִפְּנֵי]. Accordingly, the mishnah must be attributed to R' Meir. The halachah is, however, in accordance with R' Yochanan, who rules that the penalty of lashes exempts from monetary liabilities only if it is actually administered. The commentators therefore explain the mishnah according to that opinion.

גָּנַב מִשֶּׁל־אָבִיו, — *stole from his father,* [One stole a lamb or an ox belonging to his father.]

— וְטָבַח וּמָכַר, וְאַחַר־כָּךְ מֵת אָבִיו; *slaughtered or sold it, and then his father died;*

He slaughtered it or sold it during his father's lifetime, when he had not yet inherited any part of it. Although his father died before he had paid for it, and even before he was ordered to do so by the court, and now he has already inherited part of the animal, he must nevertheless pay the other heirs according to their share of the stolen animal (*Gem.* 71b).

Should he slaughter or sell the animal after his father's death, however, he is exempt from the fourfold or fivefold payment, as stated in mishnah 4. This is because the word (*Ex.* 21:27) וּטְבָחוֹ, *and slaughter it,* is construed as meaning that the slaughtering must be a completely unlawful act, and since — in this case — part of the animal already belongs to him through inheritance, his act does not fit this description (*Rav* from *Gem.* 72a).

[Surprisingly, *Tos. Yom Tov*, quoting *Rosh*, comments that this halachah is obvious, and that there is no reason for stating it in the mishnah, except to contrast it with the case in mishnah 4 of the thief who slaughters or sells the animal after the death of his father.]

— גָּנַב וְטָבַח, וְאַחַר־כָּךְ הִקְדִּישׁ — [*or*] *stole*

משניות / בבא קמא — פרק ז: מרובה [144]

7 2 and then his father died; [or] stole and slaughtered, and then consecrated — he pays the fourfold or fivefold payment.

[If] one stole and slaughtered for medicinal purposes or for dogs, if one slaughters and it is found to have an organic defect, [or] if one slaughters an ordinary animal in the Temple Courtyard, he pays

YAD AVRAHAM

and slaughtered, and then consecrated —

[After stealing and slaughtering an animal, the thief consecrated it. He is able to do so, because a thief who makes a change in the stolen item — as this one did by slaughtering it — acquires it thereby (see preface to 9:1).]

The intent of the mishnah must be that the thief consecrated the animal so that it should be used for בֶּדֶק הַבַּיִת, *repairs of the Temple*, since a slaughtered animal cannot be consecrated as an offering. Actually, even if he does not slaughter the animal, but only consecrates it for repairs of the Temple, it is tantamount to selling it, because it no longer is considered the property of the one who consecrated it, and he would therefore be liable for the four/fivefold payment. Should he consecrate it to be used as an offering, however, the sacrifice still is considered to be his property, and is not regarded as having been sold. Mishnah 4 — which states that if the thief consecrates the animal and then slaughters it, he is exempt from the four/fivefold payment — obviously refers to one who consecrates the animal to be used as an offering (*Tos. R' Akiva*).

מְשַׁלֵּם תַּשְׁלוּמֵי אַרְבָּעָה וַחֲמִשָּׁה. — *he pays the fourfold or fivefold payment.*

[In each of these cases, the thief pays the four/fivefold payments, as explained above.]

גָּנַב וְטָבַח לִרְפוּאָה — [*If*] *one stole and slaughtered for medicinal purposes*

The meat is not to be used for food, but for medicinal purposes; surely, this law is applicable if he sells it for medicinal purposes (*Tif. Yis.*)

אוֹ לִכְלָבִים, — *or for dogs,*

Although one slaughters an animal with the intention of feeding it to dogs, if the slaughter was done properly, it is valid for human consumption as well (*Meiri*).

הַשּׁוֹחֵט וְנִמְצָא טְרֵפָה, — *if one slaughters and it is found to have an organic defect,*

[He steals a lamb or an ox and slaughters it, and discovers that it has an organic defect — an injury or a malady which would not have permitted it to live for twelve months had he not slaughtered it — he is nevertheless liable for the four/fivefold payments. Although such an animal is designated by the Torah (*Ex.* 22:30) as טְרֵפָה, *torn*, an invalid slaughter is nevertheless enough to make him liable for these payments.]

הַשּׁוֹחֵט חֻלִּין בָּעֲזָרָה, — [*or*] *if one slaughters an ordinary animal in the Temple Courtyard,*

[He slaughters an unconsecrated animal that he has stolen in the Courtyard of the Temple. Unconsecrated animals may not be slaughtered within the Temple confines; if they are, they may neither be eaten nor used for any other benefit. Nevertheless, the slaughter is sufficient to make the thief liable to the four/fivefold payment according to this *Tanna*, as in the above case.]

Because benefit may not be derived from such animals, they are deemed as

בבא קמא ז/ג

אַרְבָּעָה וַחֲמִשָּׁה. רַבִּי שִׁמְעוֹן פּוֹטֵר בִּשְׁנֵי אֵלּוּ.

[ג] גָּנַב עַל־פִּי שְׁנַיִם, וְטָבַח וּמָכַר עַל־פִּיהֶם, וְנִמְצְאוּ זוֹמְמִין, מְשַׁלְּמִין הַכֹּל.

יד אברהם

no longer belonging to their owners. This occurs when the thief makes the first cut in the throat organs. He therefore should not be liable for the four/fivefold payment since a requisite for these payments is that the animal still belong to its original owner at the time of the slaughter. He cannot be liable for the first cut alone, since the liability applies only when one slaughters an entire animal. To explain why the mishnah concludes that he is nevertheless liable for these payments, the *Gemara* [72b] qualifies this case as one in which the thief began slaughtering the lamb or the ox outside the Temple Courtyard and completed the slaughter within the Courtyard *(Tos. Yom Tov)*.

According to *Rambam (Hil. Geneivah 2:8)*, who rules that the prohibition of benefiting from unconsecrated animals slaughtered in the Courtyard is Rabbinical, since Biblical law permits benefit from the flesh, the animal is deemed as still belonging to its original owner, and the thief is therefore liable for the four/fivefold payment.

מְשַׁלֵּם תַּשְׁלוּמֵי אַרְבָּעָה וַחֲמִשָּׁה — *he pays the fourfold or fivefold payment.*

As explained above, this anonymous *Tanna* — identified as R' Meir — rules that even an invalid slaughter is deemed a slaughter with regard to the four/fivefold payment. The distinction between an invalid slaughter and one which is not considered a slaughter at all is not delineated explicitly in the *Gemara*. *Chiddushei HaRan (Chullin 14b)* suggests that even if the slaughter is not valid, as long as it prevents the animal from becoming ritually con-taminated as a נְבֵלָה, *an animal that dies without having been properly slaughtered*, it is deemed a slaughter albeit an invalid one. Should the slaughter be completely disqualified, however, so that the animal does become ritually contaminated, it is considered as no slaughter whatever, and is tantamount to piercing the nostrils or tearing out the throat organs (mishnah 5).

Meiri (Chullin 14a, 81b) appears to explain that as long as the slaughter in any of these cases was performed by a Jew according to the proper procedure, it is deemed an invalid slaughter. Should it have been performed by a non-Jew or not according to the laws of kosher slaughter, it is considered as no slaughter whatever (see mishnah 5).

רַבִּי שִׁמְעוֹן פּוֹטֵר בִּשְׁנֵי אֵלּוּ — *R' Shimon exempts [him] in these two [instances].*

R' Shimon exempts the thief from the four/fivefold payment in the last two instances: the one who slaughters and finds the animal to have an organic defect, and the one who slaughters an unconsecrated animal in the Temple Courtyard. In these instances, the slaughtering — which does not make the animal fit for consumption — is invalid, and, according to R' Shimon, is therefore not deemed a slaughter as regards the four/fivefold payment. R' Shimon concurs with the Sages, however, in the instances of the thief slaughtering for medicinal purposes or for dogs. In these cases, the slaughter is valid, and the flesh may be eaten should he desire to partake of it; hence, he is also liable for the four/fivefold payment *(Rav)*.

the fourfold or fivefold payment. R' Shimon exempts [him] in these two [instances].

3. [If] according to two [witnesses] a person stole, and — according to them — he slaughtered or sold, and they are found to be false [witnesses], they pay in full.

YAD AVRAHAM

3.

The following mishnah deals with the law of עֵדִים זוֹמְמִין, *false witnesses:* Should it be discovered that witnesses testified falsely against a person, the Torah (*Deut. 19:16ff.*) ordains that they must suffer the same punishment they had plotted for the defendant. This law is not based on logic; it is a Scriptural anomaly (*Gem.* 72b). The Mishnah (*Makkos* 1:4) states that this punishment is meted out only if other witnesses testify that at the time the crime had allegedly occurred, these witnesses were with them in a place other than where the crime was said to have been committed. However, should they claim that the defendant or victim of the crime was with them at that time, it is not assumed that the first pair of witnesses testified falsely, but their testimony is void because we do not know which pair of witnesses is saying the truth (*Rambam, Hil. Edus* 18:1f.). Likewise, if the testimony of the first pair is voided in any manner other than that described above, no penalty is imposed upon the witnesses. This is derived exegetically from the above passage (*Makkos* 5a).

גָּנַב עַל־פִּי שְׁנַיִם, וְטָבַח וּמָכַר עַל־פִּיהֶם [If] — *according to two [witnesses] a person stole, and — according to them — he slaughtered or sold,*

[The same witnesses who testified that he stole also testified that he slaughtered or sold.]

וְנִמְצְאוּ זוֹמְמִין, — *and they are found to be false [witnesses],*

[It is discovered that they testified falsely concerning both the theft and the slaughter or sale.]

מְשַׁלְּמִין הַכֹּל. — *they pay in full.*

[The witnesses must pay the full four/fivefold payment to the person they accused of stealing.]

Tos. Yom Tov, quoting *Rashi,* comments that the testimony regarding the slaughter or sale was disproved first. Should the testimony regarding the theft be disproved first, however, the testimony regarding the slaughter or sale obviously becomes void automatically, since, if the person did not steal the animal, perhaps it was his legitimately, and there would be no crime in slaughtering or selling it. Consequently, the witnesses would have to pay the twofold payment, but would be exempt from the four/fivefold payment even if that testimony, too, is subsequently proved false, since it was totally ineffective in any case.

However, *Tosafos,* quoted by *Tos. R' Akiva,* contend that, even if the testimony regarding the slaughter would be disproved first, the part regarding the theft would also be disqualified, since the law is that if a witness testifies falsely, he becomes disqualified to testify from that time on. For example, if a witness testified in the month of Nissan, and that testimony is proven false by witnesses who come the following Tishri, all the testimonies given by the first witness since Nissan are disqualified. Therefore, in our case,

בבא קמא ז/ג

גָּנַב עַל־פִּי שְׁנַיִם וְטָבַח וּמָכַר עַל־פִּי שְׁנַיִם אֲחֵרִים, אֵלּוּ וָאֵלּוּ נִמְצְאוּ זוֹמְמִין — הָרִאשׁוֹנִים מְשַׁלְּמִין תַּשְׁלוּמֵי כֶפֶל, וְהָאַחֲרוֹנִים מְשַׁלְּמִין תַּשְׁלוּמֵי שְׁלֹשָׁה. נִמְצְאוּ הָאַחֲרוֹנִים זוֹמְמִין, הוּא מְשַׁלֵּם תַּשְׁלוּמֵי כֶפֶל, וְהֵן מְשַׁלְּמִין תַּשְׁלוּמֵי שְׁלֹשָׁה. אֶחָד מִן־הָאַחֲרוֹנִים זוֹמֵם, בָּטְלָה עֵדוּת שְׁנִיָּה; אֶחָד מִן־הָרִאשׁוֹנִים זוֹמֵם, בָּטְלָה כָּל־

יד אברהם

גָּנַב עַל־פִּי שְׁנַיִם וְטָבַח וּמָכַר עַל־פִּי שְׁנַיִם אֲחֵרִים, — [*If*] *according to two* [*witnesses*] *he stole and — according to two others — he slaughtered or sold*,

[Two witnesses testified that a person stole an ox or a lamb, and two others testified that he slaughtered or sold it.]

אֵלּוּ וָאֵלּוּ נִמְצְאוּ זוֹמְמִין — *and both of them were found to be false* [*witnesses*] —

[Other witnesses came and testified that both pairs of witnesses were with them at the time of the alleged crimes.]

הָרִאשׁוֹנִים מְשַׁלְּמִין תַּשְׁלוּמֵי כֶפֶל, — *the first ones pay the twofold payment*,

[The first witnesses, who had plotted to make the defendant pay the twofold payment, must pay that amount themselves.]

וְהָאַחֲרוֹנִים מְשַׁלְּמִין תַּשְׁלוּמֵי שְׁלֹשָׁה. — *and the second ones pay the threefold payment.*

[The second pair of witnesses, who plotted to make the defendant pay an additional threefold payment for slaughtering or selling the ox, must pay the amount.] Of course, should the animal in question have been a lamb, they would pay a twofold payment. The mishnah mentions only one case for the sake of brevity.]

This ruling applies only to a case in which the second pair of witnesses was proven false first. Should the first pair have been proven false first, the testimony of the second pair — that he

since the witnesses who testified about the theft were the same ones who testifed about the slaughter, and their testimony regarding the slaughter was proven false, they are automatically disqualified for the testimony regarding the theft, because both testimonies were stated together. Therefore, even if later it is discovered that they testified falsely regarding the theft as well, they are not penalized. Our mishnah — which states that they are penalized for the full four/fivefold payments — must be dealing with a case in which both testimonies were disproved simultaneously.

Tos. R' Akiva proceeds to explain that the opinions of both *Rashi* and *Tosafos* are based on the view that once testimony is contradicted, the penalty for false testimony is not administered. The halachah is, however, that הַכְחָשָׁה תְּחִלַּת הֲזָמָה, *contradiction is the beginning of disproving* — i.e., if the testimony of witnesses is first contradicted by other witnesses, and then found to be definitely false because a third pair of witnesses testifies that they were with them at the time, as discussed above, they are adjudged as false witnesses and the penalty is imposed upon them. Consequently, even if the testimony concerning the theft was disproved first, they are nevertheless still liable to be penalized for the testimony regarding the slaughter or the sale if witnesses testify that they were with them at the time.

משניות / בבא קמא — פרק ז: מרובה [148]

7
3
[If] according to two [witnesses] he stole and — according to two others — he slaughtered or sold, and both of them were found to be false [witnesses] — the first ones pay the twofold payment, and the second ones pay the threefold payment. If the second ones were found to be false [witnesses], he pays the twofold payment and they pay the threefold payment. [If] one of the second ones is found to be false, the second testimony is void; [if] one of the first ones is found to be false, the entire testimony is

YAD AVRAHAM

slaughtered or sold the animal — is voided, because the owner may have sold him the animal, and when he slaughtered or sold it, he was doing so to his own animal. Therefore, when their testimony is disproved, there is no reason to impose the penalty upon them (*Rav; Rashi*).

Similar to the comment of *Tos. R' Akiva*, cited above, *Lechem Mishneh* (*Hil. Eidus* 21:6) maintains that this follows only according to the opinion that *contradiction is not the beginning of disproving*. Therefore, since the testimony of the second witnesses is no longer effective, there can be no penalty when it is disproved. According to the halachah, however, that *contradiction is the beginning of disproving*, even if the testimony of the first witnesses is disproved first, and then that of the second ones, the latter must nonetheless pay the penalty of false witnesses.

נִמְצְאוּ הָאַחֲרוֹנִים זוֹמְמִין, — [*If*] *the second ones were found to be false* [*witnesses*],

[The witnesses who testified that the person slaughtered or sold the animal were found to be false.]

הוּא מְשַׁלֵּם תַּשְׁלוּמֵי כֶפֶל, — *he pays the twofold payment,*

[The one whom the first witnesses accused of stealing must pay the twofold payment, since their testimony was not disproved.]

וְהֵן מְשַׁלְּמִין תַּשְׁלוּמֵי שְׁלֹשָׁה. — *and they*

pay the threefold payment.

[That is, if the item that was stolen was an ox, the second pair of witnesses pay the threefold payment which they plotted to make the thief pay in addition to the twofold payment for which he was already liable. Here, too, if the stolen animal had been a lamb, they would pay an additional twofold payment.]

אֶחָד מִן־הָאַחֲרוֹנִים זוֹמֵם, — [*If*] *one of the second ones is found to be false,*

[Another pair of witnesses testified that one of the second pair had been with them at the time of the alleged slaughter or sale.]

בָּטְלָה עֵדוּת שְׁנִיָּה; — *the second testimony is void;*

The defendant must pay the twofold payment, since the testimony of the first witnesses is still in force. The second witnesses, however, are both exempt — even the one who was disproved — since witnesses are not punished unless both are proven false (*Tif. Yis.*).

אֶחָד מִן־הָרִאשׁוֹנִים זוֹמֵם, — [*if*] *one of the first ones is found to be false,*

[One of the first witnesses, who testified concerning the theft, was found to be a false witness through two other witnesses, who testified that he was with them at the time of the alleged theft.]

בָּטְלָה כָּל־הָעֵדוּת, — *the entire testimony is*

[149]   THE MISHNAH/BAVA KAMMA — Chapter Seven: *Merubah*

בבא קמא ז/ד

הָעֵדוּת, שֶׁאִם אֵין גְּנֵבָה, אֵין טְבִיחָה וְאֵין מְכִירָה.

[ד] גָּנַב עַל־פִּי שְׁנַיִם, וְטָבַח וּמָכַר עַל־פִּי עֵד אֶחָד אוֹ עַל־פִּי עַצְמוֹ, מְשַׁלֵּם תַּשְׁלוּמֵי כֶפֶל, וְאֵינוֹ מְשַׁלֵּם תַּשְׁלוּמֵי אַרְבָּעָה וַחֲמִשָּׁה. גָּנַב וְטָבַח בַּשַּׁבָּת; גָּנַב וְטָבַח לַעֲבוֹדָה זָרָה; גָּנַב

יד אברהם

void,

Since one of the first witnesses was proven false, the defendant is exempt from paying the twofold payment. The first witnesses are likewise exempt, since only one of them was proven to be false. Although the testimony of the second witnesses becomes automatically void, they are not liable, since liability applies only if the disproving witnesses testify that the accusing witnesses were with them. Also, in this case [as explained above], the witnesses to the slaughter or sale are not liable, since their testimony may be true that the defendant slaughtered or sold the animal, but he may have purchased it from its previous owners. Even if there are witnesses that he did not purchase it, they are not liable for this contradiction, because of the reason mentioned above.

Even if other witnesses later do testify that the accusing witnesses were with them there is no liability, since their testimony was already voided (Rav; Tos. Yom Tov). [As mentioned above, according to the halachah, the second pair would be liable in such a case.]

Surely, if both of the first pair of witnesses is disproved, the entire testimony is void except that, in that case, the first pair must pay the twofold payment (Tif. Yis.).

שֶׁאִם אֵין גְּנֵבָה, אֵין טְבִיחָה וְאֵין מְכִירָה — for if there is no theft, there is no slaughter and no sale.

As explained above, if we have no proof that a person stole an animal, his slaughtering or selling it does not make him liable to pay anything (Rambam, Hil. Eidus 21:6).

4.

This mishnah presents various instances in which the thief is liable for the twofold payment but exempt from the four/fivefold payment. Most of these instances are contrasted with those mentioned in mishnah 2.

גָּנַב עַל־פִּי שְׁנַיִם — [If] according to two [witnesses] one stole,

[Two witnesses testified that a person stole.]

וְטָבַח וּמָכַר עַל־פִּי עֵד אֶחָד אוֹ עַל־פִּי עַצְמוֹ — and — according to one witness or by his own confession — he slaughtered or sold,

[Either one witness testified or he himself confessed that he had slaughtered or sold the lamb or the ox.]

מְשַׁלֵּם תַּשְׁלוּמֵי כֶפֶל — he pays the twofold payment,

[He must pay the twofold payment, since witnesses testified that he stole.]

וְאֵינוֹ מְשַׁלֵּם תַּשְׁלוּמֵי אַרְבָּעָה וַחֲמִשָּׁה — but he does not pay the fourfold or fivefold payment.

Since a fine cannot be imposed upon anyone unless two qualified witnesses testify against him, he does not pay the four/fivefold payment by the testimony

[150]

4. [I]f] according to two [witnesses] one stole and — according to one witness or by his own confession — he slaughtered or sold, he pays the twofold payment, but he does not pay the fourfold or fivefold payment.

[If] one stole and slaughtered on the Sabbath; stole and slaughtered for idolatry; stole from his father,

YAD AVRAHAM

of one witness or by his own confession.

The *Gemara*, considering this to be obvious, explains that it is necessary for the *Tanna* to state this law for the following reason: Just as — in the case of one witness — should another witness come later, he joins the first one in forming a pair to impose a fine upon the defendant, so it is in the case of confession: should two witnesses come after the defendant has confessed his crime, the fine is imposed upon him. However, this rule applies only if his confession does not make him liable to pay the original amount of the theft, as in this case, in which he confessed to the slaughtering or sale only after the witnesses had testified that he stole, and the court had imposed the twofold payment upon him. Since he does not obligate himself by this confession at all — because he knows that one who admits to a crime to which he must pay a fine is exempt from paying it — it is not considered a confession of any consequence. Therefore, when witnesses subsequently testify that he slaughtered or sold, the fine is imposed upon him. Should he have confessed from the outset that he stole, however, and then witnesses came and testified to the same effect, since his confession had made him liable to pay the principal amount, it is considered to have been of consequence, and the twofold payment is not imposed when the witnesses testify (*Rav* from *Gem.* 75a-b).

גָּנַב וְטָבַח בְּשַׁבָּת; — [*If*] *one stole and slaughtered on the Sabbath;*

As explained in the commentary to mishnah 2, since slaughtering on the Sabbath is a capital crime, even if it was committed without the perpetrator being warned — in which case he does not receive the death penalty — no monetary liability is imposed upon him (*Tif. Yis.*).

גָּנַב וְטָבַח לַעֲבוֹדָה זָרָה; — *stole and slaughtered for idolatry;*

The same follows for this instance, since slaughtering an animal as a sacrifice to idols is a capital offense. A case in which one appoints an agent to slaughter the animal, would be subject to the controversy between R' Shimon and R' Meir, whether an invalid slaughtering is deemed a slaughtering [see commentary loc. cit.]. In our case, since a sacrifice offered to idols becomes prohibited even for benefits other than eating, we must qualify the mishnah as referring to one who designates this animal as a sacrifice only when he makes the very last cut in the throat organs, otherwise [as explained there] the animal would become forbidden for benefit upon the first cut, and be considered ownerless. Hence, there is no liability for the four/fivefold payment, since that penalty is applicable only if the entire slaughtering of the animal is done while it belongs to its owner (*Gem.* 71a).

THE MISHNAH/BAVA KAMMA – Chapter Seven: *Merubah*

בבא קמא ז/ד

מִשֶּׁל־אָבִיו וּמֵת אָבִיו, וְאַחַר־כָּךְ טָבַח וּמָכַר; גָּנַב וְהִקְדִּישׁ וְאַחַר־כָּךְ טָבַח וּמָכַר — מְשַׁלֵּם תַּשְׁלוּמֵי כֶפֶל, וְאֵינוֹ מְשַׁלֵּם תַּשְׁלוּמֵי אַרְבָּעָה וַחֲמִשָּׁה. רַבִּי שִׁמְעוֹן אוֹמֵר: קָדָשִׁים שֶׁחַיָּב בְּאַחֲרָיוּתָם, מְשַׁלֵּם תַּשְׁלוּמֵי אַרְבָּעָה וַחֲמִשָּׁה; וְשֶׁאֵינוֹ חַיָּב

יד אברהם

גָּנַב מִשֶּׁל־אָבִיו וּמֵת אָבִיו, — stole from his father, and his father died,

When his father dies, he inherits a share in the animal (Rav). The mishnah is apparently discussing a case in which there are also other heirs (Rav; Tos. Yom Tov).

וְאַחַר־כָּךְ טָבַח וּמָכַר: — and afterwards he slaughtered or sold;

Since he inherited a share prior to the slaughter or sale, the act was not completely unlawful, and there is therefore no four/fivefold payment (ibid. from Gem. 72a).

◆§ Acquisition of Stolen Property

Stolen goods do not become the property of the thief, and must be returned to the original owner. Even in those instances when the perpetrator does not pay the twofold payment, such as a thief who confesses to his crime, or a robber, who never is penalized with the twofold payment (see preface to this chapter), he must return the stolen article. This subject will be discussed at length in chapter 9.

There are cases, however, in which the thief or robber gains ownership of the article and must remunerate the owner for it. One method of acquiring the article is through שִׁנּוּי, *a change*: should the robber change the article, or should the article change spontaneously, its ownership is transferred to the robber — i.e., he need not return the item he stole to its owner, but must recompense him for it.

Another method is יֵאוּשׁ, *despair*: should the owner despair of recovering the article, some opinions in the *Gemara* maintain that the robber gains ownership of it. Although the halachah is that the robber does not gain ownership through despair alone, if there is a change in the name of the article (e.g., designating a hide as a tablecloth, or produce as *terumah*; consecrating an article), or a change in the possession of the article, — i.e., selling it or giving it as a gift — the thief gains ownership.

As long as the article belongs to the original owner, the thief has no power to sell it or consecrate it. Concerning the latter, the Torah (*Lev.* 27:14) states: וְאִישׁ כִּי־יַקְדִּשׁ אֶת־בֵּיתוֹ קֹדֶשׁ לַה׳, *If a man consecrates his house, making it holy to HASHEM...,* which is exegetically interpreted as meaning that just as one's house is his own, so can he consecrate only what is his own, but not stolen goods (*Gem.* 68b). The only instance in which one can consecrate a stolen article is when its owner despairs of recovering it. In that event, the act of consecration transfers it to the possession of the Temple, so that there is both despair and change of possession.

גָּנַב וְהִקְדִּישׁ — stole and consecrated

He consecrated the animal for an offering, as is often done with living animals. The *Gemara* (68b) qualifies the mishnah as dealing with a case in which the owner despaired of ever obtaining his stolen animal. In that case, the thief has the power to consecrate it. Since, through consecration, it changes possession, it becomes consecrated through a combination of despair and change of possession (*Tos. Yom Tov*).

משניות / בבא קמא — פרק ז: מרובה [152]

7
4

and his father died, and afterwards he slaughtered or sold; stole and consecrated and afterwards slaughtered or sold — he pays the twofold payment, but he does not pay the fourfold or fivefold payment.

R' Shimon says: [For] consecrated animals for which he is responsible, he pays the fourfold or fivefold payment; [for] those for which he is not

YAD AVRAHAM

וְאַחַר־כָּךְ טָבַח וּמָכַר — *and afterwards slaughtered or sold* —

Since he had already consecrated it, he was slaughtering an animal that belonged to the Temple, not to the original owner. He is therefore not liable for the four/fivefold payment.

The consecration is not considered a sale that would make him liable for selling an animal that he stole, since — even after a person consecrates an item — it is still referred to as his. For example, if Reuven consecrates an animal for an offering, it is called 'Reuven's offering' *(Tos. Yom Tov*

from *Gem.* 76a).

Should the thief consecrate it to be used for repairs of the Temple, however, and not for an offering, he is liable for the four/fivefold payment, since the animal is no longer referred to as his, and the consecration is therefore tantamount to selling (*Tos.* ad loc.).

מְשַׁלֵּם תַּשְׁלוּמֵי כֶפֶל, וְאֵינוֹ מְשַׁלֵּם תַּשְׁלוּמֵי אַרְבָּעָה וַחֲמִשָּׁה. — *he pays the twofold payment, but he does not pay the fourfold or fivefold payment.*

[In each of these cases, the thief pays only the twofold payment.]

The following segment of the mishnah deals with a thief who steals consecrated animals from the Temple. The Sages rule that he is exempt in any case from the twofold payments and thus, from the four/fivefold payment as well. They base this on the verse (*Ex.* 22:6): וְגֻנַּב מִבֵּית הָאִישׁ אִם־יִמָּצֵא הַגַּנָּב יְשַׁלֵּם שְׁנָיִם, *and it is stolen from the house of the man, if the thief be found, he shall pay twofold*, which is interpreted as applying only if *stolen from the house of the man*, but not from the Temple. R' Shimon differs on this point, as explained below.

רַבִּי שִׁמְעוֹן אוֹמֵר: קָדָשִׁים שֶׁחַיָּב בְּאַחֲרָיוּתָם, — *R' Shimon says: [For] consecrated animals for which he is responsible,*

That is, he says: 'הֲרֵי עָלַי קָרְבָּן, *I take upon myself to bring an offering.*' By this declaration, one undertakes a vow to designate an animal and bring it as an offering. Therefore, even if he set aside a specific animal for this purpose, and it dies or is stolen through no fault of his own, he must still replace it with another animal *(Rav to Megillah* 1:6).

מְשַׁלֵּם תַּשְׁלוּמֵי אַרְבָּעָה וַחֲמִשָּׁה; — *he pays the fourfold or fivefold payment;*

Since the previous owner is responsible for the animal should it die or be lost, it is considered to be in *the house of the man*. Therefore, although the animal is consecrated, when the thief slaughters it, it is as if he did so to an animal belonging to the owner. Nevertheless, since — as explained in the commentary to mishnah 2 — R' Shimon maintains that an invalid slaughter does not incur four/fivefold payment, and since slaughtering a consecrated animal outside of the Temple disqualified it, this ruling applies only if the thief slaughters the animal in the Temple Courtyard as an offering for the owner, and then the blood spills before he is able to sprinkle it on the Altar. The fact that he slaughtered it in the Courtyard

[153] THE MISHNAH/BAVA KAMMA — Chapter Seven: *Merubah*

בבא קמא
ז/ה

בְּאַחֲרָיוּתָם, פָּטוּר.

[ה] **מְכָרוֹ** חוּץ מֵאֶחָד מִמֵּאָה שֶׁבּוֹ, אוֹ שֶׁהָיְתָה לוֹ בוֹ שֻׁתָּפוּת; הַשּׁוֹחֵט וְנִתְנַבְּלָה בְּיָדוֹ; הַנּוֹחֵר וְהַמְעַקֵּר — מְשַׁלֵּם תַּשְׁלוּמֵי כֶפֶל,

יד אברהם

makes it a valid slaughtering, since he intended to sprinkle the blood on the Altar. Should the blood actually be sprinkled there, the thief would be exempt from all payments, since he would, in effect, be returning the animal to the owner, who himself would have had it slaughtered in the Courtyard for his offering. Apparently, then, the mishnah must be dealing with a case in which the blood spilled before he was able to sprinkle it.

Another possibility is that the animal had a blemish which rendered it unfit as an offering, and the thief slaughtered it outside the Courtyard before it was redeemed.[1]

R' Shimon rules that, since it was ready to be redeemed, it is as though it had already been redeemed, and the slaughtering is valid (Rav from Gem. 76b). [R' Shimon subscribes to the principle that a sacrifice is considered fit if it is ready for sprinkling the blood, and it is considered fit for food if it is ready and eligible for redemption. The potential for these acts gives them the status of having been already performed.]

Rashi points out that the animals must have become blemished before they were consecrated. Therefore, they could have been consecrated only for the repairs of the Temple, since they are unfit as offerings. Although all consecrated animals require being stood up and appraised [as stated in *Leviticus* 27:11f.: וְהֶעֱמִיד אֶת־הַבְּהֵמָה לִפְנֵי

הַכֹּהֵן וְהֶעֱרִיךְ הַכֹּהֵן אֹתָהּ, 'and he shall stand up the animal before the Kohen. And the Kohen shall appraise it ...]. Should they have been perfect at the time of their consecration and become blemished only afterwards, they could no longer be redeemed after their slaughter, since R' Shimon rules that animals consecrated for the Altar require being stood up and appraised before redemption, and, in this case, since they were slaughtered, they can no longer be stood up (Tos. Yom Tov).

וְשֶׁאֵינוֹ חַיָּב בְּאַחֲרָיוּתָם, — [for] *those for which he is not responsible*,

If a person said: הֲרֵי זוּ קָרְבָּן, *This animal shall be an offering,*' thereby setting aside a specific animal for a gift offering, and the animal is no longer available — for example, it died or was stolen — he is not required to replace it with another (Rav to Megillah 1:6). [This is because he obligated himself only to offer a specific animal.]

פָּטוּר. — *he is exempt.*

In this case, since the owner is not responsible for the offering, R' Shimon concurs with the Sages that it is not regarded as *stolen from the house of the man*, and there is therefore no liability for a twofold payment, and consequently, also not for a four/fivefold payment (Gem. 76a).

The halachah is not in accordance with R' Shimon (Rav; Rambam Commentary; Rambam, Hil. Geneivah 2:1).

---

1. [Should a sacrificial animal become blemished, it becomes unacceptable for use as an offering. It must then be redeemed by giving its value to the Temple treasury. It may then be slaughtered outside the Temple confines and eaten.]

משניות / בבא קמא — פרק ז: מרובה   [154]

responsible, he is exempt.

5. **[I**f] he sold it except for one-hundredth of it, or if he had joint ownership in it; [if] he slaughtered [it] and it became disqualified; [if] he pierced its nostrils or tore out the throat organs — he

YAD AVRAHAM

5.

מְכָרוֹ — *[If] he sold it*
The thief sold the stolen animal.

חוּץ מֵאֶחָד מִמֵּאָה שֶׁבּוֹ, — *except for one hundredth of it,*
If he sold it and retained for himself any part of it which becomes permissible to eat through slaughtering, he is exempt from paying the four/fivefold payments. This is because the phrase (*Ex.* 21:37) וּטְבָחוֹ אוֹ מְכָרוֹ, *and slaughters it or sells it,* is exegetically interpreted as meaning that, in order to be liable, he must sell every part of the animal that becomes permitted through slaughtering. However, should he retain the fleece or the horns, since they can be removed without slaughtering the animal, their retention does not exempt him from the four/fivefold payment (*Rav* from *Gem.* 78b; *Rambam, Hil. Geneivah* 2:11). *Rosh,* on the other hand, rules that even if he retains only the horns or the fleece for himself, he is exempt.

אוֹ שֶׁהָיְתָה לוֹ בּוֹ שֻׁתָּפוּת; — *or if he had joint ownership in it;*
He had joint ownership in the animal prior to the theft. Since the act of slaughter is not completely unlawful, he is exempt from the four/fivefold payment *(Tos. Yom Tov from Rashi).*

Although this has already been taught us in mishnah 4 with regard to one who stole an animal from his father and slaughtered it after his father's death — when he had inherited a part of it — we may think that the thief is exempt only in such an instance, in which the thief owns a share in every organ of the body of the stolen animal, but not if he has joint ownership in only one organ.

This mishnah, therefore, teaches us that even if the thief has joint ownership in just one organ of the animal's body, it is adjudged that the act of slaughter or sale is not completely unlawful, and he is exempt from the four/fivefold payment *(Tos. Yom Tov* from *Nimmukei Yosef).* In fact, *Nimmukei Yosef* and *Rosh* quote *Ramah* as stating that even if the thief owns only the fleece, he is exempt from the four/fivefold payments (see *Shitah Mekubetzes*).

This follows *Rosh's* ruling, stated above, that the thief is exempt from the fourfold payment if he sells the entire animal, retaining the fleece or the horns for himself *(Beis David).*

הַשּׁוֹחֵט וְנִתְנַבְּלָה בְיָדוֹ; — *[if] he slaughtered [it] and it became disqualified;*
The thief attempted to slaughter the animal properly, but did not succeed *(Tos. Yom Tov).*

הַנּוֹחֵר — *[if] he pierced its nostrils*
He did so intentionally *(Tos. Yom Tov).*

The translation follows *Rav* to *Chullin* 5:3. *Rashi* here explains: He tears from the nostrils to the heart; *Rashi* to *Chullin* 85b, however, explains: He chokes it.

Others render: *pierced the neck* *(Mussaf He'Aruch).*

וְהַמְעַקֵּר — *or tore out the throat organs —*

בבא קמא ז/ה

וְאֵינוֹ מְשַׁלֵּם תַּשְׁלוּמֵי אַרְבָּעָה וַחֲמִשָּׁה. גָּנַב בִּרְשׁוּת הַבְּעָלִים וְטָבַח וּמָכַר חוּץ מֵרְשׁוּתָם, אוֹ שֶׁגָּנַב חוּץ מֵרְשׁוּתָם וְטָבַח וּמָכַר בִּרְשׁוּתָם, אוֹ שֶׁגָּנַב וְטָבַח וּמָכַר חוּץ מֵרְשׁוּתָם — מְשַׁלֵּם תַּשְׁלוּמֵי אַרְבָּעָה וַחֲמִשָּׁה. אֲבָל גָּנַב וְטָבַח וּמָכַר בִּרְשׁוּתָם, פָּטוּר.

יד אברהם

Instead of cutting through the trachea and the esophagus with the slaughtering knife, he tore them from where they were attached *(Rav* and *Rambam Commentary* to *Chullin* 5:3).

This, too, is done intentionally, as in the preceding case *(Tos. Yom Tov)*. Whereas the Sages disagree with R' Shimon and maintain that an invalid slaughter is considered a slaughter with regard to the four/fivefold payment, in the case of piercing the nostrils or tearing out the throat organs there is no controversy — all concur that it is no slaughter at all. In the cases of slaughtering an animal with an organic defect, or ordinary animals in the Temple Courtyard, there is nothing disqualifying in the act itself; it is an outside factor that disqualifies the slaughtering — either the condition of the animal or the place where the act was done. In this case, however, he is not slaughtering the animal in the proper manner *(Rav loc. cit.;* see commentary to mishnah 2).

מְשַׁלֵּם תַּשְׁלוּמֵי כֶפֶל, וְאֵינוֹ מְשַׁלֵּם תַּשְׁלוּמֵי אַרְבָּעָה וַחֲמִשָּׁה. — *he pays the twofold payment, but he does not pay the fourfold or fivefold payment.*

[The thief pays only the twofold payment for the theft, as has already been explained in each case.]

In the second half of this mishnah as well as in the next one, the *Tanna* teaches us that a thief does not assume liability for the death or destruction of a stolen article, nor is he liable for twofold, fourfold, or fivefold payments, unless he takes it into his possession with one of the methods of acquisition, as delineated in the first chapter of *Kiddushin* 1:4 (see ArtScroll commentary ibid.).

גָּנַב בִּרְשׁוּת הַבְּעָלִים וְטָבַח וּמָכַר חוּץ מֵרְשׁוּתָם, — [If] *one stole in the owners' premises and slaughtered or sold outside their premises,*

He performed a *kinyan* (act of acquisition) on an animal standing in its owner's premises — e.g., lifting it, which is a valid *kinyan* even in the owners' premises — and then slaughtered or sold it. The mishnah does not mean literally that the slaughter or sale had to have taken place outside the owner's premises; rather, once the thief acquires the animal, anything he does with it is considered 'outside the owner's premises' *(Meiri)*.

Alternatively, the thief did not make a *kinyan* in the owner's premises, but dragged the animal out of there — thereby acquiring it through מְשִׁיכָה, *pulling* — and then sold or slaughtered it (ibid., *Tos. Yom Tov).* In this case, too, the mishnah does not mean literally that the slaughter or sale must have taken place outside the owner's premises, as explained above *(Meiri).*

Nimmukei Yosef maintains that the second interpretation applies even if the thief dragged the animal from the owner's premises into public property. Although

7:5

pays the twofold payment, but he does not pay the fourfold or fivefold payment.

[If] one stole in the owners' premises and slaughtered or sold outside their premises, or if he stole outside their premises and slaughtered or sold within their premises, or if he stole and slaughtered or sold outside their premises — he pays the fourfold or fivefold payment. But [if] he stole and slaughtered or sold in their premises, he is exempt.

YAD AVRAHAM

dragging an article out of its owner's premises into a public domain does not constitute a *kinyan* with regard to sales or gifts, in the case of theft, however, it suffices to make the perpetrator liable for accidents which occur to it, as well as the twofold payment, and — if the stolen item was a lamb or an ox — the four/fivefold payment if he subsequently sells or slaughters it.

Tosafos [and *Meiri*], however, rule that dragging the animal into a public domain does not constitute a *kinyan* even as regards responsibility for accidents and the penalties associated with theft. They qualify the mishnah as referring to a thief who drags the animal out of the owner's domain into an alley, which is a secluded place resembling one's own domain. Since one can acquire an object that he purchases or receives as a gift, by dragging it into an alley, he also becomes liable for accidents and penalties when he steals it in this manner *(Tos. Yom Tov).*

[Although *Nimmukei Yosef* and *Tosefos* make these comments on the next mishnah regarding accidents, *Tos. Yom Tov* applies them here regarding the penalties.]

או שֶׁגָּנַב חוּץ מֵרְשׁוּתָם — *or if he stole outside their premises —*
He found the animal on the road outside the owner's domain and stole it by performing a *kinyan* — e.g., dragging it *(Meiri).*

וְטָבַח וּמָכַר בִּרְשׁוּתָם, — *and slaughtered or sold within their premises,*
He brought it back into the owner's premises and slaughtered or sold it there. Obviously, he did not bring the animal there to return it to its owner (ibid.).

או שֶׁגָּנַב וְטָבַח וּמָכַר חוּץ מֵרְשׁוּתָם — *or if he stole and slaughtered or sold outside their premises —*
[He found the animal outside its owner's premises, performed an act of acquisition where he found it, and then proceeded to slaughter or sell it there.]

מְשַׁלֵּם תַּשְׁלוּמֵי אַרְבָּעָה וַחֲמִשָּׁה. — *he pays the fourfold or fivefold payment.*
[Since he performed a *kinyan*, he is liable for the four/fivefold payment.]

Tos. Yom Tov comments that the Tanna had no special reason for listing all the above cases, although it was unnecessary to do so; he cites 9:6 as a similar instance.

אֲבָל גָּנַב וְטָבַח וּמָכַר בִּרְשׁוּתָם, פָּטוּר. — *But [if] he stole and slaughtered or sold in their premises, he is exempt.*
He did not perform a *kinyan* prior to the slaughter or sale of the animal; e.g., he did not lift the animal, but dragged it while it was still in the owner's domain, which does not constitute a *kinyan*. In such a case there is no liability for the twofold payment, nor for the four/fivefold payment, since there is no penalty for slaughter or sale if there is no penalty for the theft *(Meiri).*

Should the animal still be alive, the thief must return it. Therefore, the mishnah states the exemption only in regard to the penalties, not the principal itself *(Mekoros Vetziunim* in *Rambam,* ed. Frankel, *Hil. Geneivah* 2:16, quoting *Halachah LeMoshe).*

בבא קמא ז/ו

[ו] **הָיָה** מוֹשְׁכוֹ וְיוֹצֵא, וּמֵת בִּרְשׁוּת הַבְּעָלִים, פָּטוּר. הִגְבִּיהוֹ אוֹ שֶׁהוֹצִיאוֹ מֵרְשׁוּת הַבְּעָלִים וָמֵת, חַיָּב.

נְתָנוֹ לִבְכוֹרוֹת בְּנוֹ, אוֹ לְבַעַל חוֹבוֹ, לְשׁוֹמֵר חִנָּם, וּלְשׁוֹאֵל, לְנוֹשֵׂא שָׂכָר, וּלְשׂוֹכֵר, וְהָיָה מוֹשְׁכוֹ, וּמֵת בִּרְשׁוּת הַבְּעָלִים — פָּטוּר. הִגְבִּיהוֹ אוֹ שֶׁהוֹצִיאוֹ מֵרְשׁוּת הַבְּעָלִים, וָמֵת, חַיָּב.

יד אברהם

6.

הָיָה מוֹשְׁכוֹ וְיוֹצֵא — [If] *he was taking it out by dragging* [lit., *dragging it and going out*],

The thief was dragging the animal out of the owners' premises (Rashi).

וּמֵת בִּרְשׁוּת הַבְּעָלִים — *and it died in the premises of the owner,*

The ox or the lamb died before the thief had a chance to drag it out of the owner's domain (Meiri).

פָּטוּר. — *he is exempt.*

It would appear that the thief is exempt from paying not only the twofold payment, but the actual value of the animal as well. Since he had not yet performed a *kinyan* in the process of stealing, he did not assume responsibility for the animal, and consequently, when it dies, the owner suffers the loss. Indeed, according to our editions of *Rashi*, the would-be thief is exempt from all payments. According to other editions, however, *Rashi* states that he is exempt from the twofold payment, which implies that he is liable for the value of the animal. This reading is found in *Rashi* on *Rif*, as well as in *Rav*, *Tiferes Yisrael*, and *Rambam* (Hil. Geneivah 2:16). *Tos. Yom Tov* asks why he should not be completely exempt since he did not perform a *kinyan*.

Beis David suggests that, since the entire chapter deals with the twofold payment, rather than the actual value of the animal, it is likely that this mishnah does as well. He explains the case as dealing with a thief who hurriedly drags an ox or a lamb from its owner's premises, and while doing so, inadvertently chokes it. He is therefore liable as a damager to pay for the animal, but since he made no *kinyan*, he is not considered a thief and is exempt from the twofold payment. (See *Shoshannim LeDavid*.)

הִגְבִּיהוֹ — [If] *he lifted it*

The thief lifted the animal he stole. This can take place even in the owner's domain, since lifting is a *kinyan* anywhere it is performed (*Rav; Rashi*).

אוֹ שֶׁהוֹצִיאוֹ מֵרְשׁוּת הַבְּעָלִים וָמֵת, — *or if he took it out of the owner's premises and it died,*

[He acquired it by dragging it out of the owner's premises, and it died after the theft.]

[See comments of *Nimmukei Yosef* and *Tosafos*, cited in the commentary for the previous mishnah, s.v. גָּנַב, which are relevant here.]

חַיָּב. — *he is liable.*

[The thief must pay the twofold payment].

נְתָנוֹ לִבְכוֹרוֹת בְּנוֹ, — [If] *he gave it for [redemption of] his firstborn son,*

The would-be thief gave the animal to

משניות / בבא קמא — פרק ז: **מרובה** [158]

6. [If] he was taking it out by dragging, and it died in the premises of the owner, he is exempt. [If] he lifted it or if he took it out of the owner's premises and it died, he is liable.

[If] he gave it for [redemption of] his firstborn son, or to his creditor, to an unpaid guardian, to a borrower, to a paid guardian, or to a renter, and he was dragging it, and it died in the premises of the owners — he is exempt. [If] he lifted it or took it out of the owners' premises, and it died, he is liable.

YAD AVRAHAM

a *Kohen* [priest] in order to redeem his firstborn son[1] *(Rav; Rashi)*.

He did so in the place where he stole the animal without first performing a *kinyan (Rashi)*.

אוֹ לְבַעַל חוֹבוֹ, — *or to his creditor,*
[He gave the animal to his creditor in payment of a debt.]

לְשׁוֹמֵר חִנָּם, וּלְשׁוֹאֵל, לְנוֹשֵׂא שָׂכָר, וּלְשׂוֹכֵר. — *to an unpaid guardian, to a borrower, to a paid guardian, or to a renter,*
[He gave the animal to someone to watch for him, or someone borrowed or rented it from him. The rules of these four types of guardians and the reason for the mishnah's listing them in this order are explained in the commentary to 4:9.]

וְהָיָה מוֹשְׁכוֹ, — *and he was dragging it,*
That is, the *Kohen,* the creditor, or the guardian was dragging the animal out of its owner's premises *(Rav; Rashi),* having been instructed to do so by the would-be thief *(Meiri).*

וּמֵת בִּרְשׁוּת הַבְּעָלִים — פָּטוּר. — *and it died in the premises of the owners — he is exempt.*
The would-be thief is entirely exempt; he need not pay for the value of the animal, nor is he liable for any penalties *(Rav; Rashi).* This is because neither he nor the person to whom he gave the animal had performed any *kinyan.* He is therefore not yet responsible for the animal, and, when it dies, he is exempt of all charges *(Meiri).*

הִגְבִּיהוּ — *[If] he lifted it*
[The *Kohen,* the creditor, or the guardian lifted the animal by order of the thief.]

אוֹ שֶׁהוֹצִיאוּ מֵרְשׁוּת הַבְּעָלִים, — *or took it out of the owners' premises,*
[The *Kohen,* the creditor, or the guardian dragged it out of the owner's premises by order of the thief, thereby performing a *kinyan* on his behalf.]

וָמֵת, — *and it died,*
[The animal died after being stolen.]

חַיָּב. — *he is liable.*
According to *Rashi* and *Tosafos,* the intention is that the thief is liable because he acquired the animal through the *kinyan* performed on his behalf. Although stealing is obviously a sin, and, as stated above in the commentary (5:6, 6:4), the principle of אֵין שָׁלִיחַ לִדְבַר עֲבֵרָה, *there is no agent in matters of sin,* dictates that if one instructs another to do a sin, the former is not

---

1. [As prescribed in Numbers 18:15f. et al., when a male baby who was his mother's firstborn becomes thirty days old, his father must redeem him by giving five silver shekels (*selaim* in Mishnaic nomenclature) or the equivalent thereof to a *Kohen* (see ArtScroll *Siddur, Ashkenaz* ed., p. 218).]

בבא קמא ז/ז

[ז] **אֵין** מְגַדְּלִין בְּהֵמָה דַקָּה בְּאֶרֶץ יִשְׂרָאֵל, אֲבָל מְגַדְּלִין בְּסוּרְיָא וּבַמִּדְבָּרוֹת

יד אברהם

liable for the latter's act, that rule does not apply here. This is because, as explained there, the reason for this rule is that the one who gave the instructions can claim that he had doubted that the other person would comply with his orders in defiance of the Divine will. In this case, however, the *Kohen*, the creditor, or the guardian was unaware that the animal had been stolen, and thought that it belonged to the one who had given it to him and ordered him to drag it out of the premises. Therefore, the thief is confident that his instructions will be carried out.

Darchei Moshe (*Choshen Mishpat* 348:2) cites *Nimmukei Yosef*, who differs with *Rashi* and *Tosafos* and rules that the principle that there is no agency in matters of sin applies even if the agent is unaware that he is committing a sin. Rather, he explains the mishnah to mean that if the animal dies before a *kinyan* was made, the *Kohen* or other agent is exempt; if it dies after a *kinyan* was made, the *Kohen* or other agent is liable. *Shach* (ibid. §6) disagrees with *Darchei Moshe*, construing *Nimmukei Yosef* to mean only that the thief is not liable, but not that the agent is liable. [This explanation seems difficult, however, because — if neither the would-be thief nor the agent is responsible for the theft — to whom does the mishnah refer when it says *he is liable*? See below.]

Rambam (*Hil. Geneivah* 2:16), too, explains the mishnah to mean that the guardian or other agent is liable. *Maggid Mishneh* (ad loc.), however, comments that *Rambam* interprets the case as one in which the guardian is aware that the animal does not belong to the one who gave it to him, and he is therefore liable for taking it. [*Maggid Mishneh* does not make clear whether, in the case that the agent is unaware of the animal's status,

Rambam would concur with *Tosafos* — that the thief would be liable — or with *Shach's* interpretation of *Nimmukei Yosef* — that neither is liable.]

Although it is stated in mishnah 1 that one who steals a stolen article from a thief does not pay the twofold payment, that is only if the thief had already made a *kinyan*. In this case, however, the guardian or other agent is the one who makes the *kinyan*, and it is therefore he who is considered the thief (*Tos. Yom Tov*).

Nimmukei Yosef holds that the reason given by the *Gemara* for the principle that there is no agency in matters of sin — that the sender doubts that the agent will defy the Divine will — is not conclusive. According to the conclusion of the *Gemara* (*Kiddushin* 42b-43a), this rule is not derived from logical reasoning, but is a decree of the Torah: Since it is exegetically derived that one can designate an agent for *me'ilah* [using consecrated objects for one's personal benefit] and for the slaughter or sale of stolen animals [*Gem.* 71a, *Me'ilah* 18b], this is an indication that regarding all other sins, there is no agency. Because this is an unqualified law, a distinction cannot be made between a case in which the agent was aware that he was committing a sin and one in which he was not (*Shach* loc. cit.).

Others explain that this segment of the mishnah is an entirely different matter, completely unrelated to the preceding segment. It is the case in which the owner of an animal gives it to a *Kohen* in order to redeem his son, to a creditor as payment of a debt, or to a guardian so that he should watch it. Should the animal die before being transferred to the possession of the recipient, the latter does not suffer a loss because of the animal's death. Should it die after the transfer, however, the recipient loses thereby, since he has already received the animal. In the case of a guardian, the question is whether he is liable to pay for the animal if it

7. We may not raise small cattle in *Eretz Yisrael*, but we may raise [them] in Syria or in

YAD AVRAHAM

dies. The mishnah states that he is responsible only after making a *kinyan*. *(Ravad, Hil. Geneivah* 2:16). Although the expressions used in the mishnah, *exempt* and *liable*, do not apply to the *Kohen* and the creditor, they are used in reference to the guardian. In the case of the *Kohen* and the creditor, the intention is *he does not lose*, and *he loses (Tif. Yis.)*. *Rashi*, too, cites this interpretation, but prefers the one given above, because it is unlikely that the mishnah would use an expression that applies only to one of the three cases discussed. Also, the only guardian who is liable for an accidental occurrence, such as death, to the article entrusted to him is the borrower; all others are exempt in such cases.

Mention of the four/fivefold payment is conspicuously absent in this mishnah. According to the interpretation of *Rashi* and *Tosafos* — that the thief gave the animal to the *Kohen* or the creditor — there should apparently be such a penalty, since giving a gift or paying a debt is analogous to selling, as explained in the *Gemara* (79a), which states explicitly that a thief is liable for such a payment. The reason he is not liable is that the Torah imposes this penalty only if the theft precedes the sale. In this case, however, the theft is perpetrated only with the sale itself, because the thief had not made any *kinyan* before giving it to the other person. In such instances, the Torah did not impose the penalty *(Meiri)*.

7.

[It is not surprising that this mishnah — which lists animals that may not be raised in certain places — is included in our tractate, because, among the reasons given for these strictures is that the animals should not graze in strange fields, a topic discussed in several previous mishnayos. *Tos. Yom Tov* wonders, however, why this mishnah was not placed in the beginning of Chapter 6, where it would be more appropriate.]

אֵין מְגַדְּלִין בְּהֵמָה דַקָּה — *We may not raise small cattle*
[That is, sheep and goats.]

בְּאֶרֶץ יִשְׂרָאֵל, — *in Eretz Yisrael,*
The Rabbis prohibited raising small cattle there, because they destroy the vegetation and hinder the settlement of the Holy Land *(Rav)*. This includes raising them on one's own property. Although they will not destroy the fields of others, since they destroy their owner's fields, they are considered as hindering the settlement of the Holy Land. *Tosafos* and *Rosh*, too, forbid raising the animals even on one's own property, but for a different reason *(Tos. Yom Tov)*. [They assert that the Rabbis imposed this ban lest the cattle graze in strange fields. This also appears

to be *Rashi's* reason. See *Rav* to *Demai* 2:3, *Tif. Yis.*, and *Tur (Choshen Mishpat* 409).]

They did not prohibit raising large cattle since it is impossible to import these when they are needed; small cattle, however, can be imported *(Gem.* 79b). Alternatively, the large cattle are needed constantly for plowing and carrying burdens *(Rashi)*. Moreover, they are not as numerous as the small cattle, therefore, and are more easily watched *(Tif. Yis.)*.

אֲבָל מְגַדְּלִין בְּסוּרְיָא — *but we may raise [them] in Syria*
This includes the lands conquered by King David. Since he had not yet conquered all the territory belonging to the Holy Land, these lands did not attain

[161] THE MISHNAH/BAVA KAMMA – Chapter Seven: *Merubah*

בבא קמא ז/ז

שֶׁבְּאֶרֶץ יִשְׂרָאֵל. אֵין מְגַדְּלִין תַּרְנְגוֹלִים בִּירוּשָׁלַיִם מִפְּנֵי הַקָּדָשִׁים, וְלֹא כֹהֲנִים בְּאֶרֶץ יִשְׂרָאֵל מִפְּנֵי הַטְּהָרוֹת. אֵין מְגַדְּלִין חֲזִירִים בְּכָל־מָקוֹם. לֹא יְגַדֵּל אָדָם אֶת־הַכֶּלֶב אֶלָּא־אִם־כֵּן הָיָה קָשׁוּר בְּשַׁלְשֶׁלֶת. אֵין

יד אברהם

the status of *Eretz Yisrael*, and therefore, we are not concerned about their settlement. Should the cattle raised in these areas damage anyone's property, the owner of the cattle will pay for it (*Rav; Rashi*).

וּבַמִּדְבָּרוֹת שֶׁבְּאֶרֶץ יִשְׂרָאֵל. — *or in wildernesses that are in Eretz Yisrael.*

Since there are no fields and vineyards among the forests and wildernesses, no ban was imposed on these places (*Meiri*).

אֵין מְגַדְּלִין תַּרְנְגוֹלִים בִּירוּשָׁלַיִם מִפְּנֵי הַקָּדָשִׁים, — *We may not raise chickens in Jerusalem because of the consecrated things,*

Since sacrificial flesh is eaten in Jerusalem, its purity must be preserved. The Rabbis therefore interdicted raising chickens in Jerusalem, since chickens — which habitually pick at the dunghills — may bring out pieces of dead rodents and reptiles, and ritually contaminate the consecrated flesh. Even a piece of flesh of these creatures the size of a lentil conveys ritual contamination (*Rav*, *Rashi* according to *Beis David*, *Rishon LeTzion*).

Beis David and *Rishon LeTzion* reject our version of *Rav*, which states that a bone the size of a grain of barley will bring contamination to the sacrificial flesh, since bones of a reptile do not convey contamination. *Shoshannim LeDavid*, however, explains our version of *Rav*. He maintains that the fear is not that the chickens will bring out flesh of reptiles, since, on the contrary, they will consume it and prevent it from conveying contamination. Rather, we are apprehensive that they will bring out bones containing marrow, which convey contamination even if they are as small as a grain of barley.

This prohibition applies only to allowing chickens to roam the streets. To keep them confined in coops, however, is permissible. Evidence to this is found in *I Kings* 5:3, where we find that King Solomon served fattened fowl, apparently raised in Jerusalem. Also, in *Yoma* (1:8) it is mentioned that a rooster was crowing, indicating that there were roosters in Jerusalem (*Tos. R' Akiva* from *R' Menachem Azariah* [*Rama*] of Pano, *Responsum* §85).

וְלֹא כֹהֲנִים בְּאֶרֶץ יִשְׂרָאֵל — *nor may Kohanim throughout [all] Eretz Yisrael*

Kohanim may not raise chickens throughout all *Eretz Yisrael* (*Rav; Rashi*).

As above, this applies only to allowing them to roam the streets at will; to keep them in coops is permissible (*Tos. R' Akiva*).

מִפְּנֵי הַטְּהָרוֹת. — *because of the ritually clean foods.*

Since *Kohanim* eat *terumah* and must preserve its purity, they may not raise chickens, which may bring ritual contamination to it, as described above (*Rav; Rashi*).

אֵין מְגַדְּלִין חֲזִירִים בְּכָל־מָקוֹם. — *In no place may we raise swine.*

The *Gemara* (82b) relates that when two brothers, Hyrcanus and Aristobolus, were vying for the Hasmonean kingdom, one was inside Jerusalem and the other was besieging the city from outside. Those inside

משניות / בבא קמא — פרק ז: מרובה [162]

7. wildernesses that are in *Eretz Yisrael*.

7. We may not raise chickens in Jerusalem because of the consecrated things, nor may *Kohanim* throughout [all] *Eretz Yisrael* because of the ritually clean foods.

In no place may we raise swine. A person may not raise a dog unless it is bound with a chain. We may

YAD AVRAHAM

would let down money to those outside, who would, in turn, send up sheep for the daily sacrifices. Once they sent up a pig. When it was midway up the wall, it stuck its claws into the wall and the Holy Land quaked throughout an area of four hundred parasangs[1] by four hundred parasangs. At that time, it was said: 'Cursed be he who raises swine' (*Rav*).

Tiferes Yisrael explains this figuratively: Since those on the outside had the unmitigated nerve to mock the Temple service in such a manner, all God-fearing men throughout the land trembled. Therefore, this decree was imposed.

Maharsha (to *Sotah* 49a) interprets the incident even more figuratively. He construes it to mean that because of the battle between these two brothers, Rome was able to gain a hold on the walls of Jerusalem, the Temple service was eventually curtailed, and we lost the Holy Land. Rome, representing Esau, is likened to a pig (see *Pesachim* 118b).

Tiferes Yisrael, however, rejects this interpretation on the grounds that it is unreasonable to believe that they laid a ban on raising swine because of Rome that is compared to a swine. It is likelier that a more literal interpretation is correct.

Should one raise swine for human consumption, he would violate the general prohibition of dealing with forbidden foods, as stated in *Sheviis* (7:3). The particular enactment against raising swine includes doing so to use their fat for lubricating hides or to sell fat to other Jews for that purpose, which is permissible in the case of all other prohibited species. Regarding swine, however, it was interdicted because of the aforementioned episode (*Tos. Yom Tov* from *Tos.* 83b).

לֹא יְגַדֵּל אָדָם אֶת־הַכֶּלֶב — *A person may not raise a dog*

One may not keep a dog since it bites, and a woman may miscarry if frightened by its barking (*Rav*; *Rashi*); to 4:9.

Tur and *Shulchan Aruch* (409:3) qualify this statement as referring to a fierce dog. This is implied by the mishnah's use of the definite article in אֶת־הַכֶּלֶב [lit., *the dog*]. In the *Gemara* (80a,b), we find that R' Yishmael and R' Shimon ben Elazar permitted keeping a species of dog known as כּוּפְרִי [which *Rashi* (80a) explains it as either a small dog, which does not bite, or a large dog used by hunters, which is likewise tame and does not bite; and *Aruch* explains as a small dog which barks at night in the wilderness, from כְּפָר, *a village*] (*Tos. Yom Tov*).

In contrast to the rest of the mishnah, the singular form of this statement's subject, *a person*, intimates that raising a dog is prohibited only for an individual who needs protection, but not for an entire city e.g., or border city that requires it (*Shoshannim LeDavid*).

אֶלָּא־אִם־כֵּן הָיָה קָשׁוּר בְּשַׁלְשֶׁלֶת — *unless it is bound with a chain*.

Since it is bound, people are not frightened of it (*Tos. Yom Tov*), and a woman will not be startled by its bark (*Lechem Shamayim*).

---

1. [פַּרְסָאוֹת] (sing. פַּרְסָה): *parasangs* or *Persian miles* (2.3-2.9 U.S. miles).]

[163] THE MISHNAH/BAVA KAMMA – Chapter Seven: *Merubah*

בבא קמא ח/א

פּוֹרְסִין נְשָׁבִים לְיוֹנִים, אֶלָּא־אִם־כֵּן הָיָה רָחוֹק מִן הַיִּשּׁוּב שְׁלֹשִׁים רִיס.

[א] **הַחוֹבֵל** בַּחֲבֵרוֹ, חַיָּב עָלָיו מִשּׁוּם חֲמִשָּׁה דְבָרִים: בְּנֶזֶק, בְּצַעַר, בְּרִפּוּי, בְּשֶׁבֶת, וּבֹשֶׁת.

בְּנֶזֶק — כֵּיצַד? סִמֵּא אֶת־עֵינוֹ, קָטַע אֶת־יָדוֹ,

יד אברהם

אֵין פּוֹרְסִין נְשָׁבִים לְיוֹנִים — *We may not spread nets for doves,*
That is, we may not even set traps to catch wild doves (Tif. Yis.), lest the doves belonging to the people of the city be caught in them (Rav; Rashi).

אֶלָּא־אִם־כֵּן הָיָה רָחוֹק מִן־הַיִּשּׁוּב שְׁלֹשִׁים רִיס — *unless it is thirty ris from an inhabited place.*

The trap must be at least thirty *ris* from the doves belonging to the inhabitants of the city (Tif. Yis.).
Thirty *ris* is equivalent to four *milin* (Rav; Rashi). A *ris*, or רוס, *rus*, equals 266 cubits, or strides, the numerical value of the word רוס. Hence, thirty *rus* equals 7,980 cubits, close to 8,000 cubits, which equal four *milin*, one *mil* equaling 2,000 cubits[1] (Tos. Yom Tov).

Chapter 8

1.

הַחוֹבֵל בַּחֲבֵרוֹ — *[If] one wounds another,*
[He strikes and wounds him.]

חַיָּב עָלָיו מִשּׁוּם חֲמִשָּׁה דְבָרִים — *he becomes liable to him for five categories:*
[That is, categories of payment.]

בְּנֶזֶק — *for injury,*
This applies if a permanent injury that decreases one's value was inflicted (Tif. Yis.).
This category is derived from *Exodus* 21:24: עַיִן תַּחַת עַיִן, *eye for eye,* which is traditionally interpreted as meaning that the damager make monetary restitution for the injury (Rambam, Hil. Chovel 1:2).
There is a lengthy discussion in the *Gemara* (83b,84a) concerning the derivation of this law of monetary restitution as opposed to the literal interpretation of the Biblical passages, which would dictate that the one who inflicted the wound is to be maimed in the same manner. *Rambam* (1:3) explains the Torah's intention to be that one who wounds another deserves to be wounded in the same manner. However, the court accepts money instead as ransom for the limbs of which the perpetrator should be deprived. Scripture (*Num.* 35:31) states: וְלֹא־תִקְחוּ כֹפֶר לְנֶפֶשׁ רֹצֵחַ אֲשֶׁר־הוּא רָשָׁע לָמוּת, *You shall not take ransom for the life of a murderer who deserves to die.* This implies that only for the life of a murderer is ransom not taken, but it is taken in lieu of the limbs of one who wounds. In a way, the one who wounds resembles the murderer, insofar as the limbs he destroys are dead and irreplaceable (Tos. Yom Tov).

---

1. [For approximate modern U.S. equivalents of these amounts, see *Gateway to the Talmud*, Chapter 12.]

משניות / בבא קמא — פרק ח: החובל [164]

8 1 not spread nets for doves unless it is thirty *ris* from an inhabited place.

1. [If] one wounds another, he becomes liable to him for five categories: for injury, for pain, for healing, for loss of time, and for disgrace.

For injury — how? [If] he blinded his eye, cut off

YAD AVRAHAM

That acceptance of ransom is mandatory is derived from other passages, as discussed in the *Gemara, Mechilta of R' Yishmael, Mechilta of R' Shimon ben Yochai,* et al. *Rambam* (loc. cit. §6) states emphatically: Although these rules appear plausible from the context of the Written Torah, they were all made clear by Moses at Sinai, and they have all come down to us as practical rules of law. And so did our ancestors witness being judged in the court of Joshua, and in the court of Samuel, and in every court that has been set up from Moses' time until now.

בְּצַעַר, — *for pain,*
The one who inflicted the wound must pay his victim for the pain caused thereby *(Rav).*

This is derived from the phrase (*Ex.* 21:25): פֶּצַע תַּחַת פָּצַע, *wound for wound,* which the *Gemara* (84a) interprets as meaning that even if one inflicts permanent injury on another and pays for the limb he destroyed, he must nevertheless also pay for the pain he caused him. We do not regard it as though he had purchased the limb and may remove it with whatever method he chooses, for, even in that respect, he should have removed it with a painless method. Since he cut the limb off and caused him pain, he must pay for the pain as well as the injury *(Rav).*

בְּרִפּוּי, — *for healing,*
[He must pay the amount required to heal the wound.]

This is based on *Exodus* 21:19, וְרַפֹּא יְרַפֵּא, *and cause him to be thoroughly healed,* and applies only to the wound itself or to ailments resulting from it. However, should an ailment result because the victim ignored a physician's instructions, the one who wounded him is exempt from paying for healing it *(Rav).*

בְּשֶׁבֶת, — *for loss of time,*
[He must pay for the time that the victim was unable to work as a result of the wound.] This is derived from (*Ex.* loc. cit.): רַק שִׁבְתּוֹ יִתֵּן, *only for the loss of his time shall he pay (Rav).* Similar to the case above, this applies only if the victim's inability to work is a direct result of the wound. However, should it be caused by neglect to follow the physician's orders, the perpetrator is exempt *(Rav, Tos. Yom Tov* from *Gem.* 85a).

וּבֹשֶׁת. — *and for disgrace.*
[In addition to all the above, the one who inflicted the wound must pay for the shame he caused his victim.]

This is derived from (*Deut.* 25:11*f.*): וְהֶחֱזִיקָה בִּמְבֻשָׁיו. וְקַצֹּתָה אֶת־כַּפָּהּ .... *... and [she] takes hold of his privy organs. You shall cut off her hand ....* This is interpreted to mean that the woman must pay monetary restitution for the shame she caused him *(Rav).*

[The mishnah now proceeds to explain each of these five categories in detail.]

בְּנֶזֶק — כֵּיצַד? — *For injury — how?*
[How is the amount of payment for injury determined?]

סִמָּא אֶת־עֵינוֹ, קָטַע אֶת־יָדוֹ, שָׁבַר אֶת־רַגְלוֹ, רוֹאִין אוֹתוֹ כְּאִלּוּ הוּא עֶבֶד נִמְכָּר בַּשּׁוּק — [*If*]

[165] THE MISHNAH/BAVA KAMMA — Chapter Eight: *HaChovel*

בבא קמא ח/א

שִׁבֵּר אֶת־רַגְלוֹ, רוֹאִין אֹתוֹ כְּאִלּוּ הוּא עֶבֶד נִמְכָּר בַּשּׁוּק, וְשָׁמִין כַּמָּה הָיָה יָפֶה וְכַמָּה הוּא יָפֶה. צַעַר? כְּוָאוֹ בְּשִׁפּוּד אוֹ בְמַסְמֵר — וַאֲפִלּוּ עַל־צִפָּרְנוֹ, מָקוֹם שֶׁאֵינוֹ עוֹשֶׂה חַבּוּרָה — אוֹמְדִין כַּמָּה אָדָם כַּיּוֹצֵא בָזֶה רוֹצֶה לִטּוֹל לִהְיוֹת מִצְטַעֵר כָּךְ.

רִפּוּי? הִכָּהוּ, חַיָּב לְרַפְּאתוֹ. עָלוּ בוֹ צְמָחִים —

יד אברהם

he blinded his eye, cut off his hand, [or] *broke his leg, we view him as if he were a slave being sold in the market,*

[For the purpose of computing the amount of payment, we imagine that the victim is a slave.]

The fact that he is of a higher status than a slave, making the injury that much more humiliating affects only the payment for disgrace. With regard to the payment for injury, however, all are deemed equal (*Tos. Yom Tov* from *Sma* 420:16).

וְשָׁמִין כַּמָּה הָיָה יָפֶה — *and appraise how much he was worth*

We assess how much the victim would have been worth as a slave before the injury (*Tif. Yis.*).

וְכַמָּה הוּא יָפֶה — *and how much he is worth.*

That is, how much he is worth as a slave after the injury. The victim is paid this amount since, if he becomes impoverished, he could sell himself as a bondman,[1] and the one who wounded him decreased his value, causing him a loss (*Rav; Rashi*).

Rosh objects to this interpretation, since the injury in question is a permanent one, whereas the loss sustained by a Jewish bondman is limited since he cannot sell himself for more than six years. The mishnah cannot be referring to the loss he would suffer were he to sell himself repeatedly for six-year periods, selling himself again each time the term of servitude ended, since that would amount to an astronomical sum, and the Torah's intention is to grant leniency to the perpetrator. This is evident by the fact that he pays for the loss inflicted on the body of the victim, rather than the loss of the limb itself. This is similar to the liability imposed on the owner of an animal that damages produce on a field — he pays the amount that the field decreases, rather than for the produce itself (6:2). [As explained in the commentary ad loc., when an item is viewed as part of a much larger entity, its loss is considered much less than if it is assessed on its own.] *Rosh* concludes, therefore, that the perpetrator must pay the victim's loss of value as though he were a gentile slave, who is sold for life. [Although, obviously, the victim cannot sell himself as a gentile slave, this is merely the method of computing the loss in his value.]

Indeed, the mishnah's expression, *being sold in the market,* alludes to a gentile slave, since a Jewish bondman is sold discreetly, not in the market (*Shoshannim LeDavid*).

1. [We have used the term *bondman* to refer to an עֶבֶד עִבְרִי (lit., *Jewish slave*), because the literal translation implies that the person is the property of his master — similar to land, chattels, and the like — which is untrue of any Jew. This description does apply, however, to gentile slaves (see *Kiddushin* 1:3; cf. *Gem.* ibid. 16a; *Tos.* to *Yevamos* 70b, s.v. אלמא).]

his hand, [or] broke his leg, we view him as if he were a slave being sold in the market, and appraise how much he was worth and how much he is worth.

Pain? [If] he burned him with a spit or with a nail — even on his fingernail, a place where it does not make a wound — we appraise how much such a man wishes to take to suffer such pain.

Healing? [If] he struck him, he is obligated to heal him. Should blisters arise on him — if as a result of

YAD AVRAHAM

צַעַר? — *Pain?*
[How do we reckon the amount to be paid for pain?]

כְּוָאוֹ בְשִׁפּוּד אוֹ בְמַסְמֵר — *[If] he burned him with a spit or with a nail* —
Some explain this to mean that he burned him with a spit or *stuck him with a nail (Rashi,* according to *Tos. Yom Tov).*

וַאֲפִלּוּ עַל־צִפָּרְנוֹ, מָקוֹם שֶׁאֵינוֹ עוֹשֶׂה חַבּוּרָה — *even on his fingernail, a place where it does not make a wound* —
Hence, there is no injury; only pain *(Meiri).*

אוֹמְדִין כַּמָּה אָדָם כַּיּוֹצֵא בָזֶה רוֹצֶה לִטּוֹל לִהְיוֹת מִצְטַעֵר כָּךְ. — *we appraise how much such a man wishes to take to suffer such pain.*

The more delicate a person is, the more he suffers pain *(Rav; Rashi).*

The mishnah's statement is not to be construed literally, since, before such pain is inflicted, a person would not agree to undergo it except, perhaps, for a huge sum, whereas here the pain has already been inflicted. Moreover, the Torah grants leniency to the perpetrator as explained above from 6:2. Rather, the intention is that we estimate how much such a person would pay to be spared such a pain if, for example, he were sentenced by the court to be burned with a spit, and the one who wounded him must pay this amount *(Tos. Yom Tov from Rosh).*

The *Tanna* does not say *we appraise how much this man wishes ...,* because that might imply that it refers to the man whom we imagine to be a slave, above in the mishnah *(Tos. Yom Tov).*

רִפּוּי? הִכָּהוּ, חַיָּב לְרַפֹּאתוֹ. — *Healing? [If] he struck him, he is obligated to heal him.*
[That is, he is obligated to pay for the healing.]

Should the perpetrator personally wish to heal his victim, the latter may object, saying that he does not trust him *(Gem.* 85a).

For the benefit of the perpetrator, we offer him the following option: at the outset, the court estimates how much the medical expenses to heal the wound will be; he may pay that amount and thereby satisfy the obligation, whether the figure proves to be accurate or whether the actual cost is more or less than had been estimated. If he chooses to decline this option, he must pay the day-to-day expenses of healing as they arise *(Rambam, Hil. Chovel* 2:14,16).

עָלוּ בוֹ צְמָחִים — *Should blisters arise on him* —
The translation follows *Rav,* who identifies these as white blisters. *Rashi* associates the term with the French word, *malant,* meaning *wounds (Otzar Laazei Rashi).*

The mishnah's rule applies even if the blisters appear around the wound, not on the wound itself *(Meiri).*

[167] THE MISHNAH/BAVA KAMMA — Chapter Eight: *HaChovel*

בבא קמא ח/א

אִם מֵחֲמַת הַמַּכָּה, חַיָּב; שֶׁלֹּא מֵחֲמַת הַמַּכָּה, פָּטוּר. חָיְתָה וְנִסְתְּרָה, חָיְתָה וְנִסְתְּרָה, חַיָּב לְרַפְּאתוֹ. חָיְתָה כָּל־צָרְכָּהּ, אֵינוֹ חַיָּב לְרַפְּאתוֹ. שֶׁבֶת? רוֹאִין אוֹתוֹ כְּאִלּוּ הוּא שׁוֹמֵר קִשּׁוּאִין, שֶׁכְּבָר נָתַן לוֹ דְּמֵי יָדוֹ וּדְמֵי רַגְלוֹ. בּוֹשֶׁת? הַכֹּל לְפִי הַמְבַיֵּשׁ וְהַמִּתְבַּיֵּשׁ. הַמְבַיֵּשׁ

יד אברהם

אִם מֵחֲמַת הַמַּכָּה, — *if as a result of the wound,*

The mishnah's rule applies even if they developed later as a result of the wound (Tif. Yis.).

חַיָּב; — *he is liable;*

[The one who inflicted the wound is liable also for the expense of healing his victim of the blisters that arose.]

This applies only if the perpetrator declined the option of paying what the court estimated to be the cost of healing and chose to pay the day-to-day expense instead, as explained above. Otherwise, he would be liable only for the court's predetermined amount regardless if blisters or any other condition subsequently arose, thereby increasing the expenses (Tos. 85a).

שֶׁלֹּא מֵחֲמַת הַמַּכָּה, פָּטוּר. — *[if] not as a result of the wound, he is exempt.*

The *Gemara* (85a) explains this to mean that even if the blisters develop from the wound, if they are caused by the victim's neglecting to follow a physician's orders, they are deemed as not resulting from the wound, and the offender is exempt from paying for healing them (Tos. Yom Tov).

חָיְתָה וְנִסְתְּרָה, — *[If] it healed and [then] relapsed, healed and relapsed,*

[The wound healed, then worsened, and then healed and relapsed again.]

חַיָּב לְרַפְּאתוֹ. — *he is liable to heal him.*

[The one who inflicted the wound must continue to pay for the medical expenses, since the wound is not yet completely healed.] As explained above, this would be applicable only if he had chosen to pay the day-to-day expenses of healing, but not if he had agreed to pay whatever the court had predetermined to be the total cost of healing (*Rambam, Hil. Chovel* 2:16).

חָיְתָה כָּל־צָרְכָּהּ, — *[If] it healed completely,*

The wound healed completely, and then, as a result of something other than the wound itself, it returned (Meiri).

אֵינוֹ חַיָּב לְרַפְּאתוֹ. — *he is not liable to heal him.*

[Since it came back because of something other than the wound itself, he is not responsible.]

שֶׁבֶת? — *Loss of time?*

[How do we reckon the amount to be paid for the victim's loss of time?]

רוֹאִין אוֹתוֹ כְּאִלּוּ הוּא שׁוֹמֵר קִשּׁוּאִין, — *We view him as though he were a watchman of a cucumber field,*

For the time that the victim is ill and unable to work, the one who inflicted the wound must pay him the wages of a watchman of a cucumber field. He does not have to pay more than this amount, since the victim — having lost his hand — is no longer capable of doing more difficult work than this even after he recovers from his illness (Rav; Rashi).

שֶׁכְּבָר נָתַן לוֹ דְּמֵי יָדוֹ וּדְמֵי רַגְלוֹ. — *since he has already given him the value of his hand or the value of his foot.*

By paying for the injury itself, the one who wounded the victim compen-

8 **1** the wound, he is liable; [if] not as a result of the wound, he is exempt. [If] it healed and [then] relapsed, healed and relapsed, he is liable to heal him. [If] it healed completely, he is not liable to heal him.

Loss of time? We view him as though he were a watchman of a cucumber field, since he has already given him the value of his hand or the value of his foot.

Disgrace? All depends upon [the status of] the one who disgraced and the one who was disgraced.

YAD AVRAHAM

sates for reducing him from his previous well-paying occupation — if he had one — to that of watchman of a cucumber field. Therefore, he has to pay him merely for the time he is completely idle and cannot work even as a cucumber watchman. The *Gemara* (85b) states that this is true if he loses his hand. Should he break his leg, however, he must be paid as a doorkeeper, not as a watchman of a cucumber field, since the latter position requires him to walk around the field *(Rashi)*. *Tosafos* suggest that if he breaks one leg, he is still capable of hobbling around a cucumber field and must be paid for this occupation. Should he break both legs, however, he is paid as a doorkeeper, since he will not be capable of engaging in a more lucrative occupation.

All these laws apply only to an unskilled worker. Should one injure a skilled worker and break his leg, since the latter can still engage in his profession, he must be paid for lost time as a worker at these professions to which he will return after his recovery. For example, if he is a teacher and he loses an arm or a leg, he can return to his original profession; if he is a jeweler, and loses a leg, he can still work at that craft. Such individuals must therefore be paid for the time lost as workers at these professions.

בֹּשֶׁת? — *Disgrace?*

[How do we compute the amount to be paid for disgrace?]

הַכֹּל לְפִי הַמְבַיֵּשׁ — *All depends upon [the status of] the one who disgraced*

Rav and *Rashi* comment that to be disgraced by a lowly individual is the worst sort of shame. In *Kesubos* (40a), however, *Rashi* states that it is worse to be disgraced by a middle-class person than by one of either high or low status.

[Although our mishnah deals with humiliation inflicted upon a person by striking him or the like, and the mishnah in *Kesubos* (3:7) deals with the disgrace of a woman who was seduced or forcibly violated, it appears that *Rav* in *Kesubos* equates the two cases, since he considers *Rashi's* interpretations as conflicting.]

Contrarily, *Ran* (*Kesubos* ad loc.) asserts that although, in general, one's disgrace is greatest if the offender is of middle class, in the cases of violation and seduction, however, the more lowly the perpetrator, the greater the humiliation (*Tos. Yom Tov* to *Kesubos* ibid.).

Meiri (ibid.) attributes *Rashi's* view to the logic that since an ignoble person is accustomed to shaming people, the disgrace perpetrated by him is of little consequence. *Meiri*, himself, however, rules that humiliation inflicted by a person of high status is the worst. He bases this view on *Yerushalmi*. *Pnei Moshe*, on the other hand, explains *Yerushalmi* in accordance with *Rashi* here.

[*Rambam's* ruling is unclear. In *Hilchos Chovel* (3:1), he states emphatically that

בבא קמא ח/א

אֶת־הֶעָרֹם, הַמְבַיֵּשׁ אֶת־הַסּוּמָא, וְהַמְבַיֵּשׁ אֶת־הַיָּשֵׁן, חַיָּב. וְיָשֵׁן שֶׁבִּיֵּשׁ, פָּטוּר. נָפַל מִן־הַגַּג, וְהִזִּיק וּבִיֵּשׁ, חַיָּב עַל־הַנֶּזֶק וּפָטוּר עַל־הַבֹּשֶׁת, שֶׁנֶּאֱמַר: "וְשָׁלְחָה יָדָהּ וְהֶחֱזִיקָה בִּמְבֻשָׁיו" — אֵינוֹ חַיָּב עַל־הַבֹּשֶׁת עַד שֶׁיְּהֵא מִתְכַּוֵּן.

יד אברהם

humiliation by a low-class person is the worst, while in *Hilchos Naarah Besulah* (2:4), he appears to concur with *Meiri's* view. *Bach* (*Choshen Mishpat* 420), however, does not note any discrepancy in *Rambam*, but rather explains both of his statements as conforming with each other.]

וְהַמִּתְבַּיֵּשׁ. — *and the one who was disgraced.*

The higher the status of the victim, the worse the disgrace (*Rav; Rashi*).

If he was struck when no one was looking on a part of the body that does not show, there is no liability for disgrace (*Choshen Mishpat* 420:7, *Sma* ad loc. §9).

הַמְבַיֵּשׁ אֶת־הֶעָרֹם, — [*If*] *one disgraces a naked person,*

According to *Tosafos* (86b), this applies if, for example, someone spits on him or slaps him, since he is shamed by these acts as much as a clothed person. According to *Rashi* and *Rambam* (*Hil. Chovel* 3:2), however, the only case in which a naked person experiences shame is if, after the wind had lifted up one's clothes and made him appear naked, someone came along and lifted his clothes even more. Even in such a case, the latter is not liable to pay as much as for disgracing a clothed person (*Tos. Yom Tov*).

הַמְבַיֵּשׁ אֶת־הַסּוּמָא, — *disgraces a blind person,*

Although a blind person does not see when he is disgraced, he feels it emotionally (*Tif. Yis.*).

וְהַמְבַיֵּשׁ אֶת־הַיָּשֵׁן, — *or disgraces a sleeping person,*

This applies if the person, upon awakening, realizes that he had been disgraced. The mishnah teaches us that, although he did not realize his shame at the time of the act, and when he awoke and felt the shame, the deed had already been done, it is nevertheless not regarded as being caused indirectly, and the offender is liable. If, however, the victim never became aware of his being disgraced, it is questionable whether the perpetrator is liable (*Tos. Yom Tov*). According to *Rosh*, the conclusion is that he is exempt. *Rambam* (*Hil. Chovel* 3:3), however, maintains that the question remains unresolved. Therefore, should such a person die in his sleep and his heirs seize money as payment for the disgrace, it cannot be reclaimed from them (see commentary to 2:1, s.v. חֲצִי נֶזֶק, par. beg. *Rambam's view*).

חַיָּב. — *he is liable.*

[In each of the three cases enumerated above, the offender must pay for having disgraced the person.] However, he is not liable to the same extent as one who disgraces a person who is not in one of these situations (*Tif. Yis.*).

וְיָשֵׁן שֶׁבִּיֵּשׁ, — *However,* [*if*] *a sleeping person disgraced,*

[While a person was sleeping, he disgraced someone else; e.g., he kicked him in his sleep, or fell off his bed on top of him.]

פָּטוּר. — *he is exempt.*

Since he had no intention to disgrace

משניות / בבא קמא — פרק ח: החובל [170]

8
1

[If] one disgraces a naked person, disgraces a blind person, or disgraces a sleeping person, he is liable. However, [if] a sleeping person disgraced, he is exempt.

[If] one fell off a roof, and injured and disgraced, he is liable for the injury but exempt for the disgrace, as it is said (*Deuteronomy 25:11*): *And she stretches forth her hand and takes hold of his privy organs* — one is not liable for disgrace unless he has intention.

YAD AVRAHAM

the other person, he is exempt, as explained at the end of the mishnah (*Meiri*).

נָפַל מִן־הַגָּג, וְהִזִּיק וּבִיֵּשׁ, — [*If*] *one fell off a roof, and injured and disgraced*,

[He injured and disgraced someone by falling on him.]

חַיָּב עַל־הַנֶּזֶק וּפָטוּר עַל־הַבֹּשֶׁת. — *he is liable for the injury but exempt for the disgrace*,

This applies even if he fell because he was blown off by a normal wind — he is liable for injury, pain, healing, and loss of time, but not for disgrace. Should the cause of his fall have been an unusually strong wind, he is liable only for injury (*Tos. R' Akiva* from *Gem.* 27a).

[As explained in 2:6, with regard to injury, man is always considered *muad* (forewarned); with regard to the other four categories, he is liable only if he was negligent.]

שֶׁנֶּאֱמַר: ,,וְשָׁלְחָה יָדָהּ וְהֶחֱזִיקָה בִּמְבֻשָׁיו״ — אֵינוֹ חַיָּב עַל־הַבֹּשֶׁת עַד שֶׁיְּהֵא מִתְכַּוֵּן. — *as it is said* (*Deuteronomy 25:11*): '*And she stretches forth her hand and takes hold of his privy organs*' — *one is not liable for disgrace unless he has intention*.

In other words, if he has intention to injure the other person, even though he has no intention to disgrace him, he is liable. This is derived from the term, וְהֶחֱזִיקָה, *and takes hold*, which indicates that she wished to injure him (*Tif. Yis.* from *Gem.* 27a; see *Tos. Yom Tov, Shoshannim LeDavid, Rashash* [*Mishnah Commentary*]).

The *Gemara* gives an example of one falling off a roof who turns over in order to fall on a person and cushion his fall — he is liable for disgrace as well as for injury.

According to the Torah (*Ex.* 22:18), all monetary disputes may be judged only by duly ordained judges, known as מֻמְחִים or סְמוּכִים, or in Biblical terminology as אֱלֹהִים. This ordination, called סְמִיכָה, *semichah*, was originally given by Moses to Joshua, and was continued through the generations by three judges ordaining another judge. Since this ordination could be bestowed only in the Holy Land, no monetary disputes could be litigated in Babylon or anywhere else in the Diaspora.

The Rabbis, however, made a special dispensation to allow the judges of the Diaspora to adjudicate these cases by making them the agents of the judges of *Eretz Yisrael*. This exemption was made only for common cases which involve monetary loss, including disputes concerning loans, sales, gifts, and confessions or denials of liability. Also, cases in which an animal damaged with *shen* or *regel* [see General Introduction] since, regarding these damages, its owner is considered forewarned from the outset [1:4] or cases in which a man injured an animal since man is always considered *muad* [2:6] — may be judged in the Diaspora. However, regarding cases in which an animal injures a man, or a man injures another man — since these are uncommon occurrences — the Rabbis did not make the judges of the Diaspora agents of the Holy Land's judges. The same applies to the case of one who disgraces another, since there is no monetary

בבא קמא ח/ב-ג

[ב] זֶה חֹמֶר בָּאָדָם מִבַּשּׁוֹר — שֶׁהָאָדָם מְשַׁלֵּם נֶזֶק, צַעַר, רִפּוּי, שֶׁבֶת, וּבֹשֶׁת, וּמְשַׁלֵּם דְּמֵי וְלָדוֹת; וְשׁוֹר אֵינוֹ מְשַׁלֵּם אֶלָּא נֶזֶק וּפָטוּר מִדְּמֵי וְלָדוֹת.

[ג] הַמַּכֶּה אֶת־אָבִיו וְאֶת־אִמּוֹ, וְלֹא עָשָׂה בָהֶם חַבּוּרָה, וְהַחוֹבֵל בַּחֲבֵרוֹ בְּיוֹם הַכִּפּוּרִים, חַיָּב בְּכֻלָּן.

יד אברהם

loss. In such instances, the perpetrator is placed under a ban until he accompanies his litigant to Eretz Yisrael or until he arrives at a compromise with him, coming close to the amount suggested by a judge. A judge cannot, however, sentence him to pay a fixed amount. Although the judges of the Diaspora can also not impose any fines, they may place the defendant under a ban even in such cases until the dispute is resolved, as explained above. This includes the case of an animal which inflicted damages in the category of *keren* (see General Introduction). Since the halachah is that the half-damage payment for *keren* constitutes a fine [*Gem.* 15b], it cannot be imposed by any judges except *semuchim* in Eretz Yisrael (Rav, Rambam Commentary, Tos. Yom Tov from *Gem.* 84b).

Tiferes Yisrael suggests a mnemonic for the types of cases that may be litigated in the Diaspora: אָב שֶׁר שָׂמַח, whose letters stand for: אֵשׁ, *fire*; בּוֹר, *pit*; שֵׁן, *tooth*; רֶגֶל, *foot*; שָׁכִיחַ, *common*; מָמוֹן, *restitution*; חֶסְרוֹן כִּיס, *monetary loss*.

Concerning the restoration of *semichah* and of the Sanhedrin (Supreme Court), see Sanhedrin 1:3 and Rambam, Hil. Sanhedrin 4:11.

2.

זֶה חֹמֶר בָּאָדָם מִבַּשּׁוֹר — — *This is the stringency of a man over a bull* —

[In the following respects, a man who commits a damage is judged more stringently than a bull which commits the same damages.]

שֶׁהָאָדָם מְשַׁלֵּם נֶזֶק, צַעַר, רִפּוּי, שֶׁבֶת, וּבֹשֶׁת, — *that a man pays for injury, pain, healing, loss of time, and disgrace,*

[This is explained in the preceding mishnah.]

וּמְשַׁלֵּם דְּמֵי וְלָדוֹת; — *and he pays the value of the young;*

[This is explained in 5:4.]

וְשׁוֹר אֵינוֹ מְשַׁלֵּם אֶלָּא נֶזֶק — *whereas [the owner of] a bull pays only for injury*

This is derived from *Leviticus* 24:19: וְאִישׁ כִּי־יִתֵּן מוּם בַּעֲמִיתוֹ..., *Should a man inflict a blemish upon another* ..., which is interpreted as applying to a case in which one person injures another, but not one in which an animal injures a man (Rav, Rashi from *Gem.* 26a, 33a).

Tos. Yom Tov points out that R' Akiva makes this derivation; according to the Sages, however, that verse exempts the owner of the animal only from the payment for pain. They derive the exemption from healing and loss of time from the phrase (*Ex.* 21:31) כַּמִּשְׁפָּט הַזֶּה יֵעָשֶׂה לּוֹ, *according to this judgment shall be done to it*, from where it is deduced that only the payment of ransom is due if an animal gores and kills a man, and only the damages, if it merely injures him, but not the payments for healing and loss of time. The exemption from paying for disgrace is derived from the passage dealing with that subject (*Deuteronomy* 25:11ff.),

משניות / בבא קמא — פרק ח: החובל [172]

2. This is the stringency of a man over a bull — that a man pays for injury, pain, healing, loss of time, and disgrace, and he pays the value of the young; whereas [the owner of] a bull pays only for injury and is exempt from the value of the young.

3. [If] one strikes his father or his mother, but does not inflict a wound upon them, or [if] one wounds another on Yom Kippur, he is liable for all of them.

YAD AVRAHAM

which begins by specifying: כִּי יִנָּצוּ אֲנָשִׁים יַחְדָּו..., *If men quarrel together*, and is interpreted as applying only to men and not animals — i.e., there is no liability if one's animal disgraces a man (see *Tos.* 33a, 42a).

וּפָטוּר מִדְּמֵי וְלָדוֹת — *and is exempt from the value of the young.*

[If an animal strikes a pregnant woman, thus causing her to abort her fetus, its owner is exempt from paying for the fetus.]

This is derived from the passage dealing with this subject (*Ex.* 21:22ff.) which begins: וְכִי יִנָּצוּ אֲנָשִׁים, *If men quarrel*, and is interpreted as applying only if humans do the damage, not animals (*Rav; Rashi;* see 5:4).

3.

הַמַּכֶּה אֶת־אָבִיו וְאֶת־אִמּוֹ, וְלֹא עָשָׂה בָהֶם חַבּוּרָה — [*If*] *one strikes his father or his mother, but does not inflict a wound upon them,*

The Torah states (*Ex.* 21:15): וּמַכֵּה אָבִיו וְאִמּוֹ מוֹת יוּמָת, *Whoever strikes his father or his mother shall be put to death.* According to *Sanhedrin* 11:1, this penalty applies only if one inflicts a wound upon his parent. Should he strike him and not inflict a wound, however, there is no death sentence, and, as the mishnah concludes, he is therefore liable for the five categories enumerated above — injury, pain, etc. [Had the death penalty been applicable, he would be exempt from monetary liability due to the principle of קִים לֵיהּ..., *He suffers only the more severe punishment* (see commentary to 6:5).] (*Tos. Yom Tov* from *Rashi*).

The *Gemara* (86a) questions how it is possible for one who strikes his parent without inflicting a wound to be liable for injury. It concludes that he smeared a depilatory cream on his father's head, causing the hair to fall out and never grow back, constituting a blemish. He must pay for pain, as well, because he made scratches on his father's head which caused his father pain. The healing costs involved are those required to heal the scratches. He must pay for loss of time in the case that the father was a dancer in wine houses, and would make gestures with his head, which he cannot do now because of the scratches. Finally, he must pay for the disgrace that his father suffers from these scratches.

וְהַחוֹבֵל בַּחֲבֵרוֹ בְּיוֹם הַכִּפּוּרִים, חַיָּב בְּכֻלָּן — *or* [*if*] *one wounds another on Yom Kippur, he is liable for all of them.*

[He is liable for each of the five categories discussed above.]

As stated in the commentary to 7:2, the penalty for violating the laws of Yom Kippur after having been forewarned is מַלְקוּת, *lashes*. In such cases, the perpetrator is exempt from any monetary liability incurred at the time

בבא קמא ח/ד

הַחוֹבֵל בְּעֶבֶד עִבְרִי, חַיָּב בְּכֻלָּן חוּץ מִן הַשֶּׁבֶת בִּזְמַן שֶׁהוּא שֶׁלּוֹ. הַחוֹבֵל בְּעֶבֶד כְּנַעֲנִי שֶׁל־אֲחֵרִים, חַיָּב בְּכֻלָּן. רַבִּי יְהוּדָה אוֹמֵר: אֵין לַעֲבָדִים בֹּשֶׁת.

[ד] **חֵרֵשׁ,** שׁוֹטֶה, וְקָטָן פְּגִיעָתָן רָעָה: הַחוֹבֵל בָּהֶן, חַיָּב; וְהֵם שֶׁחָבְלוּ בַּאֲחֵרִים,

יד אברהם

of the sin, because of the principle of *He suffers only the more severe punishment*. It would follow, therefore, that if one wounds another person on Yom Kippur, he should be exempt from monetary payments; yet, the mishnah rules that *he is liable*. *Rav* and *Rambam* explain that in the case of one person wounding another, the Torah imposed a monetary obligation which supersedes any penalty of lashes, whether incurred for striking a fellow Jew (*Deut.* 25:3; see *Rashi* ad loc.), or for violating any other prohibition. Hence, he is monetarily liable for wounding another on Yom Kippur. [For the exact derivation, see *Rav* and *Tos. Yom Tov.*]

This is based on the principle that the Torah gave consideration to a wounded person, that he should not lose the money due him. Therefore, just as the monetary obligation supersedes the penalty of lashes that the offender deserves for striking another person, so does it supersede the lashes he deserves for desecrating Yom Kippur.

Others hold that the lashes for striking a person are superseded because that prohibition is a lenient one in the respect that it is sometimes permitted: the agent of the court may strike a person when he metes out punishment. Accordingly, this would not apply to the lashes due for the desecration of Yom Kippur. To explain the mishnah according to this opinion, therefore, we must qualify it as referring to a case in which the perpetrator was not warned. Consequently, he is not punishable by lashes and must make restitution to the victim (*R' Akiva Eiger* to *Rambam, Hil. Chovel* 4:9 [ed. Frankel] from *Tos. Yeshanim, Kesubos* 32b; notes on *Sma*, 424:3; *Livnei Binyamin* 21:8).

הַחוֹבֵל בְּעֶבֶד עִבְרִי, חַיָּב בְּכֻלָּן חוּץ מִן הַשֶּׁבֶת בִּזְמַן שֶׁהוּא שֶׁלּוֹ — [*If*] *one wounds a Jewish bondman, he is liable for all of them except loss of time when he is his.*

[When one wounds his own bondman, he need not pay the latter for loss of time, since it is only he who loses by the bondman's inability to work. However he must pay for injury, pain, healing and disgrace.

Regarding the translation of עֶבֶד עִבְרִי as *Jewish bondman*, see footnote to mishnah 1, s.v. וְכַמָּה.]

הַחוֹבֵל בְּעֶבֶד כְּנַעֲנִי שֶׁל־אֲחֵרִים, חַיָּב בְּכֻלָּן. — [*If*] *one wounds a gentile slave belonging to others, he is liable for all of them.*

He must pay the slave's master for each of the five categories (*Meiri; Rambam, Hil. Chovel* 4:10).

רַבִּי יְהוּדָה אוֹמֵר: אֵין לַעֲבָדִים בֹּשֶׁת. — *R' Yehudah says: Slaves have no [indemnity for] disgrace.*

R' Yehudah bases his view on a phrase in the verse (*Deut.* 25:11) which is the source of the payment for disgrace (see commentary to mishnah 1, s.v. אִישׁ וְאָחִיו וּבֹשֶׁת), *a man and his brother*. This excludes gentile slaves, who are not considered brothers [as explained below] (*Rav* from *Gem.* 88a).

Rashi maintains that the slave is not

[174]

8
4

[If] one wounds a Jewish bondman, he is liable for all of them except loss of time when he is his. [If] one wounds a gentile slave belonging to others, he is liable for all of them. R' Yehudah says: Slaves have no [indemnity for] disgrace.

4. It is inadvisable to clash with a deaf-mute, a mentally deranged person, or a minor: [if] one wounds them, he is liable; but [if] they wound others,

YAD AVRAHAM

considered a 'brother' with other Jews, since he is not permitted to intermarry with them. In the margin of our editions and in *Sanhedrin* (86a), however, he explains that the slave is not deemed a brother even with another son of his own father. Since the *Gemara* (49a) interprets Scripture (*Gen.* 22:5) as equating the slave with a donkey, he and his brothers are no more related than are two donkeys born to the same mother.

Tosafos (*Sanhedrin* loc. cit.) objects to this explanation, since a proselyte — who is deemed a new person upon his conversion — has no more relationship to his brothers than the slave, and yet, he has indemnity for disgrace, even according to R' Yehudah. They therefore explain (88a and *Sanhedrin* ibid.) that whereas the offspring of a slave are not considered brothers to each other, those of a proselyte are. Consequently, proselytes are included in the indemnity for disgrace, unlike slaves.

The first, anonymous *Tanna* in the mishnah, however, does include the slave in this law, since he is a 'brother' of the Jewish people in the respect that he is obligated to observe those commandments which apply to a Jewish woman (*Tos. Yom Tov* from *Gem.* 88a).

The halachah is not in accordance with R' Yehudah (*Rav*; *Rambam Commentary*).

4.

חֵרֵשׁ, שׁוֹטֶה, וְקָטָן פְּגִיעָתָן רָעָה: — *It is inadvisable to clash with a deaf-mute, a mentally deranged person, or a minor* (lit., *contact with them is bad*):

[One who clashes with them will always lose.]

הַחוֹבֵל בָּהֶן, חַיָּב; — [*if*] *one wounds them, he is liable;*

He is liable for all five categories if they apply. A deaf-mute — even one who is so from birth — must be paid for all the categories; since he is capable of working, he is entitled to compensation for loss of time. A mentally deranged person, however, must be paid only for injury, pain, and healing. He is not entitled to collect for loss of time, because he is incapable of working, nor for disgrace, since he does not feel any shame. Even his family members experience no disgrace if one humiliates him, since his condition is the greatest disgrace to them. A minor, too, suffers no loss of time, but sometimes suffers from disgrace, depending upon his age and maturity (*Meiri* from *Gem.* 86b).

וְהֵם שֶׁחָבְלוּ בַאֲחֵרִים, פְּטוּרִין. — *but* [*if*] *they wound others, they are exempt.*

Even if they subsequently recover from their incapacities, and the minor reaches majority, they are nevertheless exempt for the injuries they inflicted

בבא קמא ח/ה

פְּטוּרִין. הָעֶבֶד וְהָאִשָּׁה פְּגִיעָתָן רָעָה: הַחוֹבֵל בָּהֶן, חַיָּב; וְהֵם שֶׁחָבְלוּ בַּאֲחֵרִים, פְּטוּרִין, אֲבָל מְשַׁלְּמִין לְאַחַר זְמַן. נִתְגָּרְשָׁה הָאִשָּׁה, נִשְׁתַּחְרֵר הָעֶבֶד, חַיָּבִין לְשַׁלֵּם.

[ה] הַמַּכֶּה אָבִיו וְאִמּוֹ וְעָשָׂה בָהֶן חַבּוּרָה, וְהַחוֹבֵל בַּחֲבֵרוֹ בַּשַּׁבָּת, פָּטוּר מִכֻּלָּן, מִפְּנֵי שֶׁהוּא נִדּוֹן בְּנַפְשׁוֹ. וְהַחוֹבֵל בְּעֶבֶד כְּנַעֲנִי שֶׁלּוֹ, פָּטוּר מִכֻּלָּן.

יד אברהם

הָעֶבֶד וְהָאִשָּׁה פְּגִיעָתָן רָעָה: הַחוֹבֵל בָּהֶן חַיָּב; וְהֵם שֶׁחָבְלוּ בַּאֲחֵרִים, פְּטוּרִין — It is inadvisable to clash with a slave or with a woman: [if] one wounds them, he is liable; but [if] they wound others, they are exempt,

They are exempt because they have no money. Anything belonging to a slave belongs to his master, and a woman's property is under the jurisdiction of her husband (Rav; Rashi). Even the melog [usufructuary] property (see General Introduction to ArtScroll Kesubos p. 6), which belongs to the wife, is in the husband's domain in that he eats the produce and inherits the property should she predecease him (Rav; Rashi).

Others rule that if she has usufructuary property, she must sell it with the understanding that the sale is binding only if her husband predeceases or divorces her. With the proceeds, she must pay the one whom she wounded (Tif. Yis., Tos. R' Akiva from Choshen Mishpat 424:9).

We do not coerce her to sell her kesubah [marriage contract][1] on the condition that the sale take effect only if her husband divorces or predeceases her, since we are confident that she will relinquish her rights to it in favor of her husband and cause a loss to the purchaser (Tos. Yom Tov, Tif. Yis. from Gem. 89a).

אֲבָל מְשַׁלְּמִין לְאַחַר זְמַן — although they must pay later.

[As will be explained below.]

נִתְגָּרְשָׁה הָאִשָּׁה, נִשְׁתַּחְרֵר הָעֶבֶד — Should the woman become divorced, or the slave freed,

After having wounded someone, this change in the status of the slave or woman occurred. Subsequently, he/she acquired property (Rav; Rashi).

חַיָּבִין לְשַׁלֵּם — they are obligated to pay.

Since, in reality, they were liable at the time of the incident and were exempt then only because they had no money, they must pay now (Rav; Rashi).

while they were considered irresponsible for their deeds (Tos. Yom Tov from Rosh). Meiri equates them to persons who committed damages by accident.

---

1. The foremost feature of the kesubah is the dower awarded the wife in the event of divorce or the husband's death (see General Introduction to ArtScroll Kesubos).

משניות / בבא קמא — פרק ח: החובל [176]

they are exempt. It is inadvisable to clash with a slave or with a woman: [if] one wounds them, he is liable; but [if] they wound others, they are exempt, although they must pay later. Should the woman become divorced, or the slave freed, they are obligated to pay.

5. [I]f] one strikes his father or his mother and inflicts a wound upon them, or [if] one wounds another on the Sabbath, he is exempt from all of them, because he is liable for his life. [If] one wounds his own gentile slave, he is exempt from all of them.

YAD AVRAHAM

5.

הַמַּכֶּה אָבִיו וְאִמּוֹ וְעָשָׂה בָהֶן חַבּוּרָה, וְהַחוֹבֵל בַּחֲבֵרוֹ בַּשַּׁבָּת, פָּטוּר מִכֻּלָּן. — [If] one strikes his father or his mother and inflicts a wound upon them, or [if] one wounds another on the Sabbath, he is exempt from all of them,

[That is, from all five categories: injury, pain, healing, loss of time, and disgrace.]

מִפְּנֵי שֶׁהוּא נִדּוֹן בְּנַפְשׁוֹ. — because he is liable for his life.

As discussed above [3:10, 6:5, 7:4], if one commits a capital offense, he is exempt from any monetary liabilities incurred at the time (Tif. Yis.). This rule applies even if he is not forewarned, in which case there is no capital punishment (ibid.; Meiri).

Although one is not liable for doing a destructive act on the Sabbath [see Shabbos 13:3], and the mishnah's case of wounding another falls into that category, it is nevertheless considered constructive in the respect that the perpetrator soothes his anger thereby (Rav; Rambam Commentary).

Should he wound an animal, however, he is liable only if he needs the blood, as Rav [Shabbos 14:1] explains (Tos. Yom Tov).

וְהַחוֹבֵל בְּעֶבֶד כְּנַעֲנִי שֶׁלּוֹ, פָּטוּר מִכֻּלָּן. — [If] one wounds his own gentile slave, he is exempt from all of them.

Although he would be liable should he kill him, he is not liable for wounding him, since others who wound the slave must pay the master (Meiri).

6.

There are many blows which cause humiliation and a little pain, but no injury. The Rabbis fixed definite payments to be paid by whoever inflicts one of these blows upon another. These payments are regarded as fines for the pain, healing, and loss of time and disgrace. Regardless of whether or not healing and idleness are required, the offender must pay this amount (Rambam, Hil. Chovel 3:8).

Tur [Choshen Mishpat 420], however, quotes Rif and Rosh [ch. 3], that these amounts are only for pain and disgrace. As regards healing and loss of time, however, the Sages could not establish a fixed amount; rather, each case is judged by its own merits (Tos. Yom Tov; see Lechem Shamayim).

Rav and Rashi maintain that these sums are only for disgrace.

בבא קמא ח/ו

[ו] **הַתּוֹקֵעַ** לַחֲבֵרוֹ, נוֹתֵן לוֹ סֶלַע; רַבִּי יְהוּדָה אוֹמֵר מִשּׁוּם רַבִּי יוֹסֵי הַגְּלִילִי: מָנֶה. סְטָרוֹ, נוֹתֵן לוֹ מָאתַיִם זוּז; לְאַחַר יָדוֹ, נוֹתֵן לוֹ אַרְבַּע מֵאוֹת זוּז. צָרַם בְּאָזְנוֹ, תָּלַשׁ בִּשְׂעָרוֹ, רָקַק וְהִגִּיעַ בּוֹ רֻקּוֹ, הֶעֱבִיר טַלִּיתוֹ מִמֶּנּוּ, פָּרַע רֹאשׁ הָאִשָּׁה בַשּׁוּק,

יד אברהם

הַתּוֹקֵעַ לַחֲבֵרוֹ — [If] one cuffs another, He formed a fist and struck him (Rav; Rambam Commentary, ed. Kaffich). According to our edition of Rambam Commentary and Meiri, he struck him with his fist on the back of his neck. In Hilchos Chovel (3:9), however, Rambam appears to have changed his interpretation, for there he explains it as referring to a slap. Rashi (here and Bechoros 80b) quotes his teacher who interprets it as a blow on the ear, but he himself explains it as shouting into the ear.

נוֹתֵן לוֹ סֶלַע; — he must give him a sela; This refers to a sela of provincial silver, which is ⅛ of a sela of Tyrian silver. The former was an alloy of one part silver and seven parts copper (Rambam, Hil. Chovel 3:10 from Gem. 36b; see General Introduction to ArtScroll Kesubos, p. 5).

רַבִּי יְהוּדָה אוֹמֵר מִשּׁוּם רַבִּי יוֹסֵי הַגְּלִילִי: מָנֶה. — R' Yehudah says in the name of R' Yose the Galilean: A maneh.
The Gemara (90b) interprets the mishnah as referring to a maneh of Tyrian silver. Tosafos (36b) note that, accordingly, since the first, anonymous Tanna rules that he must pay a sela of provinicial silver and R' Yose the Galilean rules that he must pay a maneh — which equals one hundred zuz of Tyrian silver — there is a vast difference between them. A sela is equivalent to four zuz, and a sela of provincial silver is ⅛ of a sela of Tyrian silver. The result is that R' Yose the Galilean imposes upon the offender two hundred times as much as the first Tanna. To avoid the unlikely interpretation that the two opinions differ so greatly, they conclude that the first Tanna is dealing with a case in which a poor man was the victim, whereas R' Yose speaks of a rich man. However, it does appear from the Gemara that there is some controversy between the two views (Tos. Yom Tov).

Rambam (Hil. Chovel 3:10f.), Tur (Choshen Mishpat 420), and Shulchan Aruch (ibid. §41-43) rule that the offender in this case must pay a sela of provincial silver if the victim was a respected person; if he was not, the payment would be less.

[Apparently, these authorities do not explain the controversy in the mishnah as do Tosafos. In order to explain the wide divergence in the opinions of the two Tannaim, we must conclude that these authorities construe the Gemara on 90b — mentioned above — as meaning that the amounts given by both Tannaim are in Tyrian silver, and another Gemara on 36b as disagreeing and maintaining that both Tannaim speak of provincial silver.

Meiri appears to explain the mishnah in the above manner.]

The halachah is not in accordance with R' Yehudah (Rav; Rambam Commentary).

סְטָרוֹ, — [If] he slaps him,
He does so, on the cheek, causing him great humiliation (Rav; Rashi). Rambam (Commentary and Hil. Chovel 3:9) states that he slaps him in the face.

משניות / בבא קמא — פרק ח: החובל [178]

6.

[If] one cuffs another, he must give him a *sela*; R' Yehudah says in the name of R' Yose the Galilean: A *maneh*.

[If] he slaps him, he must give him two hundred *zuz*; with the back of his hand, he must give him four hundred *zuz*.

[If] he pulls his ear, tears his hair, spits at him and the spittle reaches him, removes his cloak, or uncovers a woman's hair in the street, he must pay

YAD AVRAHAM

נוֹתֵן לוֹ מָאתַיִם זוּז; — *he must give him two hundred zuz;*

[This act is more humiliating than the one described above.]

לְאַחַר יָדוֹ, — *with the back of his hand,*

Instead of slapping him in the usual manner, he did so with the back of his hand (*Tos. Yom Tov* from *Rambam Commentary*).

נוֹתֵן לוֹ אַרְבַּע מֵאוֹת זוּז. — *he must give him four hundred zuz.*

Since this is even more humiliating to the victim, the offender must pay him this large amount (*Tos. Yom Tov* from *Rambam Commentary*).

צָרַם בְּאָזְנוֹ, — *[If] he pulls his ear,*

This follows one interpretation given by *Rav* and *Rashi*. The other is that he makes a slit in the ear.

Although making a slit in the ear involves injury as well as pain and disgrace, the amounts listed do not include the payment for injury but only the other payments [as discussed in the preface to this mishnah] (*Shoshannim LeDavid*).

Beis David maintains that *Rashi* — who mentions the second definition in connection with *Bechoros* 5:3 — does not intend to give us an alternate meaning for the term in our mishnah; rather he means that, although in *Bechoros*, where the mishnah deals with making a blemish on a firstborn animal in order to slaughter it outside the Temple, a word of the same root, צרם, means *making a slit*, here it is defined as *pulling*.

Rambam (Commentary) renders: he twists the ear.

תָּלַשׁ בִּשְׂעָרוֹ, רָקַק וְהִגִּיעַ בּוֹ רֻקּוֹ, — *tears his hair, spits at him and the spittle reaches him,*

Only if the spittle touches his body is he liable for disgrace. Should it touch his garment only, he is not liable, since such an act is analogous to disgracing him with words. From here the *Gemara* deduces that if one disgraces another with words, he is exempt from the indemnity for disgrace. *Rosh* explains that this is based on the verse: וְהֶחֱזִיקָה בִּמְבֻשָׁיו, *and she takes hold of his privy organs*, which indicates that it applies only if one disgraces another through his body, but not if he does so verbally or by spitting on his garment, in which case he is exempt (*Tos. Yom Tov*).

Rambam (loc. cit. §5) adds: The court should institute preventive measures in this matter everywhere and at all times as they see fit. If one shames a scholar — even if he does so verbally — he is liable to pay him for the disgrace.

הֶעֱבִיר טַלִּיתוֹ מִמֶּנּוּ, — *removes his cloak,*

He removed his outer garment and left him standing in the street without it; surely, this would apply if he bared his flesh (*Meiri*).

Lechem Shamayim maintains that there can be no indemnity for disgrace if he removes only his outer garment. The mishnah can mean only that he removes the garment next to his skin and bares his body.

פָּרַע רֹאשׁ הָאִשָּׁה בַּשּׁוּק, — *or uncovers a woman's hair in the street,*

בבא קמא ח/ו

נוֹתֵן אַרְבַּע מֵאוֹת זוּז. זֶה הַכְּלָל: הַכֹּל לְפִי כְבוֹדוֹ. אָמַר רַבִּי עֲקִיבָא: אֲפִלּוּ עֲנִיִּים שֶׁבְּיִשְׂרָאֵל רוֹאִין אוֹתָם כְּאִלּוּ הֵם בְּנֵי חֹרִין שֶׁיָּרְדוּ מִנִּכְסֵיהֶם, שֶׁהֵם בְּנֵי אַבְרָהָם, יִצְחָק, וְיַעֲקֹב.

וּמַעֲשֶׂה בְאֶחָד שֶׁפָּרַע רֹאשׁ הָאִשָּׁה בַּשּׁוּק. בָּאת לִפְנֵי רַבִּי עֲקִיבָא, וְחִיְּבוֹ לִתֶּן־לָהּ אַרְבַּע מֵאוֹת זוּז. אָמַר לוֹ: "רַבִּי, תֶּן־לִי זְמַן," וְנָתַן לוֹ זְמַן. שְׁמָרָהּ עוֹמֶדֶת עַל־פֶּתַח חֲצֵרָהּ, וְשָׁבַר אֶת־הַכַּד בְּפָנֶיהָ וּבוֹ כְאִסָּר שֶׁמֶן. גִּלְּתָה אֶת־רֹאשָׁהּ וְהָיְתָה

יד אברהם

He removed her headdress and left her standing bareheaded in the street (Meiri; see ArtScroll commentary to Kesubos 7:6).

נוֹתֵן אַרְבַּע מֵאוֹת זוּז — he must pay four hundred zuz.

[This amount must be paid by the perpetrator in the above cases.]

זֶה הַכְּלָל: הַכֹּל לְפִי כְבוֹדוֹ — This is the general rule: it all depends on his wealth.[1]

All the amounts listed are only if one disgraces a prominent person. Should he do so to a person of lower standing, he pays less (Rav from Gem. 91a).

אָמַר רַבִּי עֲקִיבָא: אֲפִלּוּ עֲנִיִּים שֶׁבְּיִשְׂרָאֵל רוֹאִין אוֹתָם כְּאִלּוּ הֵם בְּנֵי חֹרִין שֶׁיָּרְדוּ מִנִּכְסֵיהֶם, שֶׁהֵם בְּנֵי אַבְרָהָם יִצְחָק וְיַעֲקֹב — Said R' Akiva: Even the poorest of Jews are looked upon as though they were sons of noblemen who lost their wealth, for they are the children of Abraham, Isaac, and Jacob.

R' Akiva differs with the first, anonymous Tanna who distinguishes between people of different status. He rules that all are considered equal in this respect (Rav).

There are several interpretations of R' Akiva's view. Tosafos (86a) explain that a person's wealth is not always the criterion of his sensitivity to humiliation, for there are some wealthy people who are not embarrassed any more readily than people of high birth who lost their fortune. Similarly, there are poor people who are as sensitive to shame as people who were once rich and lost their fortune. It is therefore impossible to determine exactly which ones feel shame like people who lost their fortune, which feel more, and which less; consequently, they are all adjudged as equal with regard to the payment for disgrace. Likewise, in the cases above, if one removes someone's cloak or uncovers a woman's hair in the street, he must pay four hundred zuz regardless of whether the act was done in the presence of prominent people, before whom the victim is ashamed, or not (Tos. Yom Tov).

Rashi (loc. cit.) explains that we do not give the rich man more than the poor man when he is disgraced, since the shame of the rich knows no limits.

Meiri construes R' Akiva's opinion to

---

1. Although the word כָּבֹד is usually translated as honor, it is sometimes used to mean wealth, as in Gen. 31:1: עָשָׂה כָּל־הַכָּבֹד הַזֶּה, he amassed all this wealth. The phrase used by our mishnah also appears in Kesubos 5:9, where it has the same meaning.

[180]

8
6

four hundred *zuz*.

This is the general rule: it all depends on his wealth. Said R' Akiva: Even the poorest of Jews are looked upon as though they were sons of noblemen who lost their wealth, for they are the children of Abraham, Isaac, and Jacob.

There was an incident of one who uncovered a woman's hair in the street. She came before R' Akiva, who sentenced him to give her four hundred *zuz*. Said he to him: 'Rabbi, give me time,' and he gave him time. He waited for her until he saw her standing at the entrance of her courtyard, and then broke a jug which contained oil worth an *issar* in her presence. She uncovered her head and was scooping [it] up and

YAD AVRAHAM

be that these amounts are for the poorest people, since even they feel shame like wealthy individuals who have lost their wealth but still conduct themselves as if they were in their previous status. We do not judge the poor as people who were always impoverished and never felt any honor. Wealthy people, however, are judged on a higher scale, and receive a larger amount for their disgrace, according to the court's assessment.

The halachah is in accordance with the first *Tanna* (*Rav*; *Rambam Commentary*).

וּמַעֲשֶׂה בְּאֶחָד שֶׁפָּרַע רֹאשׁ הָאִשָּׁה בַּשּׁוּק. בָּאת לִפְנֵי רַבִּי עֲקִיבָא, וְחִיְּבוֹ לִתֵּן־לָהּ אַרְבַּע מֵאוֹת זוּז. — *There was an incident of one who uncovered a woman's hair in the street. She came before R' Akiva, who sentenced him to give her four hundred zuz.*

This woman was of low status, but R' Akiva, according to his ruling above, sentenced the man who embarrassed her to pay four hundred *zuz* just as if he would have done so to someone of higher status (*Chiddushei HaRavad*).

אָמַר לוֹ: ,,רַבִּי, תֶּן־לִי זְמַן.'' — *Said he to him:* 'Rabbi, give me time,'

[The offender said to R' Akiva, 'Give me time to raise the money to pay.']

וְנָתַן לוֹ זְמַן. — *and he gave him time.*

The court grants a defendant his request for time only in the case of disgrace, in which he did not cause his victim any monetary loss, but not in a case of damages, however, in which a monetary loss was caused (*Rav* from *Gem*. 91a).

שְׁמָרָהּ עוֹמֶדֶת עַל־פֶּתַח חֲצֵרָהּ. — *He waited for her until he saw her standing at the entrance of her courtyard,*

[This translation is given by *Rav* and *Rashi*.]

וְשָׁבַר אֶת־הַכַּד בְּפָנֶיהָ וּבוֹ כְּאִסָּר שֶׁמֶן. — *and then broke a jug which contained oil worth an issar in her presence.*

It contained a small quantity of oil that is purchased for an *issar*, a small coin (*Rav*; *Rashi*)

It does not mean a drop of oil the size of an *issar*, as in *Eruvin* 7:10, since that would be too little to use to anoint her head (*Beis David*).

גִּלְּתָה אֶת־רֹאשָׁהּ וְהָיְתָה מְטַפַּחַת וּמַנַּחַת יָדָהּ עַל־רֹאשָׁהּ. — *She uncovered her head*

בבא קמא ח/ו

מְטַפַּחַת וּמַנַּחַת יָדָהּ עַל־רֹאשָׁהּ, הֶעֱמִיד עָלֶיהָ עֵדִים וּבָא לִפְנֵי רַבִּי עֲקִיבָא. אָמַר לוֹ: "רַבִּי, לָזוֹ אֲנִי נוֹתֵן אַרְבַּע מֵאוֹת זוּז?" אָמַר לוֹ: "לֹא אָמַרְתָּ כְּלוּם; הַחוֹבֵל בְּעַצְמוֹ, אַף־עַל־פִּי שֶׁאֵינוֹ רַשַּׁאי, פָּטוּר; אֲחֵרִים שֶׁחָבְלוּ בּוֹ, חַיָּבִין. וְהַקּוֹצֵץ נְטִיעוֹתָיו, אַף־עַל־פִּי שֶׁאֵינוֹ רַשַּׁאי, פָּטוּר; אֲחֵרִים

יד אברהם

and was scooping [it] up and placing her hand on her head.

The word מְטַפַּחַת, scooping up, stems from טֶפַח, a fist, or a handbreadth — i.e., she gathered the oil in her hand. She was so stingy that she uncovered her head in order to take advantage of the little oil that had spilled on the ground, when she could have purchased such an amount of oil for an issar and anointed her head in the privacy of her home.

Others read: ... וְהָיְתָה מְטַפַּחַת וּמַכָּה and she was clapping and hitting her head with her hand. According to this version, the intention is that he broke a jug of oil belonging to her, and, in sorrow, she uncovered her head and mournfully clapped and hit her head with her hand (see Num. 24:10, Jer. 31:19, Moed Katan 3:9). Otherwise, why should she be so concerned for a little oil belonging to a stranger, and especially when it belonged to her opponent in the lawsuit?

The same episode appears in Avos d'Rabbi Nassan (3:4) with slight variations:

His friend said to him, 'I will give you advice so that you will not have to give her even a penny's worth.' He replied, 'Give me.' He said to him, 'Go, take oil worth an issar and break the jug at this woman's door.' What did the woman do? She came out of her house and was ...

The expression, take oil, appears to mean that he took his own oil, not hers. Also, since she came out of her house, it obviously was not because of mourning, because she could have done that within the confines of her house. It therefore appears that the alternate reading mentioned above is erroneous. Perhaps the correct version is: וְסָכָה, and anointing (Tos. Yom Tov).

Meiri explains that the man resorted to this tactic because he was acquainted with her stinginess.

הֶעֱמִיד עָלֶיהָ עֵדִים — He set up witnesses against her

[He placed witnesses there to see what she was doing, so that they would be able to testify against her in court.]

וּבָא לִפְנֵי רַבִּי עֲקִיבָא. אָמַר לוֹ: "רַבִּי, לָזוֹ אֲנִי נוֹתֵן אַרְבַּע מֵאוֹת זוּז?" — and came before R' Akiva. Said he to him, 'Rabbi, to this one I should give four hundred zuz?'

'Should I pay four hundred zuz to such a woman who lowers herself to uncover her hair in public for oil worth an issar? Has she not demonstrated that she does not care for her disgrace?' (Rav).

אָמַר לוֹ: — Said he to him:

[R' Akiva replied to the man.]

"לֹא אָמַרְתָּ כְּלוּם; — 'You have said nothing;

['Your argument is not legally valid.' R' Akiva proceeds to explain why.]

הַחוֹבֵל בְּעַצְמוֹ, אַף־עַל־פִּי שֶׁאֵינוֹ רַשַּׁאי, — [because if] one wounds himself, although he may not,

The prohibition of wounding oneself is derived from the section pertaining to

משניות / בבא קמא — פרק ח: החובל [182]

8 6 placing her hand on her head. He set up witnesses against her and came before R' Akiva. Said he to him: 'Rabbi, to this one I should give four hundred *zuz?*' Said he to him: 'You have said nothing; [because if] one wounds himself, although he may not, he is exempt; [yet] if others wound him, they are liable. And [if] one cuts off his own shoots, although he may not, he is exempt; [yet] if others cut off his

YAD AVRAHAM

the Nazirite, where Scripture states (*Num.* 6:11): וְכִפֶּר עָלָיו מֵאֲשֶׁר חָטָא עַל־הַנָּפֶשׁ, *And he shall atone for him for that which he sinned against the body.* One interpretation of this verse is that he sinned against his body by abstaining from drinking wine. If this is a sin, surely fasting unnecessarily or wounding oneself is a sin (*Tos. Yom Tov* from *Gem.* 91b).

To be sure, this verse deals with a Nazirite who became ritually contaminated and must recommence the Naziritic period, necessitating at least another thirty days of abstinence. The *Gemara*, however, asserts that even a Nazirite who has not become contaminated and must observe only one period of abstinence is also deemed a sinner. The difference is that in the case of the one who did not become contaminated the merit of being a Nazirite is greater than the sin committed. In the case of the one who became contaminated, however, the Torah labels him a sinner, because he repeated his sin (ibid. from *Tos.* 91b);

פָּטוּר; — *he is exempt;*

The intention is that there is no way of making him liable (*Tos. Yom Tov* from *Tos.* 91b).

אֲחֵרִים שֶׁחָבְלוּ בוֹ, חַיָּבִין. — [*yet*] *if others wound him, they are liable.*

Although he does not seem to care about his own body — since he wounded himself — others who do the same are liable (*Tos. Yom Tov* from *Tos.* 91b).

Surely, in the case of disgrace, others are liable, since one may disgrace himself (*Tif. Yis.*)

וְהַקּוֹצֵץ נְטִיעוֹתָיו, אַף־עַל־פִּי שֶׁאֵינוֹ רַשַּׁאי, — *And* [*if*] *one cuts off his own shoots,*

although he may not,

One who cuts down trees infracts the prohibition (*Deut.* 20:19): לֹא־תַשְׁחִית אֶת־עֵצָהּ, *You shall not destroy its trees* (*Tos. Yom Tov* from *Rashi*).

In fact, this verse deals with a besieging army in wartime. The intention may be so that the soldiers should have food, which they would not have if the fruit trees are destroyed. We find in *Makkos* (22a) that the *Gemara* derives the interdict of cutting down fruit trees from the end of the verse: וְאֹתוֹ לֹא תִכְרֹת, *but you shall not cut it down.* Apparently, the *Gemara* must rely on the end of the verse, which appears to be superfluous, to derive the general prohibition; otherwise, it would have been applied to wartime only, as explained above (*Tos. Yom Tov*).

The Torah forbids destroying trees only if this is done in a destructive manner. However, if they are damaging other trees or other people's property, or are costly to maintain, it is permited (*Rambam, Hil. Melachim* 6:8).

According to *Rashi's* interpretation of the *Gemara* (91b), this interdict applies even to trees which do not bear fruit. However, if wood is needed for purposes of siege in wartime, both barren and fruit-bearing trees may be cut down; but the latter should not be used unless the former are not available. *Rambam* (loc. cit.) contends that there is no stricture at all regarding barren trees. He interprets the *Gemara's* reference to barren trees, mentioned above, as actually referring to old fruit trees which no longer bear a substantial amount of fruit.

פָּטוּר; — *he is exempt;*

Tosafos explain that he is indeed

[183] THE MISHNAH/BAVA KAMMA – Chapter Eight: *HaChovel*

בבא קמא ח/ז

שֶׁקִּצְּצוּ אֶת־נְטִיעוֹתָיו, חַיָּבִים."

[ז] אַף־עַל־פִּי שֶׁהוּא נוֹתֵן לוֹ, אֵינוֹ נִמְחָל לוֹ עַד־שֶׁיְּבַקֵּשׁ מִמֶּנּוּ, שֶׁנֶּאֱמַר: "וְעַתָּה הָשֵׁב אֵשֶׁת וְגוֹ'." וּמִנַּיִן שֶׁלֹּא יְהֵא הַמּוֹחֵל אַכְזָרִי? שֶׁנֶּאֱמַר:

יד אברהם

liable for lashes for infracting the prohibition discussed above. The intention is that no monetary liability applies to him. [Compare *Tiferes Yisrael*.]

אֲחֵרִים שֶׁקִּצְּצוּ אֶת־נְטִיעוֹתָיו, חַיָּבִים — [yet] *if others cut off his shoots, they are liable.'*

They must pay for the shoots, although they are also liable to lashes for violating the prohibition discussed above. *Tosafos* explain that the mishnah may be attributed to R' Meir, who rules that even if one receives lashes he is liable for monetary payments incurred simultaneously [see *Makkos* 1:3] (*Tos. Yom Tov*). Alternatively, the mishnah is referring to a case in which the offender was not forewarned. Therefore, he is not sentenced to receive lashes, but is liable for monetary payments (ibid.; *Tos. R' Akiva*; see *Tiferes Yaakov*).

Lest one think that only in the mishnah's first case involving wounds, which cause pain, is the perpetrator liable even if the victim inflicts wounds upon himself, but not in the case of disgrace — which causes no physical pain — R' Akiva proves from the case of cutting off the shoots, in which no pain at all is involved, yet strangers are liable although the owner himself cuts off his own shoots, that this is surely so in the case of disgrace (*Tif. Yis.*).

7.

אַף־עַל־פִּי שֶׁהוּא נוֹתֵן לוֹ — *Although he pays him,*

That is, although one who wounds another pays him all the money due him for the wound (*Meiri*).

אֵינוֹ נִמְחָל לוֹ עַד־שֶׁיְּבַקֵּשׁ מִמֶּנּוּ — *he is not forgiven for it until he seeks [forgiveness] from him,*

He is not forgiven by Heaven for the anguish he caused his victim by disgracing him until the latter forgives him (*Rashi* [to *Gem.* 92a]; *Meiri*; *Rosh*; *Nimmukei Yosef*).

This is true of all sins that involve another person: although the sinner confesses his deed and repents, he is not pardoned unless he is forgiven by the one he wronged (*Meiri*; see *Yoma* 8:9).

Rambam (*Hil. Chovel* 5:9) states: One who injures another person is not like one who damages his property; the latter merely pays what he owes him, and the sin is expiated. In the case of injury, however, although he pays him for the five categories [listed in mishnah 1], the sin is not expiated even if he sacrifices all the rams of Nevaios[1] in the world, and his iniquity is not forgiven until he begs the wounded one for forgiveness and the latter grants it.

[It appears from *Rambam's* expression that the sin is not expiated at all until the offender is forgiven by the victim. As mentioned above, *Rashi*, however, maintains that only the

---

1. [Nevaios was a pastoral tribe noted for its rams (see *Isaiah* 60:7).]

משניות / בבא קמא — פרק ח: החובל [184]

shoots, they are liable.'

7. Although he pays him, he is not forgiven for it until he seeks [forgiveness] from him, as it is said *(Genesis 20:7): But now, return the wife ...*

Now, from where do we know that the one who forgives should not be cruel? It is said (ibid., v. 17):

YAD AVRAHAM

anguish caused by the disgrace is not forgiven until then. See *Sma* (422:1).]

In *Hilchos Teshuvah* (2:9), *Rambam* states that even if one robbed another person and made restitution for it, he must still ask for forgiveness. *Lechem Mishneh (Hil. Chovel* 5:9) explains that although one who damages another's property need not ask forgiveness from him after he makes restitution, one who robs another is required to do so. This is because, in the case of damage, the perpetrator derives no benefit from the victim's loss, whereas in the case of robbery, he does. Moreover, in the latter case, he causes him extreme anguish by coercing him to surrender his property to him.

שֶׁנֶּאֱמַר: "וְעַתָּה הָשֵׁב אֵשֶׁת וגו'". — *as it is said (Genesis 20:7): 'But now, return the wife ...'*

[Following Abraham's arrival to Gerar, Abimelech took Sarah from him. In a dream, God told Abimelech that he will die for having done so. After the latter pleads innocence, God tells him: *But now, return the wife of the man ...* (ibid. v. 1ff.).]

The verse continues: כִּי־נָבִיא הוּא וְיִתְפַּלֵּל בַּעַדְךָ, *for he is a prophet, and he will pray for you.* The intention is that Abimelech should appease Abraham so that he pray in his behalf, for what fool would ask someone to pray that he not die from a sin which he committed against that person, without appeasing him first? The mishnah therefore derives from here that one must seek forgiveness from the one he wronged.

The *Midrash (Bereishis Rabbah* ad loc.), however, explains the dialogue differently: Abimelech said to God: 'Who will appease him by assuring that I did not touch her?' God replied: 'For he is a prophet.' *Rashi* (ibid.) explains: 'And he knows that you did not touch her.'

According to this interpretation, Abimelech should have appeased Abraham, but, since the latter was a prophet, it was unnecessary.

The *Gemara* (92a), however, interprets the dialogue in the opposite manner. In reply to Abimelech's plea, *'O my Lord, will you slay a people though it is righteous?'* God replies: '... *for he is a prophet,'* and he has already taught (loc. cit. 18:2ff.) that when a guest comes into a city he should be asked about giving him to eat and drink and not questions concerning his wife. [Since you did not learn from him, your plea is baseless, and you deserve to die *(Rashi).*]

According to this interpretation, Abraham required appeasement. Although the explanation of the *Midrash* is closer to the simple meaning of the verse, the *Gemara* chooses the second interpretation. Since the mishnah derives from this verse that a person who is wronged must be appeased, this interpretation fits that derivation more aptly *(Tos. Yom Tov).*

וּמִנַּיִן שֶׁלֹּא יְהֵא הַמּוֹחֵל אַכְזָרִי? — *Now, from where do we know that the one who forgives should not be cruel?*

[The intention obviously is: How do we know that the one who is begged to forgive should not be cruel and refuse to do so?]

Many editions, including the Mish-

בבא קמא ח/ז

"וַיִּתְפַּלֵּל אַבְרָהָם אֶל־הָאֱלֹהִים וַיִּרְפָּא אֱלֹהִים אֶת־אֲבִימֶלֶךְ וְגוֹ'."

הָאוֹמֵר: "סַמֵּא אֶת־עֵינִי," "קְטַע אֶת־יָדִי," "שְׁבֹר אֶת־רַגְלִי," — חַיָּב. "עַל־מְנָת לִפְטֹר?" — חַיָּב. "קְרַע אֶת־כְּסוּתִי, שְׁבֹר אֶת־כַּדִּי" — חַיָּב. "עַל־מְנָת לִפְטֹר?" — פָּטוּר. "עָשָׂה כֵן לְאִישׁ

יד אברהם

nah printed with the *Gemara*, read: וּמִנַּיִן שֶׁאִם לֹא מָחַל לוֹ שֶׁהוּא אַכְזָרִי? *Now, from where do we know that if he does not forgive him, he is [considered] cruel?*

The one who was wounded should not be cruel and refuse to forgive him, for this is not the way of the Jewish people. Rather, as soon as the offender begs him and entreats him a first and a second time, and he knows that the offender repented of his sin and regrets his evil, he should forgive him. And whoever hastens to forgive is deemed praiseworthy (*Rambam, Hil. Chovel* 5:10; cf. *Hil. Teshuvah* 2:10).

שֶׁנֶּאֱמַר: "וַיִּתְפַּלֵּל אַבְרָהָם אֶל־הָאֱלֹהִים וַיִּרְפָּא אֱלֹהִים אֶת־אֲבִימֶלֶךְ וְגוֹ'" — *It is said* (ibid. v. 17): *'And Abraham prayed to God, and God healed Abimelech ...'*

The Torah does not even mention that Abraham forgave Abimelech, since he was obligated to do so. It mentions only that he prayed for him, this being a sign of his piety (*Tif. Yis.*).

From here they derived: A person should always be as soft as a reed and not as hard as a cedar; he should be easily appeased and slow to anger. When a sinner begs forgiveness of him, he should forgive him wholeheartedly. Even if he sinned grievously against him and caused him trouble, he should neither seek revenge nor bear a grudge. Every person should learn the correct behavior from our father Abraham. Is there anything worse than taking one's wife away against his will? Yet, as soon as he begged forgiveness, he forgave

him; not only that — he also prayed for him, as it is said: *And Abraham prayed to God* (*Midrash Hagadol*, Gen. 20:17).

הָאוֹמֵר: "סַמֵּא אֶת־עֵינִי," "קְטַע אֶת־יָדִי," "שְׁבֹר אֶת־רַגְלִי," — *[If] one says: 'Blind my eye,' 'Cut off my hand,' [or] 'Break my leg,'*

[One person asked this of another, and the latter complied.]

חַיָּב. — *he is liable.*

He is liable for all five categories, because it is common knowledge that no person wants to be injured [even if he asks another to do so] (*Rambam, Hil. Chovel* 5:11).

"עַל־מְנָת לִפְטֹר?" — *'On condition to be exempt?'* —

That is, even if the person to whom the request was made asked, 'Do you mean that I should maim you on the condition that I will be exempt?' (*Rav; Rashi* 93a).

חַיָּב. — *he is liable.*

Even if the one who asked to be wounded replied in the affirmative to this question, it is assumed that he did not really mean it, for people would never truly allow others to inflict pain upon them (*Rav*).

According to *Rashi*, this is true only if he answered sarcastically, meaning to say: 'Do you really think I would allow such a thing?' However, if he replies in a tone which indicates that he indeed means to answer the question affirmatively, the one who injures him is exempt. *Tosafos* (93a), on the other

8 And Abraham prayed to God, and God healed
7 Abimelech ....

[If] one says: 'Blind my eye,' 'Cut off my hand,' [or] 'Break my leg,' he is liable. 'On condition to be exempt?' — he is liable. 'Tear my clothes,' [or] 'Break my jug' — he is liable. 'On condition to be exempt?' — he is exempt. 'Do this to So-and-so on condition that

YAD AVRAHAM

hand, maintain that we construe his reply to have been made in a sarcastic sense, regardless of how he said it, since it is certain that he did not mean it seriously.

Should the one who requested that the other person wound him state explicitly, 'Blind my eye on condition that you will be exempt,' he is indeed exempt (*Rashi*).

In fact, the halachah is the same if he requested that the other person strike him or wound him rather than maim him. The reason the *Tanna* chose these cases is that they have already been mentioned in mishnah 1 (*Tos. Yom Tov*).

Others rule that even if he specifically asks the other person: 'Blind my eye [or 'Cut off my hand,' etc.] on condition to be exempt,' the latter is liable if he complies, since a person does not really allow another to maim his principal limbs (*Rambam* loc. cit.). Should he say, 'Strike me, wound me on condition to be exempt,' the other is exempt. However, if he had not stated it explicitly, only the other person asked him, 'On condition to be exempt?' even if he answers, 'Yes,' the other person is liable (*Maggid Mishneh* ad loc.).

קָרַע אֶת־כְּסוּתִי,, ,,שָׁבַר אֶת־כַּדִי״ — 'Tear my clothes,' [or] 'Break my jug' —

One person asked another to do this, and the latter complied (*Meiri*).

חַיָב. — *he is liable.*

The one who did the damage is liable, although the owner of the item permitted him to do it (*Rambam* loc.

cit.).

The *Gemara* qualifies the mishnah as dealing with an instance in which the owner of the item had given the garment or jug to the other person to watch for him. In that case, since the latter already was charged with the responsibility of guarding the objects, if the owner does not specifically exempt him, he is liable. If the owner never gave it to the other person to watch, and tells him to destroy it, the latter is exempt even if the owner did not specifically stipulate that he would be (*Tos. Yom Tov; Tif. Yis.*).

עַל־מְנָת לִפְטֹר?״ — 'On condition to be exempt?' —

The prospective damager asked, 'Do you mean that I should break it on condition that I will be exempt for doing so?' (*Rav*).

פָּטוּר. — *he is exempt.*

He is exempt even if the owner answered his question negatively. It is as though he said, 'Did I not tell it to you on condition that you be exempt?' We interpret it this way since it is not uncommon for people to allow others to cause them monetary damage (*Rav*). As explained above, according to *Rashi*, this would apply only if he had answered in a sarcastic manner; according to *Tosafos*, his reply is construed to mean this regardless of the way he said it.

Rambam (loc. cit.) explains the second one as meaning that the owner of the item said explicitly: 'Tear my clothes [or 'Break my jug] on condition that you be exempt.'

[187]   THE MISHNAH/BAVA KAMMA – Chapter Eight: *HaChovel*

בבא קמא ט/א

פְּלוֹנִי עַל־מְנָת לִפְטֹר״ — חַיָּב, בֵּין בְּגוּפוֹ בֵּין בְּמָמוֹנוֹ.

[א] **הַגּוֹזֵל** עֵצִים וַעֲשָׂאָן כֵּלִים; צֶמֶר, וַעֲשָׂאוֹ בְּגָדִים — מְשַׁלֵּם כִּשְׁעַת הַגְּזֵלָה.

יד אברהם

— ״עֲשֵׂה כֵן לְאִישׁ פְּלוֹנִי עַל־מְנָת לִפְטֹר״ — *'Do this to So-and-so on condition that you be exempt' —*
[One person tells another to do damage on condition that the latter will be exempt.]

חַיָּב, — *he is liable,*
The one who actually did the damage is liable, because one cannot serve as an agent for another in matters of sin [see commentary to 7:6]. This applies even if the one who instructed him to do it says, 'On condition that I will pay' (*Tos. Yom Tov; Meiri*).

[Apparently, their intention is that since there is no agency in matters of sin, the one who gave the instructions to do the damage cannot become liable for it.]

Although the perpetrator is liable for payment, the one who prompts him is his partner in sin and is considered a wicked man, since he misled the perpetrator and encouraged him to sin (*Rambam* loc. cit. §13).

The perpetrator is considered to have been misled, because although he was aware that the article did not belong to the one who instructed him to destroy it, he believed that he would indeed be exempt from payment as this person had assured him (*Sma* 380:6).

בֵּין בְּגוּפוֹ — *whether it is against his body*
[For example, he tells him to blind the other person's eye or cut off his hand.]

בֵּין בְּמָמוֹנוֹ. — *or against his property.*
[E.g., he says, 'Tear his clothes,' or 'Break his jug.']

Chapter 9

1.

This chapter and the one following it deal with the law of a גַּזְלָן, *robber*. A robber takes a person's property by force through one of the following methods: (1) seizing chattels from his hand; (2) entering his premises against his will and taking utensils from there; (3) seizing his slaves or his cattle and making use of them; (4) going into his field and eating the produce thereof, or (5) any similar incident.

Whoever robs is obligated to return the article he took, as it is said (*Lev.* 5:23): וְהֵשִׁיב אֶת־הַגְּזֵלָה אֲשֶׁר גָּזָל, *He shall return the loot that he robbed.* If the item was lost or becomes changed, he must pay its value. Whether he confessed on his own or witnesses testified that he robbed, he is obligated to pay only the principal [see preface to 7:1] (*Rambam, Hil. Gezeilah* 1:3,5).

If the item underwent a change while in the robber's possession, although the owner did not despair of retrieving it, the robber acquires it by virtue of the change and must pay its value as of the time of the robbery. Tradition teaches us that this is a Biblical law derived from the verse cited above, *He shall return that which he robbed:* if it is as it was when stolen, he must return it; but if it was changed, he pays its value (ibid. 2:1f.).

Actually, the ruling of the mishnah also applies to a גַּנָּב, *a thief,* who steals surreptitiously. Nevertheless, the laws are stated regarding the robber rather than the thief, since — according to the Sages — one despairs of recovering his

9:1

you be exempt' — he is liable, whether it is against his body or against his property.

1. **[I**f] one steals wood and makes it into utensils; [or] wool, and makes it into garments — he pays as of the time of the robbery.

YAD AVRAHAM

possessions from a thief, whom he does not see, but not from a robber. The *Tanna* therefore teaches us that even the robber — who does not have the benefit of the owner's despair — acquires ownership of the item he stole if it is changed. The halachah is, however, that only if the robber is a Jew does the victim usually despair of retrieving his property; but if he is a gentile, he does not. This is because Jewish courts require testimony before they order robbers to return what they took, whereas gentile courts do so even on the basis of circumstantial evidence (*Tif. Yis.* from *Choshen Mishpat* 368:1).

הַגּוֹזֵל עֵצִים וַעֲשָׂאָן כֵּלִים — [If] one steals wood and makes it into utensils;

According to the conclusion of the *Gemara* (93b), the mishnah deals with a robber who took wood that had not been planed and planed it into a pestle. This is an irreversible change to the item, since it can no longer return to its previous status of wood, and its name has been changed, having previously been called wood, and now a pestle. Should the robber steal planed wood, such as boards, and nail them together into a chair or a table, he does not acquire ownership, since this change is reversible: he can dismantle the chair and have the same boards that he had originally (*Tos. Yom Tov* from *Gem.* 93b).

If the robber steals unplaned wood and planes it without converting it into a utensil of any kind, this is not deemed a change and the item itself must be returned to the owner (*Tos. ad loc.*).

צֶמֶר, וַעֲשָׂאוֹ בְגָדִים — [or] wool, and makes it into garments —

The robber stole wool that was not spun and he made it into felt, which is an irreversible change, since the fibers can no longer be separated. Also, its name has changed: previously it had been called *wool*, and now *felt*. Should he steal spun wool and make garments out of it, he does not acquire ownership since the change is reversible: the strands can be separated and the item can be restored to its previous state of wool (*Tos. Yom Tov* from *Gem.* 93b).

Others rule that if the owner despairs of ever recovering the article, the robber acquires it even with a minor change, such as making spun wool into a garment.

In the instances that the robber does not acquire ownership, and he returns the garment or the utensil to the owner, the latter must compensate him for the improvement he made on the wool or wood (*Tif. Yis.* from *Choshen Mishpat* 361).

מְשַׁלֵּם כִּשְׁעַת הַגְּזֵלָה — he pays as of the time of the robbery.

He must pay only the value of the wood or wool and is not required to return the utensils or the garments, since he acquires them through the change (*Rav; Rashi*).

As explained in the preface, this is derived from *Leviticus* 5:23 which literally is translated: *He shall return the loot that he robbed.* Scripture adds the superfluous phrase *that he robbed* to indicate that if the stolen article is now in the same state as it was when it had been stolen, he must return it; otherwise, he must make restitution by

[189] THE MISHNAH/BAVA KAMMA — Chapter Nine: *HaGozeil Eitzim*

בבא קמא ט/ב

גָּזַל פָּרָה מְעֻבֶּרֶת, וְיָלְדָה; רָחֵל טְעוּנָה, וּגְזָזָהּ — מְשַׁלֵּם דְּמֵי פָרָה הָעוֹמֶדֶת לֵילֵד, דְּמֵי רָחֵל הָעוֹמֶדֶת לִגָּזֵז.

גָּזַל פָּרָה, וְנִתְעַבְּרָה אֶצְלוֹ, וְיָלְדָה; רָחֵל, וְנִטְעֲנָה אֶצְלוֹ, וּגְזָזָהּ — מְשַׁלֵּם כִּשְׁעַת הַגְּזֵלָה. זֶה הַכְּלָל: כָּל־הַגַּזְלָנִים מְשַׁלְּמִין כִּשְׁעַת הַגְּזֵלָה.

[ב] **גָּזַל** בְּהֵמָה, וְהִזְקִינָה; עֲבָדִים, וְהִזְקִינוּ — מְשַׁלֵּם כִּשְׁעַת הַגְּזֵלָה. רַבִּי מֵאִיר

יד אברהם

paying its value (Tos. Yom Tov from Rashi, quoting Gem. 66a; see Tos. 65b, s.v. הן).

גָּזַל פָּרָה מְעֻבֶּרֶת, וְיָלְדָה; — [If] one steals a pregnant cow, and it calves;

It did so while in the robber's possession (Meiri).

רָחֵל טְעוּנָה, וּגְזָזָהּ — — [or] a ewe bearing wool, and he shears it —

[The robber shears the ewe.]

מְשַׁלֵּם דְּמֵי פָרָה הָעוֹמֶדֶת לֵילֵד, דְּמֵי רָחֵל הָעוֹמֶדֶת לִגָּזֵז. — he pays the value of a cow ready to calve [or] the value of a ewe ready to be shorn.

And the difference between the previous value and the present value of the calf or the fleece belongs to the robber, since he acquired it through change (Rav; Rashi).

The commentators dispute whether the birth is regarded as a change in the body of the cow itself, or the shearing in the body of the ewe. Nimmukei Yosef (as explained by Tiferes Yisrael) maintains that they are not. Although the robber keeps the calf or fleece, he must return the cow or ewe as it is and pay for the decrease in its value since the time of the robbery when it was pregnant or laden with wool. Rosh, however, rules that the birth or the shearing is indeed regarded as a change in the body of the animal itself, which is therefore acquired by the robber, and he

pays the amount that the animal was worth at the time of the robbery. The Tanna uses the expressions ready to calve and ready to be shorn, although the robber pays only what the animal was worth at the time of the robbery, since some people purchase a pregnant cow with the intention of slaughtering it with the fetus, and some purchase a sheep with fleece with the intention of slaughtering it and using the fleece. Such an animal is not worth as much as an animal that is to be kept until the birth, and the calf raised, or the ewe kept for wool. The Tanna therefore states ready to calve and ready to be shorn to indicate that the robber in our case pays the higher price. This is according to Rosh's view that the robber acquires the animal (Tos. Yom Tov).

גָּזַל פָּרָה, וְנִתְעַבְּרָה אֶצְלוֹ, וְיָלְדָה; רָחֵל, וְנִטְעֲנָה אֶצְלוֹ, וּגְזָזָהּ — מְשַׁלֵּם כִּשְׁעַת הַגְּזֵלָה. — [If] one steals a cow, and it becomes impregnated while with him, and it calves; [or] a ewe, and it becomes laden with wool while with him, and he shears it — he pays as of the time of the robbery.

In such a case not only does he acquire the calf or the wool if the cow calves while in his possession or the ewe is shorn while in his possession, but even if it is still pregnant or laden when he pays, he must pay only for its value at the time of the robbery. This applies

9:2

[If] one steals a pregnant cow, and it calves; [or] a ewe bearing wool, and he shears it — he pays the value of a cow ready to calve [or] the value of a ewe ready to be shorn.

[If] one steals a cow, and it becomes impregnated while with him, and it calves; [or] a ewe, and it becomes laden with wool while with him, and he shears it — he pays as of the time of the robbery.

This is the general rule: All robbers pay as of the time of the robbery.

2. [I]f] one steals an animal, and it ages; [or] slaves, and they age — he pays as of the time of the

YAD AVRAHAM

according to *Rosh's* view, for just as calving and becoming shorn are considered changes in the animal's body, so are becoming pregnant and becoming full with wool.

Similarly, according to *Nimmukei Yosef*, just as calving and becoming shorn are not considered changes, neither are impregnation and becoming laden with fleece. The robber must therefore return the animal, and the owner pays him the difference between its original value and its present worth (*Tos. Yom Tov*).

According to *Rambam (Hil. Gezeilah 2:6f.)* the robber retains the increase in the value of the animal only if the improvement took place after the owner despaired of retrieving it.

זֶה הַכְּלָל: כָּל־הַגַּזְלָנִים מְשַׁלְּמִין כִּשְׁעַת הַגְּזֵלָה. — *This is the general rule: All robbers pay as of the time of the robbery.*

This superfluous sentence in the mishnah is construed by the *Gemara* (96b) as including the case of a thief who steals a lamb which then grows to be a ram, or a calf which then becomes a bull. The *Tanna* teaches us that he acquires the animal with this change, and if he subsequently slaughters or sells it, he is exempt from the four or fivefold payment [see 7:1] since he is slaughtering or selling his own animal. He does, however, pay the twofold payment — i.e., double the value of the animal as of the time of the theft (*Tos. Yom Tov*; see *Rashi* 65b).

2.

The following mishnah teaches us that the robber pays for the value of the stolen item as of the time of the robbery — not only if its worth has increased since then, but even if it has decreased (*Tif. Yis.*).

גָּזַל בְּהֵמָה, וְהִזְקִינָה; — [If] *one steals an animal, and it ages;*

[The animal grows old in the robber's possession.]

עֲבָדִים, וְהִזְקִינוּ — [*or*] *slaves, and they age —*

[They become old while in his possession and depreciate in value.]

מְשַׁלֵּם כִּשְׁעַת הַגְּזֵלָה. — *he pays as of the time of the robbery.*

Because aging is an irreversible change, the robber cannot return the

[191]   THE MISHNAH/BAVA KAMMA — Chapter Nine: *HaGozeil Eitzim*

בבא קמא ט/ב

אוֹמֵר: בַּעֲבָדִים אוֹמֵר לוֹ: ״הֲרֵי שֶׁלְּךָ לְפָנֶיךָ.״ גָּזַל מַטְבֵּעַ, וְנִסְדַּק; פֵּרוֹת, וְהִרְקִיבוּ; יַיִן, וְהֶחֱמִיץ — מְשַׁלֵּם כִּשְׁעַת הַגְּזֵלָה.

יד אברהם

animal or slave, since it is not in the same state as it was when he stole it (*Meiri*).

This applies also if the animal or slave permanently deteriorated in some other manner (*Gem.* 96b), such as through an incurable disease (*Rambam, Hil. Gezeilah* 3:4), even if it affected only part of the body (*Rashi* loc. cit.).

R' Chaim Soloveitchik (*Chiddushei R' Chaim Halevi, Hil. Gezeilah* 2:15) asserts that the ruling that a robber must pay for the value of the stolen item as of the time of the robbery is not necessarily dependent on his acquisition of the article. In order to be acquired, the article must undergo a complete change. Should it be only a partial change, however, although the robber does not acquire the item, he has no right to return it to the owner in its present state. Nevertheless, if the owner insists on getting back the item itself, he can demand it from the robber.

An example of this is the robber who steals a vessel and breaks it. According to *Rambam* (ibid.), the robber cannot return the item itself. However, should the owner demand the fragments, the robber must return them to him and pay him for the decrease in the item's value. *Maggid Mishneh* (ad loc.) explains that the vessel has not lost its previous state, but is still called a vessel; consequently, the owner can demand it from the robber.

Accordingly, we could not deduce from our mishnah that a robber acquires the stolen article if it changes spontaneously while in his possession. This is because the mishnah tells us only that the robber cannot return the animal or slave after it has aged or been stricken by an incurable illness. It does not state that the robber acquires the animal for himself. We might have thought that perhaps a spontaneous change is not deemed sufficient for the robber to acquire the stolen animal. In that case, should the animal improve rather than deteriorate, the owner could demand it back. Rather, the *Gemara* (96b) derives from the superfluous clause in the preceding mishnah [see commentary ibid., s.v. זֶה הַכְּלָל] that if one stole a lamb and it became a ram, he acquires it.

Other authorities, however, do not differentiate between the change by virtue of which the robber acquires the article and the change by virtue of which he cannot return it. They rule that the robber acquires the stolen article in both instances, and because of his acquisition, he can no longer return the article in its present form. The reason that the superfluous clause is necessary is because there is a difference between the cases of an animal that aged and a lamb that became a ram. Aging is a complete change, rendering the animal incapable of bearing young and of performing labor and one that is considered blemished as regards sacrifices. A lamb becoming a ram, on the other hand, is not that radical a change; it is just that the animal is now called by a different name. Therefore, from this mishnah, we would not be able to derive that the robber acquires these articles here. It is only the superfluous clause in mishnah 1 that implies that this, too, is deemed a change (*Chazon Ish* in Glosses to *Chiddushei; R' Chaim Halevi; Hil. Gezeilah* 2:15; *Achiezer,* vol. 3, 82:1, citing *Tos. Rid*).

רַבִּי מֵאִיר אוֹמֵר: בַּעֲבָדִים — **R' Meir says: In the case of slaves**

[That is, the case discussed above, in which the robber stole slaves and they aged.]

אוֹמֵר לוֹ: — **he may say to him:**

[The robber may say to the one he robbed:]

״הֲרֵי שֶׁלְּךָ לְפָנֶיךָ.״ — **'Here is your property before you.'**

R' Meir rules that slaves are adjudged as real estate, which cannot be stolen and always remains in the owner's possession. Consequently, in our case, the slaves aged in the owner's possession, and the robber is not responsible for their deterioration. The

9:2

robbery. **R' Meir says: In the case of slaves he may say to him: 'Here is your property before you.'**

[If] he steals a coin, and it cracks; fruit, and it rots; [or] wine, and it sours — he pays as of the time of the robbery.

YAD AVRAHAM

halachah is in accordance with R' Meir. The *Gemara* accounts for this ruling by proving that the text of the mishnah is erroneous and that, in fact, it is the Sages who rule that slaves are like real property, and R' Meir who rules that they are like chattels. Therefore, in keeping with the principle that we follow the majority opinion, we must decide the halachah in accordance with the view attributed by the mishnah to R' Meir *(Rav, Tos. Yom Tov from Gem. 96b).*

גָּזַל מַטְבֵּעַ, וְנִסְדַּק — [*If*] *he steals a coin, and it cracks;*

This is a change that is obvious *(Rav; Rashi).*

פֵּרוֹת, וְהִרְקִיבוּ; — *fruit, and it rots;*

That is, it became completely rotten. If, however, it rotted only partially, the robber can return the fruit in its present state *(Rav from Gem. 96b).*

Since it is usual for fruit to become partially rotten, it is deemed similar to an indiscernible damage and is not considered a change. This is analogous to the case of *chametz* on Pesach mentioned further in the mishnah *(Tos. Yom Tov from Nimmukei Yosef).*

Yerushalmi distinguishes between fruit that rots because of bacteria (according to *Chazon Ish, Glosses to Chiddushei R' Chaim* loc. cit.) and fruit that becomes wormy: in the former instance the robber must pay its original value, but in the latter, he can return the fruit in its present condition. *Shach* (363:6) explains that the comments of *Yerushalmi* and our *Gemara* are identical. *Yerushalmi* explains that fruit which decays is considered completely rotten; since the deterioration will spread through it, this is deemed a change, and the robber cannot return the fruit in its present condition. Should the fruit become wormy, however, it is deemed as only partially rotten, since this is not discernible from the outside. Such an occurrence, therefore, is not considered a change; hence, the robber may return the item as it is now.

Sma (ibid. §1) contends that only if the fruit rots completely or becomes even half-rotten, the robber cannot return it in its current state. If, however, it becomes wormy — even in its entirety — he may do so. Our mishnah, which rules that the robber cannot return the fruit, deals with fruit that has rotted. Since it is customary for fruit to become partially rotten, as long as the decay does not spread to half the fruit, the robber may return it, as *Nimmukei Yosef* explains *(Chazon Ish, Bava Kamma 20:3 and 17:15).*

R' Chaim Soloveitchik explains that if part of the fruit decays, he may return the remainder, but he must pay for what is missing. Should the entire fruit decay, he must pay for it completely.

יַיִן, וְהֶחֱמִיץ — [*or*] *wine, and it sours —*

Since the wine's taste and aroma are not the same as they had been previously, this is considered a discernible change, and therefore, the robber cannot return it in its current condition *(Tos. Yom Tov from Nimmukei Yosef).*

מְשַׁלֵּם בִּשְׁעַת הַגְּזֵלָה. — *he pays as of the time of the robbery.*

[Since each of these instances is considered a discernible change, as explained above, the robber cannot return the stolen item, but must pay for its value as of the time of the robbery.]

בבא קמא ט/ב

מַטְבֵּעַ, וְנִפְסַל; תְּרוּמָה, וְנִטְמֵאת; חָמֵץ, וְעָבַר עָלָיו הַפֶּסַח; בְּהֵמָה, וְנֶעֶבְדָה בָהּ עֲבֵרָה, אוֹ שֶׁנִּפְסְלָה מֵעַל גַּבֵּי הַמִּזְבֵּחַ, אוֹ שֶׁהָיְתָה יוֹצְאָה לִסָּקֵל — אוֹמֵר לוֹ: "הֲרֵי שֶׁלְּךָ לְפָנֶיךָ."

יד אברהם

מַטְבֵּעַ, וְנִפְסַל; — [If he steals] a coin, and it becomes disqualified;

That is, if a robber steals a coin and it becomes disqualified in that province, but is acceptable in another province, he may return the coin to the one he robbed as the mishnah concludes, and say, 'Take the coin and spend it where it is accepted' (Tos. Yom Tov from Rashi 97a).

Should the king disqualify it so that it is unacceptable throughout the entire kingdom, the robber cannot return it (Gem. 97a).

This is the ruling of Rambam (Hil. Gezeilah 3:4). Rosh, however, maintains that even if the king disqualifies it, the robber may still return it [see below].

תְּרוּמָה, וְנִטְמֵאת; — terumah, and it becomes ritually contaminated;

[He stole terumah (the portion of the crop given to a Kohen), and, while in the robber's possession, it became ritually contaminated, rendering it prohibited to be eaten or used for any benefit.]

חָמֵץ, וְעָבַר עָלָיו הַפֶּסַח; — chametz, and it is in his possession on Pesach (lit., Pesach passes over it);

[Chametz (leaven) which was in a Jew's possession during Passover may never be used for any purpose (Orach Chaim 448:3).]

This, too, is forbidden for any use. Since contaminated terumah and chametz which was in a Jew's possession during Pesach resemble other grain and bread, this is considered an indiscernible damage, and the robber may return them to the one from whom he stole them. In the case of a coin which was disqualified throughout the kingdom, however, since it had originally been the same as all the other coins in circulation but it no longer is, because another type has been minted in its stead, discernible damage is considered to have been done, and the robber may not return it (Tos. Yom Tov from Rashi 97a and Sma 363:4). As mentioned above, Rosh disagrees, contending that even if the coin is completely disqualified, the damage is deemed indiscernible, and the robber may return it.

בְּהֵמָה, וְנֶעֶבְדָה בָהּ עֲבֵרָה, — [or] an animal, and it is used for transgression,

One stole an animal and, while it was in his possession, it was used for sodomy or worshiped as a deity (Rav). [Should two witnesses testify to that effect, the animal is put to death by the court. If only one witness testifies, the court cannot condemn the animal, but it becomes disqualified to be used as an offering. Rav, Rashi and Tos. Yom Tov qualify the mishnah as referring to the latter case.]

Tiferes Yisrael explains that the case of the animal being sentenced to death is mentioned at the end of the mishnah: or is condemned to be stoned. Therefore, the commentators construe this part of the mishnah as telling us that even if the animal becomes disqualified to be used as an offering, the robber may return it, and the end of the mishnah as telling us that even if the animal is condemned to death, the robber may nevertheless return it.

משניות / בבא קמא — פרק ט: הגוזל עצים [194]

9 2   [If he steals] a coin, and it becomes disqualified; *terumah*, and it becomes ritually contaminated; *chametz*, and it is in his possession on Pesach; [or] an animal, and it is used for transgression, or becomes disqualified for the Altar, or is condemned to be stoned — he may say to him: 'Here is you property before you.'

YAD AVRAHAM

אוֹ שֶׁנִּפְסְלָה מֵעַל גַּבֵּי הַמִּזְבֵּחַ, — *or becomes disqualified for the Altar*,

The animal developed an unnoticeable blemish on the eye, thereby rendering it unfit to be offered on the Altar of the Temple *(Rav; Rashi)*.

Rashi explains that the robber may return the blemished animal, since he has done no damage to it; the fact that it cannot be brought as an offering is not considered a damage, since not all animals are destined to be offered on the Altar.

Tosafos Chadashim challenge this reasoning since it applies even if the blemish were conspicuous, and *Rashi* qualifies the mishnah as referring only to a case in which the blemish was unnoticeable. Moreover, it should apply even if the robber intentionally inflicted a blemish on the animal, as in case of the *Gemara* (98a), in which someone split the ear of another person's cow. He is exempt from paying, because the animal has really not been damaged, and the fact that he made it unfit for an offering is inconsequential, since not all animals are destined for the Altar. In the mishnah, however, the *Tanna* gives the case as one in which the animal *becomes disqualified* ..., implying that the ruling would not apply if the robber himself had inflicted the blemish.

Tosafos (98a) interpret the mishnah as meaning that the robber stole a consecrated animal — which is surely destined for the Altar — and it became blemished. In that case, only if the blemish is unnoticeable and the robber did not inflict it can he return the animal in its present condition.

Tos. Yom Tov maintains that *Rashi* gave this reason as an explanation for the case above, in which the animal was used for transgression. [That is difficult, however, since the robber may return the animal even if it is sentenced to death, which is surely a loss to the owner.]

אוֹ שֶׁהָיְתָה יוֹצֵאת לִסָּקֵל — — *or is condemned to be stoned* —

[The animal had gored a person to death or had been used for transgression, as in the beginning of the mishnah, and this was attested to by two witnesses.]

The *Gemara* (98b) explains that this *Tanna* rules that an animal may be sentenced in its absence. Therefore, the owner can have no complaint against the robber for allowing the animal to be brought to court and sentenced, since the sentence could have been given even if he had allowed the animal to flee to the pasture *(Tos. Yom Tov)*.

Although the goring or the transgression occurred while the animal was in the possession of the robber, the latter is deemed only an indirect cause of it, and is therefore not responsible for the sentencing of the animal *(Tif. Yis.)*.

אוֹמֵר לוֹ: — *he may say to him:*

[The robber may say to the one he robbed:]

„הֲרֵי שֶׁלְּךָ לְפָנֶיךָ.״ — *'Here is your property before you.'*

[Since no discernible damage has been done to the stolen item, the robber may return it in its present condition and need not pay for its decrease in value.]

בבא קמא ט/ג

[ג] **נָתַן** לְאָמָּנִין לְתַקֵּן, וְקִלְקְלוּ, חַיָּבִין לְשַׁלֵּם. נָתַן לְחָרָשׁ שִׁדָּה, תֵּבָה, וּמִגְדָּל לְתַקֵּן — וְקִלְקֵל, חַיָּב לְשַׁלֵּם. וְהַבַּנַּאי שֶׁקִּבֵּל עָלָיו לִסְתֹּר אֶת־הַכֹּתֶל, וְשִׁבֵּר אֶת־הָאֲבָנִים אוֹ שֶׁהִזִּיק, חַיָּב לְשַׁלֵּם. הָיָה סוֹתֵר מִצַּד זֶה, וְנָפַל מִצַּד אַחֵר, פָּטוּר; וְאִם מֵחֲמַת הַמַּכָּה, חַיָּב.

יד אברהם

3.

Following the previous mishnayos, which discuss cases regarding items that were damaged in the robber's possession, the *Tanna* now proceeds to deal with a craftsman who is given a utensil to repair and damages it instead.

נָתַן לְאָמָּנִין לְתַקֵּן, וְקִלְקְלוּ — [If] one gives craftsmen [something] to improve, and they spoil [it],

He gave craftsmen wood to make a utensil, and after making it, they broke it (*Rav* from *Gem.* 98b, 99a).

חַיָּבִין לְשַׁלֵּם — they are obligated to pay.

The carpenters are obligated to pay for the complete value of the utensil, not only for the wood that was given them. This is based on the principle that the craftsman does not acquire rights to the increase in the value of the utensil he creates. When he makes a utensil from the wood given him by the owner, that utensil remains the complete property of the owner; therefore, if the craftsman breaks it, he is liable for its complete value. Unlike the robber who pays for the value of the item as of the time of the robbery, the craftsman pays its current worth. The reason is that the craftsman has no intention of acquiring the utensil, but works solely for the owner; therefore, it still belongs to the latter at the time it is broken. The robber, however, wishes to keep the utensil for himself; consequently, he must pay its value as of the time of the robbery (*Tos. Yom Tov* from *Gem.*).

נָתַן לְחָרָשׁ שִׁדָּה, תֵּבָה, וּמִגְדָּל לְתַקֵּן, — [If] one gives a carpenter a chest, a box, or a closet to repair,

שִׁדָּה means *a wooden chest used as a seat for women in a coach* (*Rashi*). According to *Rav*, it appears to refer to the coach itself. [However, this definition seems unlikely; see *Tos. Yom Tov, Rashi, Nimmukei Yosef.*]

וְקִלְקֵל, — and he spoils [it],

For example, the utensil broke while the carpenter was hammering in the nail (*Tif. Yis.* from *Gem.* 98b).

חַיָּב לְשַׁלֵּם. — he is obligated to pay.

Although the carpenter is liable for the finished product even if he had originally been given only the wood, as explained in the beginning of the mishnah, the *Tanna* nonetheless states also the case of one who is given a finished utensil. Otherwise, we would think that the beginning of the mishnah refers to the case of a carpenter who received a finished utensil, and that if he is given only wood, and he damages it after finishing the utensil, he is exempt from paying the full value. Now that we know that the second part of the mishnah deals with that case, we understand that the first segment refers to one who is given wood, and that, even in such an instance, the craftsman

3. [If] one gives craftsmen [something] to improve, and they spoil [it], they are obligated to pay. [If] one gives a carpenter a chest, a box, or a closet to repair, and he spoils [it], he is obligated to pay.

[If] a builder undertakes to demolish a wall, and he breaks the stones or causes damage, he is obligated to pay. [If] he was demolishing from one side, and it fell from another side, he is exempt; but if it was because of the blow, he is liable.

YAD AVRAHAM

is liable for the full value of the utensil (*Rav* from *Gem.* 98b).

וְהַבַּנַּאי שֶׁקִּבֵּל עָלָיו לִסְתֹּר אֶת־הַכֹּתֶל וְשִׁבֵּר אֶת־הָאֲבָנִים אוֹ שֶׁהִזִּיק — [If] *a builder undertakes to demolish a wall, and he breaks the stones or causes damage*,

Through his demolition of the wall, the builder caused damage to others (*Meiri*).

The mishnah printed with the *Gemara* reads: אוֹ שֶׁהִזִּיקָן, *or he damaged them* [referring to the stones]. This reading appears in *Rif* as well.

חַיָּב לְשַׁלֵּם. — *he is obligated to pay.*

When a builder undertakes to demolish a wall, it is understood that he will not break the stones [so that they can be used for future construction] (*Meiri*).

He is liable for damages caused to others based on the principle that *Man is always muad* [forewarned] (2:6). This applies, however, only if the builder accepts the job of demolishing the wall as a contractor, in which case the owner of the wall is freed from all liability. Should he be hired per diem, however, they both share in the liability (*Meiri*;

Rabbeinu Yehonasan, quoted by *Shitah Mekubetzes*).

הָיָה סוֹתֵר מִצַּד זֶה, וְנָפַל מִצַּד אַחֵר, פָּטוּר; — [If] *he was demolishing from one side, and it fell from another side, he is exempt;*

Since he did not hammer on that side, it is deemed an accident (*Meiri*).

Others explain that since the wall did not fall because of the vibrations of the hammering, but because it became weak, the builder's actions are considered an indirect cause of the damage, and he is therefore exempt (*Aruch Hashulchan, Choshen Mishpat* 384:3).

וְאִם מֵחֲמַת הַמַּכָּה, — *but if it was because of the blow,*

[The impact of the blow caused the other side of the wall to fall down.]

חַיָּב. — *he is liable.*

He should have taken precautions not to shake the other part of the wall. This is tantamount to one who shoots an arrow and damages with it (*Rambam, Hil. Chovel* 6:11; *Meiri*).

Tiferes Yisrael comments: He is liable since he struck the wall harder than he should have.

4.

Adding to the discussion of the previous mishnah, the *Tanna* continues to deal with the subject of craftsmen who spoil the materials entrusted to them, or who do not follow the orders of the owner.

[197]   THE MISHNAH/BAVA KAMMA – Chapter Nine: *HaGozeil Eitzim*

בבא קמא ט/ד

[ה] **הַנּוֹתֵן** צֶמֶר לַצַּבָּע, וְהִקְדִּיחַתּוּ יוֹרָה, נוֹתֵן לוֹ דְּמֵי צַמְרוֹ. צְבָעוֹ כָּאוּר, אִם הַשֶּׁבַח יוֹתֵר עַל־הַיְצִיאָה, נוֹתֵן לוֹ אֶת־הַיְצִיאָה; וְאִם הַיְצִיאָה יְתֵרָה עַל־הַשֶּׁבַח, נוֹתֵן לוֹ אֶת־הַשֶּׁבַח.

לִצְבֹּעַ לוֹ אָדֹם, וּצְבָעוֹ שָׁחוֹר; שָׁחוֹר, וּצְבָעוֹ אָדֹם — רַבִּי מֵאִיר אוֹמֵר: נוֹתֵן לוֹ דְּמֵי צַמְרוֹ. רַבִּי יְהוּדָה אוֹמֵר: אִם הַשֶּׁבַח יָתֵר עַל־הַיְצִיאָה, נוֹתֵן לוֹ אֶת־הַיְצִיאָה; וְאִם הַיְצִיאָה יְתֵרָה עַל־הַשֶּׁבַח, נוֹתֵן לוֹ אֶת־הַשֶּׁבַח.

יד אברהם

הַנּוֹתֵן צֶמֶר לַצַּבָּע — [If] one gives wool to a dyer,
And he asks that it be dyed (Meiri).

וְהִקְדִּיחַתּוּ יוֹרָה — and the cauldron burns it,
The dyer complied with the owner's orders and put the wool into a cauldron of dye. He heated it excessively, however (Rav; Rashi), and the fibers of the wool became too brittle to be used for weaving a garment (Meiri).

נוֹתֵן לוֹ — he pays him
The dyer must pay the owner of the wool (Tif. Yis.).

דְּמֵי צַמְרוֹ — the value of his wool.
In this instance, there is no improvement as there is in the mishnah's following case. Therefore, the dyer must pay the owner of the wool for the entire wool that he spoiled (Rav; Rashi).

This applies only if the wool becomes spoiled immediately upon falling into the cauldron, before the dye is absorbed. Should the dye first become absorbed and then the wool spoiled, the dyer is liable for the value of the dyed wool. This follows the principle that the craftsman does not acquire rights to the increase in the item's value (Tos. Yom Tov from Gem. 99a).

צְבָעוֹ כָּאוּר — [If] he dyes it poorly,
He dyes the wool with the residue of the dye, an act which constitutes intentional damage. Therefore, in the instances below involving two amounts, both R' Meir and R' Yehudah — cited further in the mishnah — agree that the dyer receives the lower amount (Rav; Rashi). The word כָּאוּר is similar to כְּעוּר [usually, translated as ugly, repulsive] (ibid.). Indeed, some editions read: כְּעוּר (Shinuyei Nuschaos).

אִם הַשֶּׁבַח יוֹתֵר עַל־הַיְצִיאָה — [then] if the improvement exceeds the expense,
The value of the wool was enhanced to an extent exceeding the cost of the dye (Rav; Rashi). For example, the wool costed a dinar, and the dye costed a dinar, and the finished product was worth three dinars (Tif. Yis.).

Rashi [Bava Metzia 117b] explains that the expense includes the dye, the wood used for kindling, and the labor (Maggid Mishneh, Hil. Sechirus 10:4). [From Beis Yosef (Choshen Mishpat 306) it appears that this represents a different view from that of Rashi to our mishnah, cited above.]

נוֹתֵן לוֹ — he pays him
The owner pays the dyer (Tif. Yis.).

אֶת־הַיְצִיאָה — the expense;

משניות / בבא קמא — פרק ט: הגוזל עצים [198]

4. [If] one gives wool to a dyer, and the cauldron burns it, he pays him the value of his wool. [If] he dyes it poorly, [then] if the improvement exceeds the expense, he pays him the expense; if, however, the expense exceeds the improvement, he pays him [for] the improvement.

[If he gave it to him] to dye red for him, and he dyes it black; [or] black, and he dyes it red — R' Meir says: He must pay him the value of his wool. R' Yehudah says: If the improvement exceeds the expense, he pays him the expense; if, however, the expense exceeds the improvement, he pays him [for] the improvement.

YAD AVRAHAM

For example, the dinar that he spent for the dye *(Tif. Yis.).* According to Rashi in *Bava Metzia*, he pays him for all the expenses.

He pays the dyer for the money he expended, but not the full wage for the job that had been stipulated. Since he did not do anything contrary to the owner's wishes [he dyed it as the latter had instructed, albeit using inferior materials], he is not considered a robber and does not acquire the wool *(Rav; Rashi).*

וְאִם הַיְצִיאָה יְתֵרָה עַל־הַשֶּׁבַח, — *if, however, the expense exceeds the improvement,*

For example, the dyer spent three dinars on the wool, and the increase in its value is only two dinars *(Tif. Yis.).*

נוֹתֵן לוֹ אֶת־הַשֶּׁבַח. — *he pays him [for] the improvement.*

That is, in our example, the two dinars, and not the full wage. Should the stipulated wage be less than the amount of the improvement, however, he must pay him no more than the stipulated wage *(Tif. Yis.).*

לִצְבּוֹעַ לוֹ אָדֹם, — *[If he gave it to him] to dye red for him,*

[The owner of the wool gave it to the dyer to dye red for him.]

וּצְבָעוֹ שָׁחוֹר; שָׁחוֹר, וּצְבָעוֹ אָדֹם — רַבִּי מֵאִיר אוֹמֵר: נוֹתֵן לוֹ — *and he dyes it black; [or] black, and he dyes it red — R' Meir says: He must pay him*

The dyer must pay the owner *(Tif. Yis.)*

דְּמֵי צַמְרוֹ. — *the value of his wool.*

R' Meir maintains that the dyer, who did not comply with the wishes of the owner, is tantamount to a robber, and he acquires the wool with the change he performed on it by dyeing it. Should the owner desire to get the wool back, he must pay the dyer his complete wage *(Rav; Rashi).* Since the dyer did not intend to take the wool for himself, he differs from a robber in that the owner has the option of paying the complete wage and receiving the wool *(Tos. Yom Tov).*

רַבִּי יְהוּדָה אוֹמֵר: אִם הַשֶּׁבַח יָתֵר עַל־הַיְצִיאָה, — *R' Yehudah says: If the improvement exceeds the expense,*

[The improvement in the wool due to the dyes exceeds the expense of the dyeing.]

נוֹתֵן לוֹ אֶת־הַיְצִיאָה; — *he pays him the expense;*

The owner pays the dyer his expense *(Tif. Yis.).*

וְאִם הַיְצִיאָה יְתֵרָה עַל־הַשֶּׁבַח, נוֹתֵן לוֹ

[199] THE MISHNAH/BAVA KAMMA — Chapter Nine: *HaGozeil Eitzim*

[ה] הַגּוֹזֵל אֶת־חֲבֵרוֹ שָׁוֶה פְרוּטָה וְנִשְׁבַּע לוֹ, יוֹלִיכֶנּוּ אַחֲרָיו אֲפִלּוּ לְמָדַי. לֹא יִתֵּן

יד אברהם

אֶת־הַשֶּׁבַח — *if, however, the expense exceeds the improvement, he pays him [for] the improvement.*

R' Yehudah fines the dyer who did not comply with the owner's wishes, so that he should not profit from the improvement. He does not receive his wage, only his expense. Should the expense exceed the improvement, he receives payment only for the latter. If the owner wishes to pay him his full wage — for example, in an instance that the improvement exceeds the wage — he may do so *(Rav; Rashi).*

Should the owner wish to give the dyer the wool and receive payment for it, *Rambam (Hil. Sechirus* 10:4) rules that he may not do so over the objection of the dyer. In his *Commentary,* he explains that the ruling of the mishnah is for the benefit of both the owner and the dyer. Therefore, the owner has no right to override the dyer's wishes. *Maggid Mishneh* (ad loc.) quotes *Rashi,* who contends that the owner may indeed do so. *Tos. Yom Tov* explains that since, according to *Rashi* and *Rav,* the law was enacted as a fine to the dyer and as a benefit to the owner, he is entitled to relinquish that benefit over the objection of the dyer. *Tos. Yom Tov* explains *Ravad* as subscribing to this view. *Maggid Mishneh,* however, holds that *Ravad* concurs with *Rambam.*

The halachah is in accordance with R' Yehudah *(Rav; Rambam Commentary).*

5.

◆§ A Robber's Repentance

From here until the end of the chapter, the mishnah deals with the robber or thief who swears that he did not steal and later confesses his guilt. This is based on *Leviticus* 5:20-26:

> *And* HASHEM *spoke to Moses, saying: If a person sins and commits a trespass against* HASHEM, *and lies to another concerning deposit, or a loan or a robbery, or if he oppressed another, or found a lost article and lied about it and swore falsely, for one of all that a person does to sin with them. And it will come to pass that he will have sinned and will feel guilty, and he shall return that which he robbed, or the oppression that he oppressed, or the deposit that was deposited with him, or the lost article that he found, or of anything concerning which he swears falsely, and he shall pay it with its principal, and he shall add its fifth to it; to the one to whom it belongs he shall give it on the day of his guilt. And his guilt-offering he shall bring to* HASHEM, *a perfect ram from the flock, at its value for a guilt-offering to the Kohen. And the Kohen shall atone for him before* HASHEM, *and it shall be forgiven him, for one of all that he does to be guilty of.*

The intention is that if one steals and then swears falsely, denying the theft or the robbery, and subsequently, he confesses his guilt, he must pay the amount he stole — as well as a fifth of that amount as an atonement for swearing falsely — and bring a guilt-offering. This applies not only to robbery, but also to items given for safekeeping, loans, withheld wages, and lost articles that one has found and denies.

The mishnah teaches us that if the amount he stole is worth a פְּרוּטָה, *perutah* [the minimal unit of significant monetary value], he must pursue the one he stole from even to a distant land in order to return the theft. Less than a *perutah,* however, is

5. [If] one robs another of something worth a *perutah* and swears to him, he must pursue him with it even to Media. He may give [it] neither to

YAD AVRAHAM

not considered money and has no significance, since the one who was robbed relinquishes it. [Nevertheless, one may not anguish another person by stealing less than a *perutah* from him *(Sanhedrin 57a; Rashi ad loc., s.v.* צערא; see *Maggid Mishneh, Hil. Geneivah* 1:2).]

As mentioned often in the *Gemara*, the addition of a fifth of the amount required by the Torah is, in reality, a fourth of the principal — i.e., a fifth of the entire sum after this amount is added *(Rambam Commentary)*.

הַגּוֹזֵל אֶת־חֲבֵרוֹ שָׁוֶה פְרוּטָה — [*If*] *one robs another of something worth a perutah*

As mentioned above, less than this amount is not considered money, and there is no liability for it. This is derived from the last words of the passage לְאַשְׁמָה בָהּ, *to be guilty of (Tos. Yom Tov from Sifra).*

Malbim (ad loc.) explains that this is indicated by Scripture's choice of the word לְאַשְׁמָה, *to be guilty*, rather than לַחֲטֹא, *to sin*. The former term implies an act for which he must make monetary restitution — in this case, stealing anything worth more than a *perutah*; whereas חטא, *sin*, refers to an act, which, albeit improper, does not make one monetarily liable — in this instance, stealing anything worth less than a *perutah*.

Torah Temimah (ibid.) suggests that the word בָהּ, *of* [*it*], implies an item of significance — in our case, anything over a *perutah*.

וְנִשְׁבַּע לוֹ, — *and swears to him*,

He swears falsely that he did not rob him, but subsequently confesses his crime *(Rav; Rashi).*

יוֹלִיכֶנּוּ אַחֲרָיו אֲפִלּוּ לְמָדַי — *he must pursue him with it even to Media.*

His sin is not expiated until he delivers the stolen article into the hand of the person he robbed. This is derived from the phrase *(Lev. loc. cit., v. 24)* לַאֲשֶׁר הוּא לוֹ יִתְּנֶנּוּ, *to the one to whom it belongs he shall give it*. The verse refers only to one who robbed and then swore falsely (ibid.).

This is indicated by the last words of the verse, בְּיוֹם אַשְׁמָתוֹ, *on the day of his* guilt, which imply that he swore and must bring a guilt-offering *(Nimmukei Yosef).*

Rambam (Hil. Gezeilah 7:9) explains that since the robber swore that he did not rob, the owner despairs of ever recovering his property. It is therefore required that he follow him even to distant lands to return the stolen article. It appears that, according to *Rambam*, if the robber did not swear, he is not required even to notify his victim of the robbery. *Tur* (367), however, states that he must contact the owner, inform him that he robbed him of such-and-such an amount, and tell him to come and take it *(Tos. Yom Tov).*

Media is chosen as an example of a distant land. Moreover, in *Isaiah* [17:13] the Medes are depicted as a people who have no esteem for silver or gold. Even if the one who was robbed is in such a place, the robber must nevertheless return the money *(Tif. Yis.).*

Another reason for choosing Media is that people from *Eretz Yisrael* were not permitted to leave the Holy Land for mundane purposes. For the purpose of returning a stolen item, however, they were permitted, because it is a *mitzvah*. Since it was an everyday occurrence for people to go to Babylon to study Torah, the *Tanna* chose Media, a land not frequented by Jews of *Eretz Yisrael*. Alternatively, מָדַי is an abbreviation of מְדִינַת יָם, *overseas*, which includes all lands outside *Eretz Yisrael* [see ArtScroll Commentary to *Gittin* 1:1] *(Shoshannim LeDavid).*

[201] THE MISHNAH/BAVA KAMMA – Chapter Nine: *HaGozeil Eitzim*

בבא קמא ט/ו

לֹא לִבְנוֹ וְלֹא לִשְׁלוּחוֹ, אֲבָל נוֹתֵן לִשְׁלִיחַ בֵּית־דִּין. וְאִם מֵת, יַחֲזִיר לְיוֹרְשָׁיו.

[ו] **נָתַן** לוֹ אֶת־הַקֶּרֶן, וְלֹא נָתַן לוֹ אֶת־הַחֹמֶשׁ; מָחַל לוֹ עַל־הַקֶּרֶן, וְלֹא מָחַל לוֹ עַל־הַחֹמֶשׁ; מָחַל לוֹ עַל־זֶה וְעַל־זֶה — חוּץ מִפָּחוֹת מִשְּׁוֵה פְרוּטָה בַּקֶּרֶן — אֵינוֹ צָרִיךְ לֵילֵךְ אַחֲרָיו.

יד אברהם

לא יתן לא לבנו — He may give [it] neither to his son

The robber may not return the stolen item to the son of the one who was robbed, for it is not regarded as returned until it reaches the father's hand (Rav). Consequently, should he give it to the son, and the latter is robbed while he is bringing it to his father, the robber would still be liable for it, and he would be required to pay a second time (Tos. Yom Tov from Rashi). In such a case the robber's sin is not expiated until the item reaches the father's hand (Tif. Yis.).

ולא לשלוחו — nor to his agent,

[The robber may not return the stolen item to an agent of the one he robbed.]

In the *Gemara* (104a) there is a controversy between Rabbah and R' Chisda whether an agent appointed in the presence of witnesses by the person who was robbed may accept the stolen article on behalf of the latter from the robber. Rabbah maintains that he is not a valid agent. The only reason for appointing him is that since he is an honest person, the robber may wish to send the article with him and hope he will not lose it; but he does not become exempt from paying for the robbery until the item reaches the hand of the owner. [According to Rabbah, the only valid agent in such a case is one specifically appointed by the owner of the item in the presence of the robber (Tos. 104a, s.v. שליח).]

R' Chisda, however, rules that an agent appointed by the owner of the item in the presence of witnesses [even if the robber is not present] is valid. Thus, the robber becomes exempt when he delivers the article to the agent. Our mishnah, on the other hand — which instructs the robber not to give it to an agent — refers to a hireling or a lodger of the owner. In such a case, the robber does not become exempt, since these individuals were never appointed to be valid agents.

אבל נותן לשליח בית־דין — but he may give it to an agent of the court.

This is a Rabbinic enactment innovated to spare the robber the expenses of the trip, which may far exceed the amount of the theft (Rav; Rashi).

The enactment appears to be that the robber gives the money to the court's agent, who holds it until the owner calls for it. However, in that case, the mishnah did not have to mention an agent of the court at all; it should rather have stated that if there is a court in his city, he may deposit it with that court. *Tosafos* therefore interpret the mishnah differently: the robber may give the stolen item to an agent of the court, who will deliver it to the owner. The advantage is that the robber's sin is expiated immediately upon giving it to the agent, and he is no longer responsible for the article. Although the *Gemara* does state that there is a

משניות / בבא קמא — פרק ט: הגוזל עצים [202]

9
6
his son nor to his agent, but he may give it to an agent of the court. If he dies, he must return it to his heirs.

6. [I]f he paid him the principal, but did not pay him the fifth; [if] he forgave him the principal, but did not forgive him the fifth; [or] if he forgave him for both — save less than the worth of a *perutah* of the principal — he need not pursue him.

YAD AVRAHAM

Rabbinic enactment that the robber may leave the article with the court and bring his guilt-offering to the Temple, that enactment is not mentioned in the mishnah *(Tos. Yom Tov;* see *Shoshannim LeDavid, Beis David).*

וְאִם מֵת, — *If he dies,*
The one who was robbed dies *(Rav; Rashi).*

יַחֲזִיר לְיוֹרְשָׁיו. — *he must return it to his heirs.*

That is, the heirs of the one who was robbed *(Rashi).* The robber must pursue the heirs in order to return the stolen article, even as far as Media.

Although heirs of a robber do not pay the additional fifth if the stolen item no longer exists — even if they knew of the robbery and, after denying it and swearing falsely to that effect, admitted to it — the heirs of the one who was robbed must be paid the additional fifth where applicable *(Tos. Yom Tov* from *Tos.).*

6.

נָתַן לוֹ אֶת־הַקֶּרֶן, — *[If] he paid him the principal,*
[The robber returned the stolen item to its owner or paid him for its value.]

וְלֹא נָתַן לוֹ אֶת־הַחֹמֶשׁ; — *but did not pay him the fifth;*
[He did not pay him the additional fifth, which he must add because he swore falsely, as discussed above.]

מָחַל לוֹ עַל־הַקֶּרֶן, וְלֹא מָחַל לוֹ עַל־הַחֹמֶשׁ; מָחַל לוֹ עַל־זֶה וְעַל־זֶה — *[if] he forgave him the principal, but did not forgive him the fifth; [or] if he forgave him for both* [lit., *this and that*] —
[He forgave him for both the principal and the fifth.]

חוּץ מִפָּחוֹת מִשְּׁוֵה פְרוּטָה בַּקֶּרֶן — *save less than the worth of a perutah of the principal —*
[This applies to all of the above cases. Although part of the principal remains, it is less than a *perutah*.]

Even if the stolen article itself still exists, we do not fear that its price may rise and that the outstanding part of the principal will become worth a *perutah*. *(Rav, Rambam Commentary* from *Gem.* 105a).

אֵינוֹ צָרִיךְ לֵילֵךְ אַחֲרָיו. — *he need not pursue him.*
[The outstanding part of the principal does not have to be returned, since it is less then a *perutah*, as explained in the preface to mishnah 5. Although he must pay him the additional fifth, he need not pursue him for the purpose, since the verse from where we derive that he must pursue him *(Lev.* 5:24) deals only with the principal, not the fifth.]

Although the robber need not pursue his victim, if the latter comes to him, he must return to him even less than the worth of a *perutah*, since the Torah considers taking even such an amount to be theft *(Tos. Yom Tov* from

[203] THE MISHNAH/BAVA KAMMA — Chapter Nine: *HaGozeil Eitzim*

נָתַן לוֹ אֶת־הַחֹמֶשׁ, וְלֹא נָתַן לוֹ אֶת־הַקֶּרֶן; מָחַל לוֹ עַל־הַחֹמֶשׁ, וְלֹא מָחַל לוֹ עַל־הַקֶּרֶן; מָחַל לוֹ עַל־זֶה וְעַל־זֶה חוּץ מִשָּׁוֶה פְרוּטָה בַּקֶּרֶן — צָרִיךְ לֵילֵךְ אַחֲרָיו.

[ז] **נָתַן** לוֹ אֶת־הַקֶּרֶן וְנִשְׁבַּע לוֹ עַל־הַחֹמֶשׁ, הֲרֵי זֶה מְשַׁלֵּם חֹמֶשׁ עַל־חֹמֶשׁ עַד שֶׁיִּתְמַעֵט הַקֶּרֶן פָּחוֹת מִשָּׁוֶה פְרוּטָה. וְכֵן בְּפִקָּדוֹן, שֶׁנֶּאֱמַר: ,,.... בְּפִקָּדוֹן אוֹ בִתְשׂוּמֶת יָד אוֹ בְגָזֵל אוֹ עָשַׁק אֶת־עֲמִיתוֹ אוֹ־מָצָא אֲבֵדָה וְכִחֶשׁ בָּהּ וְנִשְׁבַּע

יד אברהם

Rambam, Hil. Gezeilah 7:11).

Although a robber is never required to return less than the worth of a *perutah*, in this case, since the original amount that he took was more than a *perutah*, he is required to return it *(Tif. Yis.).*

In order that we make this deduction from the mishnah, the *Tanna* states that the robber need not pursue the one he robbed to return less than a *perutah*, although this could be deduced from the preceding mishnah, which states that he must pursue him to return a *perutah's* worth, implying that he need not do so in order to return less than a *perutah's* worth.

Another reason for the mishnah's stating this rule, even though it could be deduced from the previous mishnah, is that we would think that only if the amount initially stolen had been less than a *perutah*, the robber need not pursue his victim, but if the original amount had been a *perutah* or more, even if he now owes him only less than a *perutah's* worth, he is obligated to pursue him. The mishnah therefore teaches us that, even in such an instance, he need not do so *(Tos. R' Akiva; Tos. HaRosh; Toras Chaim).*

נָתַן לוֹ אֶת־הַחֹמֶשׁ, וְלֹא נָתַן לוֹ אֶת־הַקֶּרֶן; — [If] he paid him the fifth, but did not pay him the principal;

[The robber paid the owner of the stolen item the additional fifth, but did not pay him for the value of the item itself.]

מָחַל לוֹ עַל־הַחֹמֶשׁ, וְלֹא מָחַל לוֹ עַל־הַקֶּרֶן; מָחַל לוֹ עַל־זֶה וְעַל־זֶה חוּץ מִשָּׁוֶה פְרוּטָה בַּקֶּרֶן — [if] he forgave him the fifth, but did not forgive him the principal, [or if] he forgave him for both save the worth of a perutah of the principal —

[The owner of the stolen item forgave payment of the additional fifth, or both — that and the value of the item itself, except one *perutah's* worth.]

צָרִיךְ לֵילֵךְ אַחֲרָיו. — he must pursue him.

[Since the robber owes his victim a *perutah's* worth of the principal, he must follow him even to a distant land in order to pay it.]

7.

[If] — נָתַן לוֹ אֶת־הַקֶּרֶן וְנִשְׁבַּע לוֹ עַל־הַחֹמֶשׁ, he paid him the principal and swore to him concerning the fifth,

The robber paid the principal, and the

9 7

[If] he paid him the fifth, but did not pay him the principal; [if] he forgave him the fifth, but did not forgive him the principal; [or if] he forgave him for both save the worth of a *perutah* of the principal — he must pursue him.

7. [If] he paid him the principal and swore to him concerning the fifth, he pays a fifth upon the fifth until the principal dwindles to less than the worth of a *perutah*. The same applies to a deposit, as it is said *(Leviticus 5:21f.):* ... *concerning a deposit, or a loan, or a robbery, or [if] he oppressed another, or found a lost article, and lied about it and swore*

YAD AVRAHAM

owner did not demand the fifth immediately. Later, when he did, the robber swore that he had already paid it, or that he had never been obligated to pay it *(Meiri).* Subsequently, he confessed that he did indeed owe the fifth *(Rav).*

The same applies if he did not pay the principal, but swore that he owed neither that nor the fifth, and then confessed that he had sworn falsely twice. The mishnah does not choose that case, however, since it is unusual that one would swear twice regarding the principal *(Tos. Yom Tov from Tos.).*

הֲרֵי זֶה מְשַׁלֵּם חֹמֶשׁ עַל־חֹמֶשׁ — *he pays a fifth upon the fifth*

When he confesses that he swore falsely regarding the fifth, this amount, too, becomes like the principal part of the theft, and he must pay an additional fifth of that fifth *(Rav; Meiri).*

Accordingly, he must pursue the one he robbed even to Media to return the first fifth which he swore he did not owe *(Tos. Yom Tov from Tos.).*

If he swears that he does not owe him the second fifth, and subsequently confesses, he must pay a fifth of *that* fifth in addition to the previous amounts. As long as he continues swearing to deny that he owes the last fifth in question, the cycle continues ... *(Rav).*

עַד שֶׁיִּתְמַעֵט הַקֶּרֶן פָּחוֹת מִשְׁוֵה פְרוּטָה. — *until the principal dwindles to less than the worth of a perutah.*

[That is, until the last fifth in question — which becomes like the principal, as explained above — equals less than a *perutah*. In such an instance he need not pursue his victim to pay back the last fifth.]

The fact that many fifths can be paid even for one principal is derived from Scripture's use of the plural form in the verse *(Lev. 5:24)* telling us about this payment: וַחֲמִשִׁתָיו [lit., *its fifths*] *(Rav).*

וְכֵן בְּפִקָּדוֹן, — *The same applies to a deposit,*

The same ruling applies to one who, after denying that he took an item for safekeeping and swearing to that effect, confesses: he must pay the principal, as well as a fifth, and bring a guilt-offering *(Tos. Yom Tov from Rambam, Hil. Gezeilah 7:1).*

שֶׁנֶּאֱמַר: ,,.... בְּפִקָּדוֹן אוֹ בִתְשׂוּמֶת יָד אוֹ בְגָזֵל אוֹ עָשַׁק אֶת־עֲמִיתוֹ אוֹ־מָצָא אֲבֵדָה וְכִחֶשׁ בָּהּ וְנִשְׁבַּע עַל־שָׁקֶר'' — הֲרֵי זֶה מְשַׁלֵּם קֶרֶן,

[205] THE MISHNAH/BAVA KAMMA – Chapter Nine: *HaGozeil Eitzim*

בבא קמא ט/ח

עַל־שֶׁקֶר״ — הֲרֵי זֶה מְשַׁלֵּם קֶרֶן, וְחֹמֶשׁ, וְאָשָׁם. ״הֵיכָן פִּקְדוֹנִי?״ אָמַר לוֹ: ״אָבַד.״ ״מַשְׁבִּיעֲךָ אֲנִי,״ וְאָמַר: ״אָמֵן,״ וְהָעֵדִים מְעִידִים אוֹתוֹ שֶׁאֲכָלוֹ — מְשַׁלֵּם קֶרֶן. הוֹדָה מֵעַצְמוֹ, מְשַׁלֵּם קֶרֶן, וְחֹמֶשׁ, וְאָשָׁם.

[ח] ״הֵיכָן פִּקְדוֹנִי?״ אָמַר לוֹ: ״נִגְנַב.״ ״מַשְׁבִּיעֲךָ אֲנִי,״ וְאָמַר: ״אָמֵן,״ וְהָעֵדִים מְעִידִים אוֹתוֹ שֶׁגְּנָבוֹ — מְשַׁלֵּם תַּשְׁלוּמֵי

יד אברהם

וְחֹמֶשׁ, וְאָשָׁם. — as it is said (Leviticus 5:21f.) '... concerning a deposit, or a loan, or a robbery, or [if] he oppressed another, or found a lost article, and lied about it and swore falsely — this one pays the principal, a fifth, and a guilt-offering.'

The *oppression* referred to in the verse consists of withholding the wages of a hireling (*Rav*).

Rambam (*Hil. Gezeilah* 1:4) gives the term a broader definition: an instance in which one into whose possession money belonging to someone else has come with the latter's consent, but who withholds it forcibly and does not return it upon the other's demand. Such is the case if one has a loan or a deposit or wages due him, and he claims it but cannot get it from the person who owes it to him because he is a strong and harsh person. Concerning this, Scripture states (*Lev.* 19:13): לֹא תַעֲשֹׁק אֶת־רֵעֶךָ, *You shall not oppress another.*

⋄§ Guardians Who Plead Theft or Loss

As mentioned in the commentary to 4:9, a שׁוֹמֵר חִנָּם, *unpaid guardian*, is exempt from liability for the item entrusted to him except in the case of negligence. Should he claim that the item had been stolen or lost, he swears to that effect and is exempt. If it is discovered through witnesses that he took the article for himself, then — in the case that he had advanced a plea of theft — he must pay the twofold payment just like a thief. If, however, he had claimed that the item was lost, he pays only the principal.

Should he confess that he took it for himself, he must pay the principal, a fifth, and bring a guilt-offering, regardless of whether he had pleaded theft or loss. The obligations of paying the additional fifth and bringing a guilt-offering apply only in the case of confession, as explained below.

״הֵיכָן פִּקְדוֹנִי?״ — *'Where is my deposit?'*

[That is, for example, Reuven had given his animal to Shimon, asking that he watch it as an unpaid guardian, and Reuven now comes to Shimon and says: 'Where is my deposit?']

אָמַר לוֹ: ״אָבַד.״ — *He said to him: 'It is lost.'*

[Shimon replied to Reuven: 'It is lost, and I am exempt for loss.']

״מַשְׁבִּיעֲךָ אֲנִי,״ — *'I adjure you,'*

[Reuven retorts to Shimon: 'I want you to swear that it is, in fact, lost.']

וְאָמַר: ״אָמֵן,״ — *and he said: 'Amen,'*

[Shimon, the guardian, said: 'Amen,' which means: 'It is true.' This is an acceptance of an oath, and is tantamount to swearing.]

משניות / בבא קמא — פרק ט: הגוזל עצים [206]

9
8
falsely — this one pays the principal, a fifth, and a guilt-offering.

'Where is my deposit?' He said to him: 'It is lost.' 'I adjure you,' and he said: 'Amen,' and witnesses testify against him that he ate it — he pays the principal. [If] he confessed himself, he pays the principal, a fifth, and a guilt-offering.

8. 'Where is my deposit?' He said to him: 'It was stolen.' 'I adjure you,' and he said: 'Amen,' and witnesses testify against him that he stole it — he

YAD AVRAHAM

וְהָעֵדִים מְעִידִים אוֹתוֹ שֶׁאֲכָלוֹ — *and witnesses testify against him that he ate it* —

[Witnesses came and testified that Shimon had eaten the animal entrusted to him.]

מְשַׁלֵּם קֶרֶן. — *he pays the principal.*

[As delineated above, a guardian who, after claiming that the item entrusted to him has been lost, is refuted by witnesses who testify that he took the item for himself, is liable only for the value of the article itself.]

הוֹדָה מֵעַצְמוֹ, — *[If] he confessed himself,*

[Before any witnesses had come Shimon confessed that he had eaten the animal.]

מְשַׁלֵּם קֶרֶן, וְחֹמֶשׁ, וְאָשָׁם. — *he pays the principal, a fifth, and a guilt-offering.*

[In addition to the payments, he must bring a guilt-offering.]

He pays the fifth and brings the guilt-offering only if he confesses. We learn this from the passage that deals with robbing a proselyte (see mishnah 11), where the Torah states *(Num. 5:7)*: וְהִתְוַדּוּ, *and they confess* (Rav). According to *Rambam (Commentary)* the derivation is from *Leviticus 5:23*, וְהָיָה כִּי־יֶחֱטָא וְאָשֵׁם, *And it will come to pass that he will have sinned and will feel guilty*, implying that he repents of his own volition.

8.

"הֵיכָן פִּקְדוֹנִי?" — *"Where is my deposit?"*

That is, as in the previous example, Reuven entrusted an item to Shimon, requesting that he watch it gratis, and now Reuven asks of Shimon: 'Where is my deposit?']

אָמַר לוֹ: "נִגְנַב". — *He said to him: 'It was stolen.'*

[Shimon answered Reuven: 'It was stolen, and I am exempt for theft, since I am an unpaid guardian.']

"מַשְׁבִּיעֲךָ אָנִי," — *'I adjure you,'*

[Reuven retorts: 'I want you to swear that it is indeed true, that the animal was stolen.']

וְאָמַר: "אָמֵן". — *and he said: "Amen,"*

[Shimon said: 'Amen' — i.e., 'It is true that the deposit was stolen.' As mentioned above, this is an acceptance of an oath and is tantamount to swearing.]

וְהָעֵדִים מְעִידִין אוֹתוֹ שֶׁגְּנָבוֹ — *and witnesses testify against him that he stole it* —

[Witnesses testify that Shimon himself stole the item.]

THE MISHNAH/BAVA KAMMA — Chapter Nine: *HaGozeil Eitzim*

בבא קמא
ט/ט

כֶּפֶל. הוֹדָה מֵעַצְמוֹ, מְשַׁלֵּם קֶרֶן, וְחֹמֶשׁ, וְאָשָׁם.

[ט] הַגּוֹזֵל אֶת־אָבִיו וְנִשְׁבַּע לוֹ, וָמֵת, הֲרֵי זֶה מְשַׁלֵּם קֶרֶן וְחֹמֶשׁ לְבָנָיו אוֹ לְאֶחָיו. וְאִם אֵינוֹ רוֹצֶה, אוֹ שֶׁאֵין לוֹ, לֹוֶה, וּבַעֲלֵי חוֹב

יד אברהם

מְשַׁלֵּם תַּשְׁלוּמֵי כֶפֶל — *he pays the twofold payment.*

This is based on the verse (Ex. 22:7f.): *If the thief is not found, and the householder has approached the judges ... whomever the judges condemn shall pay twofold to the other.* The intention is: *If the thief is not found* — i.e., his claim that the article was stolen is found to be false, *and the householder* — i.e., the guardian, *has approached the judges* — i.e., had already sworn that the item was stolen, he pays the twofold payment (Gem. 63b).

The mishnah chooses the case in which the witnesses testify that the guardian himself stole the item. In the case of the previous mishnah, on the other hand, in which the guardian claimed that the animal had been lost, the witnesses testify that he had actually eaten the animal. The different examples are given to point out that if the guardian claims that the item was lost, even if witnesses testify that it no longer exists — e.g., he ate it — he pays only the principal. Should he claim that it was stolen, however, even if the witnesses testify only that he himself had taken it and the stolen article still exists, he must nevertheless pay twofold (*Tos. Yom Tov* from *Tos.* 63b).

הוֹדָה מֵעַצְמוֹ — *[If] he confesses himself,*

[The guardian confesses that he stole the item.]

מְשַׁלֵּם קֶרֶן, וְחֹמֶשׁ, וְאָשָׁם — *he pays the principal, a fifth, and a guilt-offering.*

In such an instance, he does not pay the twofold payment since that is a fine, and one does not pay a fine by his own confession. We derive this principle from the verse cited above: *Whomever the judges condemn shall pay twofold to the other* — that is, only if the *judges* condemn him must he pay the fine, but not if he admits the crime himself (*Rav* from Gem. 64b).

[He does, however, pay the principal and the fifth, and must bring a guilt-offering as in the previous case.] He pays the fifth since that is to atone for his sin (*Tif. Yis.*).

9.

הַגּוֹזֵל אֶת־אָבִיו וְנִשְׁבַּע לוֹ — *[If] one robs his father and swears to him,*

[He swears falsely to his father that he had not robbed him.]

Beis Yosef is undecided whether the mishnah means to imply that the following ruling does not apply if the robber does not swear. *Darchei Moshe*, however, asserts that the mishnah does indeed mean this [since the ruling is based upon penalizing the robber for swearing falsely] (*Tos. Yom Tov*).

וָמֵת — *and he dies,*

[The father dies] and then the son confesses his crime to the other heirs of his father (*Rashi;* see *Maharsha, Pnei Yehoshua*).

הֲרֵי זֶה מְשַׁלֵּם קֶרֶן וְחֹמֶשׁ — *he pays the principal and a fifth*

Although at least part of the stolen property belongs to him as his share of the inheritance, he must still return it, since the Torah (*Lev.* 5:23) states: וְהֵשִׁיב

[208] משניות / בבא קמא — פרק ט: הגוזל עצים

pays the twofold payment. [If] he confesses himself, he pays the principal, a fifth, and a guilt-offering.

9. [I]f] one robs his father and swears to him, and he dies, he pays the principal and a fifth to his sons or to his brothers. But if he does not wish to, or if he does not have, he may borrow, and the creditors

YAD AVRAHAM

אֶת־הַגְּזֵלָה, *And he shall return the loot* — that is, the only way for one to atone for a theft is by actually returning that which he stole [unless the owner of the item forgives him *(Rambam Commentary)*] *(Rav).*

This applies only if the stolen property still exists and has not been changed *(Rav; Rambam Commentary* and *Hil. Gezeilah* 8:2f.). Otherwise, he is not obligated to give away his share, since the passage dealing with the obligation of returning stolen property refers to one who is returning the original item itself, not one who is paying for property that no longer exists or that has been changed and now belongs to the robber [see preface to mishnah 1] *(Tos.Yom Tov).*

According to *Rambam* (loc. cit.; see *Maggid Mishneh, Kesef Mishneh* ad loc.) after the robber returns the stolen property to the other heirs of his father [see below], he may take an extra part in the rest of his father's estate equivalent to his share of the principal and fifth that he gave away. This is because all that the Torah requires is that he return the stolen item, and he did so. [He may not take back the item itself, since he would thereby be negating his previous act of returning it.]

Rashi, Tosafos, and *Tur (Choshen Mishpat* 367) disagree, however, maintaining that the Biblical requirement is that he return it and not get it back in any form. The only permitted method of offsetting his loss is the one suggested by the mishnah below.

לְבָנָיו אוֹ לְאֶחָיו. — *to his sons or to his brothers.*

That is, his father's other sons, or — if there were none — his father's brothers; the robber pays them, since they inherit the father. Although the robber, too, is an heir, he must perform the precept of returning the stolen property, and therefore, he may not retain even his share of this part of the inheritance *(Rashi).*

Tosafos interpret the mishnah differently: The robber must pay his own sons the amount of the robbery. If he has no sons, he must pay his brothers, the father's sons. This is because — with regard to this part of the inheritance — we view him as though he, too, were dead, since the obligation to return it prohibits him from retaining it, and his sons or — if he has none — his brothers inherit him.

Rambam (Hil. Gezeilah loc. cit.) concurs with *Tosafos* that the terms *his sons* and *his brothers* refer to those of the robber. However, he disagrees regarding their precedence, maintaining that the brothers receive the robber's portion, and only if there are no brothers is it given to his sons. The mishnah, by stating *his sons* first, did not intend to give them precedence *(Tos. Yom Tov).* Indeed, according to *Hagahos HaGra, Rambam's* version of the mishnah reads: *to his brothers or to his sons.*

וְאִם אֵינוֹ רוֹצֶה, — *But if he does not wish to,*

The robber does not wish to surrender his share *(Rav; Rashi).*

אוֹ שֶׁאֵין לוֹ, — *or if he does not have,*

He does not have the means to be able

בבא קמא ט/י

[ט] **הָאוֹמֵר** לִבְנוֹ: "קוֹנָם, אִי אַתָּה נֶהֱנֶה מִשֶּׁלִּי," אִם מֵת, יִירָשֶׁנּוּ. בְּחַיָּיו וּבְמוֹתוֹ, אִם מֵת, לֹא יִירָשֶׁנּוּ, וְיַחֲזִיר לְבָנָיו אוֹ בָּאִים וְנִפְרָעִים.

יד אברהם

to afford surrendering his share (ibid.).

According to *Rambam*, this means he does not have brothers or sons to whom to give it (*Maggid Mishneh; Hagahos HaGra*).

לְוֶה — *he may borrow*,

He borrows the amount of the stolen property from others (*Rav*).

וּבַעֲלֵי חוֹב בָּאִים וְנִפְרָעִים — *and the creditors come and receive their payment.*

According to *Rashi* et al., this means that after the robber uses the money he borrowed to fulfill the *mitzvah* of returning stolen items, the creditors collect their payment from the robber's share of the inheritance that was given to the brothers. For example, if the robber was one of three brothers, the creditors receive payment from one-third of the inheritance.

According to *Rambam* this means that he may take the part of the stolen property which he was to have inherited and directly pay off a debt of his, give it as a gift, or give it to charity. However, he must inform the recipient that it was stolen from his father. [To be sure, the *Gemara* (109b) mentions this ruling and the other commentators agree with it. Yet they hold that this is not what the mishnah is saying.] If that is not enough to cover the debt, they collect the rest from him (*Rashi*).

According to *Rashi*, although the theft consists of chattels, which — if given as a gift — are not mortgaged to creditors (see ArtScroll commentary to *Kiddushin* 1:5), in this case it is not regarded as though the robber gives his brothers a gift; rather, he gives it to them without specifying what it is for, with the intention of fulfilling the *mitzvah* of returning stolen property. Consequently, the creditors may collect from it. The robber cannot take the money back for himself, however, since if he did so he will not have fulfilled the *mitzvah* of returning the stolen property. The fact that his creditors take the money, on the other hand, does not negate the *mitzvah* since the robber himself did not take it (*Tos. Yom Tov* from *Tos.*).

10.

The *Tanna* now discusses a case which resembles that of the preceding mishnah: a father forbids his son any benefit from his estate. As in the case above, the son can circumvent the prohibition by borrowing money and allowing the creditors to collect from his share of the estate. This is the case in which the father pronounced a vow, called קוֹנָם, *konam*, a corrupted form of קָרְבָּן, *an offering*, meaning that his property should be interdicted to his son as a sacrificial offering is interdicted to everyone.

הָאוֹמֵר לִבְנוֹ: "קוֹנָם, אִי אַתָּה נֶהֱנֶה מִשֶּׁלִּי," — [*If*] *one says to his son: 'Konam, if you benefit from what is mine,'*

The father prohibited his son to benefit from all his belongings by declaring a נֶדֶר, *neder* (loosely, *vow*), whose meaning is: 'The benefit of my property is forbidden you like an

10. [If] one says to his son, '*Konam*, if you benefit from what is mine,' and he dies, he inherits him. [But if he said it should apply] during his lifetime and after his death, and he dies, he does not inherit him, and he must return [it] to his sons or to

YAD AVRAHAM

offering' — i.e., just as a sacrifice is forbidden to everyone. The term קוֹנָם, *konam*, is a corruption of the word קָרְבָּן, *korban* (offering). [See General Introduction to ArtScroll *Nedarim*, p. 2f.]

Tur (*Yoreh Deah* 216) cites the mishnah as reading שֶׁאַתָּה נֶהֱנֶה מִשֶּׁלִּי, *what you benefit from what is mine*, which is a more correct version. The intention is: whatever you benefit from my property shall be prohibited to you like an offering (*Tos. Yom Tov*). Other editions (*Meiri, Kaffich*) read: שֶׁאִי אַתָּה נֶהֱנֶה מִשֶּׁלִּי, *that you shall not benefit from what is mine*.

אִם מֵת, יִירָשֶׁנּוּ. — *and he dies, he inherits him*.

If the father dies, the son inherits him despite the *neder*, since the estate no longer belongs to the father (*Tif. Yis.*), and he had prohibited only *his* property [see *Nedarim* 5:3, Rambam (*Hil. Nedarim* 5:6)] (*Tos. Yom Tov*).

בְּחַיָּיו וּבְמוֹתוֹ — [But if he said it should apply] *during his lifetime and after his death*,

[The father specifies that the property should be forbidden to his son both during his lifetime and after his death.]

אִם מֵת, לֹא יִירָשֶׁנּוּ — *and he dies, he does not inherit him*,

The son does not inherit the father, because it is as though he had said: 'This property is forbidden you,' in which case it remains interdicted even after it leaves the father's possession (ibid.).

The intention is not that the son has no right of inheritance. Were that the case, he would not be able to circumvent his father's prohibition through the procedure described below. Rather, it means merely that he may derive no benefit from his father's property even when it falls to him as an inheritance. The *Tanna* states, *he does not inherit him*, only to parallel the expression he used above *he inherits him*, but it is not to be taken literally (*Tos. Yom Tov* from *Ran* to *Nedarim* 47a).

וְיַחֲזִיר לְבָנָיו אוֹ לְאֶחָיו. — *and he must return [it] to his sons or to his brothers*.

Although the son never acquired the property, the *Tanna* uses the word *return*, since, in fact, the property is his, as stated above. Another version reads: יִתֵּן, *he shall give* (ibid.).

Ran (loc. cit.) comments that the mishnah's intention cannot be that the son should give the property to his brothers, since giving a gift for which one will receive something in return is considered a benefit, which he is forbidden to have from the property. We find such an instance in *Nedarim* (36b): if one makes a *neder* forbidding another person to benefit from him, he may not separate his own grain as *terumah* (the *Kohen's* portion) for the other person's stack of grain, according to the opinion that the privilege of choosing the recipient *Kohen* in such a case belongs to the owner of the stack of grain. [Since the *Kohen* may have a maternal grandfather, a non-*Kohen*, who will give a small gift to anyone that gives his grandson *terumah*,[1] it is

---

1. The *Kohen* himself is prohibited to give such a gift (*Ran* ibid. 36b). [Apparently, so are his father and paternal grandfather.]

בבא קמא ט/י — לְאֶחָיו. וְאִם אֵין לוֹ, לֹוֶה, וּבַעֲלֵי חוֹב בָּאִים וְנִפְרָעִים.

יד אברהם

deemed a benefit[1] (Ran ibid. 36b).] Here, too, the son who is prohibited to benefit from the estate of his father would be violating the latter's *neder* by receiving something from his brothers for giving them his share of the inheritance.

Rather, the mishnah means that the son merely points out the property to his brothers and says, 'My father forbade this property to me, and I do not know what to do with it. Take it for yourself and do with it as you wish.' This would not be considered a gift, but a type of הֶפְקֵר, *relinquishment* or *abandonment*. Indeed, *Rambam* (Hil. Nedarim 5:8) rules that he must tell him, 'This is my father's property which he forbade me,' similar to the case in the previous mishnah (see commentary ibid., s.v. וּבַעֲלֵי).

Beis Yosef (Yoreh Deah 216), however, permits even giving the property over directly. He reasons that the case in our mishnah and the one in *Nedarim* regarding *terumah* are not analogous. In the latter instance, the person who made the *neder* is giving the one he forbade to benefit from him grain which the former could have used for other purposes. When he, instead, designates it as *terumah* which the other person can give to any *Kohen* he wishes, the other person benefits thereby. In this case, however, the son is giving his brothers property which is of no use to him; moreover, they, too, are heirs of the deceased and have some connection to it. In such a case, there is no stricture against giving the property to them *(Tos. Yom Tov)*.

וְאִם אֵין לוֹ, — *If he does not have,*

He does not have what to eat (Rav; Rashi). Unlike the preceding mishnah, in which this phrase is construed by *Rav* and *Rashi* as meaning that one does not have the wherewithal to surrender his share, here it means that he has nothing to eat. The reason for the different interpretations is that in the first case — in which a son stole from his father, and the latter died — there is no prohibition on the money itself; it is only that the robber must fulfill the *mitzvah* of returning stolen property. Therefore, even if he wishes to use the property and pay the heirs in the manner described above, the law is lenient and allows him to do so. In this case, however, the money itself is interdicted to the son. To permit him to derive any benefit from it requires dire circumstances, such as having nothing to eat. Indeed, *Tosafos* point out the fact that our mishnah does not add the phrase אִם אֵינוֹ רוֹצֶה, *if he does not wish to*, implies that as long as he has what to eat, he may not follow the suggestion given by the *Tanna* below.[2]

Tosafos also advance another interpretation: In the preceding case, in which the robber was at fault for having committed the robbery, he may wish to fulfill the *mitzvah* of returning the property properly without any leniency. In our mishnah's case, however, the son was not at fault — his father had prohibited the property to him; thus, he certainly does not wish to lose his share of the estate. Our mishnah is therefore not explained as meaning that he has nothing to eat, but rather, as in *Nedarim* 4:7 [see footnote] it means: if he does not wish to lose his share for any reason, he may choose the alternative given below *(Tos. Yom Tov)*.

---

1. [The fact that he saves him the grain he would have to give the *Kohen* does not forbid him from doing so, since this is considered an indirect benefit (see preface to *Nedarim* 4:2, ed. ArtScroll; *Even Haezer* 70:8; *Choshen Mishpat* 128:1).]

2. *Tosafos'* comparison of this case to that of *Nedarim* 4:7, where the Mishnah specifically states וְאִם לוֹ מַה יֹּאכַל, *and he does not have what to eat*, is difficult to understand since there they — and *Rav* — comment that this is not meant literally.

משניות / בבא קמא — פרק ט: הגוזל עצים [212]

9 his brothers. If he does not have, he may borrow, and
10 the creditors come and receive payment.

YAD AVRAHAM

לֹוֶה, — *he may borrow,*
He borrows money for food *(Rav; Rashi).*

וּבַעֲלֵי חוֹב בָּאִים וְנִפְרָעִים. — *and the creditors come and receive payment.*
They receive payment from his share of the estate. Although he benefits by the fact that his debt is paid, the Mishnah [*Nedarim* 4:2] states that one may pay a debt for another who is forbidden by a *neder* to benefit from him *(Rav).* Rav *(Nedarim* ad loc.) explains that the one who pays the debt is merely preventing the creditor from demanding his money.

[As elucidated in the commentary to ArtScroll *Nedarim* (ibid.), there is no doubt that having one's debt paid for him is a great benefit. However, this benefit did not come to the debtor directly from the one who paid the debt, since the latter dealt solely with the creditor. Thus, as great as the benefit may be, it is only an indirect one. The only question is whether an indirect benefit is included in a *neder* forbidding benefit *(Rashba, Meiri* ibid.). The Gemara *(Nedarim* 33a) demonstrates that this issue is the subject of a debate in *Kesubos* 13:2, in which one opinion maintains that to eliminate a claim on someone is not the same as directly benefiting him. *Rav's* comment, cited above, follows this view. His other explanation, quoted below, is in accordance with the opinion that the removal of a claim on someone is equivalent to directly benefiting him.]

Some qualify the mishnah as referring only to a debt regarding which the borrower had stipulated that he would not demand repayment; the debtor would pay only if he wished to. Therefore, when a third person, on his own initiative, pays the creditor, he has not removed any claim from the debtor, since there had been no real claim on him, and he has not given him any benefit *(Rav* ibid.). According to this view, our mishnah, too, would be qualified as referring only to a loan which the debtor need not pay.

Another possibility is that this qualification applies only to the mishnah in *Nedarim,* not ours, because the two cases are different. Regarding the case in *Nedarim* — assuming that no stipulation had been made — since the debtor would be liable to reimburse one who pays his debt for him, paying the debt is considered benefit. In our case, however, the fact that the creditor collects his debt from the estate is not considered a benefit to the debtor from the estate.

The mishnah's plan is a suggestion for after the father's death. To be sure, it is feasible during his lifetime, as well, similar to the instance discussed in *Nedarim* 5:6. However, in this case, since the father does not want his son to benefit from his property in any manner whatsoever during his lifetime, such a plan must have his consent *(Tos. Yom Tov* from *Tos.).*

11.

Because a proselyte, by converting, has severed his consanguinity with his relatives, if he dies and leaves no heirs — i.e., children born after the conversion[1] — his property becomes ownerless. This mishnah deals with one who robbed such a proselyte and discusses how he can fulfill the precept of returning stolen property.

---

1. See footnote to 5:4, s.v. פָּטוּר.

בבא קמא ט/יא

[יא] **הַגּוֹזֵל** אֶת־הַגֵּר וְנִשְׁבַּע לוֹ, וָמֵת, הֲרֵי זֶה מְשַׁלֵּם קֶרֶן וְחֹמֶשׁ לַכֹּהֲנִים וְאָשָׁם לַמִּזְבֵּחַ, שֶׁנֶּאֱמַר: "וְאִם אֵין לָאִישׁ גֹּאֵל לְהָשִׁיב הָאָשָׁם אֵלָיו הָאָשָׁם הַמּוּשָׁב לַה' לַכֹּהֵן מִלְּבַד אֵיל הַכִּפֻּרִים אֲשֶׁר יְכַפֶּר־בּוֹ עָלָיו."
הָיָה מַעֲלֶה אֶת־הַכֶּסֶף וְאֶת־הָאָשָׁם, וָמֵת, הַכֶּסֶף יִנָּתֵן לְבָנָיו, וְהָאָשָׁם יִרְעֶה עַד שֶׁיִּסְתָּאֵב; וְיִמָּכֵר, וְיִפְּלוּ דָמָיו לִנְדָבָה.

יד אברהם

הַגּוֹזֵל אֶת־הַגֵּר — *[If] one robs a proselyte*
That is, a proselyte who has no heirs, having had no children born to him after his conversion (*Rambam Commentary; Meiri*).

וְנִשְׁבַּע לוֹ, — *and swears to him,*
[He swears falsely that he did not rob him.]

וָמֵת, — *and he dies,*
[The proselyte dies.]

הֲרֵי זֶה מְשַׁלֵּם קֶרֶן וְחֹמֶשׁ לַכֹּהֲנִים — *he pays the principal and a fifth to the Kohanim*
[I.e., the Kohanim serving in the Temple during that week [see preface to next mishnah] (*Meiri from Gem. 109b*).

וְאָשָׁם לַמִּזְבֵּחַ, — *and a guilt-offering to the Altar,*
His sin is thereby expiated. If he has not sworn, he may keep the stolen article, since the property of a proselyte who dies without heirs is ownerless, and since it is in the robber's possession, he has already acquired it (*Meiri*).

שֶׁנֶּאֱמַר: "וְאִם אֵין לָאִישׁ גֹּאֵל לְהָשִׁיב הָאָשָׁם אֵלָיו — *as it is said (Numbers 5:8):* 'But if the man has no kinsman to whom to return [the restitution for] the guilt'
The verse cannot be referring to ordinary Jews, since each of them has some kin related to him through a common ancestor, as far back — if need be — as our forefather Jacob. Obviously, then, the subject here is a proselyte who died heirless (*Rav from Sanhedrin 69b*).

הָאָשָׁם הַמּוּשָׁב לַה' לַכֹּהֵן — *[the restitution for] the guilt which is returned to* HASHEM *[goes] to the Kohen*
The *Gemara* (110a) interprets הָאָשָׁם, *[the restitution for] the guilt,* as referring to the principal, and הַמּוּשָׁב, *which is returned,* to the fifth. Scripture uses the term אָשָׁם to denote that the stolen item must be returned by day just as the אָשָׁם, *guilt-offering,* is brought during the day. Should the robber return the object at night, he has not fulfilled his obligation (*Tos. Yom Tov from Gem.* 110a; see *Rambam, Hil. Gezeilah* 8:6).

מִלְּבַד אֵיל הַכִּפֻּרִים אֲשֶׁר יְכַפֶּר־בּוֹ עָלָיו." — *besides the ram of the atonements with which he shall atone for him.'*
Since this refers to the guilt-offering which the thief must bring, the term הָאָשָׁם, mentioned earlier in the verse, must refer to the principal, as discussed above (*ibid.*).

הָיָה מַעֲלֶה אֶת־הַכֶּסֶף וְאֶת־הָאָשָׁם, — *[If] he was bringing up the money and the guilt-offering,*
The one who robbed the proselyte was bringing the principal, the fifth, and the guilt-offering to the Temple (*Meiri*).

משניות / בבא קמא — פרק ט: הגוזל עצים [214]

9
11

11. [If] one robs a proselyte and swears to him, and he dies, he pays the principal and a fifth to the *Kohanim* and a guilt-offering to the Altar, as it is said (*Numbers* 5:8): *But if the man has no kinsman to whom to return* [*the restitution for*] *the guilt,* [*the restitution for*] *the guilt which is returned to* HASHEM [*goes*] *to the Kohen, besides the ram of the atonements, with which he shall atone for him.*

[If] he was bringing up the money and the guilt-offering, and he died, the money shall be given to his sons, and the guilt-offering shall graze until it develops a blemish; it is then sold, and its money is placed in the donative-offering [chest].

YAD AVRAHAM

וָמֵת, — *and he died,*
The robber died on the way (*Rav; Rashi*).

הַכֶּסֶף — *the money*
This refers both to the principal and the fifth (*Meiri*).

יִנָּתֵן לְבָנָיו, — *shall be given to his sons,*
That is, to the robber's sons, since he had already acquired it upon the proselyte's death. He was required to bring it to the Temple and give it to the *Kohanim* as an atonement for his false oath, but now, since he is dead, no atonement is possible (*Rav; Rashi*).

וְהָאָשָׁם — *and the guilt-offering*
[I.e., the ram he had designated as a guilt-offering.]

יִרְעֶה עַד שֶׁיִּסְתָּאֵב; — *shall graze until it develops a blemish;*
This is the halachah of any guilt-offering whose owner dies; it must be kept on the pasture until it develops a blemish and can be redeemed [*Terumah* 3:3]. If, however, the owner of a חַטָּאת, *sin-offering,* dies, the animal is left to die (*Rav, Rashi* from *Gem.* 110b).

[Only upon suffering a blemish that would disqualify it as an offering may the animal designated as a guilt-offering be redeemed, but not prior to then, notwithstanding that, as in our case, the animal may not be brought as an offering because its owner has died.]

וְיִמָּכֵר, — *it is then sold,*
[The sale serves as a redemption, by means of which the animal reverts to the status of unconsecrated property, and the money given for it assumes its former sanctity. In this case, the money has the designation of a נְדָבָה, *donative offering.*]

וְיִפְּלוּ דָמָיו לִנְדָבָה. — *and its money is placed in the donative-offering* [*chest*].
The money is deposited in the chest in the Temple marked נְדָבָה, *donative offering* [see *Shekalim* 6:5 and ArtScroll commentary there], which was used for general contributions to purchase burnt-offerings for times when the Altar was unoccupied (*Rav; Rambam Commentary; Meiri; Rashi*).
The flesh of these animals was brought up on the Altar, and the hide given to the *Kohanim* (*Rashi*).

בבא קמא ט/יב

[יב] **נָתַן** אֶת־הַכֶּסֶף לְאַנְשֵׁי מִשְׁמָר, וָמֵת, אֵין הַיּוֹרְשִׁים יְכוֹלִין לְהוֹצִיא מִיָּדָם, שֶׁנֶּאֱמַר: "אִישׁ אֲשֶׁר יִתֵּן לַכֹּהֵן לוֹ יִהְיֶה." נָתַן הַכֶּסֶף לִיהוֹיָרִיב וְאָשָׁם לִידַעְיָה, יָצָא. אָשָׁם לִיהוֹיָרִיב וְכֶסֶף לִידַעְיָה — אִם קַיָּם הָאָשָׁם, יַקְרִיבוּהוּ בְּנֵי יְדַעְיָה; וְאִם לֹא, יַחֲזוֹר וְיָבִיא

יד אברהם

12.

⊷ מִשְׁמָרוֹת / **Mishmaros**

The *Kohanim* involved in the Temple service were divided into twenty-four extended families known as מִשְׁמָרוֹת, *mishmaros* (watches; sing. *mishmar*) each of which served for one week at a time on a rotating basis. The *Gemara* (*Taanis* 27a) tells us that King David and Samuel the Prophet divided the *Kohanim* and the Levites into these twenty-four groups. The *Kohanim* of the *mishmar* were privileged to offer all the sacrifices during that week and receive the parts due the *Kohanim*. Hence, they were entitled also to the principal and the fifth of what was robbed of the proselyte.

נָתַן אֶת־הַכֶּסֶף לְאַנְשֵׁי מִשְׁמָר — [If] he gave the money to the Kohanim of the watch,

The one who robbed the proselyte gave the principal and the fifth to be shared among the *Kohanim* serving in the Temple during that week (*Tif. Yis.*).

וָמֵת, — and he died,

The robber died before he was able to bring the guilt-offering (*Rav*).

אֵין הַיּוֹרְשִׁים יְכוֹלִין לְהוֹצִיא מִיָּדָם — the heirs cannot exact it from them,

The robber's heirs cannot compel the *Kohanim* to return the money given them, because the latter have already acquired it (*Rav*).

The *Gemara* (110b) explains that the money given to the *Kohanim* atones for half the robber's sin, while the guilt-offering atones for the other half. Therefore, we do not say that had the robber known that he would not live to bring the guilt-offering, he would also not have given the money to the *Kohanim* — in which case the heirs would indeed be able to exact it from them. Rather, since the money atones for half the sin, the robber's intention in giving it has been fulfilled (*Tos. Yom Tov*).

שֶׁנֶּאֱמַר: "אִישׁ אֲשֶׁר יִתֵּן לַכֹּהֵן לוֹ יִהְיֶה." — as it is said (Numbers 5:10): 'A man who gives to the Kohen — it shall be his.'

The apparent meaning of the verse is that once the money is given to the *Kohen*, it is his and cannot be taken away. Yet, in view of the *Gemara's* evidence that the money atones for half the sin, thereby fulfilling the intention of the robber, as discussed above, it is difficult to understand why the verse is necessary to teach us this law.

Tos. Yom Tov — according to *Shoshannim LeDavid's* interpretation — explains that it is the verse, in fact, which teaches us that the money atones for half the sin. Otherwise, we would think that there is no atonement at all until the robber brings the guilt-offering. *Beis David*, however, construes *Tos. Yom Tov* as meaning that the verse is an אַסְמַכְתָּא, a *Scriptural basis for a law*, and that the mishnah does not mean literally that the verse is its proof. [See *Rav*.]

משניות / בבא קמא — פרק ט: הגוזל עצים [216]

12. [If] he gave the money to the *Kohanim* of the watch, and he died, the heirs cannot exact it from them, as it is said *(Numbers 5:10): A man who gives to the Kohen — it shall be his.*

[If] he gives the money to Yehoyariv and the guilt-offering to Yedayah, he has fulfilled his obligation.

[If he gives] the guilt offering to Yehoyariv and the money to Yedayah — if the guilt-offering exists, the sons of Yedayah shall offer it; if not, he must bring

YAD AVRAHAM

◈§ Ideally, the robber should give the principal, the fifth, and the guilt-offering to the *Kohanim* of the same watch *(Sifrei Zuta, Num. 5:8; Bamidbar Rabbah, Midrash Hagadol* ibid.). Should he give them to *Kohanim* of different watches, however, he has discharged his obligation only in some instances. The mishnah now discusses the various cases, using the first two *mishmaros* that served in the Temple as examples. The first was the family of Yehoyariv; the second, that of Yedayah.

נָתַן הַכֶּסֶף לִיהוֹיָרִיב — [If] *he gives the money to Yehoyariv*

The robber gives the principal and the fifth to the family of Yehoyariv during their watch. As mentioned above, Yehoyariv was the first *mishmar* (Rav; Rashi).

וְאָשָׁם לִידַעְיָה, — *and the guilt-offering to Yedayah,*

He gives the guilt-offering to the family of Yedayah, the second *mishmar,* during their watch (Rav; Rashi).

יָצָא. — *he has fulfilled his obligation.*

[As mentioned above, the robber ideally should give both the principal and the fifth, as well as the guilt-offering to one *mishmar* of *Kohanim*.] However, as the mishnah states further, if he gives what he stole to one *mishmar* and his guilt-offering to a subsequent one, he has nevertheless discharged his obligation. In this case, the family of Yehoyariv rightfully acquires the money, and the family of Yedayah, the guilt-offering (ibid.).

According to *Chiddushei HaRavad,* this is so only if the guilt-offering has not yet been designated when he gives the money to the family of Yehoyariv. If it has already been designated, however,

he must bring the guilt-offering during Yehoyariv's watch.

אָשָׁם לִיהוֹיָרִיב וְכֶסֶף לִידַעְיָה — [If *he gives*] *the guilt-offering to Yehoyariv and the money to Yedayah —*

The robber first gave the guilt-offering to the family of Yehoyariv during their watch, and subsequently, the money to the family of Yedayah during their watch (Rav).

אִם קַיָּם הָאָשָׁם, — *if the guilt-offering exists,*

The family of Yehoyariv did not yet sacrifice it (ibid.).

יַקְרִיבוּהוּ בְּנֵי יְדַעְיָה; — *the sons of Yedayah shall offer it;*

Since the sons of Yehoyariv accepted the guilt-offering out of the proper sequence, we penalize them and give it to the sons of Yedayah, who committed no wrong by accepting the money. In such an instance both the money and the guilt-offering belong to the sons of Yedayah (Rav; Rashi).

וְאִם לֹא, — *if not,*

[That is, the guilt-offering no longer exists because the sons of Yehoyariv have already sacrificed it.]

יַחֲזֹר וְיָבִיא אָשָׁם אַחֵר. — *he must bring*

בבא קמא י/א

אָשָׁם אַחֵר, שֶׁהַמֵּבִיא גְזֵלוֹ עַד שֶׁלֹּא הֵבִיא אֲשָׁמוֹ יָצָא, הֵבִיא אֲשָׁמוֹ עַד שֶׁלֹּא הֵבִיא גְזֵלוֹ לֹא יָצָא. נָתַן אֶת־הַקֶּרֶן, וְלֹא נָתַן אֶת־הַחֹמֶשׁ, אֵין הַחֹמֶשׁ מְעַכֵּב.

[א] **הַגּוֹזֵל** וּמַאֲכִיל אֶת־בָּנָיו, וְהִנִּיחַ לִפְנֵיהֶם, פְּטוּרִין מִלְּשַׁלֵּם; וְאִם הָיָה דָּבָר

יד אברהם

another guilt-offering,

Since the robber brought the guilt-offering before giving the money, it is disqualified, as explained below. Therefore, he must bring another one (Rav).

שֶׁהַמֵּבִיא גְזֵלוֹ עַד שֶׁלֹּא הֵבִיא אֲשָׁמוֹ — for one who brings what he stole before he brings his guilt-offering

[He gives the Kohanim the amount he stole before he brings his guilt-offering.]

יָצָא, — has fulfilled [his obligation,

[The expression יָצָא, has fulfilled, connotes a post facto situation — i.e., although this is not the optimum method, if he has already done so, it is acceptable. The term seems incongruous with our case, however, since what he did is the proper procedure — to give the Kohanim the money and then to sacrifice the guilt-offering.

Perhaps the implication is that, although it is proper to give the guilt-offering to the same *mishmar* which received the money, as mentioned above, as long as he gives the money first, he discharges his obligation notwithstanding that he gives the guilt-offering to the following *mishmar*. This appears to be the intention of *Sifrei*.]

הֵבִיא אֲשָׁמוֹ עַד שֶׁלֹּא הֵבִיא גְזֵלוֹ — but] one who brings his guilt-offering before he brings what he stole

[And the offering has already been sacrificed.]

לֹא יָצָא. — has not fulfilled [his obligation].

The *Gemara* (111a) derives this from *Numbers* 5:8: [*The restitution for*] *the guilt which is returned to* HASHEM [*goes*] *to the Kohen, besides the ram of the atonements, with which he shall atone for him.* The future tense of the expression *shall atone* is construed to mean that he must pay the restitution before the atonement has been made with the ram (*Tos. Yom Tov*).

The same ruling applies to one who robs any Jew and pays him the principal and the fifth: he must pay at least the principal before sacrificing the guilt-offering (*Rambam, Hil. Gezeilah* 8:13). Indeed, *Rabbeinu Yonah* (*Shaarei Teshuvah* 4:18) cites this mishnah in conjunction with repentance for sins committed against one's fellow.

נָתַן אֶת־הַקֶּרֶן, — [If] he gave the principal,

The robber gave the principal amount of the theft to the Kohanim (*Rav*; *Rashi*).

וְלֹא נָתַן אֶת־הַחֹמֶשׁ, — but did not give the fifth,

[He now wishes to bring his guilt-offering before paying the fifth.]

אֵין הַחֹמֶשׁ מְעַכֵּב. — the fifth does not prevent [atonement].

The fact that he did not yet give the fifth does not prevent him from sacrificing his guilt-offering; however, he must pay the fifth later (ibid. *Rambam, Hil. Gezeilah* 8:13).

Tos. Yom Tov explains that the atonement is complete even without

[218] משניות / בבא קמא — פרק י: הגוזל ומאכיל

another guilt-offering, for one who brings what he stole before he brings his guilt-offering has fulfilled [his obligation, but] one who brings his guilt-offering before he brings what he stole has not fulfilled [his obligation].

[If] he gave the principal, but did not give the fifth, the fifth does not prevent [atonement].

1. [If] one stole [something] and gave [it] to his children to eat, or left [it] to them, they are exempt from paying; but if there was something

YAD AVRAHAM

paying the fifth; the latter remains merely as an obligation.

Lechem Shamayim disagrees, maintaining that, although the robber may bring his guilt-offering before paying the fifth, the atonement is pending until the fifth is paid. Alternatively, the atonement is only a partial one until he pays the fifth.

Tos. Yom Tov and *Lechem Shamayim* differ only in the interpretation of *Rav* and *Rashi*. Both agree, however, that *Rambam* considers the payment of the fifth as a debt that does not prevent the atonement at all (*Shoshannim LeDavid*).

Chapter 10

1.

The following mishnah deals with one who steals something and gives it to his children to eat, or leaves it to them as an inheritance and they consume it. It also discusses persons who are suspected of theft, and that it is prohibited to take money from them for fear that it is stolen.

הַגּוֹזֵל וּמַאֲכִיל אֶת־בָּנָיו, — [If] one stole [something] and gave [it] to his children to eat,

He gave it to them to eat, and he then died. The same would apply if he had given it to others prior to his death (*Tif. Yis.*).

וְהִנִּיחַ לִפְנֵיהֶם, — or left [it] to them,

When he died, the stolen article still existed [and fell to them as an inheritance] (*Rav; Rashi*).

This may also mean that he left over chattels, in which case the mishnah would be teaching us that movable property left to heirs are not pledged to the father's creditors (*Tif. Yis.*).

פְּטוּרִין מִלְשַׁלֵּם; — they are exempt from paying;

[The children need not pay back the one whom their father robbed.]

That is, if they consumed the stolen item even after their father's death, and the father had left them only chattels, they are exempt from paying, since they did not commit the crime, and movable property that was sold or was left to heirs is not mortgaged to creditors. Should the stolen article be extant, however, they are obligated to return it (*Rav from Gemara* 112b).

This is based on Rava's view in the *Gemara* that the possession of an heir is unlike the possession of a purchaser.

[219] THE MISHNAH/BAVA KAMMA – Chapter Ten: *HaGozeil U'Maachil*

בבא קמא י/א

שֶׁיֶּשׁ־בּוֹ אַחֲרָיוּת, חַיָּבִין לְשַׁלֵּם.
אֵין פּוֹרְטִין לֹא מִתֵּבַת הַמּוֹכְסִין וְלֹא מִכִּיס שֶׁל־

יד אברהם

Rava's intention is that if the robber sells the stolen article after the owner has despaired of retrieving it, the purchaser may keep it by dint of the owner's despair and the change of possession. An heir inheriting the item, however, is not considered a change of possession, but a transfer of the father's possession; therefore, the heirs must return the article if it still exists. Should it have been changed, they need not return it, just as their father would have been permitted to keep the article had it been changed, because he would have acquired it, as explained in chapter 9 [see preface ad loc.] *(Tos. Yom Tov).*

וְאִם הָיָה דָבָר שֶׁיֶּשׁ־בּוֹ אַחֲרָיוּת, — *but if there was something which can have a lien on it,*

That is, the robber left real estate to his heirs. The following applies even if the stolen article no longer exists *(Rav from Gem. 111b).*

חַיָּבִין לְשַׁלֵּם. — *they are obligated to pay.*

[The heirs must return the article — or if it no longer exists — pay its value to the one who was robbed.]

Since the robber left over real estate, which is mortgaged toward his debts, the heirs are liable to pay.

In practical application, however, if one robbed something and gave it to his children to eat — whether they consumed it prior to the owner's despairing of retrieving it, or sometime thereafter — and the robber died, they are liable to pay from his estate, regardless of whether he had left real property or chattels. This is because, nowadays, as a result of an enactment of the *Geonim* [6th-11th cent.] chattels are indeed mortgaged to paying back debts, including even the reimbursement of those whom one had robbed, which has the status of a debt not committed to writing, and, consequently, had not been collectable from heirs according to Talmudic law.[1]

In the event that the robber died, leaving no property to his children, and they had already consumed the stolen article, it depends when they had done so. If they had consumed it before the owner despaired of retrieving it, they are liable; if after that time, they are exempt.

This is derived from the phrase [*Lev.* 5:23], אֲשֶׁר גָּזָל, *that he robbed,* which is interpreted by the Gemara (112a) as meaning that the stolen article must be returned if it is still as it was when it had been robbed; if it no longer exists, however, it need not be returned. This cannot possibly refer to the robber himself, since he is certainly obligated to make restitution for the stolen article even if it is no longer extant, as explained in 9:1. Rather, the verse must mean that the robber's heirs are liable only if the article still exists; should it have been consumed, they are exempt. However, it is unlikely that this applies before the owner despairs of retrieving his article, since then it is still considered to be in his possession, and it is as if the heirs themselves had stolen the article and consumed it.

Although the *Gemara* (66a) derives from this phrase that a robber acquires ownership of a stolen article if it has been changed, we must perforce say that the phrase teaches us both laws. *Tosafos,* however, explain that the derivation of the *Gemara* in 111b is merely an אַסְמַכְתָּא, *a Scriptural basis for*

---

1. Although our mishnah rules that if the robber left over real estate, his heirs must reimburse the one who was robbed, this is because the latter, prior to his death, had already brought his claim to court, which gives the money in question the status of a debt which has been committed to writing *(Tos.* 111b, s.v. ואם).

משניות / בבא קמא — פרק י: הגוזל ומאכיל [220]

10
1

which can have a lien on it, they are obligated to pay. We may not change money from the customs collectors' box or from the tax collectors' purse, nor

YAD AVRAHAM

a law, and not an actual proof *(Rav; Tos. Yom Tov; Rambam, Commentary* and *Hil. Gezeilah* 4:6).

אֵין פּוֹרְטִין — *We may not change money*
That is, one may not change *selas* for *perutos (Rav; Rashi)* [or any large coins into small coins] from the sources listed below, since he benefits from money suspected of being stolen *(Rashi).* However, one may change a *sela* for a *sela* [probably meaning two shekels for a *sela,* making it more difficult for him to obtain smaller change later on *(Shoshannim LeDavid)*], since he does not benefit from the exchange *(Tos. Yom Tov).*

If one must give half a dinar toward one of these collections, and he does not have the exact change, he may give him a dinar and receive half a dinar in return, since a person takes change only so that he should not suffer a loss, and it is not considered a benefit *(Rav, Rashi* from *Gem.* 113a).

Tos. Yom Tov contends that he may even give a dinar with the intention of obtaining the small change. *Beis David* challenges *Tos. Yom Tov's* comment, since the *Gemara* (ibid.) states only that he may take back small change, although he incidentally benefits from it, but nowhere do we find that one may do so intentionally in order to obtain small change.

לֹא מִתֵּבַת הַמּוֹכְסִין — *from the customs collectors' box*
That is, from the box into which the money collected for customs is deposited *(Rav; Rashi).*

וְלֹא מִכִּיס שֶׁל־גַּבָּאִין — *or from the tax collector's purse,*
This refers to those appointed by the king to collect the head tax and the produce tax.

We may not take money from these boxes or purses because it is suspected of being stolen. From the *Gemara* [loc. cit.] it appears that a person would pay the king for the privilege of collecting the customs, and then the money he would collect would be his own. The tax collector, on the other hand, was appointed by the king to collect the taxes for him.

In either case, if the collector takes only what he is entitled to, his profession is perfectly legal, and there is no robbery or theft involved in it. This is based on the Talmudic maxim דִּינָא דְּמַלְכוּתָא דִּינָא, *the law of the land is binding according to Jewish law.* The mishnah, which considers these individuals suspect of stealing, deals with a gentile customs collector, who we assume is collecting excessive taxes; a Jewish customs collector known to do so; or any customs collector not authorized by the king. The same applies to the tax collectors. As long as they take nothing for themselves and collect only what the king instructs them to, we may exchange money from their boxes and purses. On the contrary, one may not avoid paying fair taxes levied by the king *(Rav; Rashi* to *Gem.* 113a; *Rambam, Hil. Gezeilah* 5:11f.).

Although benefiting from the collections of these individuals is legally permissible, since the taxpayers despair of recovering their money, and now that the money is being transferred into the possession of a third party, the latter acquires it through the combination of the owner's despair and the transfer of possession, the Rabbis nevertheless prohibited doing so. They deemed it unseemly to benefit from money obviously derived from robbing the people *(Tos. Yom Tov* from *Rosh; Tos.).*

[221]   THE MISHNAH/BAVA KAMMA — Chapter Ten: *HaGozeil U'Maachil*

בבא קמא י/ב

גַּבָּאִין, וְאֵין נוֹטְלִין מֵהֶם צְדָקָה. אֲבָל נוֹטֵל הוּא מִתּוֹךְ בֵּיתוֹ אוֹ מִן־הַשּׁוּק.

[ב] **נָטְלוּ** מוֹכְסִין אֶת־חֲמוֹרוֹ וְנָתְנוּ לוֹ חֲמוֹר אַחֵר, גָּזְלוּ לִסְטִים אֶת־כְּסוּתוֹ וְנָתְנוּ לוֹ כְּסוּת אַחֶרֶת, הֲרֵי אֵלּוּ שֶׁלּוֹ, מִפְּנֵי שֶׁהַבְּעָלִים מִתְיָאֲשִׁין מֵהֶן.

הַמַּצִּיל מִן־הַנָּהָר, אוֹ מִן־הַגַּיִס, אוֹ מִן־הַלִּסְטִים — אִם נִתְיָאֲשׁוּ הַבְּעָלִים, הֲרֵי אֵלּוּ שֶׁלּוֹ. וְכֵן, נְחִיל שֶׁל־דְּבוֹרִים — אִם נִתְיָאֲשׁוּ הַבְּעָלִים,

יד אברהם

וְאֵין נוֹטְלִין מֵהֶם צְדָקָה — *nor may we accept charity from them.*

[We may not accept charity from their boxes or purses for the above reason.] Moreover, by accepting charity from these sources, we encourage the collectors to continue sinning, for they feel that their charity atones for their wrongdoings *(Meiri).*

אֲבָל נוֹטֵל הוּא — *One may, however, accept*

[He may accept money for change or for charity.]

מִתּוֹךְ בֵּיתוֹ — *from his house*

That is, from the money the collector has in his house, which is not from his collection, but from his private business *(Shitah Mekubetzes quoting Rabbeinu Yehonasan).*

אוֹ מִן־הַשּׁוּק. — *or from the street.*

That is, if the customs collector or the tax collector is standing in the street and he gives someone charity or change from his pocket, the latter may accept it and need not fear that it was taken from the tax collection, since the collectors always deposit their tax money in the box or purse designated for that purpose, lest they be detected by the king *(ibid.).*

2.

The following mishnah is a continuation of the preceding one. It delineates how one may benefit from property given him by a customs collector.

נָטְלוּ מוֹכְסִין אֶת־חֲמוֹרוֹ וְנָתְנוּ לוֹ חֲמוֹר אַחֵר, — [*If*] *the customs collectors took his donkey and gave him another donkey,*

After seizing his donkey, they, out of pity, gave him one inferior to his which is obviously the property of another of their victims *(Meiri).*

The *Tanna* chooses the case of the customs collectors taking a donkey, a pack animal, because when they make a false accusation that one has not paid duty on his load, they confiscate the entire load with the donkey that is carrying it *(Lechem Shamayim).*

גָּזְלוּ לִסְטִים אֶת־כְּסוּתוֹ וְנָתְנוּ לוֹ כְּסוּת אַחֶרֶת, — [*or if*] *robbers stole his clothing and gave him other clothing,*

[Similar to the previous case, the robbers, out of compassion, gave him clothing inferior to his own that obviously belonged to one of their other victims.]

משניות / בבא קמא — פרק י: הגוזל ומאכיל [222]

10
2

may we accept charity from them. One may, however, accept from his house or from the street.

2. [If] the customs collectors took his donkey and gave him another donkey, [or if] robbers stole his clothing and gave him other clothing, they are his, since the owners despair of them.

One who rescues from a river, from a troop, or from robbers — if the owners have despaired [of them], they are his.

Likewise, a swarm of bees — if the owners have

YAD AVRAHAM

Instead of searching to see what their victims have in their clothes, robbers quickly snatch the clothes themselves and do not tarry (ibid.).

הֲרֵי אֵלּוּ שֶׁלּוֹ, מִפְּנֵי שֶׁהַבְּעָלִים מִתְיָאֲשִׁין מֵהֶן. — *they are his, since the owners despair of them.*

We assume that the owners despaired of ever retrieving their donkey or clothing. Therefore, when this second victim receives them, it constitutes a change of possession, and he acquires them for himself *(Rav)*. Since we assume that the owners despaired prior to the change of possession, it is a valid acquisition *(Tos. Yom Tov)*.

הַמַּצִּיל מִן הַנָּהָר, — *One who rescues from a river,*

[He takes things from a river that overflowed its banks and washed away someone's belongings.]

אוֹ מִן־הַגַּיִס, — *from a troop,*

That is, an army at war *(Tif. Yis.)*.

אוֹ מִן־הַלִּסְטִים — — *or from robbers —*

[He took from robbers who robbed another person.]

אִם נִתְיָאֲשׁוּ הַבְּעָלִים, הֲרֵי אֵלּוּ שֶׁלּוֹ. — *if the owners have despaired [of them], they are his.*

That is, only if the owner was heard lamenting the loss he sustained, implying that he has given up hope of ever retrieving it, may the finder keep it.

Ordinarily, however, it is not assumed that the owner despairs of recovering his property.

To reconcile the apparent contradiction between this statement and the first part of the mishnah, which states clearly that one despairs of recovering his property from a robber, the *Gemara* differentiates between a Jewish robber and a gentile one: if one is robbed by a Jew, he despairs of recovering the stolen goods, because in order to exact payment from the robber, he must summon him to a Jewish court, where only qualified witnesses are acceptable; if he has no qualified witnesses, he has no hope of recovering what the robber took from him. On the other hand, if one is robbed by a gentile, he summons him to a gentile court, where they accept circumstantial evidence, and it is much easier to recover the stolen property. Therefore, unless we hear the victim of the robbery state expressly that he has despaired of recovering his loss we do not assume that he has done so *(Rav, Rashi from Gem. 114a)*.

וְכֵן, נְחִיל שֶׁל־דְּבוֹרִים — — *Likewise, a swarm of bees —*

This expression stems from the word נַחַל, *stream,* since the bees flow like a stream one after the other, to the place where their queen flies. In this case, the swarm left another person's beehive and came in to his property *(Tif. Yis.)*.

[223]   THE MISHNAH/BAVA KAMMA — Chapter Ten: *HaGozeil U'Maachil*

בבא קמא י/ג

הֲרֵי אֵלּוּ שֶׁלּוֹ. אָמַר רַבִּי יוֹחָנָן בֶּן־בְּרוֹקָה: נֶאֱמֶנֶת אִשָּׁה אוֹ קָטָן לוֹמַר: ,,מִכָּאן יָצָא נְחִיל זֶה.'' וּמְהַלֵּךְ בְּתוֹךְ שְׂדֵה חֲבֵרוֹ לְהַצִּיל אֶת־נְחִילוֹ. וְאִם הִזִּיק, מְשַׁלֵּם מַה־שֶּׁהִזִּיק; אֲבָל לֹא יָקֹץ אֶת־שׂוֹכוֹ עַל־מְנָת לִתֵּן אֶת־הַדָּמִים. רַבִּי יִשְׁמָעֵאל, בְּנוֹ שֶׁל־רַבִּי יוֹחָנָן בֶּן־בְּרוֹקָה, אוֹמֵר: אַף קוֹצֵץ וְנוֹתֵן אֶת־הַדָּמִים.

[ג] **הַמַּכִּיר** כֵּלָיו וּסְפָרָיו בְּיַד אַחֵר, וְיָצָא לוֹ שֵׁם גְּנֵבָה בָּעִיר, יִשָּׁבַע לוֹ הַלּוֹקֵחַ

יד אברהם

אִם נִתְיָאֲשׁוּ הַבְּעָלִים, הֲרֵי אֵלּוּ שֶׁלּוֹ — *if the owners have despaired [of them], they are his.*

He may keep the bees only if the owner has despaired of recovering them (*Tos. Yom Tov* from *Gem.*).

According to Biblical law, bees — unlike chicken, geese, etc. — are ownerless and cannot be acquired by the fact that they are in one's property, since they do not always stay in his beehive and sometimes even leave his yard. However [to avoid disputes regarding bees (*Rashi*)], the Rabbis instituted that one acquires bees that nest in his beehive. The mishnah is telling us that, although a person owns the bees based only on this Rabbinical enactment, even if they left his property and entered that of another, we do not assume that he had despaired of retrieving them, therefore, no other person may take it unless he knows definitely that the first owner did indeed despair (*Tif. Yis.*, based on *Gem.* 114b; *Rambam, Hil. Gezeilah* 6:14 and *Tos. Yom Tov*).

אָמַר רַבִּי יוֹחָנָן בֶּן־בְּרוֹקָה: נֶאֱמֶנֶת אִשָּׁה אוֹ קָטָן לוֹמַר: ,,מִכָּאן יָצָא נְחִיל זֶה.'' — *Said R' Yochanan ben Berokah: A woman or a minor is believed to say: 'This swarm came out of here.'*

As a rule, women and minors are not accepted as witnesses (*Gem.* 114b). However, in this case, should the owner be seen pursuing the bees [which proves that he has not despaired of retrieving them], and a woman or a minor says innocently, 'This swarm came out of here,' since the ownership of bees is based only on a Rabbinical enactment as explained above, the Rabbis accepted the testimony of the woman or the minor (*Tos. Yom Tov* from *Gem.* 114b).

Therefore, the owner of the field the bees entered is obligated to return them to their owner (*Meiri*).

וּמְהַלֵּךְ בְּתוֹךְ שְׂדֵה חֲבֵרוֹ לְהַצִּיל אֶת־נְחִילוֹ. — *And one may go into another's field to save his swarm.*

He may do so, although he is aware that he will damage the vegetables and grain growing in the field (ibid.)

וְאִם הִזִּיק, מְשַׁלֵּם מַה־שֶּׁהִזִּיק; — *If he inflicted damage, he must pay for what he damaged;*

If, indeed, he damaged the vegetation growing in the field, he must pay for it (ibid.).

אֲבָל לֹא יָקֹץ אֶת־שׂוֹכוֹ עַל־מְנָת לִתֵּן אֶת־הַדָּמִים. — *but he may not cut off his branch with the intention of making restitution.*

If the bees have alighted on a branch

משניות / בבא קמא — פרק י — הגוזל ומאכיל [224]

10
3

despaired [of them], they are his. Said R' Yochanan ben Berokah: A woman or a minor is believed to say: 'This swarm came out of here.' And one may go into another's field to save his swarm. If he inflicted damage, he must pay for what he damaged; but he may not cut off his branch with the intention of making restitution. R' Yishmael, the son of R' Yochanan ben Berokah, says: He may even cut [it] off and make restitution.

3. [If] one recognizes his utensils or his books in another's possession, and a report of theft had gone forth in the city concerning him, the purchaser

YAD AVRAHAM

of a tree belonging to another person, although he fears that if he takes them one by one, the others will fly away, he may not cut off the branch to take them all at once even if he intends to pay for the damage, since this constitutes a permanent damage to the tree *(Rav; Meiri).*

רַבִּי יִשְׁמָעֵאל, בְּנוֹ שֶׁל־רַבִּי יוֹחָנָן בֶּן־בְּרוֹקָה, אוֹמֵר: אַף קוֹצֵץ וְנוֹתֵן אֶת־הַדָּמִים. — *R' Yishmael, the son of R' Yochanan ben Berokah, says: He may even cut [it] off and make restitution.*

R' Yishmael disagrees with his father, maintaining that this is one of the conditions limiting private property rights with which Joshua divided the land *(Tos. Yom Tov from Gem.* 114b).

Rosh accepts R' Yishmael's view as the halachah, while *Rif, Rambam* [*Commentary* and *Hil. Gezeilah* 6:14], *Ramah,* and *Rav* reject it *(Tur Choshen Mishpat* 270).

3.

הַמַּכִּיר כֵּלָיו וּסְפָרָיו בְּיַד אַחֵר, וְיָצָא לוֹ שֵׁם גְּנֵבָה בָּעִיר, — *[If] one recognizes his utensils or his books in another's possession, and a report of theft had gone forth in the city concerning him,*

[A rumor had gone forth that the utensils or books of a certain person (e.g., Reuven) had been stolen, and then he recognizes these items in the possession of someone else (Levi) who claims that he had bought them from a third person (Shimon).]

In the mishnah's case, Reuven is not accustomed to sell such articles. Since there was a report that they had been stolen, and there are witnesses that the items now in Levi's possession had once belonged to Reuven, the latter is believed that they were stolen from him *(Rav).*

Tiferes Yisrael adds that even if Reuven is accustomed to sell these items, if they are such that are customarily lent or rented out, we fear that he indeed had lent or rented them to Shimon, who then sold them to Levi. But if there are two reasons to believe that Reuven himself sold it — namely, he is accustomed to sell his utensils or books, and that these are not such that are customarily lent or hired — Levi is not required to return them. *Rosh* and *Tur (Choshen Mishpat* 357), however, rule that the fact that Reuven is

בבא קמא י/ד

כַּמָּה נָתַן, וְיִטֹּל. וְאִם לָאו, לֹא כָּל־הֵימֶנּוּ, שֶׁאֲנִי אוֹמֵר: מְכָרָן לְאַחֵר, וּלְקָחָן זֶה הֵימֶנּוּ.

[ד] **זֶה** בָּא בְּחָבִיתוֹ שֶׁל־יַיִן, וְזֶה בָּא בְּכַדּוֹ שֶׁל־דְּבַשׁ, נִסְדְּקָה חָבִית שֶׁל־דְּבַשׁ, וְשָׁפַךְ זֶה אֶת־יֵינוֹ וְהִצִּיל אֶת־הַדְּבַשׁ לְתוֹכוֹ, אֵין לוֹ אֶלָּא

יד אברהם

accustomed to sell such articles is sufficient, and Levi need not return these items to him. Since Reuven claimed that they had been stolen, he surely did not lend them; we therefore suspect that he had indeed sold them.

יִשָּׁבַע לוֹ הַלּוֹקֵחַ כַּמָּה נָתַן, — *the purchaser must swear how much he paid*,

[Levi, who claims to have purchased the utensils or books, must swear how much he paid for them.]

וְיִטֹּל. — *and he receives* [it].

Reuven pays Levi, and the latter returns the items to him. This rule applies only before Reuven had despaired of recovering these articles (*Rav; Rashi*). However, should he have already despaired, Levi would have acquired them through despair and change of possession, and he would not have to return them (*Tos.*).

Although, in the mishnah's case, Reuven has not despaired of recovering these articles, he must nevertheless compensate Levi for them. This rule, enacted by the Sages, and known as תַּקָּנַת הַשּׁוּק, *an ordinance of the market*, dictates that if one purchases an article in the open market, being unaware that the merchandise was stolen, he is entitled to the money he paid for it (*Rashi*).

Since, if one's articles are stolen, he ordinarily despairs of recovering his property [see mishnah 2], the ruling of our mishnah applies only if we see that the owner is busy searching for his utensils and has obviously not yet despaired. In the case of Hebrew books, we always assume that the owner does not despair of recovering them, since he knows that only a Jew will purchase them from the thief, and they will eventually be returned to him (*Tos.; Nimmukei Yosef*).

It is perhaps for this reason that the *Tanna* mentions both books and utensils — to denote that just as in the case of books the owner does not despair of them, so the case of utensils applies only if the owner has not yet despaired of them. Had the *Tanna* stated the halachah only with regard to books and omitted the case of utensils, we would have thought that the owner is believed that he did not sell the item only in the case of a Torah Scroll,[1] since it is forbidden to be sold, but as regards other items we would not rely on the fact that he is not accustomed to sell his utensils. Consequently, the *Tanna* teaches us that the ruling applies also in the case of utensils, and that we do rely on that fact (*Tos. Yom Tov*).

וְאִם לָאו, — *Otherwise*,

[That is, if it had not been rumored that these items had been stolen from Reuven.]

לֹא כָּל־הֵימֶנּוּ — *it does not avail him*,

Reuven cannot take them from Levi, the purchaser (*Tif. Yis.*).

---

1. Concerning the sale of other holy books, *Rosh*, quoted by *Tur* [*Yoreh Deah* 270], prohibits it, while *Beis Yosef* [ad loc.] permits it (*Tos. Yom Tov*).

משניות / בבא קמא — פרק י: הגוזל ומאכיל   [226]

10
4

must swear how much he paid, and he receives [it]. Otherwise, it does not avail him, for I say: He sold them to another, and this one purchased them from him.

4. [I]f this one came with his barrel of wine, and this one came with his jug of honey, [and] the jug of honey cracked, and this one spilled out his wine and saved the honey in it, he is entitled only to

YAD AVRAHAM

שֶׁאֲנִי אוֹמֵר: מְכָרָן לְאַחֵר, — *for I say: He sold them to another*,
We assume that Reuven, needing the money, sold them to Shimon *(Meiri).*

וּלְקָחָן זֶה הֵימֶנּוּ. — *and this one purchased them from him.*

[Levi bought it from Shimon.] And now that Reuven has money, he seeks to repossess the items (ibid.).

[Therefore, even if Reuven offers money for the items, Levi is not obligated to return them to him.]

4.

This mishnah discusses the instances in which one who saves another's property at his own expense can demand restitution for his loss *(Meiri).*

זֶה בָּא בְחָבִיתוֹ שֶׁל־יַיִן, וְזֶה בָּא בְכַדּוֹ שֶׁל־דְּבַשׁ, — [If] *this one came with his barrel of wine, and this one came with his jug of honey,*
[Two people were walking, one carrying a barrel of wine and one carrying a jug of honey.]
The honey is more expensive than the wine *(Tif. Yis.).*

נִסְדְּקָה חָבִית שֶׁל־דְּבַשׁ, — [and] *the jug of honey cracked,*
[The mishnah uses the terms חָבִית, *barrel*, and כַּד, *jug*, interchangeably. See commentary to 3:1, s.v. בַּעַל.]

וְשָׁפַךְ זֶה אֶת־יֵינוֹ וְהִצִּיל אֶת־הַדְּבַשׁ לְתוֹכוֹ, — *and this one spilled out his wine and saved the honey in it,*
[The owner of the wine spilled it out and poured the honey into his jug. Now he demands restitution for the wine he lost.]

אֵין לוֹ אֶלָּא שְׂכָרוֹ. — *he is entitled only to his wage.*
The owner of the wine can demand

from the owner of the honey only that he pay him for use of his jug and for saving the honey *(Rav; Rashi).*

The *Gemara* (115b) qualifies the mishnah as referring to a case in which something was tied around the barrel, so that the honey did not flow out immediately, but seeped out slowly. Had it flowed out immediately, since the owner was unable to save it, he would have lost ownership of it, and the one who saved it in his wine barrel could have claimed that he acquired it from a state of being ownerless *(Tos. Yom Tov).*

According to *Rambam (Hil. Gezeilah* 12:5), it becomes ownerless only when it spills out on the ground. Therefore, since the tie around the barrel prevents the honey from spilling out onto the ground, it does not become ownerless. *Rashi,* however, maintains that in a case in which the honey would have spilled out onto the ground had this person not salvaged it, it would become immediate-

[227]   THE MISHNAH/BAVA KAMMA — Chapter Ten: *HaGozeil U'Maachil*

שְׁבָרוֹ. וְאִם אָמַר: "אַצִּיל אֶת־שֶׁלְּךָ, וְאַתָּה נוֹתֵן לִי דְּמֵי שֶׁלִּי," חַיָּב לִתֵּן לוֹ.

שָׁטַף נָהָר חֲמוֹרוֹ וַחֲמוֹר חֲבֵרוֹ — שֶׁלּוֹ יָפֶה מָנֶה, וְשֶׁל־חֲבֵרוֹ, מָאתַיִם — הִנִּיחַ זֶה אֶת־שֶׁלּוֹ וְהִצִּיל אֶת־שֶׁל־חֲבֵרוֹ, אֵין לוֹ אֶלָּא שְׂכָרוֹ. וְאִם אָמַר לוֹ: "אֲנִי אַצִּיל אֶת־שֶׁלְּךָ, וְאַתָּה נוֹתֵן לִי אֶת־שֶׁלִּי," חַיָּב לִתֵּן לוֹ.

[ה] **הַגּוֹזֵל** שָׂדֶה מֵחֲבֵרוֹ, וּנְטָלוּהָ מַסִּיקִין —

יד אברהם

ly ownerless. The case in our mishnah, on the other hand, is that the tie around the barrel allows only drops to leak out, but not the remainder of the honey; consequently, the one who saved it cannot claim that he has acquired it from a state of being ownerless (*Maggid Mishneh* loc. cit.; *Choshen Mishpat* 264:5).

The mishnah appears to contradict *Bava Metzia* 2:9, where it is stated that if in the process of returning an article that one has found, he loses time from his work, he is compensated [albeit not entirely; see commentary ad loc.] for his loss. In our case, however, we do not compensate for the loss the person sustains by spilling out his wine. We pay him merely as a worker who came with an empty barrel and saved the other person's honey in that barrel.

Nimmukei Yosef, quoting *Rambam*, reconciles the two rulings by explaining that only in the case of losing time from work, which is common, did the Sages institute the payment specified in *Bava Metzia*, because they did not want to cause a person who returns an article that much of a loss. In our case, however, which is unusual, the Sages deemed it unnecessary to institute any payment for the loss of the wine, since if he had wished to be paid for the wine, he should have so stipulated with the owner of the honey, as discussed below. On the other hand, adds *Rosh* [*Bava Metzia* 2:28], in the case of returning a lost article, the finder does not see the owner and cannot stipulate that the latter pay for his loss. Indeed, should the owner be there, and he fails to stipulate this with him, he is awarded only what an unemployed worker would receive for returning the lost article. Similarly, in our case, should the owner of the honey not be there when the barrel cracks, the one who saves the honey receives compensation for his loss (*Tos. Yom Tov*).

וְאִם אָמַר: "אַצִּיל אֶת־שֶׁלְּךָ, וְאַתָּה נוֹתֵן לִי דְּמֵי שֶׁלִּי," — *But if he said: 'I will save yours, and you pay me for mine,'*

[The owner of the wine stipulated with the owner of the honey that he would save the honey only on condition that he be paid for his loss.]

חַיָּב לִתֵּן לוֹ. — *he is obligated to pay him.*

This applies only if the owner of the honey concurred with his stipulation and asked him to save it (*Tos. Yom Tov* from *Rav* to *Bava Metzia* 2:9).

Also, this rule is applicable only if the owner of the wine suffered a loss. If he did not, even if the owner of the honey had said that if he would save the honey he would give him a certain amount of money, he can claim to have been jesting, and is not liable (*Tos. Yom Tov* from *Gem.* 116a).

שָׁטַף נָהָר חֲמוֹרוֹ וַחֲמוֹר חֲבֵרוֹ — שֶׁלּוֹ יָפֶה מָנֶה, וְשֶׁל־חֲבֵרוֹ, מָאתַיִם — הִנִּיחַ זֶה אֶת־שֶׁלּוֹ וְהִצִּיל אֶת־שֶׁל־חֲבֵרוֹ, אֵין לוֹ אֶלָּא שְׂכָרוֹ. — [*If*] *a river swept away his donkey and another's donkey — his being worth a*

his wage. But if he said: 'I will save yours, and you pay me for mine,' he is obligated to pay him.

[If] a river swept away his donkey and another's donkey — his being worth a hundred [zuz], and the other's, two hundred — [and] he left his and saved the other's, he is entitled only to his wage. But [if] he said to him: 'I will save yours, and you pay me for mine,' he is obligated to pay him.

5. One who robs another of his field, and tyrants

YAD AVRAHAM

hundred [zuz], and the other's, two hundred — [and] he left his and saved the other's, he is entitled only to his wage.

Should both donkeys be of the same value, it is unusual for one to sacrifice his own to save that of the other person; but if he did so, the ruling is the same (*Tos. Yom Tov* from *Sma* 264:6). In our case, however, he expects the other person to pay him more than his donkey is worth for saving the more valuable one (*ibid.*)

וְאִם אָמַר לוֹ: ״אֲנִי אַצִּיל אֶת־שֶׁלָּךְ, וְאַתָּה נוֹתֵן לִי אֶת־שֶׁלִּי״, — *But* [*if*] *he said to him: 'I will save yours, and you pay me for mine,'*

[He stipulates that he is saving the other person's donkey only on condition that the latter pay him for his loss.]

Although the same would apply if he made this statement to a court composed of three persons, as in *Bava Metzia* 2:9, the *Tanna* chose this case to parallelize it with the one above, in which the owner is present (*Tos. Yom Tov*).

חַיָּב לִתֵּן לוֹ. — *he is obligated to pay him.*

Although these two cases are based on the same principle, the *Tanna* states his ruling in both of them. Were he to state only the case of the honey, we would think that the owner of the wine receives compensation for his wine when he so stipulates, because he spills it out by a direct act of his own hands. In the second case, however, since he loses his donkey only because he refrains from saving it, we would think that he cannot collect payment for the loss.

On the other hand, had the *Tanna* stated only the case of the donkey, we would think that only in such a case is the one who saved the other person's item not compensated for his loss if he does not so stipulate, since the loss came by itself; but, in the case of the honey, in which the owner of the wine spills it out by a direct act of his own hands, he would receive payment even had he not made any stipulation. Therefore, both cases must be stated (*Rav* from *Gem.* 116a).

5.

הַגּוֹזֵל שָׂדֶה מֵחֲבֵרוֹ, — *One who robs another of his field,*

[He compels him to leave the field and then occupies it unlawfully.]

וּנְטָלוּהָ מְסִיקִין — — *and tyrants take it —*

Tiferes Yisrael describes מְסִיקִין,

tyrants, as lords who confiscate the property of their serfs. The latter have no way of preventing them from doing so. *Rambam* (*Hil Gezeilah* 9:2) similarly explains that the king authorized oppressive officials to confiscate the field.

בבא קמא י/ו

אִם מַכַּת מְדִינָה הִיא, אוֹמֵר לוֹ: "הֲרֵי שֶׁלְּךָ לְפָנֶיךָ"; וְאִם מֵחֲמַת הַגַּזְלָן, חַיָּב לְהַעֲמִיד לוֹ שָׂדֶה אַחֵר. שְׁטָפָהּ נָהָר, אוֹמֵר לוֹ: "הֲרֵי שֶׁלְּךָ לְפָנֶיךָ."

[ו] **הַגּוֹזֵל** אֶת־חֲבֵרוֹ, אוֹ שֶׁלָּוָה הֵימֶנּוּ, אוֹ שֶׁהִפְקִיד לוֹ בַּיִּשּׁוּב, לֹא יַחֲזִיר לוֹ

יד אברהם

Rav (based on *Gem.* 116b, *Rashi* ad loc.) relates the term to סָקָאָה, *a robber*, as we find in *Onkelos*, who gives this word as a translation of צְלָצַל, *locust*, (*Deut.* 28:42) since locusts rob people of their crops.

The *Gemara* states that some read מְצִיקִים, *oppressors*. [This is perhaps *Rambam's* source.]

אִם מַכַּת מְדִינָה הִיא — *if it is a plague of the province,*

That is, the king has taken fields from everyone in the province (*Rambam*, loc. cit.).

In accordance with their translation of מְסִיקִין as *robbers*, *Rav* and *Rashi* interpret this to mean that the robbers took lands from others as well as from this person. *Meiri* explains that the robbers did not intend to steal from this person in particular, but rather are interested in taking the fields of all the people in the area.

אוֹמֵר לוֹ — *he may say to him:*

[The first robber may say to the owner of the field:]

הֲרֵי שֶׁלְּךָ לְפָנֶיךָ — *'Here is your property before you';*

Since the robber was not instrumental in the field being confiscated, he can plead that if the field had been in the possession of the owner, the same thing would have happened.

This applies only to real estate, which cannot be stolen and always remains in the original owner's possession. But if one steals chattels, he assumes responsibility for them, and is liable for any accident that may occur to them (*Meiri*).

וְאִם מֵחֲמַת הַגַּזְלָן, — *but if it is because of the robber,*

[The tyrants took the field only because it was in the robber's possession.]

חַיָּב לְהַעֲמִיד לוֹ שָׂדֶה אַחֵר. — *he must provide him [with] another field.*

[The first robber must provide the owner of the field with another one of the same value.]

The *Gemara* (116b) questions the necessity of the phrase *if it is because of the robber*. The mishnah should have merely stated: *But if not, he must provide him with another field*. It therefore concludes that the intention of the *Tanna* is to add that if the tyrants coerce the robber to show them all his fields, and he shows the stolen field among his, he must provide the owner with another field (*Tos. Yom Tov* from *Tos.* and *Rambam*, *Hil. Gezeilah* 9:3). *Rashi* explains that he did not rob the owner of the field, but he heard that the king sought to confiscate fields and suggested that he take the field belonging to this other person.

By showing the field to the tyrants, he can be sure that they will confiscate it; hence, he is liable. This is known as דִּינָא דְגַרְמֵי, *the law of garmei* [indirect causes]. In certain cases, the Rabbis imposed liability for indirectly causing damage. According to *Rosh* [9:13], this is applicable if the damage is certain to

10
6 take it — if it is a plague of the province, he may say to him: 'Here is your property before you'; but if it is because of the robber, he must provide him [with] another field. [If] a river inundated it, he may say to him: 'Here is your property before you.'

6. [I]f one robs another, or borrows from him, or deposits [something] with him in a settled region, he may not return it to him in the wilderness;

YAD AVRAHAM

occur, even though it may occur later. According to *Hagahos Asheri* [2:16], it applies only if the damage takes place immediately. In the case of our mishnah, showing it to the tyrant is tantamount to burning it *(Gem.* 117a).

Tiferes Yisrael states that the obligation of the robber to provide another field is a fine imposed upon him. [This is an undecided question in the *Gemara* (ibid.; see *Tos.* 54a). *Shach* 386:1 goes to great lengths to prove that the payment in every case of *garmei* is indeed a Rabbinic fine.]

שְׁטָפָהּ נָהָר, — [If] *a river inundated it,*
[A river flooded the field that was stolen.]

אוֹמֵר לוֹ: — *he may say to him:*
[The robber may say to the owner of the field:]

"הֲרֵי שֶׁלְּךָ לְפָנֶיךָ." — *'Here is your property before you.'*

As explained above, real estate cannot be stolen; it always remains in the possession of its rightful owner. Therefore, the robber can say: 'Here is your property before you' — i.e., — 'It never entered my possession that I should be responsible for accidents occurring to it.' The *Gemara* (117b) derives from passages in the Biblical section which deals with returning stolen property that only chattels which are intrinsically worth money are capable of being stolen. Land, not being movable, is not adjudged as stolen, but remains in the possession of its owner. Deeds of indebtedness, although they represent monetary obligations, have no intrinsic pecuniary value. Slaves are likened to land, and are therefore incapable of being stolen *(Tos. Yom Tov).*

6.

The following mishnah discusses the law of one who robbed, borrowed, or received something to watch from another person in a settled region, and under what circumstances he may return it if he meets him in the wilderness, where the owner does not have his residence *(Meiri).*

הַגּוֹזֵל אֶת־חֲבֵרוֹ, אוֹ שֶׁלָּוָה הֵימֶנּוּ, אוֹ שֶׁהִפְקִיד לוֹ בְּיִשּׁוּב, — [If] *one robs another, or borrows from him, or deposits [something] with him in a settled region,*
[For example, Reuven robbed or borrowed money from Shimon or received a deposit from him in a settled region.]

לֹא יַחֲזִיר לוֹ בַּמִּדְבָּר; — *he may not return it to him in the wilderness;*
That is, Reuven cannot compel Shimon to accept the item back in the wilderness. *Rashi* and *Rambam* (*Hil. Gezeilah* 1:7) explain that the recipient fears that the money or article will be stolen since the wilderness is not a safe

[231]   THE MISHNAH/BAVA KAMMA — Chapter Ten: *HaGozeil U'Maachil*

בבא קמא י/ז

בַּמִּדְבָּר; עַל־מְנָת לָצֵאת בַּמִּדְבָּר, יַחֲזִיר לוֹ בַּמִּדְבָּר.

[ז] הָאוֹמֵר לַחֲבֵרוֹ: "גְּזַלְתִּיךָ," "הִלְוִיתַנִי," "הִפְקַדְתָּ אֶצְלִי,"..., וְאֵינִי יוֹדֵעַ אִם הֶחֱזַרְתִּי לָךְ אִם לֹא הֶחֱזַרְתִּי לָךְ," חַיָּב לְשַׁלֵּם. אֲבָל אִם אָמַר לוֹ: "אֵינִי יוֹדֵעַ אִם גְּזַלְתִּיךָ," "אִם הִלְוִיתַנִי," "אִם הִפְקַדְתָּ אֶצְלִי," פָּטוּר מִלְּשַׁלֵּם.

יד אברהם

place. *Meiri* adds that Shimon objects to the trouble of transporting the article.

It is therefore still in Reuven's possession, and he is responsible for it until he returns it to Shimon in a settled region (*Rambam*, ibid.). If he returns it against the will of the recipient, he remains responsible for it (*Meiri*).

Should Shimon accept it willingly, Reuven is exempt from anything that happens to it (*Tos. Yom Tov*).

Rambam (Commentary) states that since this ruling is for the benefit of Shimon, should he demand the money, Reuven must return it to him.

In the case of the stolen property or the deposit, however, even if the owner demands it in the wilderness the robber or guardian need not carry it with him to return it there, since people usually do not carry such things with them (*Meiri* from *Gem.* 118a).

עַל־מְנָת לָצֵאת בַּמִּדְבָּר, יַחֲזִיר לוֹ בַּמִּדְבָּר — *on condition that he was going out to the wilderness, he may return it to him in the wilderness.*

The mishnah could not be telling us that if Shimon stipulates that he will accept the item in the wilderness, Reuven may return it to him there, because this is obvious. Rather, it refers to a case in which Shimon approaches Reuven and says to him, 'Please take this article and watch it for me, because I wish to go out to the wilderness,' and Shimon replies, 'I, too, wish to go out to the wilderness.' If Reuven gives Shimon the item in spite of what the latter said, he must accept it when Shimon returns it, even in the wilderness (*Rav* from *Gem.* 118a).

7.

The following mishnah deals with a person who is uncertain whether or not he owes money.

הָאוֹמֵר לַחֲבֵרוֹ: "גְּזַלְתִּיךָ," "הִלְוִיתַנִי," "הִפְקַדְתָּ אֶצְלִי,"..., וְאֵינִי יוֹדֵעַ אִם הֶחֱזַרְתִּי לָךְ אִם לֹא הֶחֱזַרְתִּי לָךְ — *[If] one says to another: 'I robbed you,' 'You lent me,' [or] 'You deposited with me,' '... but I do not know whether I returned [it] to you or whether I did not return [it] to you,'*

A person — for example, Reuven — claims with certainty that another — e.g., Shimon — had robbed him, borrowed from him, or agreed to watch an article of his. Shimon admits that this is true, but says that he is unsure whether or not he had already returned the item to Reuven (*Rav; Rambam Commentary* from *Gem.* 118a).

חַיָּב לְשַׁלֵּם — *he is obligated to pay.*

10
7
on condition that he was going out to the wilderness, he may return it to him in the wilderness.

7. [If] one says to another: 'I robbed you,' 'You lent me,' [or] 'You deposited with me,' '... but I do not know whether I returned [it] to you or whether I did not return [it] to you,' he is obligated to pay. But if he says to him: 'I do not know whether I robbed you,' 'whether you lent me,' [or] 'whether you deposited with me,' he is exempt from paying.

YAD AVRAHAM

This ruling applies only if Reuven claims positively that Shimon owes him money, since the obligation is certain, and the exemption from that obligation is doubtful. However, should Reuven make no claim, and Shimon tells him that he did owe him the money or articles, but is uncertain if he paid him back, the court cannot compel him to pay; nevertheless, he must do so if he wishes to fulfill his duty in the eyes of Heaven. On the other hand, if Shimon denies that he ever owed Reuven at all — even if the latter claims with certainty that he did — he is not obligated to pay even in order to fulfill his duty in the eyes of Heaven *(Tos. Yom Tov)*.

אֲבָל אִם אָמַר לוֹ: — *But if he says to him:* [Answering Reuven, who claims with certainty that Shimon owes him money, Shimon replies:]

„אֵינִי יוֹדֵעַ אִם גְּזַלְתִּיךָ", „אִם הִלְוִיתַנִי", „הִפְקַדְתָּ אֶצְלִי", — *'I do not know whether I robbed you,' 'whether you lent me,' [or] 'whether you deposited with me,'*

[He is unsure whether or not Reuven's claim is true.]

פָּטוּר מִלְשַׁלֵּם. — *he is exempt from paying.*

This is because we are in doubt as to whether or not the debt ever existed *(Tif. Yis.).*

Nevertheless, since Reuven claims with certainty that Shimon owes the money, if the latter wishes to fulfill his duty in the eyes of Heaven, he must pay *(Tos. Yom Tov from Gem. 118a).*

If Shimon refuses to pay, although the court cannot exact payment from him, they do require him to swear that he indeed does not know whether he owes the money. This oath is called a שְׁבוּעַת הֶיסֵת, a Rabbinical oath instituted in the time of the *Gemara*, to be sworn by a defendant although he is legally exempt from payment. Even if he pleads with certainty that he never owed the money, he would be obligated to swear to that effect *(Rav).*

We have explained the mishnah according to R' Nachman and R' Yochanan, who rule that if Reuven makes his claim with certainty and Shimon is unsure, the court cannot compel the latter to pay. This opinion is based upon the principle of הַמּוֹצִיא מֵחֲבֵרוֹ עָלָיו הָרְאָיָה, *the burden of proof lies on the one who seeks to exact money from the other* [3:11] — that is, if one person sues another for money, the latter does not have to pay unless it is clearly proven that he does indeed owe it. [However, if the defendant admits that he once owed money, it is assumed that the debt is still in force until *he* proves otherwise.]

R' Huna and R' Yehudah, however, maintain that בָּרִי וְשֶׁמָּא, בָּרִי עָדִיף — i.e., if one participant in the suit makes his claim with certainty, and the other is unsure, the former wins the case. According to them, the mishnah is construed as referring to instances in which Reuven does not make any claim. In the mishnah's first case — that Shimon admits that he once owed Reuven the

[233] THE MISHNAH/BAVA KAMMA — Chapter Ten: *HaGozeil U'Maachil*

בבא קמא
י/ח-ט

[ח] **הַגּוֹנֵב** טָלֶה מִן־הָעֵדֶר וְהֶחֱזִירוֹ, וּמֵת אוֹ נִגְנַב, חַיָּב בְּאַחֲרָיוּתוֹ. לֹא יָדְעוּ הַבְּעָלִים לֹא בִגְנֵבָתוֹ וְלֹא בַחֲזִירָתוֹ, וּמָנוּ אֶת־הַצֹּאן, וּשְׁלֵמָה הִיא, פָּטוּר.

[ט] **אֵין** לוֹקְחִים מִן־הָרוֹעִים צֶמֶר, וְחָלָב, וּגְדָיִים, וְלֹא מִשּׁוֹמְרֵי פֵרוֹת עֵצִים וּפֵרוֹת; אֲבָל לוֹקְחִין מִן־הַנָּשִׁים כְּלֵי צֶמֶר בִּיהוּדָה,

יד אברהם

article or money — the *Tanna's* ruling, *he is obligated to pay*, means that he must do so only if he wishes to fulfill his duty in the eyes of Heaven. In the second case, however, since Shimon is in doubt whether he ever owed the money, he is not obligated even in order to fulfill his duty in the eyes of Heaven (Gem. 118a).

The halachah is in accordance with R' Nachman and R' Yochanan (Tos. as loc.).

8.

The following mishnah deals with one who returns a stolen article, and an accident happens to it.

הַגּוֹנֵב טָלֶה מִן־הָעֵדֶר — [If] one steals a lamb from the flock,

And then the owner became aware of the theft (Rambam Commentary; Meiri).

וְהֶחֱזִירוֹ, — and returns it,

That is, the thief returns the lamb without the owner's knowledge (Tif. Yis.).

וּמֵת אוֹ נִגְנַב — and it dies or is stolen,

[After the thief returns the lamb, it dies or is stolen.]

חַיָּב בְּאַחֲרָיוּתוֹ. — he is responsible for it.

When the thief stole the lamb, it entered his possession; when he returned it, since the owner was not aware of it and thus, does not know to watch it, it is not considered a valid return, and the thief is still responsible for it (Rav; Rashi; Meiri).

לֹא יָדְעוּ הַבְּעָלִים לֹא בִגְנֵבָתוֹ וְלֹא בַחֲזִירָתוֹ, — [If] the owners were aware neither of its theft nor of its return,

[The owner of the lamb did not know that the thief stole it, nor that he returned it.]

וּמָנוּ אֶת־הַצֹּאן, — and they counted the flock,

[The owner counted the flock after the stolen lamb had been returned.]

וּשְׁלֵמָה הִיא, — and it was complete,

They found the complete number of sheep in the flock (Meiri).

פָּטוּר. — he is exempt.

That is, if the lamb died or was stolen after the owner was aware of its presence in the flock, the thief is exempt (ibid.).

The above explanation of the mishnah follows the opinion of Rav in the *Gemara* (118a), who rules that if the owner was aware of the theft, unless the thief notifies him when he returns it, the thief is still responsible for it. If the owner was aware neither of the theft, nor of the return, but he counts the flock and finds it complete, the robber is no longer responsible for the animal.

Although this is indeed the simplest interpretation of the mishnah, the Halachah rejects it and follows the view of R' Chisda instead. He rules contrarily

משניות / בבא קמא — פרק י: הגזול ומאכיל [234]

10
8-9

8. [If] one steals a lamb from the flock and returns it, and it dies or is stolen, he is responsible for it. [If] the owners were aware neither of its theft nor of its return, and they counted the flock, and it was complete, he is exempt.

9. We may not purchase wool, milk, or kids from shepherds, nor wood or fruit from watchmen of fruit; but we may purchase from women woolen

YAD AVRAHAM

that even if the owner was aware of the theft of the lamb, once he counts the flock and discovers that it is complete, the thief is no longer responsible for the animal. Should the owner be unaware of the theft, however, the thief must notify him when he returns the lamb to the flock, because once a lamb wanders away from the flock, it becomes accustomed to running out to the fields, and the owner must keep a closer watch over it.

Accordingly, the mishnah is explained as follows:

[*If*] *one steals a lamb from the flock and returns it, and it dies or is stolen, he is responsible for it* [whether the owners counted the flock or not. This applies only] *if the owners were aware neither of its theft nor of its return* [since they did not know to keep a closer watch over the lamb. If, however, they were aware of the theft] *and counted the flock and it was complete* [since they knew that the lamb had been stolen and returned, and that they should watch it closer], *he is exempt (Rav* from *Gem.* 118a-b).

Although it is logical that if the owner is unaware of the theft and, hence, does not realize that he must watch the lamb closely, the thief should be responsible for loss or theft, since the animal is now in the habit of wandering off from the flock and can fall prey to thieves, it is difficult to understand why he should be responsible for the lamb's death if it dies a natural death (*Tos. Yom Tov*).

The reason is that a lamb that has a habit of wandering off from the flock becomes fatigued, and this fatigue may have been the cause of its death. Even if it was found dead among the flock, it may have wandered off and returned (*Beis David*).

Alternatively, perhaps the lamb became fatigued from being driven by the thief, and had the owner known of the theft, he would have made sure that the animal should rest. Since the thief did not notify him, he is responsible for its death (*Tif. Yis.*).

9.

The following mishnah lists merchandise which may not be purchased, since we assume that it was stolen (*Meiri*).

אֵין לוֹקְחִין מִן־הָרוֹעִים צֶמֶר, וְחָלָב, וּגְדָיִים, — *We may not purchase wool, milk, or kids from shepherds,*

We suspect that they stole them from the flocks of their employer (*Rav; Rashi*). *Meiri* and *Rambam* (*Commentary* and *Hil. Geneivah* 6:1) state that we assume so.

וְלֹא מִשּׁוֹמְרֵי פֵרוֹת עֵצִים וּפֵרוֹת; — *nor wood or fruit from watchmen of fruit;*

Similarly, we may not purchase wood or fruit from watchmen who guard fruit orchards (*Tos. Yom Tov*), because it is assumed that they stole them from their employers (*Tif. Yis.*).

אֲבָל לוֹקְחִין מִן־הַנָּשִׁים כְּלֵי צֶמֶר בִּיהוּדָה, וּכְלֵי פִשְׁתָּן בַּגָּלִיל, — *but we may purchase from women woolen garments in Judea,*

[235]

בבא קמא י/י

וּכְלֵי פִשְׁתָּן בַּגָּלִיל, וַעֲגָלִים בַּשָּׁרוֹן. וְכֻלָּן שֶׁאָמְרוּ לְהַטְמִין, אָסוּר. וְלוֹקְחִין בֵּיצִים וְתַרְנְגוֹלִים מִכָּל־מָקוֹם.

[י] **מוֹכִין** שֶׁהַכּוֹבֵס מוֹצִיא הֲרֵי אֵלּוּ שֶׁלּוֹ, וְשֶׁהַסּוֹרֵק מוֹצִיא הֲרֵי אֵלּוּ שֶׁל־בַּעַל הַבַּיִת. הַכּוֹבֵס נוֹטֵל שְׁלֹשָׁה חוּטִין, וְהֵן שֶׁלּוֹ; יָתֵר מִכֵּן, הֲרֵי אֵלּוּ שֶׁל־בַּעַל הַבַּיִת. אִם הָיָה הַשָּׁחוֹר עַל־גַּבֵּי הַלָּבָן, נוֹטֵל אֶת־הַכֹּל וְהֵן שֶׁלּוֹ.

יד אברהם

linen garments in Galilee,

These are the women's own handiwork, and they sell them with their husbands' consent (Rav; Rashi).

וַעֲגָלִים בַּשָּׁרוֹן — **and calves in Sharon.**

This is a place where the women raise their own calves (Rav, Tos. Yom Tov). Maggid Mishneh (Hil. Geneivah 6:4) comments that calves are cheap in Sharon, and women raise them and sell them. The same appplies to similar commodities in other regions (Tos. Yom Tov).

וְכֻלָּן שֶׁאָמְרוּ לְהַטְמִין — **But [if] any of them says that they must be kept hidden,**

[They told their customers to keep their purchases hidden.]

Other editions (Yerushalmi et al.) read: "הַטְמֵן ,,וְכֻלָּן שֶׁאָמְרוּ, **But [if] any of them says: 'Hide.'**

אָסוּר — **it is prohibited.**

Because of this statement, we assume that it is stolen (Rambam, Hil. Geneivah 6:4, quoted by Tos. Yom Tov).

וְלוֹקְחִין בֵּיצִים וְתַרְנְגוֹלִים מִכָּל־מָקוֹם — **We may purchase eggs and fowl anywhere.**

These may be purchased from anyone in any place. However, even with regard to these items, if the seller tells the customer to keep them hidden, we may not purchase them (ibid.).

10.

The following mishnah deals with small particles of material that remain in the possession of craftsmen, some of which belong to the craftsman and some of which must be returned to the owner.

מוֹכִין שֶׁהַכּוֹבֵס מוֹצִיא — **Shreds of wool that the launderer pulls out**

The one who whitens the wool pulls small particles out of it when he rinses it (Rav; Rashi).

הֲרֵי אֵלּוּ שֶׁלּוֹ — **belong to him,**

Since they are small particles, the owner does not care if someone takes them. Even if one particular owner does care, the launderer may keep them in defiance of the owner's wishes. [Since it became a standard practice to do so, the launderer had accepted it on that condition] (Rav; Rashi).

וְשֶׁהַסּוֹרֵק מוֹצִיא — **but what the wool comber pulls out**

That is, what the one who combs and beats the wool pulls out with thorns resembling a comb (Rashi).

Tos. Yom Tov construes the mishnah

10 garments in Judea, linen garments in Galilee, and calves in Sharon. But [if] any of them says that they must be kept hidden, it is prohibited. We may purchase eggs and fowl anywhere.

10. Shreds of wool that the launderer pulls out belong to him, but what the wool comber pulls out belongs to the owner. The launderer may pull out three threads, and they belong to him; [if he pulls out] more than that, they belong to the owner. If it was black on white, he may take off everything and they belong to him.

YAD AVRAHAM

as dealing with one who beats a finished garment to even it out, and combs it to bring out the threads so that the weaving should not be seen.

הֲרֵי אֵלוּ שֶׁל־בַּעַל הַבַּיִת — *belongs to the owner.*
Since this is a substantial amount, people usually wish to keep it *(Rav; Rashi).*

הַכּוֹבֵס נוֹטֵל שְׁלֹשָׁה חוּטִין — *The launderer may pull out three threads,*
It was customary to weave three threads of another color at the edge of woolen garments. The launderer would pull these out, and then straighten out and beautify the garments *(Rav; Rashi).*
These were woven at a distance from the woven fabric, to preserve the garment, lest the woven part become unraveled when it is being laundered. Should these threads become loosened during the laundering process, the launderer may take them off.

וְהֵן שֶׁלּוֹ — *and they belong to him;*
The owner of the garment does not care if someone takes them *(Tos. Yom Tov* from *Tur Choshen Mishpat* 358).
[As above, the same ruling would apply even if one particular owner does care.]

יָתֵר מִכֵּן, הֲרֵי אֵלוּ שֶׁל־בַּעַל הַבַּיִת — *[if he pulls out] more than that, they belong to the owner.*

All of the threads, including the three at the edge, belong to the owner *(Tur Choshen Mishpat* 258). This is because all these laws depend upon whether the owner cares about the small amounts of wool or threads that come off a garment. Since he is not concerned about an amount that is of no use to him, if the launderer pulls off three threads, he may keep them. If he pulls off more than three threads, since they are useful, the owner cares about all of them, and does not relinquish them to the launderer. Therefore, the latter must return all of them to the owner *(Tos. Yom Tov).*

אִם הָיָה הַשָּׁחוֹר עַל־גַּבֵּי הַלָּבָן — *If it was black on white,*
Black threads were woven into the end of a white garment *(Rav; Rashi).*

נוֹטֵל אֶת־הַכֹּל — *he may take off everything*
The launderer may take off all the black threads, even if they are more than three, since black ruins the appearance of a white garment *(Rav; Rashi).*

וְהֵן שֶׁלּוֹ — *and they belong to him.*
The launderer may take them, since they were originally intended to be removed *(Rashba).*

[237] THE MISHNAH/BAVA KAMMA — Chapter Ten: *HaGozeil U'Maachil*

בבא קמא י/י

הַחַיָּט שֶׁשִּׁיֵּר מִן־הַחוּט כְּדֵי לִתְפּוֹר בּוֹ, וּמַטְלִית שֶׁהִיא שָׁלֹשׁ עַל־שָׁלֹשׁ, הֲרֵי אֵלּוּ שֶׁל־בַּעַל הַבָּיִת. מַה־שֶּׁהֶחָרָשׁ מוֹצִיא בְמַעֲצָד הֲרֵי אֵלּוּ שֶׁלּוֹ; וּבְכַשִּׁיל, שֶׁל־בַּעַל הַבָּיִת.
וְאִם הָיָה עוֹשֶׂה אֵצֶל בַּעַל הַבָּיִת, אַף הַנְּסֹרֶת שֶׁל־בַּעַל הַבָּיִת.

יד אברהם

הַחַיָּט שֶׁשִּׁיֵּר מִן־הַחוּט — [If] a tailor left over thread

He finished a job for a customer who had given him the thread, and there was still some left over (Meiri).

כְּדֵי לִתְפּוֹר בּוֹ, — enough to sew with it,

That is, thread the length of two needles (Tos. Yom Tov from Gem. 119b; Rambam Commentary, ed. Kaffich), which is the minimum length of thread with which one can sew (Maggid Mishneh, Hil. Geneivah 6:7).

וּמַטְלִית שֶׁהִיא שָׁלֹשׁ עַל־שָׁלֹשׁ, — or a patch which is three [fingerbreadths] square [lit., three by three],

The tailor evened a garment he was sewing by cutting off a small patch, measuring three fingerbreadths square [which is useful] (Rav; Rashi).

הֲרֵי אֵלּוּ שֶׁל־בַּעַל הַבָּיִת. — they belong to the owner.

Many editions (Yerushalmi; Rif; Rosh; Meiri; Rambam, Hil Geneivah 6:7) read: חַיָּב לְהַחֲזִירָן לְבַעַל הַבָּיִת, he is obligated to return it to the owner. The intention is that if the tailor could have finished the garment without leaving over enough thread to sew with, or a patch three fingerbreadths square, but intentionally finished in that manner in order to take the remaining thread or cloth, he must return it to the householder (Meleches Shlomo). [This would imply that if the remnant was not intended, the tailor may keep it. We do not find such a view in the Shulchan Aruch or the commentaries. Moreover, Meiri states explicitly that even if it occurred that a patch remained, he is obligated to return it to the owner.]

The Gemara states that if this particular customer cares about the thread and material in amounts even less than these, the tailor must return it to him. This ruling is, however, not mentioned by the halachic authorities. Tiferes Yisrael concludes that, nowadays, people are not particular about all the small amounts mentioned in this mishnah; consequently, all belong to the craftsman.

מַה־שֶּׁהֶחָרָשׁ מוֹצִיא בְמַעֲצָד — What a carpenter takes out with a plane

That is, the fine shavings that fall off the boards when the carpenter planes them to make them smooth (Rav).

[According to the French word used by Rashi, it appears that the word מַעֲצָד means a small axe. However, his description of the item fits a plane more aptly.]

[According to the Gemara (119b), it appears that מַעֲצָד and כַּשִּׁיל, mentioned below, are two types of axe — מַעֲצָד being the smaller one, and כַּשִּׁיל the larger one. (See ArtScroll commentary to Shabbos 12:1, Tos. Yom Tov ibid., Makkos 3:5.)]

הֲרֵי אֵלּוּ שֶׁלּוֹ; — belongs to him;

[Since they are thin, the owner does not care about them.]

וּבְכַשִּׁיל, שֶׁל־בַּעַל הַבָּיִת. — with a hatchet, belongs to the owner.

Since these are large chips, the owner

משניות / בבא קמא — פרק י׃ הגוזל ומאכיל [238]

10

[If] a tailor left over thread enough to sew with it, or a patch which is three [fingerbreadths] square, they belong to the owner.

What a carpenter takes out with a plane belongs to him; with a hatchet, belongs to the owner.

[If] he was working on the owner's premises, however, even the sawdust belongs to the owner.

YAD AVRAHAM

is particular about them *(Rav; Rashi).*

וְאִם הָיָה עוֹשֶׂה אֵצֶל בַּעַל הַבַּיִת, אַף הַנְּסֹרֶת שֶׁל־בַּעַל הַבַּיִת. — [If] *he was working on the owner's premises, however, even the sawdust belongs to the owner.*

[This applies to all cases; the sawdust is merely an example.]

For instance, he was a worker hired per diem *(Rav; Rashi). Tos. Yom Tov* explains that *Rav* and *Rashi* give the example of a hired worker merely because such a person usually works on the owner's premises, while a contractor normally works on his own premises. In fact, however, the same would apply to a contractor working on the owner's premises. Similarly, if a hired worker works on his own premises, the small amounts belong to him. The reason for this is that when one works on the owner's premises, the latter usually pays the overhead, and therefore wishes to keep any leftover material that can be of some use.

סליק מסכת בבא קמא

Glossary

Amora, pl. **Amoraim** (אֲמוֹרָא (אֲמוֹרָאִים: a Sage of the post-Mishnaic era quoted in the *Gemara* or other works of the same period.

bor בּוֹר: pit — the category of damages caused by a pit or similar things, including any obstacle lying on the ground upon which people or animals can stumble and injure themselves.

dinar דִּינָר: a type of coin. A silver dinar equals one *zuz*. One golden dinar is equivalent to twenty-five silver dinars.

eish אֵשׁ: fire — the category of damages caused by a fire or similar things, including any item that is carried by a normal wind and causes damages while flying.

Eretz Yisrael אֶרֶץ יִשְׂרָאֵל: the Land of Israel according to its halachically defined boundaries.

Gemara (abbr. **Gem.**) גְּמָרָא: the section of the Talmud that explains the Mishnah.

Gaon, pl. **Geonim** (גָּאוֹן (גְּאוֹנִים: (1) title accorded the heads of the academies in Sura and Pumbedisa, the two Babylonian seats of Jewish learning, from the late sixth to mid-eleventh centuries C.E. They served as the link in the chain of Torah tradition that joined the *Rishonim* (early authorities who flourished circa 1000-1500 C.E) to the *Amoraim*; (2) currently used to describe any brilliant Torah scholar.

halachah הֲלָכָה: (1) a religious law; (2) the accepted ruling; (3) [cap.] the body of Jewish law.

kares כָּרֵת: a form of excision meted out by the Heavenly Tribunal, sometimes as premature death, sometimes by one being predeceased by his children.

keren קֶרֶן: horn — the category of damages done by an animal with its horn, or any unusual damages done by an animal with intent to damage.

kesubah, pl. **kesubos** (כְּתוּבָה (כְּתוּבוֹת: (1) the agreement made between a man and his wife upon their marriage, whose foremost feature is the dower awarded her in the event of their divorce or his death; (2) the document upon which this agreement is recorded. See General Introduction to ArtScroll *Kesubos*.

kinyan קִנְיָן: an act by which property is legally acquired or transferred.

Kohen, pl. **Kohanim** (כֹּהֵן (כֹּהֲנִים: a member of the priestly family descended from Aaron.

maneh מָנֶה: a unit of weight equal to approximately 425 grams or one American pound. Also used to denote *one hundred*, as throughout this tractate, where it means one hundred *zuz*.

mishnah, pl. **mishnayos** (מִשְׁנָה (מִשְׁנָיוֹת: (1) [cap.] the section of the Talmud consisting of the collection of oral laws edited by R' Yehudah HaNasi (Judah the Prince); (2) an article of this section.

mitzvah pl. **mitzvos** (מִצְוָה (מִצְווֹת: a Biblical or Rabbinical precept.

muad pl. **muadin** (מוּעָד (מוּעָדִין: (1) considered forewarned; (2) an animal that has gored or done other damages in the *keren* category at least three times.

perutah פְּרוּטָה: the minimal unit of significant monetary value.

regel רֶגֶל: foot — the category of damages done by an animal with its foot or anything else as it walks.

shen שֵׁן: tooth — (1) damages done by an animal eating produce in a field belonging to someone other than its owner; (2) any damages done by an animal in order to derive pleasure.

shor שׁוֹר: bull, ox — the category of damages mentioned in 1:1 whose definition is controversial. See commentary ibid., s.v. *The Dispute between Rav and Shmuel*.

tam תָּם: innocent, tame — an animal that has not gored or done other damages in the *keren* category more than twice.

Tanna, pl. **Tannaim** (תַּנָּא (תַּנָּאִים: a Sage quoted in the Mishnah or in works of the same period.

terumah תְּרוּמָה: a portion of the crop sanctified and given to a *Kohen* who — together with his household — may eat it, but only if both the one who eats the *terumah* and the *terumah* itself are ritually clean.

Torah תּוֹרָה: (1) The Five Books of Moses; (2) The entire Written and Oral Law.

משניות / בבא קמא   **[240]**